WITHDRAWN

American Library Resources

Cumulative Index · 1870–1970

American Library Resources

Cumulative Index   •   1870–1970

compiled by

Clara D. Keller

American Library Association

Chicago 1981

Library of Congress Cataloging in Publication Data

Keller, Clara D., 1934-
   American library resources cumulative index, 1870-1970.

   1. Downs, Robert B. (Robert Bingham), 1903-
American library resources--Indexes. 2. Bibliography--
Indexes. 3. Library resources--United
States--Indexes. I. Downs, Robert B. (Robert Bingham),
1903-   , American library resources. II. Title.
Z1002.D6 1972 Suppl. 016.016021   81-12788
ISBN 0-8389-0341-X   AACR2

Printed in the United States of America

Preface

Since the appearance of the first and second supplements to *American Library Resources,* there has been an increasing demand for a cumulative index. That need, so frequently expressed by reference librarians and other users, is now being met by the present work. Through careful editing, an effort has been made to make the entries uniform and in some cases more complete than in the original volume. Used in conjunction with the index to the 1971–80 volume, we have a reasonably comprehensive guide to publications relating to the resources of libraries in the United States extending over more than a century.

As the earlier volumes of *American Library Resources* go out of print, the index may still be consulted to identify subjects for which holdings have been described. The descriptions located in the main volume and its supplements should be easily obtained through interlibrary communication.

Each entry in the Cumulative Index is followed by a roman numeral and an arabic number. The former refers to the main volume and decennial supplements through 1970 by order of publication. The latter is an entry number within the volume cited.

Index

Abajian, James de T., II:2586
Abbe, Cleveland, III:1367
Abbe, Dorothy, II:489
Abbey Theatre, II:1585
Abbot, Ezra, I:983
Abbott, Jacob, I:3273
Aborigines, Australia, I:2310
Abortion, III:999
Abraham, Terry P., III:2572
Absenteeism in industry, I:1581
Abstract services, I:8; III:3
ABT abstracts, II:1138
Academy of Motion Picture Arts and Sciences, I:3086
Academy of Natural Sciences of Philadelphia: manuscripts, III:1272–73
Accidents, industrial, I:2344, 2355, 2359
Accounting, I:2765–72; II:977, 1412; III:869; government, I:1863; railroad, I:2768–69
Acetylsalicylic acid, II:1165
Ackerman, Dorothy P., III:2271
Ackermann, Gertrude W., I:1051–52, 4965
Adams, Abigail, I:3942
Adams, Annette Carroll, II:595
Adams, Frederick B., Jr., III:153, 678
Adams, George, III:213
Adams, George C. S., I:3162
Adams, George M., I:3303
Adams, Hazard, II:1909
Adams, Henry, I:258, 3944; II:1633
Adams, James, I:727
Adams, James N., II:187–88
Adams, John, I:3943, 4438; II:1091, 2535
Adams, John Q., I:3944, 4438; II:2190
Adams, Joseph Q., I:3524
Adams, Léonie, I:3325
Adams, Lucile, II:1755
Adams, Marion, I:2993
Adams, Randolph G., I:684, 3886, 4395, 4533–36, 4563, 5213; III:2426
Adams, Sherman, III:2427
Adams, Sister Regina Mary, II:365
Adams, Stanley E., III:1069
Adams, Thomas R., II:350–51, 939, 2190; III:742, 2383
Adams, Zu, I:4852
Adamson Law, I:1628
Adan, Adrienne Hinds, III:757
Adcock, Lynette, II:2702
Addams, Jane, II:916
Addison, Agnes, I:2946

Adirondacks, III:3230
Adler, Betty, III:2044–45
Adler, Cyrus, I:1232
Adler, Elkan N., I:1215
Adult education, II:926–27
Advertising, I:301, 2773–80; history, III:916
AE, II:1871–72
Aerial photography, I:2569
Aerodynamics, I:2575
Aeronautics, I:2545–81; II:1324–38; III:1587–1602; in agriculture, II:1345; periodicals, I:2573, 2576
Aeropolitics, I:2l26
Aerospace Corporation Aerospace Library: serials, III:1587
Aesop, I:3723, 3730; II:1980
Afghanistan, II:2358, III:2828
Africa, I:4193 (13–14, 18); history, I:4366–87, II:2434–62, III:152, 2922–96; periodicals, II:2460
Africa, North, III:2822
Aged, medical care, II:1196
Agee, James, III:1980
Agnese, Battista, I:3841, 3865
Agricultural cooperatives, II:1365, 1369; III:1620–21, 1627, 1634, 1929
Agricultural credits, I:2602 (7, 23)
Agricultural economics, I:2620–39; II:1364–76; California, II:1364
Agricultural engineering, I:2594; II:1357
Agricultural experiment stations, I:2598 (4), 2613–14
Agricultural extension, I:2599 (18)
Agricultural laborers, II:1368, 1374
Agricultural marketing, I:2599 (7), 2602 (37, 43), 2623–24
Agricultural museums, I:2599 (29)
Agricultural periodicals, I:2602 (18), 2610–14; II: 1117, 1360–63; III:1625, 1635, 1642–43
Agricultural relief, I:2626 (41–42, 45, 50, 52–53, 76, 84, 92)
Agriculture, I: 2183, 2591–2673; II:1345–1411; III:1609–94; Alabama, I:2626 (15); California, I:2626 (31); China, II:1347; England, I:2599 (24), 4257; Europe, II:1356; Greece, I:2626 (39); Oklahoma, I:2626 (21); Rumania, I:2626 (49); Switzerland, I:2626 (35); U.S. history, I:2599 (26, 32–33, 35), 3615–19; Virginia, I:2593
Aguilera, Francisco, I:3710; III: 2257

Aiken, Walter H., I:2204
Air brakes, I:2513
Air conditioning, I: 2528
Air freight, I:2560, 2578
Air pollution, II:1323; III:1700, 1704–05
Air raid protection, I:5478, 5493
Airplane manufacture, I:2568
Airports, I:2567
Aitchison, Clyde Bruce, III:2428
Akron University, Bierce Library: English and American literature, I:3390
———Rubber Division Library: chemical technology, union lists, II:1425–26
Alabama: authors, I:3255; economic conditions, II:718; history, I:4711–14, III:3161
Alabama History Commission, I:4711
Alabama Polytechnic Institute Library, I:178
Alabama State Dept. of Archives and History: Alabama authors, I:3255; Alabama history, I:4713; Civil War, III:3078; newspapers and periodicals, I:283
Alabama Supreme Court Library, I:1669
Alabama, University, Business Library: Alabama economic conditions, II:718
———Library: Alabama history, I:4714; biological periodicals, II:1114; catalog, I:179; Confederate imprints, II:2536–37, III:3072; Hearn, Lafcadio, II:1702; Heflin, James Thomas, II:2143; Jeffers, Robinson, II:1715, III:2037; Louisiana history, I:4874, 4891; manuscripts, II:240; rockets and space travel, III:1588; Shelby Iron Works, II:1430
———Medical Center Library: history of medicine, II:1243, III:1472
———School of Law Library: periodicals, III:1038
Alagia, Damian P., II:400
Alamán, Lucas, II:2745
Alaska, history, I:4193 (6), 5279; II:2575, 2582–83; III:3162–63
Alaska Library Association: periodicals, III:202
Alaska State Library: state publications, III:24
Alaska, University, Library: Alaska Commercial Company, III:899; serials, III:203
Albania, I:4323; II:2347
Albany, N.Y., authors, I:3250

Albany Institute and Historical and Art
	Society Library: Albany authors,
	I:3250
Albaugh, Gaylord P., III:735
Albee, Louise B., I:3139
Albers, C.C., I:2432
Albertus Magnus, I:623
Albrecht, Otto E., I:3000; II:1512
Alchemy, III:1385; manuscripts, I:2276
Alcott, Louisa May, III:1981
Alden, John, II:319, 345; III:2210
Alden, John E., I:549, 865, II:1774
Alden, John R., I:4486
Aldine Press, I:234, 604; II:314, 323
Aldrich, Thomas B., I:3274
Aleut language, I:3187
Aleutian Islands, I:5280
Alevizos, Theodore, III:2274
Alexander, Helen P., III:2922
Alexander, Martha, II:1229
Alexandria Library (Virginia): catalog, III:170
Alfriend, Reece, III:886
Algebra, I:2220
Algonquian languages, I:3177
Algren, Nelson, III:1982
Allason, William, I:5215, 5220
Allegheny College Library: catalog, I:180;
	Lincoln, Abraham, I:4027, II:2163
Allegheny County Law Library, I:1670
Allen, Albert H., I:709, 720–21, 745–
	46, 751–53, 845
Allen, Don C., I:664
Allen, Edison B., III:2407
Allen, Francis P., I:2329
Allen, Francis W., I:3688
Allen, Frederick Lewis, II:2092
Allen, George, I:3120
Allen, Hardee, II:764, III:1034
Allen, Henry T., II:2093
Allen, Hervey, II:1663–65
Allen, Ira, I:5210
Allen, James E., Jr., III:2429
Allen, Jay, I:3015
Allen, Jessie M., II:1388
Allen, Julius W., II:1270
Allen, Kenneth S., III:680
Allen, Lafon, I:5496
Allen, Robert V., III:795, 3001, 3162
Allen, Ruth, III:1458
Alliott, Hector, I:4718
Allis, Frederick S., Jr., III:2554, 2589, 2607
Allison, Antony Francis, II:596
Allison, William H., I:1199
Almanacs: Connecticut, I:4692; Kentucky
	I:4697; Maine, I:4702, Massachusetts,
	I:4703, New Hampshire, I:4702; New
	Jersey, I:4694; New York, I:4699,
	4701; Rhode Island, I:4693; South
	Carolina, I:4707; United States,
	I:4691, 4695–96, 4698, 4700, 4704–
	06, II:2580–81, III:3293; Vermont,
	I:4702; Virginia II:2579, III:3292
Almond, Nina, I:5519
Almonds, I:2628 (23)
Alphabets, III:480
Alston, R. C., III:1909
Altheide, Dorothy P., III:614
Altschul, Eugen: II:658

Altschul, Frank: II:313
Altsheler, Brent, I:2297
Alvord, Clarence W., I:4248, 4816
American Academy of Arts and Letters:
	literary manuscripts, II:247
American Antiquarian Society Library:
	American almanacs, I:4691; American
	directories, III:2669; American
	printing history, I:685–86, III:497;
	American watch papers, II:2486;
	ballads, I:3221; Bible, I:1014; British
	newspapers, II:211; Bunyan, Paul,
	III:2146; business history, I:2742;
	Cambridge (Mass.) Press, I:765;
	catalog, I:181, III:163; Civil War,
	I:4597; collections, I:4396, II:2468,
	2472; colonial era, I:4497–98,
	II:2517; Eddy, Isaac, I:881; Florida
	newspapers, I:406; French and Indian
	War, I:4499–4500; Gibbon, Edward,
	I:3994; juvenile literature I:3801;
	Mather family, I:4071, 4076, 4523;
	manuscripts, I:497; New England
	sermons, I:4624; New York City
	newspapers, I:388; oneirocritica, I:961;
	penmanship, III:1944; poetry, I:3231;
	portraits, I:2947, 2950; rare books,
	III:443; Rhode Island almanacs,
	I:4693; Royal primers, I:700; Stearns,
	Samuel, I:4097; Vermont imprints,
	III:638; West Indian and Burmudian
	newspapers, I:451
American Assoc. for State and Local History,
	I:4397
American Association of Law Libraries:
	directory, I:1761, II:782, III:984
———Southwest Chapter: foreign legal
	periodicals, III:1039
American Assoc. of Museums, I:2157
American Assoc. of Port Authorities, I:2118
American Baptist Historical Society, II:549
———Library: catalog, I:1056
American Benedictine Academy, II:607
American Bible Society, III:701
———Library: catalog, I:1015
American Board for Foreign Missions, II:529,
	536–38
American book-prices current, I:2
American Catholic Historical Society Library:
	American history, I:4587; American
	Catholic history, I:1155; archives,
	I:1175, III:748
American Chemical Society, Chemical
	abstracts, I:2251, II:1110; Cincinnati
	Section, I:2195; Library, I:2264
American Colonization Society, I:1397
American Council of Learned Societies, II:261
American Council on Education, I:68
American drama, I:3232–38; II:1650–53,
	1697; III:1964, 1969, 1971
American Entomological Society, I:2330
American Federation of Labor, III:969
American fiction, I:3239–49; II:1654–62;
	III:1972–79
American Foundation for the Blind, I:1917;
	II:143–44
———Library: blindness, II:915; catalog,
	III:191

American Fur Company, I:4593
American Geographical Society Library:
	African collection, III:2935; catalog,
	I:3822, 3824, III:2352, 2354; map
	collection, I:3823, III:2353; New York
	City maps, I:3913; reference collection,
	I:3867; South American maps, I:2277,
	3926; South Seas, I:3172; U.S.
	geographical publications, I:3828
American Historical Association: European
	history, I:4228
———Committee for the Study of War
	Documents: World War II, II:2770–
	2800
American Home Missionary Society, I:1051–
	52
American Imprints Inventory: Alabama, I:708;
	Arkansas, I:710; Arizona, I:711;
	California, I:717; Idaho, I:730–31;
	Illinois, 732; Iowa, I:742; Kansas,
	I:744; Kentucky, I:748, 751–53;
	Louisiana, I:755; Massachusetts, I:774;
	Michigan, I:785; Minnesota, I:787;
	Missouri, I:793; Nebraska, I:796;
	Nevada, I:797; New Jersey, I:803,
	806; New Mexico, I:809; New York,
	I:817–18, 827; Ohio, I:847;
	Tennessee, I:873–75; Washington,
	I:887; West Virginia, I:889; Wisconsin
	I:891, II:474; Wyoming, I:894
American Indian, I:154, 2599 (23), 4486–96,
	4498–4500; II:254, 1002, 1119,
	2499–2516; III:3020, 3027–44,
	3145; folklore, III:2345
American Institute of Accountants Library:
	accounting, I:2765; bookkeeping,
	I:2772, catalog, I:2766
American Institute of Electrical Engineers,
	I:2481–82
American Institute of Mining Engineers,
	I:2495
American Institute of Pacific Relations,
	II:2367
American Jewish Historical Society Library:
	collections, II:634; Franks family
	letters, III:759; manuscripts, III:760
American Library Association: Art Reference
	Round Table, I:2830, II:1441;
	Committee on Foreign Documents,
	I:49; Committee on Library
	Cooperation with Latin America,
	I:452; Junior Members Round Table,
	I:1; Office for Adult Education, I:59
American library directory, I:69, III:86
American Library in London: Whitman, Walt,
	II:1757
American literature, I:3219–3347; II:1618–
	19, 1622, 1627, 1632–1773;
	III:1944–2101, 2103
American Mathematical Society, I:2209
American Merchant Marine, I:2130
American Missionary Association, I:1053;
	III:821–22
American Museum of Natural History Library:
	serials, III:243
American Numismatic Society Library:
	catalogs, I:2903, III:1775
American Oriental Society Library, I:3795

American Patent Law Association Library, I:1671

American Philatelic Society, I:2045

American Philosophical Society Library: American Indian, II:1119, 2500, III:3027–28, 3030–31; Beccaria, Giambatista, II:2098; catalog, I:182, III:1275; collections, II:2258; Darwin, Charles, II:1047; Franklin, Benjamin, I:3982, 3987; genetics, III:1407; instruments and models, III:1274; Iroquois folktales, II:1002; manuscripts, III:1276, 1278; Parsons, Elsie Clews, II:1003, physics history, III:1375; portraits, III:1706; Rafinesque, C.S., II:1041; science history, III:1278, 1307; U.S. history, I:4398, 4538, 4542

American poetry, I:3219–31, 3356, 3359; II:1644–49; III:1964–70

American Railroad Association, Economics and Finance Dept. Library: catalog, III:920

American Red Cross, I:1919, 5524

American Russian Institute Library, I:4310

American Scientific Congress, I:3825

American sketch book (magazine), II:157

American Society of Civil Engineers, I:2454, 2505–06

American Society of Genealogists, III:2650

American Society of Mechanical Engineers, I:2473

American Sunday School Union, III:2315

American Telephone and Telegraph Co., I:2767

American Type Founders Co., I:928, 932

American University Library: serials, III:275, 286

Americans in Paris, II:2085

Ames, A. D., publisher, III:609

Ames, Charles Lesley, II:2380–81

Ames, Herman V., I:5140–42

Ames Foundation, I:1762

Amhara history, I:4368

Amherst College Library: Amherstiana, I:2022; French and Indian War, I:4515; serials, III:234; Wordsworth, William, I:3576

Amish Church, II:547–48

Ammunition, I:5419

Amo Julián, II:1949

Amory, Harcourt, I:2232, 3446

Amphibians, I:2338

Amundsen, Leiv, I:4198

Amusements, I:3086–3145

Amylases, I:2800

Amzalak, Moses Bensabat, II:725

Anabaptists, II:555

Ander, O. Fritiof, I:367, 4304; II:676, 940, 2168

Anderl, Robert G., III:1526

Andersen, Hans Christian, I:3632; II:1929, 1933

Anderson, Alice G., III:1348

Anderson, Bart, II:2675

Anderson, Benedict R., II:2429

Anderson, Charles A., II:570–71

Anderson, Fanny, III:1501, 1560

Anderson, Frank J., III:1839, 2380, 2424

Anderson, Frederick, II:1754

Anderson, Gerald H., II:533; III:712

Anderson, Gregg, I:773

Anderson, Hazel A., II:783

Anderson, Henry J., I:2158

Anderson, Jack, III:1873

Anderson, James, III:2526

Anderson, John, III:2430

Anderson, Lorene, II:2618

Anderson, Margaret, III:2689

Anderson, Maxwell, III:1983–84

Anderson, Robert B., I:1763–64, 4487

Anderson, Russell H., I:4135

Anderson, Sherwood, I:3275

Andover Theological Seminary Library, I:984, 4071

Andreassen, John C. L., II:2629

Andres, John E., II:436

Andrews, Avery D., II:2316

Andrews, Clement W., I:318

Andrews, Edward Deming, II:625

Andrews, Faith, II:625

Andrews, Frank De W., I:5005

Andrews, Patricia, III:1113, 1118, 1136, 1177, 1202, 3109–16

Andrews T. Coleman, III:2431

Andrews, Wayne, I:3992

Andrews, William L., I:614

Anesthesia, I:2375, 2416

Angell, Joseph Warner, Jr., I:3605, II:1916

Angelus Studio, I:5135

Angle, Paul M., I:4026, 4039

Anglemyer, Mary, III:866

Anglo-Egyptian Sudan, II:2451

Animal culture, I:2635–39; II:1377–82; III:1657–63

Animal industry, II:1378–82

Ankenbrand, Frank, I:3918

Annan, Gertrude L., I:4394, II:1222

Anne, Queen of England, II:2286

Annmary Brown Memorial, I:615–16

Anonyms, I:15

Antarctic Region, II:2763, 2766–67; III:3395, 3402–3; maps, II:2044

Anthony, Robert O., I:4062

Anthracite coal, I:2293

Anthrax, II:1153

Anthropology, I:134, 2307–14, 2626 (89), 2847, 3864; II:651, 1003, 1115, 1118–20; III:795, 1412

Antiphonaries, II:266

Antrim, Edward, I:1714

Apel, Willi, I:3001

Apian, Peter, II: 2021

Apiculture, I:2599 (21), 2639

Appalachians, III:3133

Appel, Alfred, III:2184

Apple industry, I:2626 (19)

Applegate, Howard L., III:938, 2416, 2493, 2914

Appleseed, Johnny, I:3268

Appleton, John B., I:4657

Aquatic biology, III:1417

Aquilera, Francisco, II:1950–52, 1962

Arabian nights, I:3771

Arabian Peninsula, II:2458

Arabic history, I:4369, III:181

Arabic languages, I:3170

Arabic literature, I:3767–68, 3770–71, 4202, 4369; III:2810

Arabic manuscripts, II:276, 1986–87

Arai, Hirotake, III:2901

Arbitration: industrial, I:1641, 1654; international, I:1821

Archaeology, II:1001, 1115; III:1726

Archer, Horace Richard, II:1618

Archer, John, II:1223

Archibald, Raymond C., I:3952

Architecture, I:2874–2902; II:1453, 1456–66; III:1722, 1729, 1738–52; American, I:2886; colonial, I:2874; English, I:2885, 2928; Greek, I:2884; history, III:1720; library, II:68; Pennsylvania, I:2845; school, II:1460

Archives, U.S., I:4416–31, 4465, 4472, 4477

Archives of American Art, III:1707

Arctic Institute of North America, II:2761

Arctic warfare, I:5405

Area College Library Cooperative Program (Pa.): serials, III:204

Arents, George, I:2640–42; II:1383, 1386, 1627, 1786

Arents, Prosper, II:1784

Argentine history, I:5289; III:3326–27

Argonne National Laboratory Library: serials, III:1326

Ariosto, Ludovico, II:1948

Aristotle, I:3722; II:1968; III:2280

Arithmetics, I:2213, 2216, 2221, 2226

Arizona Dept. of Library and Archives: newspapers, III:299; state publications, III:25

Arizona, history, I:4715–18

Arizona Pioneers' Historical Society, III:3371

Arizona State Library: catalog, I:183

Arizona State University: percussion library, III:1795

Arizona Statewide Archival and Records Project, I:1272

Arizona Territorial Library: catalog, I:183

Arizona University, Bureau of Audiovisual Services: educational films, III:1785
———Library: Arizona history, I:4715; Brazil, III:3330; Mexican writers, I:3694; serials, I:284; University of Arizona publications, II:941

Arkansas: government publications, I:23, II:18, III:26; history, I:4719–27, II:2584–85, III:3164–65

Arkansas Folklore Society, II:1559

Arkansas Foundation of Associated Colleges: periodicals, III:205

Arkansas Geological Survey, State Map Library, I:3826

Arkansas History Commission: Arkansas history, I:4719, 4721, II:2584; Arkansas newspapers, II:189; Barrow, John C., II:2097; Bliss, Calvin Comins, II:2100; Eno, Clara Bertha, II:2123; Fulton, William Savin, III:2500; Oldham, Kie, I:4720; Trimble, Robert W., II:2217; Woodruff, William E., II:2239

Arkansas Legislative Council, Research Dept., II:834

Arkansas Library Commission, III:3164–65

Arkansas State History Museum, I:4719

Arkansas, University, Library: Arkansas folk songs, III:1559; Arkansas history, I:4723, II:2585; Brough and Remmel papers, II:2104; Fletcher, John Gould, II:1696; government research reports, II:834; Ozark region, II:2557; state publications, I:23, II:18, III:26
Armajani, Yahya, I:545
Armenia, I:4213
Armenian Apostolic Church, I:1081
Armenian manuscripts, II:2323
Armitage, Merle, III:670
Armstrong, A. Joseph, I:3430, 3432
Armstrong, Charles E., III:2355
Armstrong, Eva V., I:2252–55, 2268
Armstrong, Margaret, III:675
Armstrong, Mrs. A. Joseph, II:1814
Armstrong, Nellie C., I:1794
Arnade, Charles W., II:2597–98, 2732
Arnakis, G. G., II:2362
Arndt, C. O., I:4363–65
Arndt, Karl J. R., III:206, 3411
Arnett, Benjamin William, II:557
Arnold, H. H., II:2094
Arnold, Matthew, II:1805
Arnold, Nancy I., III:1019
Arrian, Anabasis, II:1965
Art: auctions, I:2842; Byzantine, II:1445; Indian, I:2381; Latin American, I:2841, 2848, 2852–54; medical, III:1497, 1504; medieval, II:1442; Negro, I:2832–33; Oriental, II:1444; Pennsylvania, I:2845; periodicals, I:2830, II:1441; sales catalogs, II:1448
Art Institute of Chicago Library: art periodicals, III:1708
Arthur, Chester A., II:2095; III:2432
Arthurian romances, I:2151–52
Artigas, Jose Gervasio, I:5281
Arvidson, Lloyd A., III:2014
Asakawa, Kanichi, I:3777
Asbestos, I:2465
Asch, Sholem, I:1237
Ash, Lee, II:72; III:87, 1444
Ashby, Charlotte M., II:2069, 2071, 2074; III:800, 1106, 1128, 1132, 1685, 1750, 3369
Ashcom, Benjamin B., III:2258
Ashendene Press, III:669
Ashley, Robert P., II:1823
Asia: history, I:4328–65, II:2352–2433, III:2793–2921; South Asia, II:2324, 2359, 2375–85, 2410
Asia Society, III:2793
Asian Americans, III:3003–4
Asian history, III:2793–2921
Aspirin, II:1165
Assemblies of God, I:1197
Associated Colleges of Central Kansas: serials, III:201
Associated Knit Underwear Manufacturers of America, I:2807
Association books, I:3204; II:285
Association for Asian Studies: Chinese periodicals, III:347; East Asian collections, III:2853
Association for Recorded Sound Collections, II:2674

Association of American Railroads, I:5205
Association of Casualty and Surety Executives, I:1946
Association of Research Libraries, I:368
———Committee on National Needs, II:2375
———Foreign Newspaper Microfilm Project, II:210
Association of Southeastern Research Libraries, III:95
Association of the Bar of the City of New York Library, I:1672, 1765–66
Assyria, I:4214
Astor Library, I:231–32, 3796
Astrology, II:1084
Astronomy, I:2229–44; II:1084–89; III:1292–93, 1364–71; 1567; Arabic, II:1084
Athapascan languages, I:3178
Athletics, I:3129–38
Atiyeh, George N., III:2924
Atkinson, Fred W., I:3232
Atkinson, Geoffroy, I:3827
Atkinson, Gloria L., III:1208
Atlanta Public Library: Georgia counties, I:4811
Atlanta University Library: African collection, III:2953; Civil War, III:3076; manuscripts, II:248; Negroes, I:1385, II:681
Atlantic neptune, I:2124
Atlas, Mona F., III:2533
Atomic bomb, I:2502
Atomic power, I:2179, 2181–82; II:1097–99
Atwood, Albert W., II:89
Atwood, Alice C., I:2315
Auburn University Library: East European and Russian literature, III:2740; engineering, III:1565; English and American literature, III:2103; Latin American collection, III:3294; medical periodicals, III:1527; speech and hearing sciences III:192
Auction catalogs, I:9
Audio-visual aids, I:2602 (28)
Audubon, John James, II:1131–32, 1134; III:1434, 1761
Augustana College Library: catalog, I:184; children's books, II:2002; European history, I:4229; Lincoln, Abraham, II:2168; Swedish Americans, I:367, II:940; Swedish history, I:4304; Swedish immigration, II:676
Ault, Ruth Genevieve, II:1498
Auslander, Joseph, I:3189
Austin, Mary, I:4654
Austin, Robert B., III:1473, 1496
Australia: history, I:5371, 5373, II:2756, III:3400; literature, II:1794
Austria, history, III:2703–9
Austria-Hungary, history, III:2704, 2706, 2708–9
Autographs, I:483, 488, 503, 509, 511, 552, 569, 578, 612
Automobile industry, I:1635, 2544
Automobile parking, I:2135; II:1305
Automobile tires, I:2542
Automotive history, II:750, 958; III:1569
Avant, Julius H., III:329–30

Avery, Ellen Walters, I:555
Avery, Laurence G., III:1983–84
Avery, Mary, I:1200
Avianus, I:3733
Aviation, maps, II:2041
Aviation, military, history, II:900, 1326
Avins, Wesley, III:220
Ayer, Edward E., II:2511, 2758
Ayer, Joseph C., I:1003
Ayer, Mary F., I:369
Ayres, Frank C., I:2698
Ayton, Mauree W., II:1274
Azhderian, Helen Wentworth, II:1513
Aztec manuscripts, III:408

Baatz, William H., II:1706
Babb, James T., I:4399, II:2558
Babbitt, Charles J., I:1854
Babcock, Charles E., I:5324
Babine, Alexis V., I:3745
Babson Institute Library, I:2184
Babylonian history, I:4200, 4214, 4217
Babylonian seals, II:2265; III:2809
Bach, Johann Sebastian, II:1556
Bachmann, George T., III:624
Bacillus anthracis, II:1153
Backus, Edythe N., I:3011
Backus, O. P., II:1971
Backus, Richard C., I:1736
Bacon, Francis, I:3421–22, II:1806
Baden, Anne L., I:971, 1355, 1486–87, 1505, 1510, 1526, 1537, 1558–59, 1563, 1867–69, 1888, 1947, 2130, 2358–59, 2494, 2544, 2696, 2777, 2826, 3117, 5378, 5410, 5419
Baer, Carlyle S., I:54
Baer, Elizabeth, I:762, III:444, 1745
Baer, Karl A., II:1183–85
Baginsky, Paul B., I:4522
Bagley family, III:2433
Baha'i Assemblies, I:1196
Bahnsen, Jane E., II:90
Baig, Samuel, I:2172
Bail, Hamilton Vaughan, II:1654
Bailey, Louis J., II:60
Bailey, Philip J., I:3423–24
Bailey, Rosalie Fellows, II:2242
Bailey, Thomas P., I:969
Bailyn, Bernard, III:3058
Bakelite, I:2814
Baker, C. H. Collins, I:2948; II:1467; III:2138
Baker, Carlos, III:2022
Baker, Charles E., I:4023
Baker, Eugene C., I:5185
Baker, Frank, III:726–28
Baker, Frank S., I:3431
Baker, George H., I:3191
Baker, Mary E., I:285, 4136
Baker, Ray S., I:3945
Baker University Library: Bibles, I:1016
Bakken, Douglas A., III:811, 2460, 2568, 3217
Bako, Elemer, III:1, 1910, 2286, 2743
Balas, Leslie, III:519
Balbus, Catholicon, II:334
Balch, Ruth, I:955
Balderston, Katharine C., I:3472

Baldner, Ralph W., III:2244
Baldwin, Loammi, I:2713
Baldwin, Muriel F., I:2931
Baldwin, Thomas W., II:1877
Baldwin-Wallace College, Bach Library,
    II:1556
Balearic Islands, I:4296
Baley, Zena, II:1993
Balkans, I:4193 (4), 4238, 4323–24;
    II:2337–47
Ball, Joyce, III:796
Ballads, English and American, I:769, 783,
    2147, 3221, 3227, 3355; III:2109
Ballantyne, Agnes Louise, II:515
Ballard, James F., I:2417
Ballendine, John, II:2384
Ballenger, T. L., II:2499
Ballinger, Richard A., III:2434
Ballet, I:3023
Baltic states, III:2768–70
Baltimore and Ohio Railroad, I:2059; II:994
Baltimore, history, I:4898, 4910
Baltimore Museum of Art: calligraphy,
    III:1780; maps, II:2017
Baluchistan, II:2358
Balys, John P., III:2768–70
Balzac, Honoré de, III:2247
Banana industry, I:2628 (19)
Bancroft, George, III:3141
Bancroft, Hubert H., I:4676; II:2699
Bandy, W. T., II:1939
Bangor Public Library: Maine history, I:4896,
    III:3197
Bangorian controversy, I:1006
Bank for International Settlements, I:1478
Bank of the U.S., I:1476, 1495
Banker, Howard J., I:2201
Banking, I:1476–1503
Bankruptcy, I:1492, 1498
Banks, Joseph, I:4252
Banks, Paul N., III:1386
Bannon, John Francis, II:597
Banta, David Demaree, II:2614
Baptist Church, I:1056–72, 1207; II:549–52;
    III:721–22; periodicals, II:552
Baptist Mission Press, I:746
Barbados, history, III:3337
Barbeau, Marius, II:2500
Barber, Delta C., II:173
Barberini family, I:2714, 2717
Barck, Dorothy C., I:2699
Barclay, Julius P., II:1685
Bard family, I:5030
Barden, Bertha R., II:65; III:83
Barez, Reva R., II:1853
Baring, Alexander, II:2096
Barlow, Francis, II:1481
Barlow, Joel, I:3276; II:1666
Barlow, Robert, II:1650–51
Barlow, Samuel L. M., III:2435
Barnard, George Grey, III:1760
Barnard, Henry, I:1961
Barnason, Gudrun, I:3606
Barnes, Bonnie J., III:2287
Barnes, Cynthia, II:1313, 1316, 1318, 1320–
    21
Barnes, Dorothy L., II:162
Barnes, Helen V., II:1388

Barnes, John S., I:5452
Barnes, Russell F., II:162
Barnes, Suzanne, II:2708
Barnes, Warner, III:1992, 2144
Barnett, Abraham N., II:656
Barnett, Claribel R., I:2601 (16)
Barnett, George E., I:1645–46
Barnett, John, I:3094
Barnhardt, Edward Nelson, II:2801
Barnhart, J.H., I:2300
Barnhart, John H., III:1428
Barnum, P. T., III:2436
Baron, Hans, III:2724
Baroque art, III:1721
Barreda, Nicolás de la, II:2503
Barrett, Clifton Waller, II:1632, 1634, 1700,
    1704, 1709, 1718, 2474
Barrett, Ellen Catherine, II:2248, 2587
Barrett, Lawrence, I:3095
Barrie, James M., II:1807, III:2136
Barringer, G. Marlyn, III:852
Barrow, John C., II:2097
Barrow, John Graves, II:516
Barry, David F., II:1501
Barry, Jeannette, II:1171, 1186
Barry, Louise, II:2620
Barry, Rozanne M., III:392
Barter commerce, I:2626 (40)
Barthold, Allen J., I:370
Bartlett, Hazel, I:3035
Bartlett, Henrietta C., I:3419, 3514–16,
    3530, 3541
Bartlett, John R., I:4501, 5160
Bartlett, Kenneth F., I:2239, 2382; III:1114
Bartlett, Mary Ellen, III:544
Bartlett, Phyllis, II:1863
Bartlett, Richard, III:1908
Bartók, Bela, III:1861
Bartolomei, Roy, III:2589, 2607
Barton, George A., I:4204
Barton, Mary N., III:445
Barton, William E., I:4051
Bartow, Barbara, II:572
Bartram, John, II:1122
Bartram, William, II:1122
Baruch, Bernard, III:2410
Basanoff, V., I:1080
Baseball, I:3134
Baskerville, John, I:682–83
Basler, Roy Prentice, II:2162
Bass, Harry W., II:972–73
Bassan, Maurice, III:2016
Bassett, John S., I:5090–91
Bassett, Theda, II:172
Batchelder, John D., I:511, 610–11
Bates, Albert C., I:723, 1767, 3802, 4692,
    4756
Bates, George H., I:5382
Bates, James Wesley, II:819
Bates, W. N., I:3722
Bator, Victor, III:1861
Batsel, John, III:732
Batson, Walter, III:2468
Batteau, D. Wayne, II:1612
Battle Abbey, I:4275
Batts, Grover C., II:922
Baudelaire, Charles, II:1939
Bauer, Harry C., I:116

Bauer, K. Jack, II:2769
Bauer, Robert V., II:1670
Baugh, Virgil E., II:736, 851, 860, 867, 914,
    1464; III:1102, 1647
Baughman, Roland, I:593, 716; II:279, 284,
    494, 1997, 2221–22; III:453, 660,
    1757
Baum, Joan H., II:1682, 1997
Baum, L. Frank, II:1997
Baum, P. F., I:3506; II:1867
Baumgardt, David, I:958, 1514; II:514
Baumgartner, Leona, I:3660
Bausman, Lottie M., I:5143
Baxter, Charles N., I:4595
Baxter, James P., I:4086
Baxtresser, Betty B., III:615, 1608, 1661
Bay, J. Christian, I:132, 1156, 2159
Bay psalm book, I:768, 783; II:542
Bayden, David D., II:1557
Bayley, Daniel, II:1562
Baylor University Library: Browning, Robert
    and Elizabeth Barrett, I:3430, 3432–
    33, II:1814, 1816, III:2143; music
    collection, III:1815; serials, I:306;
    Texas history, I:5190
Beach, Helen, I:1932
Beaches, I:2288
Beal, Edwin G., Jr., I:3778; II:2366, 2409,
    2425
Beale, Joseph H., I:1762, 1764, 1768
Bealer, Lewis W., I:5281–82
Beall, Rachel H., I:2932
Beane, L. E., I:2827
Bear, James A., Jr., II:2579; III:3292
Beardsley, Arthur S., I:1769
Beardsley, Aubrey, I:2909; II:1473
Beardsley, Richard K., II:1115
Beardsley, Theodore S., Jr., III:2259
Bearings (machinery), II:1432
Beasley, Roger, III:385, 3313
Beatty, Arthur, II:1908
Beauharnais, Eugene, I:4283
Beaumarchais, Pierre, I:3650, 4560
Beaumont, Francis, I:3372
Beaumont, William, I:2412, III:1500
Bebout, Lois, III:1353
Beccaria, Giambatista, II:2098
Beck, Lucy, III:2288
Beck, Richard J., II:1015
Beck, Sydney, III:1796
Becker, Carl, I:4849
Becker, R. H., III:3308
Beckett, Samuel, III:1982
Beckford, William, II:1667
Bedford County, Penn.: history, I:5157
Bedinger, Margery, I:2793
Bee culture, III:1658
Beebe Town Library, I:4915
Beef cattle, II:1381
Beer, William, I:286
Beerbohm, Max, I:3425; II:1808
Beers, Henry Putney, II:2466; III:3106–7,
    3135
Beethoven, Ludwig van, I:3043–44; III:1867
Beggars, I:1921
Behrens, William B., I:2248
Beinecke, Edwin J., II:1888, 1890; III:2226
Beinecke, Frederick W., II:2740

Beinecke, Walter, Jr., II:1807, 1888, 1890, 2740

Bela Bartók Archives, III:151

Belgian Congo, I:4373; III:2759

Belgium, history, I:4193 (3); III:2719

Belknap, George N., II:431–32; III:612–13, 3241

Bell, Alexander G., I:3946

Bell, Barbara L., III:850

Bell, Daniel, III;786

Bell, J. Fred, II:719

Bell, James Ford, II:2061–62, 2522–27

Bell, Janet E., III:3177

Bell, Martha S., I:2138; II:1308

Bell, Matthew J., III:564

Bell, Millicent, II:478

Bell, Whitfield J., Jr., II:1039, 1223, 2125, 2154; III:1278, 1308

Bellamann, Henry, I:3678

Bellamy, Lauretta M., II:1913

Bellamy, V. Nelle, III:713

Bellis, Genevieve, II:387

Belt, Elmer, Library of Vinciana: illustrated books, II:488; Nightingale, Florence, II:1225; Vinci, Leonardo da, II:1482

Bemis, Samuel F., I:1404

Bender, Albert M., I:598

Bender, Harold S., I:1091

Bender, John E., I:1476

Benedict, Russell, I:1770

Benedictines, II:605, 607; III:749

Benedictis, Jack de, I:453

Bengston, Betty Grimes, III:520

Benjamin, Hazel C., II:757

Benjamin, John A., II:1224

Benjamin, Judah P., I:3947

Benjamin, Mary A., I:1157; III:3059

Benjamin, Philip M., I:4027; II:2163

Bennett, Archibald F., II:2647

Bennett, Arnold, II:1797; III:2137

Bennett, Elaine C., II:735

Bennett, Emily F., II:401

Bennett, Jo Ann Waite, II:1133

Bennett, Josiah Q., III:489

Bennett, Norman Robert, III:2928

Bennett, Paul A., III:658

Bennett, Richard, I:580, 605

Benny, Jack, III:1875

Benson, Adolph B., I:3625–26

Benson, Nettie L., I:1405; II:475, 1040, 2741; III:2273, 3348

Bentley, Gerald E., III:1762, 2211

Bentley, Richard, II:256

Bentley, William, I:180

Benton, Elbert J., I:4646

Benton, Joel, I:813

Benton, Josiah H., I:1118

Benton, Mildred, III:88, 102

Benton, Rita, III:1797, 1811

Benton, Thomas H., I:3948

Berg, Fanny K., II:506

Berg Collection, New York Public Library: Blake, William, II:1809; Dickens, Charles, II:1829; Emerson, Ralph Waldo, II:1690; English and American literature, II:1622, 1787–89; Great Britain, history, II:2236; Hawthorne, Nathaniel, II:1701; Masefield, John,

II:1861; Meredith, George, II:1863; Pardoe, Julia, II:1868; pseudonyms, II:1623; Shaw, George Bernard, II:1881; Thoreau, Henry David, II:1748–49; Whitman, Walt, II:1765

Berge, Wendell, II:2099

Berger, Abraham, III:761

Bergson, Henri, I:950

Bergstrom, Doris M., III:575

Bering Strait, maps, II:2062

Berkeley, Francis L., Jr., I:2743; II:91, 2148, 2198

Berkeley, George, I:995; II:517

Berkeley Public Library: city planning, I:2873

Berkenmeyer, Wilhelm Christoph, II:520

Berkowitz, David S., III:481

Berkshire Athenaeum: Melville, Herman, II:1726

Berlin, Charles, III:762

Bermuda, history, I:5343

Bernath, Frances A., III:2845

Berner, Richard C., II:955; III:1679, 2613

Bernson, Alexander, III:2382

Berrien, John MacPherson, III:2437

Berry, W. J. C., I:1765

Berryman, Clifford K., I:2921

Berryman, John R., I:1729

Berthier, Alexander, I:4558

Berthold, Arthur B., I:70

Berthrong, Donald J., I:4608

Berton, Peter A., II:2407; III:2889

Bertrand, Marcella M., III:576

Beshers, Mary Jane, II:370

Bestor, Arthur E., Jr., I:1512; II:2613

Bethany Biblical Seminary: serials union list, II:541

Bethel, Elizabeth, I:4475, 4773, 5387, 5434, 5531; II:2549; III:943

Bethel College and Theological Seminary: Baptist archives, II:551

Bethel College Historical Library: Mennonites and Anabaptists, II:555, III:725

Betten, Francis S., I:4230

Betts, Raymond F., II:2119

Beveridge, William, I:491

Bewick, Thomas, II;1129

Beyer, George R., III:3245

Bhutan, III:2828

Bible, I:234, 572, 1014–46, 1227; II:264, 294, 297, 303, 523–28, 583, 932; III:698–711; in drama, I:3368

Biblia Pauperum, II:273

Bibliographical Center for Research, Rocky Mountain Region: Colorado newspapers, III:300; periodicals union list, 1:287

Bibliographical Planning Comm. of Philadelphia, I:71, 117

Bibliographie géographique internationale: I:3828

Bibliography: American, I:13; Dutch, II:16; East European, II:2277, 2284, 2327; English, I:13; French, I:20; general, I:1–22, II:1–17, III:1–18; German, I:20, 468, III:12; international, I:59; Italian, I:20; Latin American, II:476, III:4; national, I:4, II:12–13, III:17; Polish, III:8, Russian, I:21, II:14, 142, 2327; III:14; Slavonic, I:11; subject, I:6

Bibliotherapy, II:1195

Biddle, George, II:1489

Biel, Nicholas, II:2538

Bien, Corabel, II:1348, 1381

Bierce, Ambrose, II:289

Bigelow, Frank B., I:371

Bigelow, Kennard and Co., I:2715

Bigg, Norwood N., III:974, 1092

Biggert, Elizabeth C., II:2668

Bill of Rights, I:1841, 1848, 4578, 5231

Billings, Harold W., II:1884

Billington, Ray Allen, II:2218, 2467, 2559; III:3137

Bimetallism, I:1480

Bingham, Hiram, II:2723

Binsfeld, Edmund L., II:626

Bioanalytic technology, II:1138

Biographical dictionaries, III:2

Biography, I:1997, 3935–4134; II:2078–2241; III:2407–2649

Biological sciences, I:2297–2314; II:1114, 1116–17, 1138, 1162, 1232; III:1289, 1407–20; periodicals, I:2300–02, 2306, 2390, 2610, II:1067, 1114, 1215, III:1414, 1417

Biomedicine, III:1415

Bird, Dorothy Margaret, III:592

Bird, Margaret, II:1305

Bird, Nancy, III:2301

Bird, R. M., II:1668–69

Birdsong, Robert E., I:1934

Birgitta, Saint, II:609

Birkbeck, Morris, I:1374

Birmingham Public Library, I:3255, 4635, 4640

Birth control, III:999

Bischoff, W. N., II:2501

Bishop, Crawford M., I:1737

Bishop, David F., III:585

Bishop, Delbert A., III:1027

Bishop, Eleanor C., III:881

Bishop, William W., I:665, 4240

Bishop Museum Library: Pacific region, III:3394

Bitting, Katherine L., I:2582

Bitzer, David R., I:1017

Bixler, J. Seelye, III:2033, 2610

Black, George F., I:963–67, 2310, 3401, 4271–72, 4368

Black, George N., I:4823

Black, Hester M., II:1785, 1896, 1911

Black, J. William, I:1571

Black, Matthew W., III:1874

Black, Patti Carr, II:2539; III:3073, 3089

Black, Robert K., I:3375

Black Sun Press, II:478

Blackouts, I:5477

Blackstone, William, I:1732; II:801

Blair, Albert U., II:996

Blair, Austin, I:4944

Blair, Emma H., I:5374

Blair, Mirpah, II:2674

Blair, Samuel, II:572

Blake, S. F., II:1389

Blake, William, I:2949, 2980, 3426; II:303, 1467, 1809–11; III:1767, 2138

Blanchard, Linn R., I:5362

Blanck, Jacob N., I:3803–04; II:1633; III:1945
Blankinship, Anne G., III:2289
Blast cleaning, I:2474
Blast furnaces, I:2475
Blatt, Genevieve, II:2676
Blegan, Theodore C., II:2646
Blind, I:1917; II:915; books for, II:143–53, III:191, 193, 195–200
Bliss, Calvin Comins, II:2100
Bliss, Carey S., II:1573
Bloch, Ernest, III:1862
Bloch, Joshua, II:320, 635
Block books, II:273
Blondheim, David S., I:3163
Blood, II:1150, 1231
Bloomer, Gertrude, II:1074, 1214
Bloomer, Robert O., I:3921
Blosser, Susan K., III:3130
Bluhm, Heinz, II:1917
Blum, Albert A., III:952
Blumann, Ethel, I:4729; II:2589
Blunden, Edmund, III:2139
B'nai B'rith, I:1987
Boak, A. E. R., I:4208
Boardman, Samuel L., I:759
Boardman, Thayer M., II:765, 773
Boatman, Mildred, I:3855
Boatner, Maxine Tull, II:2132
Bobbitt, Mary R., I:2154
Bocker, Dorothy, II:1166, 1177, 1179, 1190, 1192
Bodde, Derk, I:3779; II:2376
Bode, Carl, II:1750
Bodin, Jean, II:670
Boeninger, Hildegard R., II:2298
Boewe, Charles, II:1041–42
Bogan, Louise, II:1628
Boger, Lorise C., III:345, 1363
Bolander, Louis H., I:5472
Bolivar, Simón, I:3949–51
Bolivia, history, I:5289, 5323; II:2754; III:3329
Boll, T. E. M., III:2221
Bolton, Charles K., I:4916
Bolton, Henry C., I:2196
Bombard, Owen W., II:956–57
Bombs and bombing, II:1294
Bonaparte, Charles Joseph, II:2101
Bonaparte, Louis-Lucien, I:3154
Bonaparte, Napoleon, III:2579
Bond, John W., III:1756
Bond, Richmond P., I:454, 3376
Bond, W. H., II:241, 1898; III:436
Bone, II:1193
Bonn, George S., III:1327
Bonneau, Ward, III:521
Bonner, Amy, II:1670; III:1985
Bonney, Edward, II:1671
Bontemps, Arna, I:1386; II:1677
Bonus pay, I:1624
Book design, I:927–48
Book illustration, I:673, 914–17, 2912–14, 2953, 2957, 2960; II:286, 292, 305, 485–88, 1480–81, 1492; III:651–57, 1710; American, II:655; French, III:653, 656–57; Icelandic, I:3612; Italian, II:282, 304; Japanese, III:654;

New England, III:651–52; oriental, I:3781
Book jackets, III:663
Book of Common Prayer, I:985, 1118, 1137; II:582–83, 2287
Book reviews: technical, I:2435
Bookbinding, I:524, 527, 568–69, 572, 604, 611, 918–26; II:286, 292–93, 298, 305, 505; III:464, 675–80
Bookkeeping, II:977
Bookmaking, I:539
Bookplates, I:54–55, 57, 60; II:60, 62; III:81; Jewish, III:776
Books, deterioration, I:61
Books of Hours, I:519, 985
Booktrade, I:65
Book-worms, I:63
Booth, Ada P., I:3235
Booth, Bradford A., I:3561; III:2127
Booth, John Wilkes, III:2438
Borchard, Edwin M., I:1734, 1756, 1759
Borden, Elizabeth B., II:1009
Bordin, Ruth, II:2229
Boreman, Arthur I., I:5243
Born, Lester K., I:3164; II:1, 261; III:425
Borneo, history, I:4358; III:2917
Borowski, Felix, II:1514
Borrenstein, David A., I:806
Borrow, George, II:303
Bossuet, Jacques B., I:3651
Boston: history, I:4917, 4919; maps, I:3896–98
Boston Athenaeum Library: Adams, John Quincy, I:3944; catalog, I:185, III:164; Catholicism, II:598; Civil War, I:4597; Confederate imprints, I:4595, II:2541; Great Britain, history, I:4257; Halliwell-Phillipps, James O., I:3543; printing history, I:582, 927; rare books, II:277; Washington, George, I:4105; Western Americana, II:2568
Boston College Library: Latin America, I:5285; Thompson, Francis, I:3559; university archives, II:948
Boston Elevated Railway Co. Library, I:2132
Boston, Engineering Dept., I:3896–97
Boston Medical Library: manuscripts and incunabula, I:2417
Boston Museum of Fine Arts: Indian art, I:2831; La Fontaine, Jean de, I:3652
Boston Navy Yard, I:5465
Boston Philatelic Society, I:2044
Boston Public Latin School, I:1995
Boston Public Library: Adams, John, I:3943, II:2091; American Revolution, III:3054; anthropology, I:2312; architecture, I:2875–76; astronomy, I:2231; Bailey, Philip James, I:3423; Barbados, III:3337; Beethoven, Ludwig van, I:3044; Biblia Pauperum, II:273; Book of common prayer, I:985, 1118; Boston music history, I:3063; Boston printing, I:687; Brome, Richard, I:3429; Browning, Robert and Elizabeth Barrett, I:3431, II:2815; catalog, I:186–87, 4184; Civil War, I:4597; Columbus, Christopher, I:3961; costume, I:2936; dance, I:3104; Dante, Alighieri, I:3674, 3681;

Defoe, Daniel, II:1827, III:2157; Dickens, Charles, II:1828; Dryden, John, I:3466; English Bible, I:1018; English literature, I:3349, III:2104; Far East history, I:4342; films, III:1786; fore-edge paintings, II:1478; foreign language books, I:3201; Franklin, Benjamin, I:3974, 3989, II:2126; French literature, I:3635; genealogy, I:4137; German literature, I:3581, 3583, 3592; Great Britain, history, I:4249–50, 4257; Griswold, Rufus W., I:3286; Halliwell-Phillipps, James O., I:3543; historical fiction, I:3193; Horace, I:3726; incunabula, I:617, 630; Italian literature, I:3661; Johnston, David C., III:1753; Judaism, I:1216, II:644–45; juvenile literature, I:3805, 3809; landscape gardening, I:2856, III:1664; manuscripts, I:483–84; maritime history, III:3123; Massachusetts history, I:4917–19, 4927; Mather family, I:4076; medieval manuscripts, III:429; music, I:3002; New England history, I:4625–28, III:3124; newspapers, III:301 Paris history, II:2302; periodical, I:166; philately, I:2044; photographs, III:1781, Prescott, W. H., II:2195; printing history, I:581–82, 927; Psalms, II:542; rare books, II:281–82; Royal primer, I:700; Russian music, III:1798; Seneca, I:3738; serials, I:288; Shakespeare, William, I:3516–19, III:2210; social reform, I:1254; Spanish dictionaries, I:3165; Spanish history, I:4297; Spanish and Portuguese literature, I:3690–91, 3695, III:2260; Swift, Jonathan, I:3551; Thackeray, William Makepeace, II:1901; theater history, III:3087; Tosti engravings, I:2955; Washington, George, I:4106–07; West Indies, I:5284, II:2750; Western Americana, II:2568; women, history, I:2139
Boston Social Law Library, I:1673
Boston Society of Natural History Library, I:2298
Boston University Libraries: Africa, I:2434, 2436–37, 2441, III:2925–27; architectural history, III:1738; archives II:948; catalog, II:126, III:165, 174; chemistry, I:2266; history of nursing, III:1474–75; medical library catalog, I:2361; philately, II:978; School of Education films, III:1787; 20th century authors, III:1918; Van Gulick, R. H., III:2634; Whitman, Walt, III:2090
———New England Institute of Inter-American Affairs: Latin America, I:5285
Boswell, James, I:3427–28
Boswell, Jane E., II:1097
Botanical illustration, III:1432
Botany, I:2315–28, 2601 (42); II:1121–27, 1232; III:1421–33; medical, I:2323, II:1140; Micronesian, II:1124; periodicals, I:2317, 2321

Botkin, B. A., I:4596
Bourguina, Anna, III:2762
Bourke-White, Margaret, III:1783
Bourland, Benjamin P., I:3683
Bourland, Caroline B., I:3690
Bourne, Henry E., I:4288, 5527
Bowden, Ann, III:2171
Bowden, Clyne N., III:3006
Bowden, Edwin T., II:302, 527, 1710, 1712;
    III:2078
Bowdith, Nathaniel, I:3952
Bowdoin, W. G., I:60
Bowdoin College Library: catalog, I:188;
    German language, I:3158; Hawthorne,
    Nathaniel, III:2017–18; Longfellow,
    H. W., III:2017; Maine history,
    I:4892, 4896
Bowen, Dorothy, II:1637, 1758
Bowen, Helene L., III:1175, 1180
Bowen, Jean, III:1799
Bowen, Richard LeBaron, II:2635
Bowerman, Elizabeth G., I:2450
Bowers, Fredson, I:3362, 3511; II:1759–60,
    1873
Bowker, Howard F., I:2904
Bowker annual, III:89
Bowles, Edmund A., III:1800
Bowles, William Lisle, II:1812
Bowman, Albert H., III:3074
Bowman, J. R., I:4539
Bowman, Jacob N., I:5239
Bowman, Ned A., III:1746
Boxer, C. R., II:2311; III:2913
Boxing, I:3131
Boyce, Benjamin, III:2105
Boyce, George K., II:92, 270, 1619
Boycotting, labor, I:1658
Boyden, William Llewellyn, II:919
Boyer, Blanche B., III:428
Boyer, Calvin James, III:721
Boyer, David S., II:93
Boys, R. C., I:3350
Brackenridge, Henry H., I:3953
Brack, O. M., Jr., III:2176
Bracker, Jon, III:2048, 2050
Bradford, John, I:749
Bradford, William, III:588
Bradley, Isaac S., I:4658, 5257
Bradley, James J., II:958
Bradley, Lawrence J., III:752, 2616
Bradley, R. H., I:1711
Bradley, Will, II:1468
Bradstreet, John, I:4497
Brady, John G., II:2582
Brady, Mathew B., I:4610; II:1504, 1506;
    III:3103
Bragdon, Henry W., I:4132
Bragg, Clara W., I:3318
Bragg, Thomas, III:2439
Brahms, Johannes, I:3047, 3049
Braille books, I:17
Brain, physiology, II:1147
Brainerd, Erastus, II:2102
Braithwaite, William Stanley, III:2440
Bramsbäck, Birgit, II:1886
Brand, Denis, I:756
Brand, Katharine E., I:3945, 3967, 4099,
    4133; II:2114, 2213, 2232–34

Brandeis, Louis Dembitz, II:2103
Brandeis University Library: archives, II:948;
    incunabula, III:481
Brann, Harrison Allen, II:573–74
Branner, Robert, II:1442
Brantley, Rabun L., I:373
Brasch, Frederick E., I:2229–30, 2245;
    II:1043; III:1309, 1321
Bray, Robert S., III:193
Bray, Ruth K., I:1618, 1840; II:770–71
Brayer, Herbert O., I:372, 2054
Brazil, I:4193 (8); history, I:4292, 5286,
    5313, 5345, II:2746, III:2731, 3330–
    36; literature, III:2263
Bread making, I:2626 (2)
Breckenridge, James M., I:792
Breckenridge, William C., I:792
Breitenbach, Edgar, II:1483
Brennan, Minnie Elizabeth, III:616
Brennan, William J., Jr., II:828
Brenni, Vito J., III:2088
Brent, Charles Henry, II:587
Breton literature, I:3743
Brett, Philip, II:1567
Breuer, Ernest Henry, II:711, 796, 830;
    III:1015
Brewer, Frances J., II:1998
Brewer, Luther A., II:1840–41; III:2177
Brewing, I:2795
Brick, I:2783
Brickett, Margaret F., III:953
Bridgeport Public Library: Barnum, P. T.,
    III:2436; Catholic books, I:1158
Bridgers, Frank E., III:2412, 2421, 2666
Bridges, Katherine F., III:2466
Bridges, Robert, II:2233; III:2140
Bridges, I:2516
Bridgewater, Dorothy W., I:3975–76; II:1666
Bridgman, Jon, III:2962
Brien, John Smith, III:2441
Briggs, Grace M., II:945
Briggs, Michael J., III:2994
Briggs, Rose T., I:4939
Briggs, Walter B., I:3310
Brigham, Clarence S., I:374–75, 4597, 5161;
    II:211, 1825, 2468; III:302–3
Brigham Young University Library, III:136;
    Mormons, II:568; Victorian collection,
    III:2106, 2691, 2695, 2700
Bright, Franklyn F., I:4613
Brincklé, Gertrude, I:2914
Brinks, Herbert, III:3203
Brinner, William M., III:764
Brinton, Ellen S., I:972, 978, 4633; II:507
Brinton, Margaret, I:2384
Briscoe, Ruth L., I:2402
Brisman, Shimeon, III:763
Bristol, Roger Pattrell, II:352, 402, 2528;
    III:495
Bristow, Joseph Little, III:2442
British Central Africa, I:4375
British Commonwealth sessional papers,
    II:819
British East Africa, I:4375; II:2449
British Guiana, I:5347
Britton, Allen P., II:1562
Britton, Roswell S., I:3780
Broadwater, Aloha P., III:1189–90, 3419

Brock, Clifton, III:803
Brock, Mabel D., III:1068
Brockett, Paul, I:2545
Brockton Public Library, I:3202
Broderick, John C., III:2091, 2584
Brody, Fannie M., I:289
Brogan, Howard O., II:2318
Bromberg, Eric, II:2575
Brome, Richard, I:3429
Bronson, Leisa, I:1567
Brontë, Charlotte, I:3386
Bronx County, N. Y., history, I:5038
Brook Farm, I:1512
Brooke, Rupert, II:289
Brookline, Mass., history, I:4916
Brooklyn, N. Y., history, I:1462, 5041, 5054
Brooklyn Botanic Garden Library: history of
    botany, I:2316; periodicals, I:2317
Brooklyn Museum Library: Egyptology,
    I:4199; illuminated manuscripts,
    I:518–19
Brooklyn College Library, II:107; Slavic
    literature, III:2734
Brooklyn Public Library, catalog, I:189;
    chess, I:3121; Civil War, I:4598;
    costume, I:2937; earthquakes and
    volcanoes, I:2278; English fiction,
    I:3377; juvenile literature, III:2315;
    Polar regions, I:5380
Brooks, Aurelia E., I:3433
Brooks, Charles F., II:1090
Brooks, Charles Timothy, II:1672
Brooks, Jerome E., I:2642
Brooks, Philip C., III:3418
Brooks, Robert P., I:4799
Brooks, Van Wyck, III:1986
Brough, Charles H., II:2104
Brougham, John, II:1813
Broughton, Leslie N., I:3572–73
Broussard, Ray F., II:2733
Browder, Philip P., I:1540
Brower, Edith, III:2060
Brower, Philip P., I:2828
Brown, Alan S., III:3207
Brown, Alexander, I:4502
Brown, Allen A., I:3002, 3087
Brown, Ann D., I:1267, 1532, 1556, 1851,
    1864–65, 1891, 1894, 1904–05,
    2115, 2146, 2526, 2670, 2899, 2998,
    3316, 4079, 4325, 4393, 4644, 4778–
    79, 5349, 5355, 5357, 5408–09;
    II:2492
Brown, Carleton F., I:3351; III:2122
Brown, Charles Brockden. III:1987
Brown, Clement R., II:1109
Brown, E. K., II:1675
Brown, Elisabeth P., II:1403
Brown, Gertrude L., III:3009
Brown, Guy A., I:225
Brown, Herbert R., I:3239
Brown, Horace, I:3869
Brown, Howard M., III:1801
Brown, Ida C., II:2545; III:3211
Brown, Ira V., I:882
Brown, Joe C., III:2101
Brown, John, II:2105
Brown, John, Jr., III:2443
Brown, John Stillman, III:2444

Brown, Julie K., III:630
Brown, Karl, I:139, 281, 2149, 2448, 2689, 3133
Brown, Leighton B., I:4982
Brown, Lloyd A., I:3879; II:2052
Brown, Ralph H., I:3880
Brown, Ralph M., 4077
Brown, Robert B., I:3721
Brown, Sanborn C., II:1044
Brown, Stanley W., II:736
Brown, W. N., I:3772
Brown, Walter F., III:2445
Brown, Walter V., I:2688
Brown, Warren, I:376
Brown, William Compton, III:2446
Brown University, I:2021
————John Carter Brown Library: American
    federation era, III:3055; American
    history, I:4401–03, 4485, 4577,
    II:2469, 2472, III:3045–49; American
    Indian, II:2502; American
    printmaking, I:2993, III:1766;
    Antarctica, III:3395; Brown family,
    I:2728; 15th-century imprints, I:618;
    Florida history, I:4798; Hispanic
    Americana, II:2731; Latin American
    imprints, I:896–98, 902; Latin
    American newspapers, I:479; Lima,
    Peru, imprints, I:896–97; maps,
    III:2356–57; Mexican history,
    II:2737, 2744; navigation, I:2243; New
    England history, II:2553; New England
    maps, III:2383; Northwest Passage,
    III:3049; Rhode Island imprints, I:868;
    U.S. colonial period, I:4501, 4527,
    II:2517; West Indies, III:3338
————Photographic Laboratory, I:5286
————Library: African history, III:2928;
    American drama, I:3222, III:1964,
    1969, 1971; American history,
    III:3002; American poetry, I:3219,
    3222, 3231, II:1644, III:1964, 1969;
    American songs, I:3051; Audubon,
    John James, III:1434; Black Sun Press,
    II:478; calligraphy, III:1777; catalog,
    I:190; 15th-century imprints, I:618; fly
    fishing, III:1904; Harris collection,
    II:1560; Hay, John, II:2141, III:2518;
    Kaser, Arthur L., II:1581; Latin
    American imprints, II:476; Law,
    Andrew, II:2161; Lincoln, Abraham,
    I:4028, 4059; Morris, William, II:490;
    Napoleon Bonaparte, I:4084; Negro
    songs, I:3220; Presidential campaign
    songs, III:1849; psychic science,
    II:509, 512; Shakespeare, William,
    III:2213; 16th-century imprints, II:308;
    Thoreau, Henry D., III:2076; whaling,
    II:726; Whitman, Walt, II:1769
Browne, Margaret F., I:5447
Browne, Maurice, II:1586
Browning, Elizabeth B., I:3431; II:1815;
    III:2141–42, 2144
Browning, James R., II:784
Browning, Robert, I:3430–33; II:1814–17;
    III:2141–44
Brownson, Orestes Augustus, III:2447
Brubaker, Robert L., III:2475, 2540, 3180

Bruccoli, Matthew J., II:1674
Bruce, Anne, III:230
Bruce, David W., I:628
Brumbaugh, A. J., I:68
Brumbaugh, Robert S., III:2284
Brun, Christian, II:2060; III:2406
Bruner, Helen M., I:118
Brunner, Henry S., III:1431
Brunnschweiler, Tamara, III:371
Bruno, Giordano, II:1943
Bry, Doris, II:1499
Bryan, M. M., II:2018
Bryan, Mary Givens, II:2243, 2601
Bryan, Mina R., III:1802
Bryant, Douglas W., I:4404, 5407
Bryant, William C., I:3277; II:1673; III:1988
Brydges, James, I:4265
Bryn Mawr College Library: fifteenth century
    books, II:328; medieval history,
    II:2274; serials, I:320
Bryson, Thomas A., III:748
Buchan, John, III:2145
Buchanan, Briggs W., II:2265; III:2809
Buck, Solon J., I:4817
Buckley, Amelia King, II:1377
Buckman, Thomas R., II:1050
Bucks County Historical Society Library:
    periodicals, I:290
Buddhism, I:1214, II:632
Budé, Guillaume, II:670
Bueckler, John, II:1940
Buell, George Pearson, III:2441
Buffalo and Erie County Historical Society:
    Porter, Peter B., III:2592
Buffalo Historical Society Library: Buffalo
    periodicals, I:342; manuscripts, I:5022
Buffalo Museum of Science: history of
    science, I:2185
Buffalo Public Library: Buffalo periodicals,
    I:342; chemical serials, II:1101;
    German books, I:3584; Mark Twain,
    II:1755
Buffalo, University Library: American
    literature, I:3251; Hawthorne,
    Nathaniel, I:3288; Joyce, James,
    II:1843, 1848, III:2185; Stevens,
    Wallace, II:1645
————Medical School Library: medical
    periodicals, I:2386
Buffum, Imbrie, I:3654
Bühler, Curt F., I:619–20, 646; II:321–22,
    329, 582
Building and loan associations, I:1500
Bukharin, Nikolai I., III:2759
Bulgaria, I:4323; II:2347; history, III:2771–
    73
Bullen, Henry L., I:928
Bulley, Joan Sumner, III:643
Bullock, Charles J., I:1456
Bullock, Helen D., I:2857, 4010, 4029
Bulwer-Lytton, Edward, I:3405
Bunker Hill, I:3853, 4564
Bunnell, Ada, I:2388
Bunyan, John, I:233–34, 3434–35; III:2146
Burbank Public Library: Western history,
    III:3153
Burch, Franklin W., III:3408

Burckhardt, Jakob, II:670
Bureau of Railway Economics Library:
    accounting, railway, I:2768–69; hours
    of work, I:1627–29; labor relations,
    I:1634, 1651; pensions, I:1601;
    railroads, I:2055–95, 2483, 2507–12,
    II:987–89; transportation, I:2745;
    waterways, I:2110–17
Burke, Redmond A., II:323
Burke, Thomas, II:2106; III:2448
Burke, William J., I:3149
Burks, Ardath W., II:2367
Burlington Railroad, I:2103
Burma, I:4359; III:2828, 2839
Burmese literature, I:3787; II:1982
Burndy Library: history of science, II:1045;
    III:1310
Burnett, Charlene R., III:565
Burnett, Whit, III:1976
Burnette, O. Lawrence, III:407
Burney, Fanny, I:3436
Burnham, John M., I:191
Burnham, Phyllis B., III:3214
Burns, Robert, II:289, 1818–19; III:2147
Burns, Robert W., III:1284, 1680
Burns, II:1183
Burr, Aaron, I:3954; II:2107
Burr, Nelson R., I:4001, 4128, 4818; II:627,
    1451
Burton, Arthur G., II:2203; III:2384
Burton, Clarence M., I:4647
Burton, Robert, II:1791
Burton, Robert Edward, II:2257
Burton, Theodore E., I:3955
Burton, William L., III:3085
Busby, William, I:2163
Buschke, Albrecht, I:3122
Bush, Alfred L., III:408, 1946, 2123, 3037
Bush, Cynthia B. G., III:1754
Bush, Martin H., III:1755
Bush, Sargent, Jr., III:2041
Business and commerce, I:2674–2780;
    II:1412–24; III:869–951; biography,
    II:959, 965; cycles, I:2031; finance,
    III:880; forecasting, III:878; history,
    I:2698–2744, II:955–77, III:899–
    919; indexes, II:723; periodicals,
    III:883; services, I:64, 2685, 2692;
    statistics, III:886
Business Historical Society, I:2698, 2700,
    2706
Businessmen, photographs, I:2680
Busse, Gisela von, III:85
Butler, Benjamin F., III:2449
Butler, Nicholas M., I:3956
Butler, Pierce, I:643, 929
Butler, Ruth L., I:455, 485, 3174–75, 4503,
    5287
Butler, Samuel, I:3437–39
Butler, Smedley Darlington, III:2450
Butler, William E., III:1052
Butter oil, I:2598 (5)
Butterfield, Lyman H., I:4011
Butterfield, Margaret, II:60, 2116, 2206, 2657
Butterworth, Charles C., II:523, 932
Butts, Patricia, III:2945
Bynner, Edwin Lassetter, III:1989
Byrd, Anne R., II:1590

Byrd, Cecil K., I:4030; II:388, 829, 1722; III:543, 3189
Byrd, Ruth Evelyn, II:1127, 2157
Byrd, William, II:1567, 2108
Byrns, Lois, III:1947
Byron, George Gordon, I:3440–43; II:1820–21; III:2148

Cabeen, David C., I:3656
Cabell, James Branch, II:1674; III:1990
Cabon, Adolphe, I:456
Cabot, John, I:3957
Cabot, Sebastian, I:3957
Cacao, II:1394
Cadbury, Henry J., I:1142, 4071; II:517–18, 590
Cadenhead, Ivie E., II:2734
Cadillac, Antoine de la Mothe, I:4943, II:2637
Cagle, William R., III:3189
Cahoon, Herbert, II:1620, 1634, 1725, 1844, 1847
Cairns, Margaret, II:449
Caldwell, Anne E., III:1187
Caldwell, Edward, I:4665
Caldwell, Erskine, II:289
Caldwell, Norman W., II:242
Cale, William E., III:522
Calhoun, J. C., II:2190
California: fiction, I:3240–41; government publications, I:24–25; history, I:572, 4728–50, II:2586–92, III:3166–67; maps, I:3899–3903
California Academy of Sciences, I:2160
California, Dept. of Industrial Relations, I:4744
California Historical Society Library: American imprints, III:517; Californiana, I:4749–50, II:2588; Kirsten Flagstad collection, III:1816; manuscripts, II:2586
California Historical Survey Commission: county archives, I:4728
California Institute of Technology Libraries, serials, III:1328
California Library Association: California local history, III:3166; California periodicals, I:291; newspapers, I:377; serials, I:292
———Children and Young People's Section: children's book illustrations, III:2290
———Committee on Local History: California local history, I:4729, II:2589
———Documents Committee: state publications, II:19
———Regional Resources Committee: California library special collections, I:73; foreign dictionaries and grammars, II:1595
California literature, II:1637
California State Archives: genealogical research, III:2651
California State Library: accounting, II:1412, III:869; California fiction, I:3240–41; California history, I:4730; catalog, I:192–193; education, II:923, III:1236; genealogy, I:4138;

management, II:1413, III:870; maps, I:3829; newspapers, II:192; personnel, II:1414, III:871; state publications, I:25, II:20, III:27; supervision, II:1415; technical and scientific books, II:1253, III:1279
———Law Library: administrative law, III:985; capital punishment, III:989; catalog, I:1674; comparative negligence, III:990; computers in law practice, III:991; contested elections, III:992; debtors rights, III:997; freedom of information, III:986; gun legislation, III:988; mentally irresponsible, III:987; military service and law, III:993; ombudsmen, III:994; periodicals, III:1040; population control, III:999; public employee labor relations, III:995; reapportionment, III:996; riots and demonstrations, III:998
———Sutro Library: California maps, I:3899; Catholic Church, I:1159; English pamphlets, I:666; English poor laws, I:4251; Fernandez de Lizardi, J. J., I:3716; Hebraica, III:764; Iceland, I:4252; Italian history, III:2725; Jews in England, I:4253; Latin Americana, III:3297; Mexican pamphlets, I:3696; New England history, I:4629; Protestant Reformation, I:986; research materials, I:118, II:94
California State Mining Bureau Library, I:2496
California State University Library (Fresno): Afro and Mexican Americans, III:823, 2929
———(Long Beach): Mexican Americans III:3372; Negroes, III:818
———(Los Angeles): Afro-American studies, III:2930; Mexican-American studies, III:3373
———(San Diego): astronomy, III:1364; Kepler, Johann, III:1368; literature of time, III:1369
California Supreme Court, I:1771
California, University, Anthropology Library (Berkeley): primates, III:1409
———Bancroft Library (Berkeley): California history, II:2560–61; catalogs, III:3138; Fernandez de Lizardi, J. J., I:3718–19; Jesuit letters, I:4677; Larkin, Thomas Oliver, II:2590; library history, I:4675–76; manuscripts, I:4679, 4685, III:3139; maps, III:2358; Mexican history, II:2735, 2737, III:3374; New Mexico, II:2656; Portuguese archives, II:2312; Utah, II:2698–99; Western Americana, II:2566, III:3149
———Biomedical Library (Los Angeles): acquisitions, III:1445; guide, III:1507; medical history, II:1225, III:1476–77; Pacific Southwest Regional Medical Library Service, III:1447; serials, III:1528–29
———Business Administration Library (Los Angeles): art of administration,

III:874; business and economic history, III:875; foreign materials, III:872; reference guides, III:873; serials, III:876
———Center for South Asia Studies (Berkeley): acquisitions, II:2377, III:2824; periodicals, II:213
———Center for Southeast Asia Studies (Berkeley): Indonesia, III:2840; Philippines, III:2912; Vietnam, III:2848
———East Asiatic Library (Berkeley): catalog, III:2854; collections, II:2369
———Elmer Belt Library (Los Angeles): Vinci, Leonardo da, II:1482
———Engineering and Mathematical Sciences Library (Los Angeles): guide, III:1566: periodicals, III:1567
———Extension Media Center (Berkeley): 16mm films, III:1789
———Geology-Geophysics Library (Los Angeles): serials, III:1391
———Giannini Foundation (Berkeley): agricultural economics, II:1364
———Institute of Industrial Relations (Berkeley): theses and dissertations, II:747
———Law Library (Berkeley): research guide, II:785
———Libraries: resources, II:111, III:138
———Library (Berkeley): aesthetics, I:949; Artigas, Jose Gervasio, I:5281; Berkeley, George, I:995; bookbinding, I:918; California maps, I:3900; Californiana, II:2592; catalog, I:194, III:166; Chinese periodicals, III:348; city planning, I:2873; directories, I:4178; education, I:1949; ethics, I:969; foreign periodicals, II:212; French writing, I:3641; gastronomy, II:1339; German literature, I:3592; German philology, I:3160; history of science, II:1046; Horace, II:1963; international studies, II:811; Japanese American evacuation, II:2801; labor, II:748, 752; Larkin, Thomas Oliver, III:2545; Latin American history, I:5282, III:3308; music, II:1516, 1525; racial minorities, III:3004; rare books, I:3157; redwoods, II:1399; resources, I:138; Russian newspapers and periodicals, I:453; serials, I:293; Spain and Spanish America, I:4290, III:2730; Tartini, Giuseppe, II:1557; theology, I:987; Twain, Mark, II:1754; Uruguay, I:5281; working class movements, II:753
———(Davis): Asian Americans, III:3003; Mexican Americans, III:3375; Negroes, III:819; rare books, II:278, III:446; serials, III:207
———(Los Angeles): arid lands, II:2562; Armenian collection, III:2899; Benny, Jack, III:1875; bookbindings, III:675; California history, I:4731; catalog, III:167; children's books, II:1994, 2005; Chinese collection, III:2869; civil defense, I:5480; Cole, Cornelius,

II:2111; collections, I:163; Cook, Captain James, III:2469; decorative designers, III:1709; detective fiction, III:1934; Dickens, Charles, III:2158; dictionaries, II:1596; Durrell, Lawrence, III:2168; ecology, III:1408; English fiction, II:942,1782, III:2127; English language, III:1911; English literature, I:3392–94; frontier, II:2563; German literature, I:3590; guide, III:137; Hebraica and Judaica, III:765–67; illustrated books, II:488; incunabula, III:482; Japanese collection, III:2899; Jewish studies, III:765; juvenile literature, III:2291; Latin America, III:3324; letters of American statesmen, III:2408; medieval and Renaissance studies, III:2685; Mexican Americans, III:3376; Monitor and Merimac, III:3075; music, I:3003, II:1515; numismatics, III:1776; oral history, III:2675; Orientalia, II; 2372; physical sciences, III:1295; Portuguese collection, III:2261; rare books, III:447; Rexroth, Kenneth, III:2058; Rosecrans, William Starke, III:2604; Russian literature, III:2755; Sanskrit collection, III:2835; serials, III; 208; Slavic studies, III:349; Southern hymnody, III:1803; special collections, II:95, 115, 280; Spinoza, Baruch, II:508; Western history, III:3140; Wilde Oscar, II:1904; Zangwill, Israel, II:1915
———(San Diego): American Revolution, III:3056; English and Italian literature, III:2107; European integration, III:2682; Latin literature, III:2275
———(Santa Barbara): Cabell, James Branch, III:1990; Hook, Sidney, III:681; typography and book design, III:659; Wyles collection, II:2164, III:2549
———Lick Observatory Library (Mt. Hamilton): catalog, I:2233
———Music Library (Berkeley): Bloch, Ernest, III:1862; Italian instrumental music, III:1806; Italian Libretti, III:1804; Mozart, Wolfgang Amadeus, III:1863
———School of Law Library (Los Angeles): copyright law, III:1001; entertainment industry, III:1002; Latin American law, III:1046; maritime law, III:100; oil and gas, III:1004; patents and trademarks, III:1003, water, III:1005
———Scripps Institution of Oceanography Library (La Jolla): catalogs, III:1392–94
———Visual Science Information Center (Berkeley): serials, III:1329
———Water Resources Center (Berkeley): archives, III:1568; Pacific coast, II:1500; reports, II:1315–16, 1319–20; theses, I:1313–14, 1317; water pollution, II:1318; watershed management, I:1321

———William Andrews Clark Library (Los Angeles): collections, I:667; Dickens, Charles, I:3458; Harte, Frances Bret, I:3287; library history, I:119; manuscripts, I:494, II:1618; Montana, I:4990; musicians, I:3014; Stricker, Thomas Perry, I:713; Wilde, Oscar, I:3568–69
Calkin, Homer L., II:677, 739, 744, 908
Callan, John Lansing, III:2451
Calligraphy, I:2916–17; II:254, 265, 289, 1469–71; III:1777–80; Chinese, III:1779
Calloway, Ina Elizabeth, III:3076
Cam, Gilbert A., I:1604, 1901, 2867; II:720
Cambell, Helen H., II:1139
Cambodia, III:2828
Cambridge (Mass.) Press, I:765, 781
Cambridge Public Library, I:3675, 4920
Camden and Amboy Railroad, I:2061
Cameron, K. W., I:1119
Cameron, Kenneth Walter, II:1688
Cameroon, Africa, III:2931, 2960
Cammack, Eleanore, III:729
Cammack, Floyd M., III:3396
Camouflage, I:5412
Camp, Charles, L. II:2570
Campbell, Edward G., I:5574
Campbell, Frank C., I:3045; II:1568
Campbell, Jean, I:511, 550, 610
Campbell, Ruth B., I:3243
Campbell, W. J., I:3978
Campion, Eleanor Este, II:9
Camus, Jean Pierre, III:2248
Canada, Mary W., III:2292
Canada, history, I:1375, 4388–94; II:2463–65; III:2997–3000
Canada Bureau of Statistics: I:1269
Canada Public Archives: Canadian maps, II:2053
Canaday, Dayton W., II:550
Canadian Pacific Railway Co., I:2062
Canal boats, I:2105
Canal Zone Library-Museum: Panama collection, III:3349
Canals, I:2112–14, 2726; II:1308–09
Cancer, II:1144, 1173
Cancer Research Laboratories, I:320
Cannon, Carl L., I:72, 481
Cannon, Lucius H., I:1927
Canny, James R., I:3321
Cantu, Jane Q., III:1478
Capek, Karel, II:1979
Caperton, Mary, III:3292
Capital punishment, I:1850, 1852; III:989
Capital University Library: periodicals, II:170
Capon, Ross B., III:743
Cappon, Lester J., I:378, 882, 1072, 1140, 4405, 5211; III:2652
Carbeau, Ada S., III:3340
Carberry, Hilda M., I:294
Carder, Marguerite L., III:1722
Cardozo, Manuel S., I:5288
Careers, I:1987–91
Caribbean area, I:4193 (7, 26), 5283, 5332, 5349; II:618, 2718; III:3317, 3337–47
Caricatures and cartoons; II:1474–75; medical, II:1244

Carleton College Library: periodicals, II:162, 169
Carlson, William H., I:73, 3627
Carlsten, Alan W., II:539
Carlton, Robert G., III:394, 2735, 2787
Carlyle, Thomas, I:3960
Carmack, Elizabeth M., I:1468
Carman, Bliss, I:3348
Carman, Harry James, II:2470; III:3005
Carmelites, II:621
Carmody, Francis J., II:1084
Carnegie, Andrew, III:2452
Carnegie Endowment for International Peace Library: acquisitions, II:812; conscientious objectors, I:5388; conscription, I:5389; intervention, I:1803; peace and war ethics, I:973–76; war profiteering, I:5389; war referendum, I:1350
Carnegie Institute of Technology: vocational information, II:936
———Hunt Botanical Library: early botanical books, II:1121, 1123; III:1421, 1423
Carnegie Institution of Washington, I:3; III:1365
Carnegie Library of Pittsburgh: air conditioning, I:2528; catalog, I:249; chemical technology, I:2781–92; coal industry, I:1552; electric heat, I:2583; engineering, I:2455; floods, I:2520–21; forestry, I:2651; gyroscope, I:2540; industrial accidents, I:2344; iron and steel, II:1427, III:1695; juvenile literature, I:3806–07; II:1995; lampblack, I:2345; manufactures, I:2808–12; mechanical engineering, I:2474–77; metals, I:2256; mica, I:2279; mining, I:2497; Morgan, George, I:4083; music, I:3004, II:1526, 1564; ophthalmia neonatorum, I:2343; ornithology, I:2331; Pennsylvania history, II:2677; philately, I:2045; Pittsburgh, II:2678; Pittsburgh imprints, I:853; railroad and road, I:2513-15; sand, I:2280; scientific and technical literature, I:2162, 2197, 2435–36, II:1259, III:1564; scientists, I:2161; Scotland, II:2285; sewage disposal, I:2530–31; smoke, I:2529, 2532; sodium nitrate, I:2257; soil conservation, I:2666; technical writing, II:1254; trade-names, I:2773; waterglass, I:2258; World War I, I:5497; X-ray, I:2246
Carolson, Carol, III:2659
Carp, Robert A., III:1006
Carpenter, Edwin H., Jr., II:1484, 2227, 2735
Carpenter, Kenneth E., III:854
Carpenter, Kenneth J., II:1963
Carpenter, Malinda Fannye, II:367
Carpenter, Zoe Irene, III:545
Carr, Lucile, III:2166
Carr, Mary Callista, III:2165
Carr, Virginia, II:2157
Carroll, Dewey Eugene, II:324
Carroll, Horace B., II:2689
Carroll, Lewis, I:3445–48, II:1082–83

Carruthers, Ralph H., I:63
Carson, Hampton L., I:1719
Carson, Jane, II:2703
Carson, Josephine R., II:1216
Cartels, I:1564, 1567
Carter, Clarence E., I:4504
Carter, Constance, I:930, 3662
Carter, George E., III:3077
Carter, John, II:1839
Carter, Landon, III:2453
Carter, Phyllis G., II:659–60
Carter family, III:2454
Cartier, Jacques, I:4391
Cartography, I:3837, 3877
Cartoons, I:2921, 2959; II:1475;
    III:1753–55
Cartularies: I:4285
Carty, William Edward, III:2455
Carus, Paul, III:684
Carvely, Andrew, III:2822
Carver, George Washington, II:2109
Carver, Jonathan, I:4514
Carver, Marjorie, II:1704, 1718; III:1997,
    2073, 2095, 2603, 2621, 2639
Cary, Austin, I:2652
Cary, Richard, II:2078; III:1991, 2027,
    2030, 2038, 2059, 2222, 2238, 2409,
    2449
Case, Arthur E., I:3352
Case, Lynn M., II:2279
Case, Margaret H., III:2825
Case Institute of Technology Library: serials,
    I:357, II:179
Casey, Silas, III:2456
Cassady, Theodore J., I:1446; II:2604
Cassel, Abraham Harley, II:353
Cassidy, Phoebe A., III:1500
Castañeda, Carlos E., I:988, 5186, 5289,
    5337; II:2755
Casting, I:2460
Castlemon, Harry, I:3803
Caswell, John Edwards, II:2762
Cataloging, I:59
Catechisms, I:990
Cathedral Rare Book Library: Biblical and
    liturgical texts, III:698
Cather, Willa, II:1675–76; III:1991
Catholic Historical Society (St. Louis),
    I:1174
Catholic Library Association: periodicals,
    I:1160, II:155, III:209
Catholic University of America Library:
    Bryant, William Cullen, III:1988;
    classical literature, III:2278;
    Clementine collection, III:1916; Denis,
    Ferdinand, I:5312; Evans, Luther H.,
    II:67; Maryland history, I:4897;
    patristic literature, II:595; periodicals
    and serials, I:395, III:275, 286;
    Portuguese and Brazilian history,
    I:5288, 5290, 5310, III:2731; rare
    books, I:3697; Stearns, Foster, II:599
Cathon, Laura E., II:1995
Catoe, Lynn E., III:1598
Cattell, James McKeen, II:922; III:2457
Cattle trade, I:2636, 4687–88
Caudill, Watson G., I:1447; II:716, 983, 1335
Caughey, John W., I:4676

Cavagna Sangiuliani, Antonio, I:4299
Cavanagh, G. S. T., II:1140, 1226–27;
    III:1311, 1480
Cavanaugh, Cortes W., I:3462
Cavender, Curtis H., I:1094
Cawley, F. Stanton, I:3607
Caxton, William, I:650, 655; II:322, 335, 343
Celestina, II:1955
Cellophane, I:2815
Cellulose, I:2602 (24, 44)
Celtic literature, I:3742–44; III:2110
Cement, I:2829
Censorship, II:287
Center for Research Libraries: Belgian Congo,
    III:2931, 2959; catalog, III:168;
    Handbook, III:139; missionary
    archives, III:714; newspapers, III:304;
    pharmaceutical periodicals, III:1562;
    research materials, III:140; scientific
    serials, III:1330
Central America: government publications,
    I:46; history, I:5304, 5321; III:3138,
    3348–58, 3378
Central Michigan College Library: Michigan
    history, II:2636
Central New York Reference and Resources
    Council: serials, III:210
Central State College Library: Negro
    periodicals, II:678
Centralization of government, I:1903
Century Association Library: Graham
    collection, I:195; rare books, I:551
Century of Progress Exposition, I:2443
Ceramics, I:2799; III:1696
Cervantes, Miguel de, I:595, 3709–15;
    II:1952, 1962, 2315; III:2270–71
Cesnola, Luigi Palma di, II:2317
Ceylon, III:2828; publications, III:2919
Chafey, Sister Stella James, II:417
Chaffee, Edmund B., III:2458
Chamberlain, Jacob C., I:3304
Chamberlain, Ellen F., I:1819, 2035, 2107,
    2136–37
Chamberlin, Waldo, I:1467, 1639
Chambers, Jay, III:1709
Chambers, Moreau B. C., III:579
Chambers, Orville T., II:1213, 1217
Chambers, Washington Irving, III:2459
Chambers of commerce, I:2039
Chandler, Marilyn Eve, II:2576
Chaney, Ralph W., III:1400
Chapbooks, I:836, 2147–48, 2150; II:1792;
    III:2109
Chapin, Edward L., Jr., II:2591
Chapin, Howard M., I:688, 2638, 3917,
    4130, 4693
Chapin, Peter, I:2638
Chaplin, W. E., I:379
Chapman, John, I:3268
Chapman, Lily M., I:4635
Chapman, Samuel M., III:2460
Chapple, A. J. V., II:1822
Charanis, Peter, II:2273
Charcoal, activated, III:1699
Charities and corrections, I:1917–24
Charles I of England, I:4250, II:2292
Charles II of England, II:1774
Charleston, S. C., history, I:5171

Charleston Library Society: South Carolina
    history, I:5164; South Carolina
    newspapers, II:190
Charlotte (N.C.) Public Library: textiles,
    II:1428
Charlton, Henry B., I:3520
Charmion, Shelby, II:1949
Charno, Stephen M., III:350, 393
Charters, W. W., II:928
Charters, English, I:4262
Chase, Franklin H., I:5023
Chase, Gilbert, I:3073, 3076; III:1833
Chase, Lawrence B., III:1589
Chattanooga, University, Library: Civil War,
    III:3074
Chaucer, Geoffrey, I:3379, 3404; II:335
Chausson, Ernest, I:3047
Chautauqua County Historical Society:
    Tourgée, Albion W., III:2631
Chaves, Francisco, III:3325
Chavez, Angelico, II:2655
Checkers, III:1905
Cheever, Lawrence O., III:318, 546
Chekhov, Anton P., I:3751, 3753
Chemical abstracts, I:2251; III:1381
Chemical technology, I:2781–2806; II:1425–
    37; III:1695–99
Chemical warfare, I:5390, 5424, 5494
Chemistry, I:2251–76; II:1062, 1100–1110;
    III:1381–90; periodicals, I:2251,
    2259, 2261–64, 2271–73, 2275,
    2610, II:1100–1101, 1103, 1108,
    1110, III:1381
Chemists' Club Library, I:2264
Chen, Simon, II:371
Chenery, Winthrop H., I:363
Cheney, Frances, I:1271, 1564, 3230, 5422
Cheng, Sheng-Wu, II:2386
Chermock, Ralph L., II:1114
Cherokee Indians, I:4486; III:3038
Cheshire, Joseph Blunt, II:586
Chess, I:3120–26; II:1001; III:1261, 1905
Chester, James, I:5403
Chester County Historical Society, II:2675
Chesterfield, Philip D. S., I:3413, II:2110
Chestnutt, Charles Waddell, II:1677–78
Cheverus, John Louis de, II:598
Cheyney, E. P., I:4231
Chicago and North Western Railway Co.,
    I:2063
Chicago Art Institute, Ryerson Library:
    Japanese and Chinese illustrated
    books, I:3781; surrealism, II:1476
Chicago Historical Society: American history,
    I:4476; business history, I:2738;
    Chicago imprints, II:386; Lewis and
    Clark expedition, I:4540; manuscripts,
    II:2611; newspapers, I:396; Peoria
    (Ill.) imprints, I:737; Presidential
    campaigns, II:666; Stowe, Harriet
    Beecher, II:1745
Chicago Joint Reference Library: periodicals,
    I:1856
Chicago Law Institute Library, I:1676–77
Chicago Library Club: directory, I:74; serials,
    I:296
Chicago Library of International Relations:
    Central and South America, I:5291

Chicago Municipal Reference Library: catalog, I:1872; municipal legislation, I:1873; subways, I:2133

Chicago Public Library: American history, I:4476; Catholic books, I:1161; Chicago and Cook County publications, I:1875; Civil War, II:2540; fiction, I:3378; foreign language books, I:3203; foreign language newspapers and periodicals, I:297; Greenland, I:5381; historical novels, I:3194; Latvian books, I:3746; Masaryk, Thomas Garrigue, I:4069; municipal government, I:1874; philosophy, religion, medicine, I:196; Russian literature, I:3747; Scandinavian books, I:3628–29; social sciences, I:1255; Visual Materials Center, II:1574

——Omnibus Project: early American imprints, I:689; Latin America, I:5293; Negro art, I:2832

Chicago Scottish Rite Library, I:1935

Chicago Theological Seminary Library: missionary records, I:1051–52

Chicago, University, Center for Children's Books: II:1993

——Committee on Southern Asian Studies, II:2378; accessions, III:2826

——Department of New Testament: Rockefeller McCormick New Testament, I:1020

——Far Eastern Library: II:2373; III:2855; acquisitions, III:2856; Chinese history, III:2870–74; Chinese periodicals III:351; Japanese periodicals, III:352

——Institute for Far Eastern Librarianship: Chinese library resources, III:2872; Chinese studies, III:2873; Japanese reference works, III:2900

——Law Library: acquisitions, III:1010; criminal law, II:832; evidence, II:786; Llewellyn, Karl N., III:1007–8; Rheinstein, Max, III:1009; Soviet law, III:1048; torts, II:787; Yugoslav foreign trade law, III:1047

——Library: II:96; Africa, III:2932, 2993; American drama, I:3232; American history, I:4476; atlases, I:3830; Bibles, I:1019; Chicago and Cook County publications, I:1875; Chicago private agencies, I:1918; Chinese books, I:3782; collections, I:120; constitutional conventions, I:1833; Cromwell, Oliver, I:4254; East Asiatic books, I:4352; English civil war, I:4254; 15th-century books, I:621; geographic serials, I:3832; German fiction, I:3582; Goethe, Johann Wolfgang von, I:3595; Greenland, I:5381; Hebraica, III:768; illuminated manuscripts, III:433; juvenile literature, III:2294; Kentucky history, I:4856, II:2624; library surveys, II:59; Lincoln, Abraham, I:4050–51; little magazines, II:161; manuscripts, I:486, II:258, III:428; medical history,

I:2412; medieval and renaissance manuscripts, III:428; medieval European history, I:4232; middle American ethnology, I:2311; Mongolian collection, III:2882; newspapers, I:380; Nicholas Bacon manuscripts, III:2692; Ohio River Valley history, II:2624; Oriental books, I:3782, 3791; rare books, III:448; Renaissance, III:1919; 17th-century plays, I:3363; South Asian collection, III:2827; special collections, III:155; Ukrainian literature, III:2748; unemployment, I:1659

——Oriental Institute: Arabic manuscripts, III:2812

——Program on contemporary China, III:2874

——School of Commerce Library: U.S. National Recovery Administration, I:1460

Chicago writers, II:1642

Chiera, Edward, I:4225–26

Chilcote, Ronald H., III:2961

Child, Sargent B., I:5

Child labor, I:1664–68

Child psychology, I:959

Childs, James B., I:43–47, 50–51, 1804; II:53–54

Chile, history, I:5289, 5311, 5330; III:3296, 3359

Chiles, Rose P., I:4068

Chin, Elisabeth May, III:557

China, history, I:4328–36, 4342, 4356; II:2359, 2376, 2386–2408, 2410; III:181, 2869–98

Chinantec Indians, II:2503

Chinard, Gilbert, I:4541

Chinchona, I:2598 (9)

Chinese Americans, I:1381

Chinese gazetteers, III:2884

Chinese literature, I:3779–83, 3785–86; 3788–94; II:1983–84, 1989, 1992; III:2860, 2869

Chinese reference works, III:2875

Chinookan languages, I:3179

Chippewa Indians, III:3035

Chisholm, William W., I:1717

Chiswick, Jeanne Hunnicutt, III:3291

Chiu, A. K'aiming, I:3783; II:2368; III:2875

Chow, Dorothy Wei, III:2653

Christian art, I:2844

Christian churches and sects, I:1056–1213; II:539–631; III:719–56

Christian Science Church, I:1073–74

Christie-Miller, Sydney R., I:4505

Christmas, I:526, 528, 2156

Chromium, I:2808

Chung, E. W. H., III:2876

Chung, Yong Sun, III:2909

Chung-min, Wang, II:2405

Church, Elihu D., I:3391, 4506

Church, George Earl, III:2461

Church, Randolph W., II:2292

Church, William Conant, II:239

Church and state, I:1006

Church Historical Society Library: Liberia

papers, III:713; Protestant Episcopal Church, III:739

Church libraries, III:692

Church of Jesus Christ of Latter Day Saints Genealogical Society, III:2654

Churchill, William, I:3172

Churchill, Winston, II:2127, III:2462

Cincinnati history, I:5114

Cincinnati Public Library: adult reading books, I:197; Inland Rivers Library, III:3006; Lincoln, Abraham, I:4031

Cincinnati, University, Library: Burnam collection, I:191; Greek literature, II:1964

——Medical College: history of medicine, II:1228

Cincinnati Young Men's Mercantile Library Association, I:198

Circus, I:3112, 3115; III:1902

Citadel, Mark Clark, III:1144

Citrus fruits, I:2646; II:1391

City College Library, New York: Russian history, III:2749

City planning see Urban planning

City University of New York Libraries: periodicals, III:211

Civil defense, I:5476–95; II:894, 899; III:1164

Civil Service, I:1857, 1861–62, 1864–66; II:840, 862, 929; III:1073–75

Civil war, English, I:4250, 4254, 4263

Civil War fiction, II:1657, 1661

Cizevsky, Dmitry, II:1972–73

Clagett, Helen L., I:1735, 1738–44; III:3377

Clandestine publications, I:5513, 5545–46, 5578

Clapp, Clifford B., I:4124

Clapp, William F., II:1290

Clare, John, II:1822

Claremont College Library: California water problems, I:2533; Chinese collection, III:2877; Latin American history, I:5293; Pacific area, I:4343–44; Pacific coast steamship companies, I:5450

Clark, Alexander P., II:243, 255, 2235; III:2074

Clark, Charles E., III:1948

Clark, Ethel B., I:552

Clark, Evert M., II:524

Clark, Frederick C., I:2813

Clark, George R., I:3958, 4555, 5229

Clark, Georgia H., II:2585

Clark, Grenville, III:2463

Clark, John C. L., I:4097

Clark, Jonas G., I:553

Clark, Josephine A., I:2601 (20)

Clark, Kenneth W., I:1021–22; II:579–80, 2266–67; III:699

Clark, Lucy Trimble, II:491, 1672, 1700, 1704, 1709, 1718; III:1970, 1989, 1997, 2073, 2095, 2603, 2621, 2639

Clark, Mark, III:1144

Clark, Maryanne, III:258

Clark, T. D., I:405; II:2554

Clark University Library: Clark Memorial Collection, I:553; serials, I:298; World War I, I:5498

Clark, William Andrews, Library: I:667; Dickens, Charles, I:3458; English literature, I:3392–94; manuscripts, II:1618; Wilde, Oscar, I:3568

Clarke, David E., III:2962

Clarke, J. F., I:905

Clarke, Jack Alden, II:746

Clarke, Marian G. M., III:474

Clarke, Prescott, III:360

Clarkson, Richard W., II:1612

Clary, Ann Roane, II:462

Clary, William W., II:945

Classification: agricultural, I:2602 (30); engineering, II:1263, III:1570; library, I:66, II:65, III:83

Clay, Albert T., I:4217

Clayton, B. A., I:4336

Clayton Act, II:731

Clayton-Torrence, W., I:5230

Cleland, Robert G., I:4738

Cleland, Thomas Maitland, III:668

Clemence, Stella R., I:5359

Clemens, Samuel, see Mark Twain

Clemens, Walter C., III:1150

Clementi, Muzio, I:3046

Clements, William L., I:4406

Clemons, Harry, I:75; II:119–20, 1095

Clemson College Library, I:199

Clendening, John A., III:1406

Clendening, Logan, II:1226, 1236

Cleveland, Grover, II:2158; III:2464

Cleveland Hearing and Speech Center Library: serials, I:357; II:179

Cleveland Health Sciences Library: serials, III:1530

Cleveland, history, I:5117

Cleveland Institute of Art Library: serials, I:357, II:179

Cleveland Medical Library: Nicolaus Pol collection, I:2420; serials, I:357, II:179

Cleveland Medical Library Association: serials, III:1531

Cleveland Museum of Art Library: serials, I:357, II:179

Cleveland Museum of Natural History Library: serials, I:357, II:179

Cleveland Public Library: British history, I:4255–56; business and technology, II:1416, III:877; Catholic books I:1162; chess, I:3125–26, III:1905; China, II:2394; Drehem tablets, I:4205; English ballads, I:3355; environmental pollution, III:1700; films, III:1788; folk dances, I:3088; folklore, I:2153, III:1261–63; French history, I:4284; German literature, I:3585, II:1918; Negro spirituals, I:3053; newspapers, III:305; Oriental literature, I:3797; orientalia, I:2153; Polish books, I:3748, II:1974; theatre collection, III:1876; vocations, I:1988; White collection, II:1001

Cliff dwellings, I:2309

Clifford, William, I:2170

Clift, G. Glen, II:792, 2625–26

Climatology, I:2238, 2662; II:1090–94

Cline, Clarence L., II:1864

Cline, Howard F., II:2503; III:2359

Clinton, George, I:3959, 5022

Clinton, Henry, I:3886, 4534, 4561–62

Close, Virginia L., II:1575

Clough, Arthur Hugh, III:2150

Cloutier family, III:2466

Clubb, Louise George, III:2254

Coad, Oral S., III:1972

Coal industry, I:1552, 1565; III:1405

Coal mines, nationalization, I:1504

Coale, Robert P., III:3295–96

Coats, Nellie M., I:2203

Cobb, Gwendolin B., II:2312

Cobb, Jessie E., III:3078

Cobb, Maud B., I:4800

Cobb, Ruth, I:2198

Cobbett, William, III:2151

Cobden-Sanderson, T. J., III:678

Cochran, Alexander D., I:537

Cochrane, Henry Clay, III:2465

Cocks, J. Fraser, III, III:864

Coe, William R., I:4678; II:2573

Cofer, Diane, III:238

Coffin, Lewis C., II:2, 1016

Cognasso, Ernestine, III:3336

Cogswell, George Ralston, III:1739

Cogswell, Joseph G., I:231

Cohen, Boaz, I:1217

Cohen, Joseph, II:1607

Cohen, Morton N., III:2192

Cohen, Nina, III:296

Cohen, Selma Jeanne, III:1807

Coker, C. F. W., III:2465, 3063, 3250

Coking, I:2784

Colburn, Gail C., III:2178

Colby, Elbridge, I:3481

Colby College Library: Abbott, Jacob, I:3273; association books, I:3204; Butler, Benjamin F., III:2449; Butler, Samuel, I:3438; Cather, Willa, III:1991; Connolly, James Brendan, I:3278; Cuala Press, II:347; Deland, Margaret, I:3281; 1850 books, I:584–85; Hardy, Thomas, I:3006, 3475–79, II:1838; Higginson, Thomas Wentworth, III:2027; Housman, Alfred Edward, I:3483; Howells, William Dean, III:2030; incunabula, II:339; James, Henry and William, I:3298, III:2033; Jewett, Sarah Orne, I:3301, II:1720, III:2038; journal, I:167; Kelmscott Press, I:668, II:492; Lee, Vernon, II:1859; Lincoln, Abraham, I:4032; Lovejoy, Elijah Parish, I:4063; Mann, Thomas, III:2238; manuscripts, II:244; O'Grady, Standish, II:1866; Omar Khayyam, II:1990; Pope, Alexander, I:3501; Presidential autographs, II:2078; Richards, Laura E., III:2059; Robinson, Edwin Arlington, I:3326, II:1741, III:2060–62; Russell, George W., II:1871–72; Schweitzer, Albert, III:2610; Stephens, James, III:2222; Synge, J. M., II:1897; U. S. Presidents' letters, III:2409; Waterville imprints, II:393

Cold storage, I:2599 (10), 2602 (11)

Cole, Arthur H., I:1457, 2674–75, 2701–05; II:723

Cole, Betty Joy, I:2273

Cole, Cornelius, II:2111

Cole, Eva A., I:1997

Cole, G. Glyndon, III:3227

Cole, George W., I:3391, 3398, 4007, 4506–07

Cole, Joan E., III:2295

Cole, Maud D., II:357; III:708

Cole, Toby, I:3749, 4310

Coleman, Earle E., II:1255; III:449, 2672

Coleman, Edward D., I:3368–69

Coleman, J. Winston, I:4854

Coleridge, Hartley, III:2152

Coleridge, Samuel T., I:3360, 3449; III:2152

Coles, Harry L., I:5499

Colgate University Library: Baptist history, I:1057, 1071

Colgrove, Arline W., I:4255–56

Colhoun, Edmund Ross, III:2467

Colket, Meredith B., Jr., III:2666, 3239

Collamore, H. Bacon, II:1853

Collective bargaining, I:1589

College of St. Catherine Library: perodicals, II:162, 169

College of St. Thomas Library: periodicals, II:162, 169

College of the Bible Library: Disciples of Christ, III:723

College of the City of New York Library: catalog, I:200; special resources, II:107

Colleges and universities, I:1997–2022; II:939–52; III:1252–60; in fiction, II:942

Collier, Cleveland E., III:1187

Collier, Thomas, I:776

Colliflower, Charles, E., II:424

Collins, Philip, III:2159

Collins, Robert O., III:2933

Collins, Rowland L., III:2230

Collins, Sara Dobie, III:573

Collins, Varnum L., I:802

Collins, Victor, I:3154

Collins, Wilkie, I:3387; II:1823

Collison, Robert Lewis, II:1596; III:1911

Collmann, Herbert L., I:3353

Colmer, William M., III:2468

Columbia: government publications, I:44; history, III:3296, 3323, 3360–62

Colon, Maria Luisa, II:437

Colonial Dames of the State of New York, I:4139

Colonial Williamsburg: American Revolution, II:2529; archives, II:2704; manuscripts, II:2702; Virginia history, III:3050

Colonization, I:1370–84

Colorado: authors, I:3253; government publications, I:26; history, I:4751–55, II:2593

Colorado River, I:4686, 4689

Colorado State Board of Library Commissioners, I:26

Colorado, State Historical Society, Division of State Archives and Public Records:

Colorado imprints, I:722; railroads, II:990–92; Shafroth, John Franklin, II:2207; state publications, III:28
Colorado State Library, I:201
Colorado State University Libraries: chemistry serials, I:2259; serials, I:299; social sciences, III:784; Western American literature, III:1949
Colorado Supreme Court Library, I:1678
Colorado, University, Library: children's literature, II:1996; history, III:2670; music education, II:1517; serials, I:300, III:212; Spanish plays, II:1953
Columbia Broadcasting System Reference Library, I:2484
Columbia Conserve Company, II:967
Columbia University Avery Architectural Library: architectural periodicals, III:1740; catalog, I:2877, II:1456, III:1739, 1742; collections, I:2893–95; early architectural books, I:2901; Greek revival architecture, I:2884; house plan books, I:2878; Louis Henry Sullivan drawings, III:1747; obituary index, III:1741
——College of Pharmacy Library: catalog, I:2369
——College of Physicians and Surgeons: Florence Nightingale collection, II:1141
——East Asian Library: Chinese collection, II:2396, III:2878; Chinese Communist movement, II:2387–88, 2390; Chinese periodicals, III:353; Korea, II:2423; Mao Tse-tung, II:2389; Western language acquisitions, III:2857
——International Affairs Library: periodicals, III:1058
——Law Library: acquisitions, III:1012; catalog, III:1011; Pollard and Redgrave holdings, III:1013
——Libraries: accounting, I:2770–71; American history and genealogy, I:4453; autographed books, I:203; Babylonian tablets, I:4200; Baum, L. Frank, II:1997; Bergson, Henri, I:950; Bibliotheca Columbiana, I:121; bookbindings, III:676; Brook farm, I:1512; business collection, I:1458; Butler, Nicholas Murray, I:3956; Carroll, Lewis, I:3445; catalog, I:202; Chekhov, Anton P., I:3751; Civil War records, I:4599–4600; college history, I:1998, II:947; Connecticut history, I:4762; Cooper, James Fenimore, I:3279; Coptic papyri, II:2271; Crane, Stephen, II:1682; drama and literary criticism, I:3191; economic history, I:1452, 1466; education, I:1950; English and American literature, III:2108; epigraphy, II:1598; Far East, II:2352; Firdausi, I:3798; German literature, I:3592; Goudy, Frederic William, III:660; grammars, I:3151; Greek papyri, I:4201, II:2268; Grotius, Hugo, I:1806; Hamilton, Alexander, II:2137; hornbooks, I:1985; Islamic

manuscripts, II:276; Italian literature, II:1947; Japanese collection, I:3784; Johnson's Dictionary, II:1597; King's College, I:947; Latin American maps, I:3926; Limited Editions Club, II:493; Lincoln, Abraham, I:4033; manuscript collections, II:245; Marlow, Christopher, I:3493; mathematics, I:2158, 2209, 2212–13, 2219, 2221–26; Mathews, Brander, I:3205; medicine, II:1142; Montesquieu, Charles de S., I:3656; musical scores, I:203; Near East collections, I:4202; Olcott, Thomas Worth, III:901; oral history, II:2259; Oriental manuscripts, I:535; Ottoman Empire, II:2348; pageants, I:3109; photography, I:2994; Plimpton manuscript collection, I:496, 570; Poe, Edgar Allan, I:3318; printing history, I:586; Pulitzer prizes, II:943; railroads, I:2956, II:997; rare books, I:554–55, II:279; resources, II:118; Rackham, Arthur, III:1757; Russian history, II:2326; Russian newspapers, II:214; science, I:2158, II:1017; Shakespeare, William, I:3531; Swift, Jonathan, III:2227; Tammany, I:1925; textbooks, III:1251; Thomson, James, I:3560; trade catalogs, I:2686; typography, I:928, 931–32, II:494; Washington, George, II:2221–22; weights and measures, I:2740
——Medical Library: plastic surgery, III:1446
——Oral History Research Office: oral history, III:2676–77
——School of International Affairs: Lehman, Herbert H., III:2548
——School of Library Service Library: catalog, III:79
——School of Mines Library: catalog, I:2498
——Teachers College Library: catalog, III:169; nursing history, I:2403; rare books, I:555; schoolroom decoration, I:2932; serials, III:243
Columbus, Christopher, I:3961–62, 4508, 4521, 4530; II:2112, 2498
Comer, Hubert E., III:1022
Commission government, I:1893
Committee of Ancient Near Eastern Seals, I:4203
Common law, I:1693, 1719; III:1018
Communal settlements, I:1512–13
Communism, I:1514; II:2387–90, 2395, 2397; III:786, 813–14
Communities, I:2602 (46)
Community centers, I:2898
Comonfort, Ignacio, II:2733
Comparative negligence, III:990
Compton, LaNell, III:3164
Compulsory military training, I:5408–09, 5422
Computers, II:883–84; III:991
Conat, Mabel L., I:1879
Conchology, III:1438
Concord Antiquarian Society Library: Emerson, Ralph Waldo, III:2005

Concord (Mass.) Free Public Library: Emerson, Ralph Waldo, II:1689
Concordia Historical Institute: Lutheran Church, II:553; III:724
Concrete, I:2461
Condit, Anna R., III:230
Condon, Patricia A., III:1645, 1699
Confederate Memorial Hall, New Orleans, I:3969
Confederate Memorial Literary Society, I:4601, 4620
Confederate Museum Library: manuscripts, I:4601; newspapers, I:440
Confederate States of America: literature, I:3227, 3257, 4595, 4601–04, II:298, 1647, 2004, 2536, 2541, 2544; muster rolls, II:2542; postal covers, I:2046; publications, I:4611, 4620; war records, II:2549
Conference of Eastern College Librarians, I:301
Conference of Historical Societies, I:4185
Conferences, international, I:311; II:815–17
Conger, John L., I:4942
Congregational Church, I:1075–78
Congresses: international, I:311; medical, I:2377
Congreve, William, II:1824; III:2153–54
Conklin, Dorothy G., I:2456
Conklin, Edwin G., I:4542; II:1047
Conlan, Ann A., II:455
Conlan, Eileen M., III:510
Connally, Ernest Allen, II:1461
Connally, Thomas Edmund, II:1843
Connally, Tom, II:2113
Connecticut: authors, I:3252; history, I:4756–65, III:3168
Connecticut College for Women, Palmer Library: Wordsworth, William, I:3570
Connecticut Examiner of Public Records, I:4757
Connecticut Historical Society: Connecticut authors, I:3252; Connecticut history, I:4758–60; Connecticut imprints, I:723–24; Washington, George, I:4108
Connecticut State Library: archives, I:4756, III:3168; cemetery records, I:4141; church records, I:1201, II:628; Connecticut houses, I:2879, 2889; employers' liability, I:1642; government publications, III:29; Johnson family, I:4762; law collection, I:1679; Library history, I:122; manuscripts, I:4761; periodicals, III:213; printing history, I:587; probate files, I:4142; subject collections, III:90; Webster, Noah, II:2226
Connecticut, University, Library: periodicals, II:180; reference materials, II:5
Connelly, D., Boiler Co., I:2730
Conner, Helen West, III:637
Conner, John M., II:926
Connolly, James B., I:3278
Connolly, Terence L., I:3559
Connor, Jeanette T., I:4780
Connor, R. D. W., I:4407, 5144
Connor, Seymour V., II:2690

Conover, Helen F., I:982, 1270, 1356, 1362–64, 1383, 1413, 1415, 1472, 1499, 1522, 1621, 1820, 1916, 1930, 1986, 2031, 2504, 2778, 2806, 2935, 3762, 4286, 4303, 4307, 4316, 4323, 4334, 4338, 4340, 4373, 4376–77, 4379, 4384–85, 4495, 4645, 5361, 5372, 5383, 5415, 5491–92, 5547, 5552–53, 5556; II:13, 697–98, 2263, 2282–83, 2435, 2450–57; III:17, 84, 387, 2974–75

Conrad, Joseph, I:3379, 3450–51; II:289, 1616

Conscientious objectors, I:5888

Conservation of natural resources, III:862–68, 1097

Consortium of Western Universities and Colleges: newspapers, III:307

Constitution, U.S., I:1401–02, 1834–36, 1839, 1844–45, 1847–48; II:828

Constitutional conventions, I:1833, 1837–38, 1849, 1854

Constitutional law and history, I:1260, 1833–49; II:828–31; III:1069–71

Constitutions, state, I:1849; II:829–30

Construction industry, II:1439–40

Consular service, I:1826

Consumers' cooperatives, I:1509

Container cars, I:2509

Containers, I:2777

Contract farming, II:1370; III:1626

Convict labor, I:1580, 1593

Conway, G. R. G., II:2734, 2743

Conway, William E., I:3569

Cook, C. Donald, II:118

Cook, Captain James, III:2469

Cook, Doris E., II:1697, 2226

Cook, Dorothy E., I:2942

Cook, Elizabeth, I:3429

Cook, Elizabeth C., I:381

Cook, Eugene B., I:3122, 3124

Cook, Olan V., I:645; II:337

Cook, Roy Bird, III:2470

Cook, Ruth V., II:1457

Cook, William B., Jr., I:4199

Cookery, I:2583–85, 2587–89; II:1341–44; III:1603

Cooley, Elizabeth F., I:879

Cooley, Laura C., I:4732

Coolidge, Bertha, I:3495

Coolidge, Calvin, I:3963; III:2471

Coomaraswamy, Amanda K., I:2831

Cooper, James Fenimore, I:3279; II:1632, 1679; III:1992

Cooper, John A., II:712

Cooper, Martha K., I:5121

Cooper, Peter, I:3964

Cooper Union Library, I:2457, 3964

Cooperation, I:1509–11, 2602 (41)

Coover, James B., III:1844

Copernicus, Nikolaus, I:2230

Copinger, Harold B., I:906

Copinger, Walter A., I:989

Copper, I:2806

Coppet, Andre de, II:2485

Coppin, Levi Jenkins, II:685

Coptic manuscripts, I:4216, 4218–19, 4222, 4227; II:2271

Copybooks, I:2024; II:1469–70

Copyright: records, I:19, 589, 703, 735; law, III:1001

Corbin, John B., III:2663

Corbitt, D. L., I:5106; III:3091

Corey, Herbert, II:1680

Cork oak, I:2598 (7)

Corn, I:2626 (87)

Corn laws, I:1543

Cornell University, Collection of Regional History: acquisitions, I:5024

————Dept. of Asian Studies: Indonesian serials, III:354; Thailand, III:2844–45

————Dept. of Communication Art: journalism, III:404

————Libraries: American history, I:4463, II:2471; anti-Masonic literature, III:1234; architecture, I:2880; bee culture, III:1658; Bible, I:1023; Brazil, II:2746; Chinese collection, II:2408; Chinese gazetteers, III:2879; Chinese periodicals, III:355–56; Chinese reference books, III:2880; Dante, Alighieri, I:3676; East and Southeast Asia, III:2858; entomology, III:1436; French Revolution, I:4233; hotel administration, II:1340; Icelandic literature, I:3608–09, 3611–23, II:1928, 1930–31; Indonesia, II:2429–30; Indonesian publications, III:2841; industrial and labor relations, II:749; Joyce, James, II:1845, III:2186; Lafayette, Marquis de, III:2543; Lavoisier, Antoine Laurent, III:1382; Lewis, Wyndham, III:2040; manuscripts, III:415; mathematics, I:2210; New York State history, II:2568, 2660, 2738; North Vietnam, III:2849; nutrition, II:1343; Petrarch, Francesco, I:3685; Protestant Reformation, I:4233; Rice Poultry Library, II:1378; Romansch language, I:3166; Russian literature, I:3750; Russian serials, III:357; serials, III:214; Shakespeare, William, II:1878; Shaw, George Bernard, III:2219; Southeast Asia, III:2829; Thai literature, III:2845; Vesalius, Andreas, III:1319; Wordsworth, William, I:3571–73, II:1906, III:2233

————New York State School of Industrial and Labor Relations: catalog, III:955; guide, III:954; railroad collection, III:956

————Poultry Library: poultry husbandry, III:1657

————Regional History and University Archives: George Bancroft papers, III:3141

————Southeast Asia Program: Borneo, III:2917

Corning, Howard, I:2706–07

Cornwallis, Charles, I:4567

Corporations, I:2675, 2677

Corré, Alan D., III:483

Correctional institution libraries, III:1229

Corrosion, metal, I:2256

Corsi, Edward, III:2472

Cortés, Vicenta, III:3378

Cortisone, II:1184

Cost of government, I:1523

Cost of living, I:1561

Costa Rica, I:5296, 5304, 5321; III:3353

Costabile, Salvatore L., III:617

Costume, I:2936–45

Cotten, Bruce, I:5092

Cotton, John, I:1007

Cotton, I:2626 (44, 61, 63, 91), 2628 (8–9, 18, 22), 2648

Cotton textile industry, I:2626 (57), 2628 (3, 7), 2825

Coues, Elliott, I:2332

Coufal, Evelyn, II:372

Coulter, Edith Margaret, II:2592

Coulton, George G., I:4232

Council of Higher Educational Institutions in New York City, III:91

Council on Foreign Relations Library: catalog, III:1059; resources, I:1805, 1810

Counciling, retirement, II:751

County government, I:1875, 1886, 1888–90

County histories, U. S., II:2487, 2618, 2677

Courtenay, Purviance, I:4543

Courtesy, I:970

Coventry, Rose, III:3179

Coverdale Bible, I:1035

Covington, Samuel F., I:5123

Cowan, Robert E., I:714, 4731

Cowan, Robert G., I:4731

Coward, Hester H., II:2614

Coward, Robert Y., II:2614

Cowden, Laura, II:389

Cowdrey, Mary Bartlett, II:1492

Cowles, Katharine C., I:778

Cowley, John D., I:1772

Cowper, William, III:2155

Cox, Carolyn, I:1581

Cox, Raymond S., II:2806

Coy, Owen C., I:4728

Cozzens, James Gould, II:1681

Crabtree, Loren W., III:1227

Craftsmanship, I:2725

Crage, Thomas Joseph, II:438

Craig, Edward Gordon, III:1890

Craig, James L., III:1436

Craig, Mary E., I:457

Cramer, Dorothy, II:1163–64

Crandall, Marjorie Lyle, II:2541

Crandall, Ruth, II:959

Crane, Evan Jay, II:1102

Crane, Hart, II:1993–94

Crane, Ronald S., I:458

Crane, Stephen, I:3280; II:289, 1682–84, 2155

Crane, Verner W., I:3977

Crapsey, Adelaide, III:1995

Crask, Catherine, III:1710

Crawford, Dorothy, III:1877

Crawford, J. P. W., I:3698–3700

Crawford, Leila, II:439

Crawford, Susan, III:1451

Creighton, Alice, III:1435

Cremation, I:2347

Cremation Association of America, I:2347

Crikelair, George F., II:1446

Criminal law, I:1850–52, 1933; II:832

Criminology, I:1698, 1926–33
Crittenden, Charles C., I:382, 4397
Crittenden, John J., I:3965
Crocker, Templeton, I:4749
Cromwell, Oliver, I:3960, 4250, 4254
Crosby, Sumner McKnight, II:1860
Cross, Arthur L., I:4267
Cross, Robert John, II:2391
Cross, Wilbur L., I:3470–71
Crossey, J. D. M., III:2935
Crouch, Mary F., III:2526
Crouch, William H., III:1049
Crowne, John, I:3452
Crowther, Simeon J., III:1307
Cruikshank, George, I:673, 2910–11, 2920,
    3458; II:1830
Cruikshank, Isaac, I:2910
Cruikshank, Robert, I:2910
Crusades, I:254
Cryptogamic botany, I:2320
Crystal Palace exhibition, II:1255
Cuala Press, II:347
Cuba, I:4193 (34); II:2753; history, I:5301,
    5344, 5346, 5364, 5367, III:3363–69;
    maps, I:3932
Culbertson, William S., III:2473
Cullen, Countee, II:248
Culver, James H., II:71
Cumming, William P., II:2054; III:2385
Cummings, Hubertis M., II:1308
Cundall, Frank, I:899
Cuneiform inscriptions, I:503, 4200, 4202,
    4204–05, 4220, 4225–26
Cunninghame Graham, R. B., I:3453
Curran, Terence J., II:2300
Currie, Florence B., I:123
Currier, Margaret, I:683, 2307–08
Currier, Thomas F., I:1951, 1982, 3344,
    3653, 5500; II:1703
Currier and Ives, I:2968
Curti, Merle E., I:2023
Curtis, Carolyn, I:2103
Curtis, Florence R., I:58
Curtis, Lewis P., I:5501
Curtis, Nathaniel C., II:2881
Curtis Publishing Co., I:3978
Curtiss, Benjamin De F., I:4531
Curvey, Mary F., III:3397
Cusenza, Joan, III:2347
Cushing, Harvey, I:2364, 2384, 2404
Cushing, Leonard J., III:2619
Cushman, Esther C., I:4028
Cushman, Helene L., II:1385
Cusick, Margaret R., I:2720
Custer, George A., I:3966
Cuthbert, Norma B., I:4511–12
Cutler, Manasseh, I:3915
Cutting, Helen Frances, III:625
Cutts, Elmer, I:3773
Cuyler, Louise E., II:1518
Cybernetics, II:953
Czechoslovakia, I:4318, II:2344; history,
    III:2774–75

Dabbs, Jack Autrey, I:5289, 5337; II:2755;
    III:3383
Daehler, Mary K., II:1341
Daguerre, Louis, II:1507

Dahl, Folke, II:215
Dailey, George, III:3245
Dains, Frank Burnett, II:1104
Dairying, I:2599 (6), 2626 (71, 97)
Dakota Indians, III:3035
Dale, Jane Catherine, II:1996
Daley, Charles M., I:622–23
Dallas Public Library: serials, I:306, 315;
    theatre collection, III:1878
Dalphin, George R., II:2019–20
Daly, Lloyd W., II:1965
Daly, Lowrie J., II:606
Damon, Samuel Foster, I:3220; II:1560
Dams, I:2524
Dana, Maria T., I:1999
Dancing, I:3104; II:1578; films, III:1873
Danes, Doris L., III:2296
Danforth, Margaret V., III:2297
D'Angelo, Susan, III:2629
Daniel, Katherine D., III:3193
Daniells, Lorna M., III:878–79
Daniels, Josephus, I:3967; II:2114
Dante, Alighieri, I:3674–84; II:1940
Dante Society, I:3677
Danubian Federation, II:2280
Darling, Louise, III:1447
Darlington, William, II:1227
Dart, Henry P., I:4875
Dart, Thurston, II:1567
Darter, L. J., I:4078
Dartmouth College Library: Adams, Sherman,
    III:2427; Alaska, II:2583; American
    Indian collection, III:3029; American
    newspapers, II:2532; Burns, Robert,
    II:1818; Canadian books, III:661,
    Cervantes, Miguel de, III:2270;
    Cesnola, Luigi Palma di, II:2317;
    Christian history, II:539; Civil War,
    II:2538, III:3077; Clark, Grenville,
    III:2463; climatology, II:1091; Crane,
    Stephen, I:3280; Cunninghame
    Graham, R. B., I:3453; Dresden
    imprints, I:800; French literature,
    II:1935; Frost, Robert, I:3285; globes,
    II:2019; Hale, John P., III:2512; health
    of Eskimos, III:1448; illustrated books,
    III: 651–52; incunabula, III:484;
    Lindsay, Vachel, I:3303; marine
    atlases, II:2020; motion picture scripts,
    II:1575; New Hampshire and Vermont
    maps, III:2389; New Hampshire
    printing, I:798; newspapers, III:308;
    political science, I:1344; prints,
    II:1488; rare books, II:289, III:450;
    Rastell press, I:674; Saint-Gaudens,
    Augustus, III:1756; Spanish collection,
    III:2262; Stefansson collection,
    II:2763, 2765, III:3398–99; Stevens,
    Wallace, III:2072; Taggard,
    Genevieve, I:3333; Thomas, Isaiah,
    I:766; Ticknor, George, III:2081;
    Weeks family, III:2645
———Tuck School: business administration,
    I:2676
Darwin, Charles R., I:2190; II:1047, 2533
Data processing, II:884
Date palm, I:2650
Daubert, Richard D., III:936

Daughters of the American Revolution
    Library: Evans, Luther Harris, II:67;
    genealogy, I:4143
Daughters of the Republic of Texas, III:3262
Daumier, Honoré, II:2959
Davenport, Frances G., I:4257
Davenport, Marcia, III:1996
David, Charles W., II:2120; III:2474
David, Hans T., I:3069
Davidson, Katherine H., III:800, 1183, 1749,
    1751
Davies, David, I:1835; III:1274
Davies, Geoffrey, II:576
Davies, John D., III:2023, 2410, 2648
Davis, Andrew M., I:2000, 2004, 4921–22
Davis, Caroline H., I:3109
Davis, Curtis Carroll, II:2238
Davis, David, III:2475
Davis, Doris S., III:2571, 2595, 2632
Davis, Dorothy R., III:2337
Davis, Elizabeth Gould, II:1351, 1353, 1367,
    1371–73, 1408; III:1644
Davis, Emily G., I:2354
Davis, Godfrey, II:1874
Davis, Harry, I:3089
Davis, Herbert F., I:3552
Davis, Innis, I:5252
Davis, James J., II:2115
Davis, Jefferson, I:3968–69; III:2476
Davis, Katharine Norman, II:463
Davis, Marie L., II:1408
Davis, O. L., Jr., III:3079
Davis, Richard B., I:3511; II:1873
Davis, Richard Harding, III:1997
Davis, Sarah Marie, II:2472
Davis, Vashti Atkins, II:403
Davison, Archibald T., II:1520
Davy, Edgar W., III:2955
Dawson, Edgar, I:4766
Dawson, John P., III:1050
Dawson, Sister Avelina, II:600
Day, Cyrus L., I:2007
Day, Emily L., II:1348
Day, George E., I:1055
Day, Gordon M., III:3029
Day, James M., III:1141, 2386, 2400, 3257,
    3266
Day, Jerome J., III:2477
Day, John, II:1598
Day, Joseph P., I:2747
Day, Mahlon, II:2015
Day, Richard E., I:5025
Dayton, William A., II:1393
Dayton Public Library, I:204
Deal, N. Harvey, II:97
Dean, Elva, III:2667
Dean, Hazel, I:2390
Dean, Helen E., I:77
Dearborn, James M., I:4595
Debating, I:3218
DeBenko, Eugene, III:2934, 2945
DeBow, James D. B., I:322
Debt, public, I:1527–28
Debtors' law, III:997
Decalcomania, II:2926
Decatur Public Library, I:4156
DeCharms, Elizabeth Graves, II:325
Decker, Eugene D., III:3080

Decker, Patricia, II: 1477
Declaration of Independence, I: 4547, 4556, 4571, 4584; II: 2530–31; III: 3060
Decoration and design, I: 2875, 2890, 2923–35
DeCoster, Cyrus C., II: 1954
Dedmond, Francis B., II: 1748
Deering, F. P., I: 1720
Defense financing, I: 1521
Defoe, Daniel, I: 3454–57; II: 1825–27; III: 2157
DeForest, John H., I: 4589
DeForest, John W., I: 4589
DeGolyer, E. L., II: 1054–57
DeGruson, Gene, III: 1954
Dehydrated foods, I: 2586, 2598 (6), 4193 (21)
De la Mare, Walter, II: 1798; III: 2156
DeLand, Fred, I: 1924
Deland, Margaret, I: 3281
Delaware, history, I: 4766–72; II: 2594; III: 3169–71
Delaware and Hudson Co., I: 2070
Delaware Historical Society Library: catalog, I: 4767; Delaware history, III: 3171; Delaware newspapers, I: 446
Delaware, Lackawanna and Western Railroad Company, III: 938
Delaware Public Archives Commission, I: 4144, 4768; II: 21, 2200; III: 3169–70
Delaware State Archives: Ridgely family, I: 4768, II: 2200, III: 2597
Delaware State Library: catalog, I: 205; law books, I: 1680
Delaware, University, Library: China trade papers, II: 2399; Delaware history, III: 3171; Delaware newspapers, I: 446; history of chemistry, III: 1383; maps, I: 3840; newspapers, III: 309; Samoa, I: 5382; University history, I: 2006, II: 946
DeLerma, Dominque-René, III: 1864
Delgado, David J., III: 3289
Delivery of goods, I: 2080, 2094
Delmatier, Royce Deems, II: 191
DeLong, Chester W., III: 1462
Delta County, Colo., I: 2628 (21)
Deming, Robert H., III: 2187
Demobilization, military, I: 4193 (28), 5554
Democracy, I: 1357
Democratic Party, II: 717
Demography, I: 1272–1343; II: 661–65; III: 797–800
Demorest, Rose, I: 853
Dempster, Margaret, I: 4034
Dengue, II: 1154
Denis, Ferdinand, I: 5312
Denison, Barbara, II: 65; III: 83
Denison University Library: periodicals, II: 170
Denker, David D., II: 2580
Denmark, history, I: 4306
Dennis, George T., III: 2725
Dentistry, I: 2353, 2387, 2393, 2400; III: 1461; periodicals, I: 2387, 2393, 2400, III: 1543
Denver Art Museum: African art, I: 2833; anthropology, I: 2847
Denver Public Library: aeronautics, I: 2555; African art, I: 2833; American music,

I: 3054; anthropology, I: 2309; Arabic manuscripts, I: 536; architecture, II: 1458; Colorado writers, I: 3253, 4752; folk music, II: 1521–22; mathematics, I: 2211; metals, I: 2793; music education, I: 3008; science, II: 1018; sociology and business, II: 654; technical books, I: 2437; Western history, II: 1501, 2564–65, 2571–72, III: 3142–43
Denver, University, Library: Judaica, III: 769; serials, I: 302
DePaul University Library: Napoleon Bonaparte, I: 4085
DePauw University Library: Harte, Bret, II: 1698; Methodism, III: 729
Depew, Ganson G., I: 3415
DePeyster, John W., I: 5046, 5088
Depressions, economic, I: 1483
DePuy, Henry F., I: 4488
DeRenne, Wymberly J., I: 4804, 4809–10
Der Nersessian, Sirarpie, III: 439
Dertien, James L., III: 215
Deschamps, Margaret B., II: 575
Design copyright, II: 1269
Detective stories, II: 1740; III: 1934–35, 1937, 1939
Detmers, Arthur C., Jr., III: 2592
Detroit: history, I: 4943, II: 2638; maps, I: 3904
Detroit Public Library: architecture, I: 2882; automotive history, I: 2541, II: 958, III: 1569; biological serials, I: 2301; Blair, Austin, I: 4944; Burton Historical Collection, I: 4647, 4650–51, II: 1502, 2472, 2638; Cadillac, Antoine de la Mothe, I: 4943; catalog, I: 206; city government, I: 1876; costume, I: 2938; Detroit maps, I: 3904; economic cooperation, I: 1509; electric utilities, I: 2030; films, I: 1576–77; flouridation, II: 1322; French books, I: 3642; furniture, I: 2923; German books, I: 3586; Greenaway, Kate, II: 1998; industrial arts, I: 2438; Joy, James F., II: 2151; labor in auto industry, I: 1635, II: 750; Michigan history, I: 4943–45, II: 2639, 2642; Michigan state planning, I: 2858; Netherlands, music, II: 1523; preretirement counseling, II: 751; public utilities, I: 2032; Richard, Father Gabriel, I: 4945; Stowe, Harriet Beecher, II: 1746; technical literature, I: 2439; Thailand, II: 2433; Washington, George, II: 2222; Whitman, Walt, I: 3339, II: 1761
Deutrich, Mabel E., II: 629; III: 719, 1221, 1225, 3067
Deutsch, Herman J., I: 1202
de Valinger, Leon, Jr., III: 2597, 3169
Devan, Thomas A., III: 3355
DeVille, Winston, III: 3196
DeVoto, Bernard, II: 1685
DeWaal, Ronald B., III: 1949
Dewey, Thomas E., II: 2116
Dewing, Charles E., II: 2767
DeWolf, James, I: 5162
Dexter, Franklin B., I: 2001

Dexter, Gordon, I: 2120
Dexter, Henry M., I: 1075
Dextrins, I: 2800
D'Happart papers, II: 2301
Dial, magazine (Chicago), II: 238
Dialects: American, I: 3152; European, I: 3154; French, I: 3162; German, I: 3158; Japanese, II: 1606
Diamond drilling, I: 2480
Diaries, I: 4630
Diaz, Albert James, II: 3, 2656, 2716
Díaz, Porfirio, II: 2732
Dibdin, Thomas Frognall, III: 2478
Dibner, Bern, II: 1045; III: 1310
DiCesare, Mario A., III: 1906
Dichter, Harry, II: 1569
Dickens, Charles, I: 3405, 3458–64; II: 1828–30; III: 2158–66
Dickinson, Emily, I: 3282; III: 1998–99
Dickinson, Jacob McGavock, II: 2117; III: 2479
Dickinson, Lenore M., III: 662
Dickinson, Z. Clark, II: 721
Dickinson College Library: Sandburg, Carl, III: 2064
Dickson, Frederick, I: 3470
Dickson, Sarah Augusta, II: 1383, 1386, 1627, 1786; III: 1671
Dictionaries, I: 7, 550, 3147, 3155–56; II: 1595–97, 1599–1600; III: 1911; French and Provencal, I: 3162; Latin, II: 1601, 1603; scientific and technical, I: 2172; Slavic, I: 3169, II: 1604, III: 1913; Spanish, I: 2172, 3165
Diesel motors, II: 1274
Dietz, Ambrose P., I: 4730
Dikewood Corporation: serials, III: 216
Dillard, Henry B., I: 3482
Dillon, Howard W., III: 151
Dillon, Richard H., II: 4, 75; III: 3297
Dime novels, I: 3244; II: 1656, 1659
D'Innocenzo, Michael, III: 3228
Dinstel, Marion, III: 2927
Dion, Dora E., III: 523
Diorama, I: 2887
Directories, I: 7, 4178–83; II: 2257; American, III: 2669; commercial, I: 2039, 2816; New York, I: 4179–81
DiRoma, Edward, III: 957–58
Disability benefits, II: 771
Disarmament, I: 1817, 1827; II: 885; III: 1150, 1162–63
Disaster relief, I: 2066
Disasters, II: 1034
Disciples of Christ, I: 1079, III: 723
Disease prevention, I: 2355
Displaced persons, I: 5552, II: 2282
Dissertations, I: 1967, 2015
District of Columbia, history, I: 4773–79, II: 2595–96
District of Columbia Bar Assoc. Library, I: 1681
District of Columbia Grand Lodge Library, I: 1936
District of Columbia Public Library: Catholic books, I: 1163–64; juvenile literature, III: 2332

Disturnell, John, I:3934
Divorce, I:980–82
Dixon, Elizabeth I., III:2675
Dixon, Maxey R., I:1501
Dobell, Bertram, I:588
Dobson, John, III:2154
Dock, George, I:2362
Docke, I:2323
Dockweiler, J. F., I:1773
Doctrina Christiana, I:907
Dodge, Sally, II:1306
Dodgson, Charles L., II:1082–83
Doe, Janet, I:2405
Doelle, J. A., I:4946
Doesborgh, Jan van, I:4527
Dogs, I:2638; police, II:874
Doheny, Estelle, I:572; II:297
Dolan, Rosemary, II:1195
Doll, Eugene E., I:854
Domestic allotment plans, I:2626 (4l)
Dominican Republic, I:4193 (35), 5363, 5365
Donahue, Eileen C., II:418
Donahue, Jane, III:3051
Donaldson, Ella, III:1489
Donaldson, Gordon, III:880
Donati, Lamberto, II:601
Doneghy, Virginia, II:2524
Donne, John, I:3465
Donnelly, Frederic D., Jr., II:404
Donnelly, Ignatius, III:2480
Donnelly, Joan Angela, II:394, 767
Donnelly, Ralph W., II:2542
Donohup, Mildred D., III:1398
Donovan, Alan B., III:2034
Donovan, Frank P., I:3206
Donovan, General William H., III:3414
Dorame, Gilbert, III:867
Dorbin, Sanford, III:1990
Dorez, Léon, II:2278
D'Orleans, Louis, II:1937
Dorn, Georgette M., III:3318
Dornbusch, Charles E., II:156, 1655; III:1142, 3081
Dorosh, John T., I:21, 3168; II:14; III:3163
Doss, Mildred A., II:1204
Doster, James F., II:1430
Dostoevsky, Feodor, II:1972
Doty, C. Stewart, II:2310
Doty, Marion F., I:2267
Doughty, Arthur G., I:4388
Douglas, John R., III:1416
Douglas, Norman, II:289
Douglas, Stephen A., III:2481
Douglass, Frederick, I:4605
Doumani, George A., III:1373, 3403
Dover Public Library: New Hampshire history, I:5000
Doves Press, I:667
Dowd, Aelred, II:1524
Dowell, E. Foster, I:1895
Downes, Olin, III:1824
Downing, J. Hyatt, III:2000
Downing, Margaret B., I:1165
Downs, Robert B., I:78–83, 4197, 5039; II:76, 280; III:30, 92–94, 136
Dowse, Thomas, I:221
Doxsee, Ruth, II:1515
Doyle, Francis R., III:1061

Doyle, Mary, II:1999
Drainage, agriculture, II:1408
Drake, Mayo, III:1540
Drake, Milton, III:3293
Drake, Thomas E., I:4088; II:591
Drama, I:3191–92; II:1610–11; American, I:3232–38, II:1650–53, III:1971; English, I:3362–74, II:1777, III:2123–26; French, I:3633–34, III:2245; German, I:3580; Italian, II:1941; medieval, II:1610; Spanish, I:3687–89, II:1953–54, 1958, III:2258, 2264–65
Drama recordings, I:3213
Dramatic music, I:3037
Draper, Greta H. Balfour, III:524
Draughon, Wallace R., II:2244
Drawing, I:2909–22; II:1467–75, 1479–80; III:1753–55
Dreier, Katherine S., II:1905
Dreiser, Theodore, I:549; II:1686–87
Drepperd, Carl W., I:2915
Drew, Fraser Bragg, II:1860
Drewry, Elizabeth B., I:4781
Drolleries, II:1800
Dromgoole, Edward, III:2482
Dropsie College Library: Genizah fragments, I:1219
Drug control, I:2357
Druids, I:966
Drummond, Herbert W., II:192
Drury, Clifford M., III:511
Drury, Francis K. W., I:316, 2199
Dryden, John, I:3466–67
Dubester, Henry J., I:1333, 1335, 1339, 1341; II:663–64
Dubose, LaRocque, II:1676
Dubuar, Paul S., II:2576
Ducasse, Curt J., II:509
Duckles, Vincent, II:1525; III:1806
Dudley, Laura H., I:2957
Dudley, Miriam Sue, III:3376
Dufalla, Dennis, J., III:1804
Duff, Edward G., I:624
Duignan, Peter, III:380, 2933, 2935–37, 2965
Duino, Russell, II:2209
Duke University, Divinity School Library, III:687
————Library: advertising history, III:916; Alabama pamphlets, I:706; American literature, III:1951; American Revolution, I:4543; art history, III:1716; Bibles, III:699; Brazilian collection, I:5313; British Commonwealth, II:819; British documents, II:55; British history, III:2693; Bryant, William Cullen, II:1673; building arts, II:1459; Byron, George Gordon, II:1821; classical literature, III:2281–83; Confederate children's books, III:2292; county histories, II:2487; Dante, Alighieri, I:3678; emblem books, II:1621; Emerson, Ralph Waldo, I:3283; English literature, III:2105; French history, I:4289; Greek manuscripts, II:2266–67, III:699; Greek New

Testament, I:1022; Hispanic collection, III:2732; history of science, III:1311; Italian history, III:2726; Italian literature, II:1942; Italian pamphlets, III:2253; League of Nations II:813; Mahan, Alfred Thayer, I:4068; manuscripts, I:4637–38, II:259, III:419–20; medical history, II:1229, 1240, III:1480–82; medieval and Renaissance studies, III:2282–83, 2687–88; Methodist collection, III:726–28; music collection, I:3020; Negroes, III:820; newspapers, I:383, 433; North Carolina folklore, III:1264; North Carolina history, I:5110; O'Shaughnessy, Arthur, II:1867; painting and drawing, II:1479; Peruvian collection, I:5294, 5333; Purviance, Samuel, I:4543; race relations, I:1400, II:680; radical organizations, III:808; research holdings, I:124; Rossetti, Dante Gabriel, I:3506; science serials, I:2200, II:1071, III:1345; serials, III:217; social science periodicals, II:652; Southern history, I:4636–38, III:3134; Southern literature, I:3254, 4636; utopias, III:815; Whitman, Walt, I:3340–41, II:1762–63, III:2092
Dulany, Bladen, III:2483
Dulles, John Foster, II:2118; III:2410, 2679
Dumbarton Oaks Library: rare books, I:552
Duncan, Withrop H., I:4408
Duniway, David C., I:5502
Dunklin, Gilbert T., I:3574
Dunlap, Ann B., III:2386
Dunlap, Fanny, I:4933
Dunlap, Leslie W., I:4035; II:246, 1743, 2165, 2171–72
Dunlap, Mollie E., I:1387
Dunlap, Sara, I:4475
Dunn, Barbara Butts, III:631
Dunn, Caroline, I:4066, 4145
Dunn, George, I:1796
Dunn, James Taylor, II:2659
Dunn, Roy S., III:3129
Dunne, Peter M., I:4677
Dunsany, Lord, III:2167
Duplin County, N. C., history, I:5109
Dupont, Julie Andree, III:626
DuPont de Nemours & Co. Technical Library, I:303
DuPont family, II:2119–20
Duquesne University Library: African collection, III:2942; Hebraica and Judaica, III:770; vocational guidance, II:936
Durden, Robert F., III:820
Dure, Charlotte A., I:1705
Durham, Philip, II:1656, 1758; III:3140
Durkin, Joseph T., I:3663
Durling, Richard J., III:1495, 2505
Durnbaugh, Donald F., II:353
Durrell, Lawrence, III:2168
Durrett, Reuben T., II:2624
Durrie, Daniel S., I:5270
Durrie, Isabel, I:5270
Duryea, Samuel B., I:597

Dust explosions, I: 2534
Dutch-American Historical Commission, III: 3203
Dutcher, George M., I: 4187, 4279
Duvoisin, Roger, III: 2320
Dwiggins, W. A., II: 489
Dwight, Edward H., III: 1761
Dwight, Theodore, F., I: 3937
Dyce, E. J., III: 1658
Dyeing, I: 2804
Dyer, Arthur, I: 5462
Dysentery, I: 2346
Dysinger, Robert E., II: 1897

Eaker, Ira C., II: 2121
Eala, Quintin A., II: 217
Eames, Marian, II: 1578; III: 1886
Eames, Wilberforce, I: 690, 767–68, 834, 990, 3831, 4091, 4096, 4521
Earthquakes, I: 2278; III: 1948
Earths, II: 2282
East, Mona, II: 1902
East Asia, III: 2853–2911
East Asian bibliography, III: 2862
East Germany, II: 2299; III: 2702
East India Company, II: 975
East-West Center Library: acquisitions, III: 2859; Asian history, III: 2798; Japanese collection, III: 2901
Eastern Michigan University Library: city planning, III: 1727
Eastern Orthodox Church, I: 1080–81
Eastern Regional Public Library System (Boston): serials, III: 218
Eastern Washington State College Library: periodicals, III: 219
Eastham, Lucy Beale, III: 632
Eastham, Melville, II: 2028
Eaton, Charles C., I: 2677
Eaton, Dorothy S., I: 3942; II: 2518; III: 2641
Eaton, Vincent L., I: 3292, 4134, 4659; II: 247, 1735, 2166, 2518–19
Eberlein, Alfred, III: 959
Eberstadt, Charles, II: 2167
Eberstadt, Lindley, II: 433
Echenrode, H. J., I: 5212
Echeverria, Durand, II: 2530
Echols, John M., III: 354, 2841, 2917
Eckel, John C., I: 3459
Eckels, George M., I: 4254
Eckhoff, Mark G., II: 702; III: 1063
Eckler, Albert R., I: 2708
Eckman, Florence, III: 548
Ecology, III: 1408
Economic assistance programs, II: 688, 691–93, 699–700, 705–06, 1261, 2374
Economic entomology, I: 2598 (8)
Economic planning, I: 1562, 1569
Economics, I: 1420–32, 1452–1570, 2599 (27, 31); II: 651, 718–46; III: 852–68; African, II: 693; French, I: 1459 Japanese, II: 728, III: 859; Latin American, I: 1454, 1465, II: 688, 692; Near East, II: 693; Philippines, II: 694; Rumanian, II: 730; Russian, I: 1472; Southeast Asia, II: 694
Economics of war, I: 5560
Ecuador, history, III: 3323, 3370

Eddas, I: 3613, II: 1930
Eddy, George S., I: 3980; II: 2128
Eddy, Harry L., I: 2091
Eddy, Henry H., I: 3914; II: 2679
Eddy, Isaac, I: 881
Edel, Leon, II: 1713
Edelstein, J. M., II: 1122, 1770, 2543; III: 2107, 2551, 2685
Eder, Phanor J., I: 1736
Edes, Peter, I: 759
Edgar, Campbell C., I: 4210
Edgeworth, Maria, I: 3468
Edie, Evelyn C., II: 440
Edmands, John, I: 4258
Edmonds, Albert S., I: 883
Edmonds, Cecil K., I: 669
Edmonds, John H., I: 4923
Edmunds, Albert J., I: 1143
Edmunds, Charles C., I: 1026
Edmunds, John, II: 2223; III: 1850
Education, I: 1949–2029; II: 922–52; III: 792–93, 1236–60; elementary, I: 2026; higher, I: 1997–2022, II: 939–52, III: 1252–60; periodicals, III: 1247; secondary, I: 1995–96, 2026
Edwards, Clyde S., II: 193
Edwards, Everett E., I: 2615, 4109
Edwards, Hugh, II: 1476
Edwards, Jonathan, I: 3970–71; II: 2122
Edwards County, Ill., I: 1374
Eells, Richard, I: 2546–47
Egbert, Donald D., I: 522
Egbert, Victor, II: 2979
Egerer, Joel W., III: 2131, 2163
Egerton, Thomas, I: 4260
Eggs, I: 2628 (4)
Egnal, Freda, III: 771
Egypt, history, I: 4199, 4211–12, 4370; II: 2291, 2451
Eichhorn, Hermene, I: 3055
Einstein, Albert, I: 2245, 3041
Eklund, Myrtle J., I: 4268
Elections, I: 1365–69; III: 992
Electoral college, I: 1367
Electric utilities, II: 1348, 1351; Soviet, II: 1276
Electronics, III: 1377
El Hadi, Mohamed, M., III: 358
Eliot, George, I: 3386; II: 1831
Eliot, Jared, I: 2618
Eliot, John, Indian Bible, I: 767; II: 2498
Eliot, Margaret S., I: 4409, 4432
Eliot, T. S., II: 1832; III: 2001–4
Elisséeff, Serge, II: 2392
Elizabeth II, Queen of England, II: 2287
Elkins, Kimball C., I: 1144, 1351, 3610
Elkins, William M., II: 2477
Ellen, John C., Jr., III: 310
Eller, Catherine S., I: 1732
Eller, Mabel H., I: 2360
Ellesmere, Francis E., I: 3521
Ellingwood, Raymond M., III: 1008
Elliott, Agnes M., I: 1942
Elliott, Fannie Mae, II: 1672, 1709; III: 1997, 2095, 2639
Elliott, Mary B., I: 3811
Ellis, Ethel M. Vaughn, III: 825
Ellis, John T., I: 1166

Ellis, Mary B., II: 2136
Ellis, Ralph N., II: 1128
Ellis, William A., I: 5457
Ellison, Rhoda C., I: 707; II: 194
Ellison, Robert S., II: 2160
Ellmann, Richard, III: 2231
Ellsworth, George S., II: 2698–99
Elmer, Minnie, III: 1806
El Salvador, history, III: 3354, 3357
El-Zehery, Mohamed Hussein, III: 893
Elzevir press, I: 906; II: 311, 317
Emancipation Proclamation, II: 2167, 2543
Embargoes, I: 1853
Emblem books, II: 1621, 1624–25; III: 1931
Emeneau, Murray B., I: 3774
Emerich, J. Oscar, I: 1670
Emerson, Guy, I: 5503
Emerson, John, III: 1863
Emerson, Ralph W., I: 3251, 3264, 3283; II: 1632, 1688–90; III: 2005
Emery, Alice Sproat, II: 2000
Emich, Madelaine, II: 1526
Emig, Wilmer J., I: 385
Emory University Library: Charles Forrest Palmer collection, III: 1728; chemistry serials, II: 1062; Civil War, I: 4602; Confederate postal covers, I: 2046; Davis, Jefferson, I: 3968; Georgia counties, I: 4811; history of books, II: 309; incunabula, II: 324; indexing services, III: 3; newspapers, II: 195, III: 311, Presidents collection, II: 2079; special collections, I: 125–26, 556, II: 77, III: 141
Employers' liability, I: 1642–44
Employment, I: 1566, 1586
Enamel, I: 2790
Encephalitis, II: 1166
Encyclopedias, I: 7; III: 2, 10
Engel, Mary Louise, II: 3001
Engineering, I: 2448–49, 2454–2581; II: 1022, 1256, 1263–1323; III: 1291–93, 1565–86, 1591; automotive, I: 2540–44, III: 1569; electrical, II: 1275–76, III: 1577; ethics, I: 2455; history, I: 2457, 2468, II: 1266; hydraulic, I: 2520–27, III: 1582; industrial, II: 1267; marine, I: 2503–04; mechanical, I: 2473–80, II: 1272–74; mining, I: 2495–2501, II: 1277–81; periodicals, I: 2458, 2462, 2473, 2481–82, II: 1072, III: 1586; sanitary, I: 2528–39
Engineering index, I: 2458
Engineering Societies Library: bearings, II: 1432; casting, I: 2460; catalog, I: 2454, 2482, III: 1572; concrete, I: 2461; construction, I: 1439; diamond drilling, I: 2480; Engineering index, I: 2458; filing, classification, and indexing, I: 2678, II: 1263, III: 1570; granular materials flow, III: 1571; highway engineering, I: 2505; machinery foundations, I: 2478, II: 1273; metal bonding, II: 1431; pallets, I: 2459; reference collection, III: 1574; serials, III: 243; shell molding, II: 1433; solar heating,

II:1272; technical periodicals, I:2440, 2462, 2473, 2481, 2495, III:1573; unionization of engineers, II:1264
Engineers, I:2161
English, Elisabeth D., I:5170; II:298
English, Thomas H., I:556; III:95
English drama, I:3362–74; II:1777; III:2123–26
English fiction, I:3198, 3375–89; II:942, 1778–83; III:2127–35
English language, III:1909
English literature, I:3349–3579; II:124, 1618–19, 1622, 1627–28, 1774–1915; III:2103–2234; periodicals, I:3409, III:2117; Victorian, I:3399, 3405, II:1790, 1793, 1796, III:2106
English poetry, I:3225, 3349–61; II:1774–76; III:2122
Engraving, I:2954–93; II:305, 1483–97; III:1763–74; copper, II:1484; wood, I:2954, 2957, 2960, 2965, 2993, II:1485–86, 1492
Engstfeld, Caroline P., I:3255
Eno, Clara Bertha, II:2123
Enoch Pratt Free Library: Baltimore history, I:4898; genealogy, III:2653; Mencken, H. L., III:2044–45; Poe, Edgar Allan, I:3319; Shapiro, Karl Jay, I:3330
Entertainment industry, law, III:1002
Entomology, I:2321, 2599 (20), 2601 (55); II:1385, 1397; III:1436
Environmental control, III:1700–05
Ephrata Cloisters, I:854
Epictetus, I:3734; II:1966
Epigraphy, II:1598
Episcopal Seminary of the Southwest Library: archives, II:588, III:740
Epstein, Dena J., III:1865
Epstein, Fritz T., II:1919, 2294, 2299
Equitable Life Assurance Society, I:1682
Erasmus, Desiderius, II:523; III:452, 2484
Ercilla, Alonso de, II:1959
Erdelyi, Gabor, III:382, 2029
Erdman, David V., II:1809
Erie Railroad Company, III:939
Eritrea, I:4381
Erosion, I:2667 (1), 2669 (1)
Erskine, Robert, I:4552
Eskimos: health, III:1448; language, I:3180
Espelie, Ernest M., II:2002, 2168
Espey, John J., III:675, 1709
Essex County (Mass.), Law Library, I:1684
Essex County (N. J.), Bar Assoc. Library, I:1683
Essex Institute Library: business history, I:2707, 2729; China, history, I:4328; Oriental numismatics, I:2905; Whittier, John Greenleaf, I:3345
Esterquest, Ralph T., II:1103; III:1479
Estes, David E., II:2079
Esthetics, I:949
Estonia, II:2341
Etcheverry, Bernard A., II:1319
Ethics, I:969–71
Ethiopia, I:4366–68, 4379, 4381
Ethiopic languages, I:3171
Ethnography, bibliography, III:14
Ethnology, American, I:2311

Etiquette, I:2154
Ettlinger, J. R. T., II:2352
Europe, history, I:4228–4327; II:2273–2351; III:2682–2792
Euthanasia, III:999
Evangelical Church, I:1082–84
Evans, Charles, I:691; II:350–52, 354, 357, 360, 1282; III:495–97
Evans, Clara T., I:54
Evans, Frank B., II:2679; III:3247
Evans, Lola Blasingame, II:248
Evans, Louise, I:340
Evans, Luther H., I:1830, 3972, 4259, 5187; II:67
Evans, Marjorie D., III:170
Evanston Public Library: music collection, I:3009; vocational guidance, I:1989
Evelyn, John, I:3469
Everett, Alexander Hill, II:2136
Everett, Edward, II:2136
Everly, Elaine, III:1036, 1113
Evidence (law), II:786
Ewing, Donald, II:780
Ewing, Thomas, Sr. and Jr., III:2485–86
Ewing, William S., II:253
Exchanges, international, II:2
Executives, II:1286
Exhibits, I:2602 (45), 2628 (17)
Explosives, I:5419
Expositions. I:2452
Ezekiel, Jacob, I:1218

Faber du Faur, Curt von, I:3587; II:1920, 1927; III:2235
Fables, I:3727, 3730, 3733
Fagan, Carolyn K., III:1677
Faigel, Martin, III:1711
Fair, Judy, III:66
Fairbank, John K., I:4329; II:2393
Fairchild, Herman LeRoy, III:2487
Fairchild family, I:5263
Fairs, I:2452; II:1255, 1262
Falconieri, John V., II:1941
Falconry, II:1593
Falk, Sawyer, III:2488
Falkland Islands, I:5361; II:2766
Fall River Law Library, I:1685
Falmouth, Va., I:5215, 5220
Fancher, Pauline M., III:2243
Far East, II:2366–76
Faris, Nabih Amin, I:531–32
Faris, Robert, III:1000, 1046
Farkas, Cathrine Ann, III:627
Farley, Alan W., II:390, 2618
Farley, Earl, II:287, 1051, 1104
Farm labor, I:2602 (4), 2626 (26, 64, 72, 95)
Farm management, III:1656
Farm mechanization, II:1371
Farm migration, I:2602 (38)
Farm mortgages, I:2626 (47)
Farm production, I:2602 (49)
Farm taxes, I:2626 (94)
Farm tenancy, I:2602 (2), 2626 (70, 85)
Farman, Hafez F., II:2432
Farmer, David R., III:709, 2057, 2205, 2242
Farmhouses, I:2602 (19)
Farmington Plan, Association of Research Libraries, II:88; III:134

Farnsworth, Dorothy, II:822
Farquhar, David M., II:2353
Farragut, David G., III:2489
Farrand, Max, I:1833, 4762
Farris, Betty R., II:1230
Farris, Donn Michael, III:687
Fascism, I:4301
Fassett, Frederick G., I:386
Faulkner, William, II:1616, 1691–94; III:2006–08
Faust, Barbara Louise, III:3082
Faw, Walter Wagner, III:2490
Fawcett, Marion, III:1307
Faxon, Frederick W., I:3207
Fay, Bernard, I:4544
Faye, Christopher U., I:625, 1024; II:1966; III:436
Faye, Helen, II:1443
Fayer, Margaret L., I:3256
Fayssoux, Callander I., I:5341
Feamster, Claudius N., I:3965
Fearing, Daniel B., I:55, 3140–43
Federal Reserve Banking System, I:1479
Federal-state relations, II:848–49, 870
Federalist Party, I:1448
Fehl, Philipp, III:1712
Fein, John M., II:2717
Feinberg, Charles E., II:1761, 1768; III:2091
Feinman, Valerie, III:287
Feldman, Mary Helen, III:2298
Fellman, Jerome D., I:3832; II:2024–25
Felt, Thomas E., III:2481
Felton, Samuel M., II:2098
Fenderich, Charles, II:1496
Fenton, Roger, I:4236
Fenton, William Nelson, II:2504–06
Fenyo, Mario D., III:3345
Ferguson, Faith Crawford, II:1147
Ferguson, Henry, III:373
Fernández, Oscar, III:359, 2263
Fernandez de Córdoba, Joaquin, II:2736–37
Fernandez de Lizardi, J. J., I:3716–19
Ferrand, Gabriel, I:3797
Ferries, II:1309
Ferris, Ruth, II:1503
Fertilizers, I:2602 (27)
Fessenko, Tatiana, III:2767
Fessler, Aaron L., II:196
Fiction, I:3193–3200; II:1612–17; III:1934–41; American, I:3239–49, II:1654–62, III:1972–79; English, I:3375–89, II:942, 1778–83, III:2127–35; French, I:3635–40, III:2244; German, I:3581–82; Italian, II:1946; Spanish, I:3690–93
Field, Alston G., I:2709
Field, Carolyn W., III:2299
Field, Rachel, III:2332
Field, William B. O., I:3491–92
Field Museum Library, I:2311, 2333
Fielding, Henry, I:3470–71; III:2169
Fields, James T., II:289
Fields, Joseph E., II:2188, 2531
Fifth columns, I:5543, 5555
Figenbaum, Muriel C., II:1478
Filar, Leo, I:2475
Filby, P. W., III:1778, 1930
Filing systems, I:2678; II:1263; III:1570

Film libraries, II:1327–29
Filson, John, I:3907, 4855, 4859
Filson Club, II:792
Finance, I:36; III:896
Finch, Herbert, III:3141
Finch, Jeremiah S., I:3488–89
Findly, Elizabeth, III:333
Fine, Ruth, I:2356
Fine arts, I:2830–3145; II:1441–1594;
    III:1706–1903
Finger, Frances L., III:482
Fingerson, Ronald L., III:451, 2438, 2511
Fink, Albert, I:2058
Finland, II:2319
Finley, Katherine P., III:1879
Finley, Samuel, II:572
Finneran, Helen T., III:1374, 1609, 1650
Finney, Charles G., I:1211
Finney, Theodore Mitchell, II:1527
Finno-Ugrian languages, III:1910, 2286
Finotti, J. M., I:1167
Finzi, John Charles, II:1904
Firdaust, I:3798
Fire departments, I:1884
Fire prevention, I:2410
Fire protection, I:5480
Firearms, I:5419; II:1283; III:3148
Firestone Tire and Rubber Company, II:974
Fireworks, I:5419
Fisch, Max H., I:2420
Fischer-Galati, Stephen A., III:2790
Fischmeister, Marie Antonie, III:549
Fish, Arthur M., II:2636
Fish, Carl R., I:5258
Fish, Daniel, I:4036
Fish, fisheries and fishing, I:55, 2334, 2338–
    39, 2637, 3139–45
Fish protein, III:1605
Fishbein, Meyer H., II:735, 741, 744; III:900,
    960
Fisher, Harold H., I:4186
Fisher, Irving, III:853, 861
Fisher, Irving Norton, III:853, 861
Fisher, Jennie D., I:227
Fisher, Mary Ann, II:2561
Fisher, Oneita, III:1713
Fisher, Ruth Anna, II:2096
Fisher, Samuel H., I:776
Fisher, Walter L., II:2124
Fishing, II:1594
Fisk University Library: American Missionary
    Association, I:1053, III:822; Chestnutt, Charles Waddell, II:1677–
    78; Civil War, III:821; Gershwin,
    George, I:3056, 3079, III:822;
    Johnson, Charles S., II:655; Negroes,
    I:1389, III:821–22; sociology, II:655;
    special collections, III:822
Fiske, Minnie Maddern, III:2491
Fiske, Pliny, I:2054
Fiske, Willard, I:3165, 3676, 3685
Fitch, Cornelia, III:2041
Fitch, Elizabeth H., I:3935
Fitch, John, I:3891
Fitz, Reginald, II:2363, 2406
Fitzgerald, Edward, Rubáiyát, II:1990
Fitzgerald, F. Scott, II:1695
Fitzgibbon, Russell H., III:138

Fitzpatrick, John C., I:4117–18, 4120
Fitzpatrick, William H., III:1462
Fitzroy, Alexander, I:4859
Flagg, Charles A., I:4924, 5027
Flags, I:1347, 5413
Flagstad, Kirsten, III: 1816
Flaherty, David H., III:3125
Flanagan, John T., II:1635, 1743; III:2065
Flanders, Bertram H., I:304
Flanders, Louis W., I:692
Flanders, Ralph B., I:305
Flanders, Ralph E., III:2492–93
Flaxman, John, III:1763
Fleck, Ursula, II:1160
Fleisher, Edwin A., I:3016, 3030; II:1542
Fleischmann, James J., II:740
Fleming, Thomas P., II:1017, 1142
Flemish literature, I:1784
Fletcher, Harris F., I:3496–97; II:1601–02,
    1865, 2026
Fletcher, John Gould, II:1696
Fletcher, Joseph J., III:618
Flick, Alexander C., III:2494
Flick, Frances J., II:1402–04
Flint, F. C., I:2781
Flisch, Julia A., I:4801
Floods, I:2520–21, 2525, 2628 (13); II:1310
Floras, I:2321; II:1389
Florence, history, I:4300
Florida, fiction, II:1658; government
    publications, I:27; history, I:4780–98,
    II:2597–2600, III:3172; maps,
    I:3905, II:2064
Florida Agricultural and Mechanical
    University Library: Negroes, III:824
Florida Atlantic University Library: catalog,
    III:171; government publications,
    III:31
Florida Library Assoc.: Floridiana, I:4782
Florida State Dept. of Agriculture: surveyors'
    field notes, II:2599
Florida State Historical Society: Spanish
    Florida, I:4780, 4793
Florida State Library, Florida fiction, II:1658;
    government publications, III:32
Florida State University Library: juvenile
    literature, III:2300–02, 2335, 2340;
    Negroes, II:824
Florida, University, Libraries: Caribbean,
    II:2718, III:3339–40; chemistry
    serials, II:1062; collections, II:77;
    Cuban acquisitions, III:3363; Florida
    history, I:4786, II:2597; Florida news-
    papers, I:406; forestry, I:2652; govern-
    ment publications, I:27, II:22, III:33;
    Latin American history, I:5297; Latin
    American political parties, III:809;
    Seminole Indians, I:4489; special
    collections, III:142; Vietnam, III:2850;
    Wright, John Buckland, III:1764
Florists and floriculture, III:1669
Flour milling, I:2626 (2)
Flower, George, I:1374
Flowers, George W., I:4636
Flute, I:3021
Fly fishing, III:1904
Flynn, Jane M., III:550
Flynn, John T., III:2495

Flynn, Raymond P., I:5495, 5568
Foerster, Adolph M., II:1570
Foglesong, Hortense, I:4410
Foley, Clair, II:2003
Folger Shakespeare Library: acquisitions,
    I:3524, II:1876; catalog, III:172; early
    English books, I:671, 3419, II:307;
    English plays, I:3374; Italian plays,
    III:2254; manuscripts, III:409;
    resources and history, I:3520, 3522–
    23, 3540, II:124, 1875, III:162
Folk, Edgar E., I:207; II:1643
Folk dances, I:3088
Folk music, I:3024, 3028, 3052–54, 3067,
    3073–75, 3077; II:1521–22, 1539,
    1559, 1565–66; III:1262, 1840–43;
    African, III:1841
Folkes, John G., III:312
Folklore, I:2147–56; II:1001–06, 1635;
    III:1261–67; Brazilian, I:2149;
    Greek, III:1917
Folksongs, Ohio, III:1854; Virginia, III:1859
Folsom, Josiah C., II:1368, 1374
Folsom, Morrill G., II:1319
Food: preservation, I:2599 (4); production and
    distribution, I:4193 (17); supply,
    I:2599 (9), 2626 (82)
Foos, Donald D., III:3269
Foote, Henry W., I:1047
Foote, Lucy B., I:755
Forbes, Charles H., I:3736
Forbes, Harriette M., I:4630
Forbes, Robert Bennett, III:2496
Forbes, Ruth D., II:1396
Forbes, William Cameron, II:2757
Force, Manning Ferguson, III:2497
Force, Peter, I:4022, 4548, 4553
Force, William Q., I:4553
Ford, Elizabeth, I:4347
Ford, Ford Madox, II:1797; III:2170
Ford, Henry, I:3973
Ford, Paul L., I:195, 693, 814, 1884, 3981,
    3996–98, 4126, 4545
Ford, Worthington C., I:387, 769, 3221,
    4411, 4546, 4925–26, 5295
Ford Motor Company, II:956–57, 960
Fordham University Library: Jesuits, II:610
Fore-edge paintings, I:2953; II:1478
Foreign aid, II:688, 692–93, 699–700, 705–
    06, 1261, 2374
Foreign relations, I:1375, 1404–18; II:686–
    709, 2721; III:1058–68
Foreign trade, I:2038, 2040–42; III:1047, 1119
Foreman, Carolyn T., I:851
Foreman, Edward R., I:815
Foreman, Grant, I:5130
Foreman, Paul B., III:843
Forest, A. N., I:3633
Forest fires, I:2602 (34), 2655
Forest History Foundation, II:1400, 1406–07
Forest products industry, I:2653, 4193 (19)
Forestry, I:2601 (24, 76), 2602 (36), 2651–
    65, 2856; II:1393, 1399–1407;
    III:1679–94; history, III:1633;
    periodicals, I:2663; tropical, III:1689
Forgeries, II:290, 1802–03
Forman, Sidney, II:904; III:676
Formosa, II:2404

Fornaroli, Cia, II:1578
Forrestal, James, III:2410
Forster, Walter Otto, II:553
Fort, Gilberto V., III:3364
Fort Wayne Public Library: periodicals, III:220
Fort Worth Public Library: serials, I:315
Fortuine, Robert, III:1448
Fosberg, F. Raymond, II:1124
Fossils, I:2296
Foster, John, I:687, 771
Foster, Ludmila A., III:2750
Foster, O. D., III:2498
Foster, Stephen C., I:3083; II:1569
Fourth of July, I:4572
Fowler, Lawrence Hall, III:1745
Fowler, Mary, I:3676, 3685
Fox, Edith M., II:2660
Fox, Edward W., III:2543
Fox, Helen M., II:1384
Fox, John L., III:1467
Fox, Louis H., I:388
Fox, Film Corporation, I:3090
Foxwell, Herbert S., I:2727
Fraenkel, Josef, III:772
Fraktur, II:268
Francastoro, Girolamo, I:3660
France, I:4193 (3); government publications,
    I:49; history, I:123, 4279−89,
    II:2300−2310, III:2710−18
Francis Bacon Foundation Library, II:1806
Franciscans, II:603
Franck, Marga, II:181
Franco, Diane Marion, III:537
Frank, John C., I:2112, 3224
Frankenberg, Celestine G., III:1725
Frankfurter, Felix, III:2499
Franklin, Aurelia W., II:405
Franklin, Benjamin, I:684, 690, 3936, 3974−
    90; II:128, 2098, 2125−30, 2512,
    2533; III:3147
Franklin, E. M., I:3395
Franklin College, Library: Indiana history,
    II:2614
Franklin D. Roosevelt Library: American
    Indians, II:2509; World War II,
    II:2802
Franklin Institute Library: catalog, I:2441,
    2492; serials, III:1331
Fraser, Robert S., III:1999, 2248, 3037
Frawley, Margaret Lenora, III:551
Frazee, Helen D., III:173
Frazier, E. Franklin, I:1388
Frazier, Sandy, III:288
Frederick, Wayne A., III:2554
Frederick the Great, I:3960
Free Europe Committee, II:686
Free speech, I:1359−60
Free Speech League, III:1071
Freedley, George, I:3091; II:1579;
    III:1880
Freedom of information, II:697; III:986
Freedom of press, I:1360−61
Freedom of seas, I:1818, 1820
Freeman, Douglas S., I:4601; II:2131
Freeman, Edmund A., I:2059
Freeman, John F., III:3028, 3030−31
Freeman, Walter E., III:831

Freemasons, I:559, 1935−42; II:919−20;
    III:1234; Supreme Council Library,
    I:2163, II:919
Freeney, Mildred, II:1678
Freer Gallery of Art: Armenian manuscripts,
    III:439; library catalog, III:1714;
    Mongolian manuscripts, II:2353
Freeze-drying of foods, III:1606
Freides, Thelma, III:343
Freight rates, I:2631
Freimann, Aaron, I:599; III:773
Freitag, Ruth S., III:291, 805, 1615
Frelinghuysen, Peter H. B., Jr., II:984
French A. D. W., I:4163
French, Hannah Dustin, II:1870; III:677
French, Robert D., I:3507
French Africa, I:4376
French and Indian War, I:4499−4500, 4515
French bibliography, I:20
French drama, I:3633−34; II:1936; III:2245
French fiction, I:3198, 3264, 3635−40;
    III:2244
French in North America, II:2466
French Institute Library: Louis XVII, I:3648
French language, I:3162; dictionaries, III:1915
French literature, I:123, 3633−59; II:1935−
    39, 2306−08; III:2244−51
French Revolution, I:578, 4233, 4279−82,
    4287−89; II:2303−04, 2310;
    III:2710−11, 2716
French West Africa, II:2456
Freneau, Philip, I:3284
Freud, Sigmund, II:1616
Freudenheim, Tom L., III:777
Frewen, Moreton, I:4687
Frey, Ellen F., I:3340; II:1763; III:2092
Frick, Bertha M., I:884, 2212−13
Frick Art Reference Library: medieval and
    Renaissance manuscripts, II:267
Friede, Juan, III:3388
Friedenwald, Herbert, I:4119, 5346
Friedman, Lee Max, III:759
Friedmann, Robert, I:1092
Friedrich, Gerhard, I:1370
Friedrich, W. H., II:1966
Friedus, A. S., I:3769
Friend, Llerena B., II:157, 495, 3691;
    III:635−36, 3144, 3258
Friend, William L., I:1800
Friendland, Louis S., I:4412
Friends, Society of, II:589−94
Fries, Adelaide L., I:5093
Frisian literature, I:3161
Fritz, Emanuel, II:1399
Frontier, American, II:2563
Frost, Anaclare, III:1533, 1559
Frost, John Eldridge, II:1719−20
Frost, Mary C., III:1021, 1024
Frost, Pattie P., I:4155
Frost, Robert, I:3285; III:2009−11
Frozen food industry, I:2628 (2)
Fry, Joshua, II:2055
Fry, Mary Isabel, II:576
Fry, William H., I:3080
Frye, Roland M., III:493
Fuch, James R., II:1280
Fuels, solid, II:1437
Fuller, Donald F., II:949

Fuller, Grace H., I:1348, 1451, 1488, 1492,
    1498, 1511, 1533−34, 1592, 1624,
    1828, 1841, 1847−48, 1870, 1923,
    2117, 2294, 2898, 3155−56, 4061,
    4327, 4381, 5279−80, 5373, 5411−
    12, 5418, 5460−61, 5548−49, 5554
Fuller, Minnie N., III:1661
Fulton, John F., I:2260, 2270, 2364, 2416,
    3660; II:2205; III:1506
Fulton, Robert, I:3991, 5051; II:1309
Fulton, William Savin, III:2500
Fungus infections, II:1177
Funk, Anneliese M., I:854
Funk, Charles E., Jr., III:90
Fur trade, I:1555
Furber, Holden, II:2183
Furnald, Sara L., II:216
Furnas, Robert W., III:2501
Furness, Horace Howard, III:1874
Furniture, I:2890, 2923−25, 2928, 2930
Furuseth, Andrew, I:1592
Fyfe, Arthur W., Jr., I:2798

Gabler, Anthony J., I:460
Gadd, L. H., I:1703
Gaeddert, G. Raymond, I:389
Gages, I:2479
Gaine, Hugh, I:814
Gaines, Jacquelyn M. Melcher, III:3387
Gaines, Peter Welch, II:2535
Gaines, Pierce W., III:3057
Galaxy, magazine (New York), II:239
Galbreath, C. B., I:333
Gale, Frederick C., III:3218
Galilei, Galileo, III:1315
Gallatin, Albert, I:3992; III:2502
Gallatin, Albert E., I:2909, 3425; II:1808
Gallaudet, Edward Miner, II:2132
Gallaudet, Peter Wallace, II:2132
Gallaudet College Library: deafness and deaf,
    III:194
Gallaudet family, II:2132
Gallier, James, II:1466
Galloway, John A., II:2651
Gallup, Donald, I:3331; II:1631; III:667,
    1950, 2001
Galsworthy, John, II:1833
Gambet, Adrien, I:3123
Gamble, William B., I:2465, 2558, 2797,
    2820, 2822, 2997, 3108
Gambrill, Georgia, I:4172; II:2253; III:2660
Game animals, I:2341
Gammons, Harold Winsor, II:2169
Gandhi, Mahatma, II:2133
Ganfield, Jane, II:1117; III:787
Gangrene, gas, II:1178
Gans, Edward, III:1776
Ganz, Margery, III:2690, 3025
Gardel, Luis D., II:2719
Gardella, Robert, III:796
Garden Center of Greater Cleveland Library:
    serials, II:179
Gardening, I:2602 (15), 2643; II:1384;
    III:1664
Gardiner, C. Harvey, II:2194; III:3312
Gardiner, George L., II:655
Gardinier, David, III:2960
Gardner, Charles S., I:3785, 4330

Gardner, Elizabeth A., I:1565, 2042, 2650, 3820, 4324
Gardner, Isabella, III:2012
Gardner, Ralph D., III:2303
Garfield, James A., I:3993
Garfield, Jane, II:1072
Garford, Arthur Lovett, III:2503
Garland, Hamlin, III:2013–14
Garloch, Lorena A., II:1663–64, 2301
Garner, Jane, III:3298
Garner, W. W., I:2644
Garnett family, II:1801
Garrett, Robert, I:487, 544–46
Garrett Biblical Institute: Methodist manuscripts, I:1095
Garrick, David, II:1834
Garrison, Curtis W., I:514, 2710; III:2574
Garrison, Ellen, III:3110
Garrison, Fielding H., I:2385, 2421
Garrison, George P., I:5188
Garrison, Guy G., III:96
Garrison, Lucy McKim, III:1865
Garvan, Mabel B., I:4466
Garvey, Eleanor M., III:653, 657
Gary, Elbert H., I:1749, 1795
Garza, Ben, III:3375
Gas, II:1278
Gas, natural, I:2281
Gaskell, Elizabeth C., I:3386
Gaskill, Nelson B., I:694
Gassett, Henry, I:1940
Gassner, George, II:1580
Gaston, William, III:2504
Gastronomy, I:2582; II:1339
Gately, Charles, II:419
Gates, Alice J., I:2440
Gates, Charles M., I:4660
Gates, Elizabeth, I:2261
Gates, Francis, II:748, 752
Gates, William E., III:408
Gatley, Flora McKenzie, III:566
Gaul, John J., I:2519, 2995
Gay, Alice, II:1717
Gay, Ernest L., I:127, 3653
Gay, Frederick L., I:127, 4631
Gay, George H., I:127
Gay, Henry N., I:3663–64, 3668, 3673
Gazetteers, Chinese, I:4336
Gearhart, Frank Hobart, II:936
Gecker, Sidney, II:1781
Geiser, Samuel W., I:306
Geissman, Erwin W., II:610
Genealogical Forum, II:2245
Genealogical Society of Pennsylvania: manuscripts, I:4146; II:2246
Genealogical Society of Utah: family histories, I:4147
Genealogy, I:141, 4135–77, 5179; II:254, 2242–57; III:163, 2650–68; periodicals, III:2652
General Society of Mechanics and Tradesmen Library: architecture, I:2883
General Theological Library (Boston): catalog, I:991
General Theological Seminary Library (New York): American church history, I:1134; collections, II:583; gospel manuscripts, I:1026; Gutenberg Bible,

II:326; Latin Bibles, I:1025; manuscripts, II:584; periodicals, I:999
Genetics, III:1407; plant, I:2328
Genthe, Arnold, II:1511
Geography, I:2283, 3822–3934; II:2017–77; III:1292–93, 2352–2406; American, I:3869–3934, II:2052–77, III:2382–2406; Antarctica, II:2044; Japanese, II:2023; periodicals, I:3832, 3851, II:2024–25; Slavic, II:2048; Yugoslav, II:2049
Geology, I:2086, 2277–95; II:1111–13; III:1292–93, 1391–1406; Maryland, III:1398; Mississippi Valley, I:2287, III:1396; North America, III:1395; Virginia, I:2285; Washington, II:1113; West Virginia, III:1406
Geopolitics, I:1453
George, Albert J., III:2247
George, Henry, I:1519
George III, King of England, II:2293
George IV, King of England, I:2928
George Washington Masonic Museum: music collection, III:1851
George Washington University Library: international law, I:1803; peace, I:973–75; serials, III:275; war, I:1350, 5388–89
George Williams College: Civil War, I:4606
Georgetown University Library: Catholic Bibles, I:1038; Catholic books, I:1182, 1187; Early English books, II:345; papal autographs, I:1157; serials, III:275, 286; special collections, I:56
Georgi, Charlotte, III:874
Georgia: history, I:4799–4814, II:2601–03, III:3173; maps, I:3906
Georgia Dept. of Archives and History: Civil War, III:3083; Georgia history, I:4808, 4811, II:2601
Georgia Historical Society, I:4811; II:2603
Georgia Institute of Technology Library: resources, II:77; science and technology, III:1281; serials, II:1062, III:1332
Georgia Library Association: Georgiana, II:2602
Georgia State Law Library, I:1686
Georgia State Library: Georgia history, I:4802, 4811; government publications, II:23–24, III:34
Georgia, University, Library: catalog, I:208; Confederate imprints, III:3084; Georgia history, I:4799, 4811; McIntosh, Lacklan, III:2561; Olin Downes papers, III:1824; resources, II:77
Geoscience Information Society, III:1395
Gerdts, Elaine E., II:1444
Germain, George, I:4536
German, Mark, III:3114
German Americans, I:1370–71, 1380
German archives, World War II, II:2770–2800, 2803, 2818
German bibliography, I:20, 468
German drama, I:3580
German fiction, I:3581–82

German literature, I:3580–3605; II:1639, 1916–27; III:2235–42
Germanic languages, I:3157–61, 3624
Germany: government, I:53; government publications, I:53; history, II:2294–99, III:2701–02, 3415–16
Gerould, James T., I:4269
Gerow, Bert A., II:1118
Gershenson, Judd, III:2756
Gershwin, George, I:3056, 3084; II:1568; III:822
Gesamtkatalog der wiegendrucke, I:626
Gesner, Conrad, III:2505
Gessiness, Gernard, I:2195
Gest, Erasmus, III:2506
Ghana, Africa, III:2977
Gheorghiu, Raoul, II:820
Gibbon, Edward, I:3994
Gibbons, Mother Mary Rosario, II:368
Gibbs, Clayton R., II:831
Gibbs, Robert Coleman, II:1772
Gibson, A. M., II:2507, 2670
Gibson, Charles, III:3032
Gibson, Mary Jane, III:2986
Gibson, Reginald W., III:2200
Gibson, Wilfred Wilson, II:1835
Gibu, Morio, III:2901
Giddings, Joshua R., I:5116
Gide, André, II:1616
Giefer, Gerald J., II:1313, 1315–18
Gieger, Bayard J., I:4733
Giffen, Helen Smith, II:197
Gigedo, Revilla, II:2735
Gilbert, Allan H., I:3678; II:1942
Gilbert, Felix, II:2295
Gilbert, John, I:3113
Gilbert, W. H., I:1500
Gilchrist, Agnes Addison, III:1743
Gilcrease Institute: Spanish inquisition, II:2734
Gildea, Matthew Edward, III:558
Gilder, Rosamond, III:3091
Gildersleeve, Hallet, II:246
Gilfillan, Ellen, III:429
Gilkey, M. A., I:4176
Gill, Eric, III:447
Gillespie, William H., III:1406
Gillett, Charles R., I:4276–77
Gillett, Theresa, III:3331
Gillette, William, II:1697
Gilliam, Franklin, II:1801
Gillis, I. V., I:4345, 4354
Gilmer, Gertrude C., I:307–08
Gilmore, Barbara, I:770
Gimbel, Richard, II:1736; III:2160
Giroux, Richard, I:5432; III:1179, 3352
Girsch, Mary Louise, III:2304
Gissing, George, II:1836
Glasgow, Ellen, III:2015
Glass, Carter, II:2134–35
Glass, I:2781, 2796, 2799
Glavin, Mary A., III:2029
Glazer, Sidney, I:4346, II:2363
Glazier, Kenneth M., III:380, 1143, 2957–58
Glazier, William S., II:271
Gleason, Frances E., I:1158
Gleason, Margaret, III:2655
Gleaves, Albert, III:2507

Glenk, Robert, I:4887
Glenn, Bess, I:5448; II:784
Glidden, Sophia H., I:2711
Gliders, I:2580
Glossaries, scientific, I:2165
Gnudi, Martha T., III:1446, 1477
Goan, Fava E., I:309
Godard, Doris, I:4397
Goddard, Jeanne M., III:3158
Goebel, Wallace B., III:1110
Goethals, George Washington, III:2508
Goethe, Johann W. von, I:3595–99; II:1917, 1924
Goff, Frederick R., I:557–58, 577, 589, 627, 908, 3010, 3962, 4547–48; II:264, 327, 342, 373, 484, 1613, 1929, 2021, 2170, 2519; III:485–88, 1907, 2938
Goggin, Daniel T., III:1064–65, 1653, 3108
Gohdes, Clarence, I:3283; III:1951
Gold, Neil Newton, III:901
Gold standard, I:1480
Goldbeck, Gwendolyn Owens, III:577
Goldberg, Merle, III:593
Golden, Arthur, III:2093
Goldenbaum, Mary Bacon, III:525
Goldsmith, Alfred F., I:3342; III:2092
Goldsmith, Oliver, I:3472–73
Goldwater, Walter, III:221
Gollin, Richard M., III:2150
Gómez de la Serna, Ramón, III:2272
Gomperz, Heinrich, II:511
Gondos, Victor, Jr., I:5533; II:740
Gondra, Manuel E., I:5289; II:2755
Góngora y Argote, Luis de, I:3720
Gonzaga University Library: Gerard Manley Hopkins, III:2172
Gooch, Donald W., II:1375, 1380
Good, Terry W., III:1686
Goode, Paul Killian, III:619
Goodhart, Howard Lehman, II:328
Goodman, Marie Cleckner, II:2022
Goodnight, Scott H., I:3588
Goodrich, F. L. D., I:779
Goodrich, Nathaniel L., I:3195
Goodspeed, Charles Eliot, II:1870
Goodspeed, Edgar J., I:486
Goodwin, Noma L., I:4543, 4638
Goold, Clarissa L., I:3208
Gordan, John D., I:3322, 3400, 3556; II:1608, 1622, 1636, 1690, 1701, 1749, 1756, 1765, 1787, 1788–89, 1829, 1836, 1861, 1881, 2286; III:1483, 1955, 2113, 2115, 2128, 2137, 2212
Gordan, Phyllis W. G., II:328, 2274
Gordon, Cyrus H., II:2354
Gordon, Jacques, II:1552
Gordon, Norma S., III:1398
Gordon, Reginald B., I:2192, 2282, 2479, 2486
Gordon, Vesta Lee, III:718
Gorham, Rex, I:2149
Göring, Hermann, I:2991
Gorky, Maxim, I:3761
Gorokhoff, Boris, II:2320
Gorokhoff, Cecilia J., II:2729
Goshen College, Mennonite Historical Library, I:1092

Gosnell, Charles F., I:5028; II:2520
Goss, W. F. M., I:2468
Gossman, Mildred, III:3145
Gotlieb, Howard B., II:1667; III:3412
Gotschall, William C., II:292
Gott, John Kenneth, II:464
Goudy, Frederic W., I:939, 946; II:504; III:660
Gough, Richard, II:975
Gould, John, II:1135
Gould, Marie, II:1381
Goult, Virginia B., I:4085
Gourley, James E., II:2585, 2587
Government: U.S. Federal and state, I:1895–1915, II:834–71, III:1072–1140; Great Britain, I:1915; Latin American, II:876; local, II:872–75
Government publications, I:23–53, 223; II:18–58; III:19–78; Alaska, III:24; Arizona, III:25; Arkansas, I:23, II:18, III:26; Brazil, III:23; California, I:24–25, II:19–20, III:27; Chicago, I:1875; Colombia, I:44, III:23; Colorado, I:26, III:28; Connecticut, III:29; Cuba, III:23; Delaware, I:21; Florida, I:27, II:22, III:31–33; Georgia, II:23–24, III:34; France, I:49; Germany, I:53, II:53–54; Great Britain, I:1434, II:55, 819; Hawaii, III:35–36; Idaho, III:37; Illinois, II:25, III:38; Indiana, II:26, III:39; Iowa, II:27, III:40; Kansas, II:28, III:41–42; Kentucky, III:43; Latin America, I:43–48, III:23; Louisiana, I:755, II:30, III:44; Maine, II:31, III:45; Maryland, II:32; Massachusetts, III:46–47; Mexico, I:48, III:23; Michigan, II:33, III:48; Minnesota, I:32–33, III:49–50; Mississippi, III:51; Missouri, II:34, III:52; Montana, II:35; Nevada, II:36, III:53; New Hampshire, I:35, II:37, III:54; New Jersey, III:55; New York, I:37, 1882–83, II:38–39, III:56–57; North Carolina, II:40, 45, III:58; North Dakota, III:59; Ohio, II:41, III:60–61; Oregon, II:42, III:62; Pennsylvania, III:63; Philippines, II:56–57; Rhode Island, I:38, III:64; South Carolina, III:65; Tennessee, II:43, III:67; Texas, II:44, III:68; United States, I:23–42, 1722, II:18–52, III:24–78; Utah, II:48, III:72–73; Virginia, I:41, II:51, III:74–75; Washington (State), I:42, II:50, III:76; West Virginia, II:51, III:77; Wisconsin, III:78
Government purchasing, II:842–43
Goy, Peter A., III:2749
Grabhorn, Jane, II:502
Grabhorn Press, I:716; II:362, 364, 502
Grade crossings, I:2508
Grady, Catharine C., I:105
Graf, Dorothy W., II:2594
Graff, Everett D., I:5195; II:2552, 2559
Graff, George P., III:3206
Graham, Ida Hervey, III:1449
Graham, James L., I:195
Graham, Janet, III:685, 695
Graham, John W., I:962; II:509, 512

Graham, Mary E., I:310
Graham, Philip, II:1707
Graham, Richard Marr, II:1479
Graham, Robert B. C., II:289
Graham, Walter J., I:310
Grametbaur, Agnes B., II:2056
Grammars, I:3147, 3165; II:1595, 1602
Grand Lodge of Iowa Library, I:1937
Grand Rapids Public Library, I:2924
Granger movement, II:2647
Granier, James A., I:3706
Granniss, Ruth S., I:935, 938
Granovsky, A. A., III:2751
Grant, Elliott M., II:1935
Grant, Isabelle, II:1877
Grant, Ulysees, III:2509
Grants in aid, I:1840, 1842, 1923; II:770, 870
Grape industry, I:2626 (36)
Graphic arts, II:1449
Gratwick Laboratory Library: medical periodicals, I:2386
Graves, E. Sharon, III:2232
Graves, F. P., I:1952
Graves, William B., I:1895–96; II:849
Gray, Asa, I:2190
Gray, Francis C., I:2984
Gray, John C., I:1774
Gray, Phyllis Anne, II:602
Gray, Roland, I:1774
Gray, Ruth A., I:1967, 4362–63, 4387
Gray, Thomas, I:3474; II:1837
Gray, Virginia R., III:808
Great-books lists, II:284, 295
Great Britain: foreign relations, II:2290; government publications, II:55, 819; history, I:490, 4242, 4248–78, II:2285–93, III:2691–2700
Great Britain, Historical Manuscripts Comm., I:4260–61
Great Britain, Ministry of Reconstruction, I:1473
Great Britain, Parliament, I:4273
Great Lakes, maps, I:3881, 3909
Greater Hartford Librarians Club, II:5
Gredler, Charles R., III:2736
Greece, history, I:4238, 4325; II:2351
Greek literature, I:237, 3722–24, 3727, 3730, 3734–35, 3740–41; II:517, 1602, 1964, 1968–69; III:2274, 2276, 2278–81, 2283–85
Greek manuscripts, II:2266–68, 2270
Greek ostraca, I:4198, 4207
Greely, Adolphus W., I:28–29
Greely, Georgiana Mathews, III:497
Green, Duff, III:2510
Green, Harriet E., I:1448
Green, O. H., I:3700
Green, Ralph, II:496
Green, Robert S., II:1436
Green, Rosalie B., III:437
Green, Samuel A., I:695, 771–72
Green, Thomas, I:723
Greenaway, Kate, I:572; II:1998
Greenbaum, Milton, I:5366
Greene, Belle Da Costa, I:565
Greene, Evarts B., I:4509; II:2521
Greene, Jane, I:1541
Greene, Nathanael, I:4538

Green and, I:5381
Greenlee, William B., II:2311, 2314
Greenly, Albert H., I:3312; II:421, 2463, 2550, 2640
Greenwood, Arthur M., II:2500
Greenwood, Jane L., I:1775
Greenwood, John, I:2971
Greenwood, Robert, III:512
Greer Sarah, I:1857−58, 1860, 1877
Greg, Walter W., I:3364
Gregory, James, III:3018
Gregory, Julia, I:3034
Gregory, Winifred, I:52, 311, 362, 366
Greming, Anne E., III:279, 281−82, 284
Greming, Richard C., II:176−77
Grey, Lady Jane, I:3995
Gribben, Lenore S., III:1935
Grieder, Elmer M., I:1859
Griffin, A. P. C., I:1419, 1545, 2050, 4094, 4105, 4582, 4663, 4708, 5344, 5346, 5350−51, 5376−77, 5384
Griffin, Grace G., I:1404, 4413, 4469
Griffin, Lloyd W., II:2152
Griffin, Max L., I:312
Griffin, Ray B., III:2511
Griffin, Warren B., III:1025
Griffith, Albert H., I:4037
Griffith, Connie G., II:249; III:3194
Griffith, H. W., I:269
Griffith, Reginald H., I:3442, 3502
Grimes, Maxyne Madden, II:2539; III:3073, 3089
Grinstead, S. E., I:1389
Griswold, Ada T., I:448
Griswold, Rufus W., I:3286
Griswold, Stephen B., I:1709
Groce, George C., II:1450
Grolier Club: American literature, III:1952; Americana, II:2474; art collection, I:934, 937; book binding, I:919; collections, I:933, 935−36; English literature, III:2111; 15th century books, II:329; great-book lists, II:295; history of science, III:1312; Italian books, I:3665; mezzotints, I:2958; microscopic books, I:590; printing history, I:628−29; typography, I:938
Gropp, Arthur E., I:5340; II:64, 220; III:4
Grossman, Moses H., I:1789
Grossmann, Jorge, II:876
Grosvenor Library, I:559, 1188, 1191, 2262, 2386, 3057, 3354
Grotney, Mina Jane, III:3379
Grotius, Hugo, I:1806−07
Grote, Joseph Della, III:2728
Grover, Wayne C., II:960
Groves, Esther P., III:513
Grulee, Clifford G., II:1203
Gryzybowski, Kazimierz, II:2321; III:2786
Gsovski, Vladimir, I:4311; II:821
Guam, I:5385
Guatemala, history, I:5304, 5321; III:3348, 3355, 3358
Guarule, I:2602 (10), 2667 (4)
Gudger, Eugene W., I:2334
Guerber, Louise, I:2309
Guerra, Francisco, III:1484
Guerrilla warfare, II:1288

Guggenheim, Daniel, II:1324
Guianas, I:3931, 4394, 5358
Guild, Edward C., I:3158
Guilford College Library: Quaker history, III:746
Gulick, Charles Adams, II:753
Gullans, Charles B., III:675, 1709
Gulley, L. S., I:4721
Gummere, Amelia M., I:5029
Gun legislation, III:988
Gundry, L. D., III:1277
Gurland, A. R. L., II:672
Gutenberg, John, I:581; II:334
Gutenberg Bible, I:569, 637, 661; II:326, 330−31, 333, 338, 528
Guthorn, Peter J., III:2387−88
Guthrie, Chester L., I:1553
Gutsch, Milton R., I:5189; II:2689
Guzzetta, Anthony J., III:2635−36
Gwyer, Joseph A., II:1088
Gynecology, II:1230
Gypsies, I:2155; II:1007
Gyroscope, I:2540
Gyulahazi, Maria, III:2305

Haas, Emma B., II:1410
Habeas corpus, II:833
Haber, Tom Burns, II:1805
Haferkorn, Henry E., I:390, 2287−88, 2569, 4588, 4652
Hafstad, Margaret R., III:2360
Hage, George S., III:325
Hagedorn, Ralph, I:1246, 2164; II:1048
Hahn, Allen W., III:1527
Haight, Gordon S., I:4589; II:1831
Haines, Donal H., I:2746
Hair, May Jane, II:2569
Haiti, I:4193 (40); II:2748; history, III:3344
Hale, Carolyn L., I:4178
Hale, George Ellery, III:1365
Hale, John P., III:2512
Hale, Nathan, II:2136
Hale, Richard W., III:2671
Haley, Emilie L., I:1162
Halik, Glen, II:1528
Hall, Drew B., I:4892
Hall, Edward B., I:3092−94
Hall, Glendora, II:941
Hall, John W., II:2411
Hall, Lillian A., I:3095−99, 3101
Hall, Louise, II:1459; III:2687−88
Hall, Robert B., II:2023
Hall, Ruth Louise, III:526
Hall, W. S., I:2906
Hall, Wilmer L., I:1542, 5228; II:49
Haller, Mark H., II:1390
Halley, Fred G., I:5466, 5468−69, 5572
Halley, Gail Kern, II:441
Hallidie, Andrew S., I:987
Halliwell-Phillips, James O., I:3543
Halper, Benzion, I:1219
Halpern, Kathryn D., III:620
Halpern, Sybil, III:2774
Halsband, Robert, III:2227
Halsell, Willie D., II:2648
Halverstott, Lyle J., II:869
Ham, Edward B., I:4632
Ham, F. Gerald, III:313, 812, 961, 979, 3279

Hamer, Elizabeth E., I:5470
Hamer, Philip M., II:250; III:410
Hamill, Alfred E., II:1007
Hamilton, Alexander, I:3996−98; II:2137
Hamilton, George Heard, II:1480
Hamilton, Joseph G. de R., I:4639
Hamilton, Kenneth G., II:558−59; III:733
Hamilton, Milton W., I:1941; II:2150
Hamilton, Sinclair, I:914; II:486−87; III:655
Hamilton, William B., III:2693
Hamlin, Arthur T., I:3291, 4366
Hamlin, Omer, Jr., III:1537
Hamlin, Talbot F., I:2878, 2884
Hamline University Library: periodicals, II:162, 169
Hamman, Frances, II:1529
Hammer, Victor, II:500
Hammond, George P., I:4679, 5015; II:2590; III:2545, 3139
Hammond, James, I:236
Hamond, Sir Andrew Snape, III:2513
Hampton Institute: Negro collection, I:1390
Hamrick, Lillian A., II:46
Hamtramck, John Francis, II:2138
Hancock, Eva, II:450
Hancock, Harold B., III:902
Hand, Learned, III:1016
Handel, George Frederick, III:1868
Handicapped, I:1578
Handicrafts, I:2935
Handwriting, I:3214
Hanford, James Holly, II:667; III:2047
Hanke, Lewis, I:5296
Hanlin, Frank S., II:1840
Hanna, Archibald, Jr., II:2508, 2582; III:2145, 3146
Hannay, Annie M., II:1366
Hannesson, Jóhann Sigurjónsson, II:1930−31
Hansen, Ralph W., III:3350
Hanson, Howard, II:1572
Hanson, J. C. M., I:621
Haquinius, Eric, I:2292
Haraszti, Zoltan, I:617, 630, 2231; II:281− 82, 2091, 2302
Harbeck, Charles T., I:5449
Harbin, Dorothy, III:314
Harbors, I:2118, 2125, 2523
Hardin, Floyd, I:959, 4291
Harding, George L., I:715
Harding, Jane D., I:2151
Harding, Walter Roy, II:1750−51; III:2005
Harding, Warren G., III:2514
Hardwicke, Robert E., I:2281
Hardy, James D., Jr., III:2710, 2716
Hardy, Thomas, I:3006, 3405, 3475−80; II:1838; III:2171
Hargett, Lester, I:4490; II:430
Haring, Clarence H., II:2747
Haring, Douglas G., III:2907
Hariot, Thomas, I:5213
Harkness, Edward S., II:300
Harkness, Mary Stillman, II:299
Harlow, Neal Roten, II:2057
Harman, Eleanor Randall, III:586
Harman, Marian, II:1966
Harmar, Josiah, I:4661; II:2138
Harmon, Frances, I:3914
Harmonia, II:2209

Harmsen, Thyrus G., II:2475
Harmsworth collection, Folger Library, II:307
Haro, Robert P., III:3299
Harper, George M., I:3574
Harper, J. Russell, III:222
Harper, Josephine L., II:2715; III:3288
Harpster, John W., III:3244
Harriman, Averell, III:2515
Harriman, Florence Jaffray, II:2139
Harrington, Janice B., I:5422
Harrington, Thomas F., I:2407
Harris, Caleb F., I:3222
Harris, Chauncy D., I:3832; II:2024–25
Harris, James D., II:1308
Harris, Joel Chandler, I:556
Harris, Phoebe M., III:3159
Harris, Ray Baker, II:919–20
Harris, Richard, II:1668–69
Harrison, Benjamin, III:2516–17
Harrison, Guy B., I:5190
Harrison, John P., II:2721, 2742; III:3319
Harrison, Robert W., II:2476
Harrison, Thomas P., Jr., I:2432
Harrison, William H., II:2140
Harrisse, Henry, I:4510
Harrow, Stefan M., III:3066
Harrsen, Meta P., I:1027; II:269–70
Hart, Donn V., II:217; III:383, 2802
Hart, Richard H., I:3319
Hart, Weldon, III:1869
Harte, Francis Bret, I:3287; II:1633, 1698–
    1700
Hartford Seminary Foundation: Arabic
    collection, I:3771; manuscripts, II:630
Hartford Theological Seminary Library:
    religious periodicals, I:1001
Hartsook, Elizabeth, I:4907
Hartwell, Edith, I:2002
Hartzell, James, III:2058
Harvard, John, I:250
Harvard College: archives, I:2000, 2004,
    2008; broadsides, I:2005; history,
    I:2020
Harvard Law School Assoc., I:1776
Harvard University: archives, I:2003, 2009,
    2012–13; graduates, I:2014
——Andover-Harvard Theological Library:
    periodicals, III:688
——Arnold Arboretum Library, I:2322;
    catalog, I:2318; incunabula, I:657
——Blue Hill Meteorological Observatory
    Library, II:1090
——Bureau of Economic Research in Latin
    America, I:1454
——Chinese-Japanese Library: Japanese
    collected works, II:2412
——Dept. of Architecture Library: II:1457
——Division of Engineering and Applied
    Physics Library: guide, III:1575;
    periodicals, III:1576
——Dumbarton Oaks Library: Byzantine
    studies, II:1445
——East Asian Research Center: Chinese
    newspapers, III:360
——Education Library, II:924
——Engineering Library, I:2456, 2467
——Farlow Herbarium and Library:
    cryptogamic botany, I:2320, 2327

——Fine Arts Library: book jackets,
    III:663; reference materials, III:1715
——Fogg Art Museum Library, I:2840;
    II:1446; Far Eastern art, II:1444;
    prints, II:1487; Spanish photographs,
    I:2996; Washington, Lafayette,
    Franklin exhibition, I:3936
——Graduate School of Business
    Administration, Baker Library, I:2674,
    2681–82, 2703; Adam Smith
    collection, I:1455; agricultural history,
    III:1613; Aldrich library, I:2712;
    aviation, I:2564; Baldwin collection,
    I:2713; Barberini and Sciarra-Colonna
    families, I:2717; Barberini collection,
    I:2714; bibliographies of economics,
    III:854; Bigelow, Kennard & Co.,
    I:2715; Briggs-Stabler papers, I:2726;
    business forecasting, III:878; business
    history, I:2679–80, 2698, 2700, 2706,
    2711–27, II:965, 968–70; business
    indexes, II:723; business manuscripts,
    I:2702, 2716, 2720; catalog, III:903;
    China trade, III:2883; colonial
    craftsmanship, I:2725; company
    records, I:2708; corporations, I:2675;
    De Wolf family papers, I:5162;
    economic history, III:855; European
    railroads, I:2097, II:993; flour milling,
    I:2734; guide, II:722; inland
    waterways, III:921; Israel Thorndike
    papers, I:2711; Kress Library of
    Business and Economics, I:2704–05,
    2719, 2727, 2733, II:961–63, 975,
    III:912; labor relations, I:1636; liquor,
    I:2718; manuscripts, II:964, 968;
    maritime history, I:2122, II:998;
    Medici manuscripts, I:2721, 2724,
    4300; motion picture industry, I:2722;
    New England business history, I:2723;
    Poor Publishing Co., I:2701; Samuel
    Snow records, I:2737; ''South Sea
    Bubble,'' I:1477; South Sea Company,
    III:905; special collections, I:2683;
    street railways, II:1000; Suez Canal,
    I:2123; surveying, I:2726; textile
    machinery, I:2817; trade cards, I:2774;
    transportation, II:1421, III:922; U.S.
    agriculture, I:2616; U.S. railroads,
    I:2098; U.S. transportation, I:2747
——Graduate School of Design Library:
    catalog, III:1729
——Graduate School of Education Library:
    guide, III:1237; periodicals, III:1238
——Gray Herbarium Library, I:2325; plant
    index, III:1422
——Harvard-Yenching Institute Library:
    China, I:4329, II:2393; Chinese book
    catalog, I:3783; Korean collection,
    III:2910; Ming encyclopedias,
    III:2875; Oriental collection, II:2392;
    resources, I:3786, II:2368
——Houghton Library: association books,
    II:285; books and manuscripts, III:452;
    cookbooks, II:1341; Erasmus,
    Desiderius, III:2484; illustrated books,
    III:653; imaginary books, III:1920;
    Johnson, Samuel, III:2182; manuscript

collections, II:241; rare books, I:560–
    61; Russian literature, II:1975; science
    fiction, II:1612, 1614; Vienna,
    III:2703; William King Richardson
    library, II:286; young authors, III:1921
——Institute of Geographical Exploration:
    Northern Polar region, I:3833
——Isham Memorial Library: early music,
    II:1520; photographs, I:3001
——Lamont Library: catalog, II:127
——Landscape Architecture Library:
    landscape architecture and city
    planning, I:2860, II:1454–55
——Law School Library, I:1763, 1782,
    1790, 1792; accessions, I:1777, 1791;
    Annual legal bibliography, III:1014;
    catalog, I:1687, 1774; Chinese law,
    III:1051; Current legal bibliography,
    II:788; early American legal treatises,
    I:1783; early English law books,
    I:1764, 1768, 1796; foreign business,
    III:888; foreign law, III:1050; guide,
    II:789; international law and relations,
    I:1809, III:1060; Law School history,
    I:1776; rare books, II:790; Soviet law,
    III:1052; special collections, I:1778–
    79, 1784, 1793; treaties, III:1061;
    U.S. Supreme Court, biography,
    II:2080
——Library, I:67, 151; Aesop, I:3723;
    Africa, I:4366, III:2923, 2939–40;
    Aldrich, Thomas Bailey, I:3274;
    American drama, I:3238; American
    history, III:3007, 3024; American
    literature, III:1953; American poetry,
    I:3356; American Revolution, III:3058;
    Americana, I:4435; Arabic, Persian,
    and Ottoman Turkish collections,
    III:2810; archives, I:2003–05, II:948;
    astronomy, I:2232; ballet music,
    III:1809; Barlow, Francis, II:1481;
    Barnett, John, I:3094; Baroque book
    illustration, II:485; Barrett, Lawrence,
    I:3095; Beaumont, Francis, I:3372;
    Beerbohm, Max, I:3425, II:1808;
    Berenson Library, III:1711; Berkeley,
    George, II:517; bibliography, III:5;
    bookplates, I:55, 57; Bossuet, Jacques
    Benigue, I:3651; Boston Public Latin
    School, I:1995; Browning, Robert,
    I:3431; Bulgarian collection, I:905;
    business and economics, I:1457;
    businessmen, II:959; Byrd, William,
    II:1567; Canadian history and
    literature, I:4389, III:2997; Capek,
    Karel, II:1979; Carman, Bliss, I:3348;
    Carroll, Lewis, I:3446; catalog,
    I:209–11; Celtic literatures, I:3743–
    44, III:2110; Cervantes, Miguel de,
    I:3713; chapbooks and ballads, I:2147,
    III:2109; Charles Sumner collection,
    I:259; charters, English, I:4262; chess,
    I:3123; children's books, I:3808;
    China, Japan, Korea, III:2860; Chinese
    collections, I:3783, 3786, III:2881;
    city planning, III:1730; Civil War,
    U.S., I:4621; Civil War, English,
    I:4263; classical literature, I:3724,

Harvard University Library (cont.)
3740; Coleridge, Samuel T., I:3360, 3449; collections, I:127, 209; copybooks, II:1470; Cromwell, Oliver, I:3960; Crowne, John, I:3452; Cruikshank illustrations, I:2910; Crusades, III:2686; Czechoslovakia, I:4318; Daguerre photographs, II:1507; dancing, I:3104; Dante, Alighieri, I:3677, 3681; decorated papers, III:662; Dibdin, Thomas Frognall, III:2478; Dickens, Charles, I:3460; Donne, John, I:3465; Dostoevsky, Fedor, II:1672; drolleries, II:1800; economics, II:724, III:857; education, I:1951, 1953, 1960; Eliot, T. S., II:1832; English history, I:4257; English literature, I:3396–97; English novels, I:3376, 3381; English plays, I:3374; English poetry, I:3352, 3356; engravings, I:2984; European and world history, III:2683; Fernandez de Lizardi, J. J., I:3717–18; Festus, I:3423; 15th century books, I:631; fine arts collection, I:2834, 2837; fishing, I:3139–43; Fletcher, John, I:3372; Florentine woodcuts, I:2957; Forbes, William Cameron, II:2757; French African colonies, I:4376; French fine printing, III:647; French literature, I:3644; French newspapers, I:459; French Revolution, I:4280; Frisian books, I:3161; general literature, III:1922; geographical exploration, I:3842; German literature, I:3592; Gibbon, Edward, I:3994; Gilbert, John, I:3113; Goethe, Johann Wolfgang von, I:3596; government, III:801; guides, II:944; Harry Elkins Widener collection, I:209, 274, 2910; Harvard archives, I:2000, III:1252, 1257; Harvard in fiction, II:1654; Hebrew books, I:1248, III:774, 783; Heine, Heinrich, I:3600; Herbert, George, I:3358; Hofmannsthal, Hugo von, I:3603, II:1922; Hogarth, William, I:2992; Hollis, Thomas, II:669; Icelandic literature, I:3606–07, 3610, 3624; illuminated manuscripts, II:265; Indochina, I:4347; Irish literature, II:1795; Italian literature, I:3662–64, 3666; James, William, I:3299; Japanese books, I:3786; Jewett, Sarah Orne, I:3300; Johnson, Samuel, I:3485; Judaica, II:636, III:762; Keats, John, I:3487, II:1849; labor history, III:966; Lamb, Charles, II:1851; Latin American literature, III:3300; Latin American manuscripts, I:5303; Latin American maps, I:3926; Latin American periodicals, III:361; Lee, Arthur, I:4549; Leech, John, I:3492; Lermontov, Mikhail Y., I:3754; Lessing, Gotthold, I:3604; Library bulletin, I:168; Lincoln, Abraham, I:4038; literary recordings, I:3213; Lowell, James Russell, I:3305; Luther, Martin, I:4064; Majakovskij,

Vladimir, II:1977; Maltese press, I:911; manuscripts, I:488–89, 508; maps, II:2018; Marty, André, III:856; Mather family, I:4071, 4075; medical history, II:1231; Melville, Herman, I:3310, II:1730; Middle East, III:2823; Milton, John, I:3498; Minoan writing, II:2269; minstrels, I:3097; mission records, II:529, 536–38; modern Greek, III:2274; Molière, Jean Baptiste, I:3653, 3655; Montaigne, Michel E. de, I:3655; Napoleon Bonaparte, I:4280, II:2309; Nelson, Admiral Horatio, I:4086; Noh dance prints, I:2974; nonbook materials, II:122; North America, I:4414; Norton, Charles Eliot, I:3314; ornithology, I:2342; Ottoman Empire, I:2348; periodicals, III:223; Persian collection, III:2810–11; Persius, I:3728; Peruvian imprints, III:649; Petrarch, II:2462; philosophy, I:951; physics, II:1096; poetry, II:1609; political science, I:1349; Pope, Alexander, I:3503; Portugal and Brazil, I:4292; Portuguese literature, I:3702; printing history, I:582, 927; prompt books, I:3119; public administration, I:1859; Quakers, I:1142, 1144; radiology, history, III:1485; rare books, I:579; reference collection, III:6–7; religion, I:985, II:518; Rilke, Rainer Maria, III:2240; Risorgimento, I:3663–64, 3668, 3673; Roman de la Rose, I:3643; Romance languages and literatures, I:3167; Roosevelt, Theodore, II:2202, III:2601; Roulstone bookbindings, III:677; Rousseau, Jean Jacques, I:3657; Rumford scientific drawings, II:1044; Russian books, I:4312; Russian history, II:2752; Russian literature, III:2750; Russian periodicals, II:225; Sarton, George, II:1049; Scandinavian literature, II:1932; science books, I:2194; science history, I:2187; science journals, III:1333; Shakespeare, William, I:3526, 3541, 3543, III:2213; 16th century imprints, II:308; Slavic collection, I:4319, III:2737; Slovak literature, II:1973; Southern Asia, III:2828; Spanish Armada, I:4293; Spanish fiction, I:3690; Sparks, Jared, I:4415, 4439; Sterne, Laurence, III:2224; Stevenson, Robert Louis, I:3549; subject distribution, II:106, 108; Swift, Jonathan, I:3551; Tennyson, Alfred, II:1898; textbooks, I:1982; theatre collection, I:3092–3101, 3103, 3113, 3119, 3238, II:1591, III:1881, 1903; theology, I:992; Thirty Years' War, II:2276; Thomas à Kempis, I:989; Thoreau, Henry David, II:1748, 1752; Tibetan collection, II:1981; tobacco, I:2645; treaties, I:1808; Trotsky, Leon, II:2322; typography, I:930; utopias, I:1351; Venezuela, history, I:5335;

Virginia, history. I:5216; Walpole, Horace, I:3564, 3566; Washington, George, II:2225; West African languages, I:3188; Western Americana, II:2568; Wolfe, Thomas, I:3346; women, III:1268; Wordsworth, William, I:3360, 3577; World War I, I:5500, 5503, 5537–38; World War II, I:5540; Yiddish collection, I:1242
——Lucien Howe Library of Ophthalmology, II:1152
——Medical Library: early American imprints, III:1478; guide, III:1508; legal medicine, I:2365; Library history, I:2363, 2406, 2409; Medical School history, I:2407; rare books, III:1479; serials, III:1534; Warren Library, I:2366
——Museum of Comparative Zoology Library, I:2335; II:1137; catalog, III:1437
——Observatory Library: II:1085
——Peabody Museum Library: I:2307–08; catalog, III:1410–11
——Public Administration Library, II:871
——Semitic Museum: Arabic manuscripts, I:3767
Harvey, Edward L., I:4265
Harvey, John, III:692
Harvey, Perry W., I:682
Harvey, William, I:2411; II:1234, 1248
Harvin, Marie, II:1165
Harwell, Richard B., I:2046, 3257, 3968, 4603; II:77, 1062, 2105, 2544; III:2017, 3084
Harwood, Thomas Frank, II:2555
Harzberg, Hiler, I:2939
Haselden, R. B., I:490
Haskell, Daniel C., I:281, 329, 424, 675, 1240, 1926, 2689, 2907, 3192, 3236, 3647, 3913, 4367, 4450, 4454, 4594, 5319; II:993
Hass, Emma B., II:817
Hassall, Albert, I:2374, 2380
Hasse, Adelaide R., I:1420–32, 5062, 5064, 5066
Hastings, Henry, II:98
Hastings, Reginald R., I:4261, 4264, 4266
Hastings, William T., III:2213
Haswell, Anthony, I:782
Hatch, Benton L., II:393
Hatch, W. H. P., I:1026
Hatfield, Henry R., I:2772
Hathaway, Richard J., III:3204
Hatheway, Nicholas, I:1685
Hatzfeld, Herta, II:622–23; III:756
Haubold, Marcia Ann, III:2711
Hauke, Lewis, III:2461
Havens, James M., II:1091
Haverford College Library: cuneiform tablets, I:4204; manuscripts, I:533; Morley, Christopher, I:3313; Otsego purchase, I:5029; Penn, William, I:4088; Quaker collection, I:1145, 1148, 1154, II:589, 591; serials, I:320; William Pyle Philips collection, II:283
Haviland, Virginia, III:2306, 2341–42

Hawaii, I:485, 2121, 5384; II:2511; III:3020, 3174—78
Hawaii Dept. of Planning and Economic Development, III:1282
Hawaii Library Association: Hawaiian documents, III:35; serials, II:158, III:224
Hawaii State Library: government publications, III:36; Hawaiian history, III:3174—75
Hawaii, University, Center for . . . East and West: Korean history, III:2911
——East-West Library: Philippine newspapers, III:362
——Library: Asian history, III:2798; electrical engineering, III:1577; Hawaiian history, III:3176—78; Pacific islands, III:3396; physics, III:1376
Hawaiian language, I:3174
Hawes, Lilla M., II:2603; III:2561
Hawes, Lloyd E., III:1485
Hawkins, Dorothy L., I:726—27
Hawkins, R. R., I:3347
Hawkins, Richmond L., I:3643, 3657
Hawks, Emma B., I:2601 (18)
Hawley, Edith J. R., I:3834
Hawley, Emma A., I:3271
Hawley, Lorene Anderson, II:390
Hawthorne, Julian, III:2016
Hawthorne, Nathaniel, I:3251, 3288—89; II:1632, 1701; III:2017—19
Hay, John, II:2141; III:2518
Hayden, Horace E., I:3646, 4281
Hayes, Catherine, III:2614
Hayes, Rutherford B., I:3999—4000; II:2142; III:2519
Hayes Memorial Library: letters and papers, I:3999; pamphlets and periodicals, I:4000
Haykin, David J., I:939
Hayne, Paul H., I:3254
Hays, Alice N., II:951
Hays, I. Minis, I:3982
Hayward, Elizabeth Gardner, II:1418
Hayward, John, II:1943
Hayward, Ruth P., I:4122
Hazelton, Louise, III:111
Hazelton, Philip A., II:766
Hazen, Allen T., I:3486, 3565
Hazen, Margaret P., I:2796
Head, Edwin L., I:4734
Head, Mary Joe, III:1174, 1180
Healey, George Harris, II:1906
Healy, Frances, III:594
Healy, Mary Agnes, III:595
Heaney, Howell J., II:801, 2477; III:2070
Heard, John P., III:862
Hearn, Lafcadio, I:3290; II:1702
Heartman, Charles F., I:696—97, 3320—21, 3338, 3953, 4550, 4694; II:683
Hébert, John R., III:2403
Hebrew Education Society: Lesser library, II:1232
Hebrew literature, I:4202
Hebrew periodicals, I:289
Hebrew Union College Library: Alsatian Jewish inventories, II:646; American Jewish archives, I:1245, II:638, 640,

III:758; bookplates, III:776; catalog, III:775; 15th century Hebrew books, II:641; Jacob Ezekiel collection, I:1218; Jewish music, I:3042; Jewish newspapers and periodicals, II:637; Spinoza collection, II:506
Hecht, Arthur, II:979—82
Heckewelder, John, II:560
Heckscher, William S., II:1624
Hedges, James B., I:2728
Hedrick, Ellen A., I:2601 (41)
Heers, William H., I:1902
Heffron, Paul T., III:963
Heflin, James Thomas, II:2143
Hegel, G. W. F., I:954
Hegg, Eric A., II:1498
Heifitz, Anna, I:3751, 3753—54
Heilbron, Bertha L., II:1504
Heiman, Monica, III:2249
Heindel, Richard H., I:2188
Heine, Heinrich, I:3600—02
Heintze, James R., III:1851
Heintz, Grete, III:2718, 3415
Heiss, Willard C., III:744
Heitman, Sidney, III:2759
Helbig, Richard E., I:1371
Held, Ray E., I:5297
Helicopters, police use, II:875
Hellman, Florence S., I:1347, 1489, 1493, 1525, 1562, 1863, 1889, 1905, 1909—11, 2040, 2293, 2451—52, 2485, 2664, 2871, 3306, 3761, 3973, 4065, 4339, 4358, 4380, 4383, 4386, 4583, 4689, 5275, 5347—48, 5358, 5391, 5459, 5550—51, 5555
Hellman, Lillian, III:2020—21
Hellmann, George, II:603
Helly, Dorothy Oxman, II:529
Helton, H. Stephen, II:705, 707, 865, 907, 2730, 2809; III:1064, 3418
Heltzel, Virgil B., I:970
Hematology, II:1150
Hemingway, Ernest, II:1616; III:2022—24
Hemphill, William E., I:1141, 2019
Henderson, Archibald, II:1882—83; III:2220
Henderson, James P., I:4001
Henderson, James W., III:19
Henderson, Robert W., I:3129, II:1592
Henderson, Rose, I:1391
Hendrick, George, II:2133
Hendricks, Donald D., III:97—99
Hendrickson, G. L., I:3725
Henkle, Herman H., II:1143, 1203
Henley, Lillian E., I:4829
Hennepin, Louis, I:4884
Hennepin County, Minn., Medical Library: serials, I:2302
Henry, Edward A., I:4856
Henry, Mary T., II:1678
Henry, Patrick, II:2533
Henry County, Tennessee, III:3253
Henry Shaw Botanical Garden Library: serials, II:168
Henthorn, William E., III:2911
Hepburn, William M., I:739, 2468, 3309; II:1266
Heppner, Francis J., III:3407
Heraldry, I:4163, 4166, 4175

Herbals, I:2323, 2424, 2532; II:1121, 1125, 1228; III:1421, 1427, 1430
Herberstain, Sigismund, I:4311
Herbert, Arthur S., III:700
Herbert, George, I:3358
Herbert, Hilary Abner, III:2520
Hergesheimer, Joseph, III:2025—26
Hering, Hollis W., I:1054
Hermannsson, Halldór, I:3608—09, 3611—23; II:1928
Herdnon, Dallas T., I:4719
Hernandez, Francisco, II:1040
Herrick, Marvin T., III:2255
Herrick, Mary D., I:4032; II:530, 2436—37; III:165, 174, 2926
Herrick, Myron T., I:4002
Herrman, Augustine, II:2063
Herschel, John, III:1323
Hershkowitz, Leo M., III:759
Hersholt, Jean, II:1613, 1929, 1933
Hertzberg, Harry, I:3112
Hertzog, Carl, II:495
Hess, Henry E., I:1944
Hess, Mildred, II:2665
Hetrick, Marjory H., III:1703
Hettich, Ernest L., I:4571
Heuser, Frederick W. J., I:3589
Heusser, Albert H., I:4552
Hewett, Anna B., I:1145
Hewlett, Leroy, III:3036
Heya-Kiss, Maria, II:1976
Heyer, Anna H., I:3012
Hiatt, Caroline W., I:1597
Hibernation, I:2336
Hickerson, Joseph C., III:1841
Hickman, Roger W., II:1096
Hicks, Carroll Ann, III:1696
Hidy, Muriel E., I:2729
Hiebert, Ray E., III:405
Higashiuchi, Yoshio, II:2413
Higginbotham, S. W., II:2680
Higgins, Helena, III:1097
Higginson, Thomas W., I:2139; III:2027
Highways, I:2505; II:1305—07; III:931—32, 940, 942, 949
Hildeburn, C. S. R., I:855
Hildreth, Richard, I:4412
Hiler, Hilaire, I:2940
Hiler, Meyer, I:2940
Hilgenbrink, Roger, III:1026
Hill, David S., I:84
Hill, Edward E., II:1411; III:1108, 1112, 1655, 1663, 3042
Hill, Edwin C., I:1458
Hill, Esther C., I:4850
Hill, Frank P., I:802, 3233
Hill, J. Douglas, II:2047
Hill, James J., Jr., III:2176
Hill, Knute, III:2521
Hill, Richard S., I:3013; II:1530
Hill, Robert W., II:299—300, 1309, 1742, 2224, 2479
Hill, Roscoe R., II:531
Hill, William H., I:816
Hilliard, Jack B., III:2571, 2630
Hillquit, Morris, III:981
Hills, Margaret T., III:701
Hillyer, Robert Silliman, III:2028

Hilton, Ronald, I:5300; II:2722
Hinckley, Lyman, I:5365
Hinding, Andrea, III:1228
Hinduism, II:633
Hingham (Mass.) Public Library, II:489
Hinkle, Mary Pickford, II:1936
Hintz, Carl W., I:85; II:78
Hirsch, Felix E., I:5030
Hirsch, Rudolf, III:411, 417
Hirst, David W., II:2236
Hisatsune, Kimi, II:633
Hispanic Society of America Library:
    antiphonaries, II:266; book collection,
    I:212; catalog, III:3301; Celestina,
    II:1955; Cervantes, Miguel de,
    I:3711–12, 3715; collections, I:2836,
    II:100–102; early books, I:594–95,
    II:310, III:3302; Fernandez de Lizardi,
    J. J., I:3719; Góngora y Argote, Luis
    de, I:3720; Hispanic-American history,
    I:5308; incunabula, I:594, 634; Irving,
    Washington, I:3293, II:1711;
    manuscripts, I:492–93, 2836, II:266;
    Mexicana, II:2737; portolan charts,
    I:3835–36; Prescott, William
    Hickling, I:4090; Spanish drama,
    I:3687; Spanish fiction, I:3690;
    Ticknor, George, I:4100; woodcuts,
    I:2960
Historical and Philosophical Society of Ohio
    Library: Cincinnati history, I:5114;
    Ohio history, I:5115; resources,
    II:2480, III:158; Western U.S. history,
    I:4680
Historical Foundation of the Presbyterian and
    Reformed Churches Library: books and
    manuscripts, I:1103; church catalogs,
    II:577; Kentucky history, I:4871;
    records and minutes, I:1104, II:578
Historical Records Survey: business records,
    I:2730; Confederate archives, I:4604;
    Cuban papers, I:5301; Du Simitière
    papers, I:4513; federal archives
    inventory, I:4417–31; manuscripts,
    I:4416, 4432; musicians, I:3014;
    project reports, I:5; ship registers,
    I:2749–63; transportation, U.S.,
    I:2748
——Alabama: county archives, I:4712;
    imprints, I:708; Protestant Episcopal
    archives, I:1120; vital statistics,
    I:1273–74
——Arizona: county archives, I:4716;
    imprints, I:711
——Arkansas: Christian Science archives,
    I:1073; county archives, I:4722; news-
    papers, I:394; vital statistics, I:1275
——California: Bixby collection, I:4741;
    county archives, I:4742–43; Harte,
    Francis Bret, I:3287; imprints, I:717;
    manuscripts, I:4740; Snyder collection,
    I:4739; state archives, I:4744; vital
    statistics, I:1276–77
——Colorado: county archives, I:4751;
    Jewish archives, I:1220; vital statistics,
    I:1278
——Connecticut: Lutheran archives,
    I:1086; municipal archives, I:4763;

Protestant Episcopal archives, I:1121;
    vital statistics, I:1279
——Delaware: church archives, I:1087;
    county archives, I:4769
——District of Columbia: Bell, Alexander
    Graham, I:3946; church archives,
    I:1122; Douglass, Frederick, I:4605;
    Force papers, I:4553; municipal
    archives, I:4774; musicians, I:3058
——Florida: Baptist archives, I:1058;
    county archives, I:4784; forestry,
    I:2652; manuscripts, I:4783; Spanish
    land grants, I:4785; vital statistics,
    I:1280–81
——Georgia: Baptist archives, I:1059;
    county archives, I:4803; maps, I:3906;
    vital statistics, I:1282
——Idaho: county archives, I:4812;
    imprints, I:730–31; vital statistics,
    I:1283
——Illinois: Chicago imprints, I:732; Civil
    War, I:4606; county archives, I:4820;
    manuscripts, I:4819; Methodist
    manuscripts, I:1095; Presbyterian
    archives, I:1105; state archives,
    I:4821; vital statistics, I:1284–85;
    Wyoming imprints, I:894
——Indiana: county archives, I:4830; vital
    statistics, I:1286
——Iowa: county archives, I:4845;
    imprints, I:742; manuscripts, I:4843–
    44; vital statistics, I:1287
——Kansas: county archives, I:4851;
    imprints, I:744; vital statistics, I;1288
——Kentucky: county archives, I:4857;
    imprints, I:748; vital statistics, I:1289
——Louisiana: Confederate letters, I:4607;
    Jewish archives, I:1221; manuscripts,
    I:4877–79; municipal archives,
    I;4880; newspapers, I:397; parish
    archives, I:4881; state archives,
    I:4882–83; vital statistics, I:1290;
    World War I, I:5504
——Maine: municipal archives, I:4893
——Maryland: county archives, I:4899;
    Protestant Episcopal archives, I:1123;
    Williams papers, I:4433
——Massachusetts: county archives,
    I:4931; Darwin, Charles, I:2190;
    imprints, I:774; Knox papers, I:4927;
    manuscripts, I:4928–29; municipal
    archives, I:4930; proclamations,
    I:4932; Protestant Episcopal
    manuscripts, I:1124; Universalist
    archives, I:1193; vital statistics, I:1291
——Michigan: Baptist records, I:1060;
    Church of the Nazarene archives,
    I:1194; county archives, I:4950;
    Dearborn church archives, I:1203;
    Evangelical archives, I:1082–83;
    imprints, I:785; Jewish archives,
    I:1222; manuscripts, I:4947–48;
    Methodist archives, I:1096; municipal
    archives, I:4949; Pilgrim Holiness
    Church archives, I:1195; Presbyterian
    archives, I:1106; Protestant Episcopal
    archives, I:1125; Roman Catholic
    archives, I:1168; Salvation Army,

I:1204; state archives, I:4951; vital
    statistics, I:1292–93
——Minnesota: county archives, I:4961;
    imprints, I:787; manuscripts, I:4960;
    vital statistics, I:1294–95; World War
    I, I:5505
——Mississippi: county archives, I:4975;
    Jewish archives, I:1223; newspapers,
    I:392; Protestant Episcopal archives,
    I:1126; vital statistics, I:1296
——Missouri: archives, I:4984; Baptist
    archives, I:1061–62; county archives,
    I:4986; court records, I:4983; imprints,
    I:793; manuscripts, I:4985; vital
    statistics, I:1297–98
——Montana: county archives, I:4991;
    Montana papers, UCLA, I:4990; vital
    statistics, I:1299–1300
——Nebraska: county archives, I:4995;
    imprints, I:796; manuscripts, I:4994;
    vital statistics, I:1301
——Nevada: county archives, I:4998;
    imprints, I:797; Protestant Episcopal
    archives, I:1127; Roman Catholic
    archives, I:1169; vital statistics, I:1302
——New Hampshire: county archives,
    I:5003; manuscripts, I:5001; municipal
    archives, I:5002; Roman Catholic
    archives, I:1170; vital statistics, I:1303
——New Jersey: Baha'i archives, I:1196;
    Baptist archives, I:1064; Christian
    Reformed archives, I:1107;
    Congregational archives, I:1076;
    county archives, I:5008; Evangelical
    archives, I:1084; imprints, I:803;
    manuscripts, I:5006; municipal
    archives, I:5007; naturalization
    records, I:4148; Presbyterian archives,
    I:1108; Protestant Episcopal archives,
    I:1128; Salvation Army, I:1205;
    Unitarian archives, I:1192; vital
    statistics, I:1304
——New Mexico: county archives, I:5016;
    imprints, I:809; vital statistics, I:1305
——New York: Batavia imprints, I:818;
    county archives, I:5035, 5037; Gerrit
    Smith papers, I:5031; manuscripts,
    I:5032–33, 5036; maps, I:3910;
    municipal archives, I:5034; Protestant
    Episcopal archives, I:1130; Utica
    imprints, I:817; vital statistics,
    I:1306–08
——New York (City): Armenian Apostolic
    archives, I:1081; Eastern Orthodox
    archives, I:1081; Lutheran archives,
    I:1088; Methodist archives, I:1097;
    Presbyterian archives, I:1109;
    Protestant Episcopal archives, I:1129;
    Quaker archives, I:1146; Reformed
    Church archives, I:1110
——North Carolina: Baptist archives,
    I:1063; Bartlett Yancey papers, I:5094;
    historical records, I:5097; manuscripts,
    I:5095–96; Moravian archives,
    I:1099; state archives, I:5098–5102;
    vital statistics, I:1309
——North Dakota: county archives, I:5112;
    vital statistics, I:1310–11

——Ohio: county archives, I:5118; Governors' papers, II:2666; imprints, I:847; Joshua Giddings manuscripts, I:5116; municipal archives, I:5117; Roman Catholic archives, I:1172; state archives, I:5119

——Oklahoma: church archives, I:1206; county archives, I:5132; state archives, I:5131; vital statistics, I:1312

——Oregon: county archives, I:5133, 5137; manuscripts, I:5134, 5136; photographs, I:5135; vital statistics, I:1313

——Pennsylvania: county archives, I:5147, II:2681; manuscripts, I:5145–46

——Philadelphia: newspapers, I:395

——Rhode Island: Baptist archives, I:1065; municipal archives, I:5163; Quaker archives, I:1147; vital statistics, I:1314–15

——South Carolina: county archives, I:5165

——South Dakota: county archives, I:5173; vital statistics, I:1316

——Southern California: manuscripts, I:494

——Tennessee: Baptist archives, I:1066; county archives, I:5177; imprints, I:873–75; Jewish archives, I:1224; manuscripts, I:5175–76; vital statistics, I:1317–18

——Texas: colonial archives, I:5191; county archives, I:5192; newspapers, I:393; vital statistics, I:1319

——Utah: county archives, I:5204; Ogden newspapers & magazines, I:313; state archives, I:5203; vital statistics, I:1320

——Vermont: county archives, I:5207; municipal archives, I:5206

——Virginia: Baptist archives, I:1067–69; county archives, I:5214

——Washington: church archives, I:1208; county archives, I:5240; imprints, I:887; vital statistics, I:1321–22

——West Virginia: Arthur Boreman letters, I:5243; churches, I:1209; county archives, I:5248; Francis Pierpont letters, I:5244; Henry Matthews letters, I:5245; imprints, I:889; J. J. Jacob letters, I:5246; maps, I:3925; Presbyterian archives, I:1111; Protestant Episcopal archives, I:1132; vital statistics, I:1323–24; William Stevenson letters, I:5247; wills, I:4149

——Wisconsin: Assemblies of God archives, I:1197; county archives, I:5261; Disciples of Christ archives, I:1079; imprints, I:891; Jewish archives, I:1225; manuscripts, I:5259; Moravian archives, I:1100; municipal archives, I:5260; newspapers, I:391; Protestant Episcopal archives, I:1133; Roman Catholic archives, I:1173; state archives, I:1897–98, 5262; United Brethren archives, I:1198; vital statistics, I:1325–26

——Wyoming: county archives, I:5272; vital statistics, I:1327–28

Historical societies, I:4185, 4397

Historical Society of Western Pennsylvania, I:398

History, I:4184–5578; II:2258–2818; III:2670–3421; ancient, I:4198–4227, II:2264–72; medieval, I:4230–32, 4234–35, 4243–44, II:2273–74, III:2685–90; oral, III:2674–81; sources, III:2671–72

Hitchcock, Henry R., I:2886; III:1744

Hitchcock, Jeannette M., I:2764

Hitchcock, Ripley, II:1684

Hitchings, Sinclair H., II:496

Hitler, Adolf, II:2295

Hitti, Philip K., I:3768

Hittites, I:4215

Hitz, Benjamin D., II:1675

Ho, Don Tchengton, II:1063

Hoaxes, I:3211

Hobbs, Cecil C., I:3787, 4348, 4359; II:1531, 1982, 2384, 2406; III:2837

Hodges, John C., II:1824

Hodges, John I. H., III:143

Hodgson, James G., I:30, 2259, 2263

Hoernlé, Reinhold F. A., I:951

Hofer, Philip, I:520, 921, 2837; II:485, 1481

Hoffleit, Dorrit, II:1085

Hoffman, Arthur S., III:1957

Hoffman, Morris, III:889

Hoffman, Paul P., III:2056, 2454, 2513, 2547

Hoffman, William H., I:4084

Hofmannsthal, Hugo von, I:3603; II:1922

Hofstra University Library: Radin, Paul, III:1412

Hogan, Beecher, II:1716

Hogan, Charles B., I:3508

Hogan, Jane S., III:596

Hogan, William R., I:4879

Hogarth, William, I:2992

Hokkaido, Japan, III:2902

Holbrook, Franklin F., I:4962

Holcroft, Thomas, I:3481

Holdcamper, Forrest R., II:1291; III:898, 946, 1082, 1085, 1089–91, 1101, 1104, 1109, 1121, 1131, 1135, 1181, 1304, 1600, 3417

Holden, Edward S., I:2233, 2241, 5427–28

Holden, William, I:239

Holgate, Josephine, I:1508

Holl, George, II:1339

Holl, Jack Monroe, III:1234

Holland, Dorothy G., II:159

Holland, F. R., Jr., II:2556

Holland, Harold E., III:1313

Holland, Jeanette B., II:1486

Holland Society of New York Library: Dutch Reformed Church, I:1112–13; Grotius, Hugo, I:1806

Hollander, Jacob H., II:719

Holley, Edward G., III:99, 3259

Hollins College Library: printing history, I:596

Hollis, Thomas, II:667, 669

Holloway, O. W., II:2351

Holman, Winifred Lovering, II:2701

Holmes, Dorothy P., I:5

Holmes, Henry W., II:924

Holmes, Jane M., III:233

Holmes, John, III:2029

Holmes, Oliver Wendell, II:1703–04

Holmes, Pauline, I:1995

Holmes, Ruth E. V., I:3697

Holmes, Thomas J., I:920, 3355, 4072–74

Holt, Albert C., I:5178

Holt, Anna C., I:2366, 2409

Holt, Daniel D., III:1144

Holt, Henry, publisher, III:498

Holt, John, II:425

Holt, Roland, I:3089

Holverstott, Lyle J., I:1501, 1871; III:1066, 1135

Holweck, F. G., I:1174

Holy Cross College Library: Newman, John Henry, II:604

Home economics, I:2582–90, 2599 (18); II:1339–44; III:1603–08

Homer, II:1969

Homer, Dorothy R., II:679

Homer, Rachel Johnston, III:1781

Homer, Thomas J., I:288; II:160

Homer, Winslow, I:2912; II:1492

Homsher, Lola M., I:2635

Honduras, I:5304, 5321; British, I:5348

Honnold Library for Claremont Colleges: Burton, Robert, II:1791; Hispanic-American history, II:2725; Oxford University, II:945; water resources, II:1316

Hons, Fred W., III:1027

Hook, Alice P., II:2480

Hook, Sidney, III:681

Hooker, H. Donn, II:861

Hoole, William S., I:314–15; III:315

Hoover, Herbert, III:2522

Hoover Institution, see Stanford University, Hoover Institution

Hopewell, Helen J., II:878

Hopkins, Edna Alethia, II:374

Hopkins, Gerard M., I:4003; III:2172

Hopkins, Kenneth, III:2173

Hopkinson, Francis, I:549

Hopp, Ralph, I:2474

Hoppe, A. J., I:3437

Hopper, Elizabeth G., I:2612

Hopper, Hazel W., II:2615

Hoppo Chiiki, Japan, III:2904

Horace, I:3726, 3729, 3737, 3739; II:1963

Horan, Walt, III:2523

Horecky, Paul L., II:230–32, 479, 2340; III:395, 2738

Horn, Andrew H., II:6

Horn, Jason, II:624

Hornberger, Theodore, I:2189

Hornbooks, I:1983, 1985

Horner, Harlan H., II:2165

Horner, Henry, I:4048

Hornicek, John, I:4318

Horology, I:549

Horsch, John, I:1093

Horses, III:1659; racing, II:1377

Horst, Irvin B., III:644

Horticultural Society of N.Y. Library, I:2604

Horton, Louise, III:2567

Horton, S. Wentworth, III:2524

Horvath, Michael J., III:2776

Horwitz, Herbert J., III:976, 1106, 1120, 1127, 1129, 1678
Hoskins, Janina W., III:8, 648, 3008
Hospital service, railroad, I:2092
Hostetler, John Andrew, II:547
Hotchkiss, Jedidiah, I:3883, 3895; II:2065
Hotel management, II:1340
Houchin, Margaret, III:567
Houdini, Harry, I:3114
Hough, Franklin B., I:4111
Houghten, Mattie L., I:2794
Houle, André, II:355
Hours of work, I:1627–33
House, Albert V., III:2435
House, Edward M., I:4004
House plans, I:2878–79, 2889, 2896
Houser, Gloria W., III:1345
Housing, I:5479; cooperative, II:733
Housman, Alfred E., I:3482–83; II:1839; III:2174–75
Houston, Samuel, I:4005; III:3263
Houston, William Churchill, III:2525
Houston list of scientific and technical serial publications, III:1334
Houston Public Library: genealogy, I:4173
Houston, University, Library: American Revolution, III:3059; Bibles, III:702; Huxley, Aldous, III:2181; Negro periodicals, III:840; newspapers, III:316; scientific and technical serials, II:1073; Texana and Western Americana, III:3259–60
Hovey, Richard, II:1705
Howard, E. Stuart, III:1028
Howard, Francis G., II:1742, 2144
Howard, Richard C., III:348, 353
Howard Memorial Library: Confederate publications, I:4611; Louisiana publications, I:755
Howard University Library: African collection, II:2439, 2441, 2447, III:2922; Moorland Foundation collection, I:1392, III:2438–39; Negroes, I:1398, III:825–27; serials, III:275, 286
Howe, Daniel W., I:4831
Howe, W. T. H., I:3288
Howell, Hannah Johnson, II:267
Howell, James, I:3484
Howell, Margaret A., III:1020
Howells, William Dean, I:3291; II:1706–09; III:2030–32
Howes, Wright, II:2481; III:3009
Howey, R. S., II:725
Howland, A. C., I:4234
Howren, Robert, III:1912
Hoyt, Edward A., II:2700
Hoyt, William D., Jr., I:4590, 4900, 4909
Hrdlicka, Adolph E., II:605; III:2550
Hsia, Tao-tai, III:1054, 1056
Hsüeh, Chun-tu, III:2888
Hu, David Y., III:399
Hu, Shih, II:1983
Huang, C. K., III:2861
Hubach, Robert R., II:2551; III:3136
Hubbard, Gardiner G., I:2988
Hubbard, Geraldine H., I:4613
Hubbard, James M., I:3518

Hubbard, Lucias L., I:3551
Hubbard, Theodora, I:2859–60
Huber, Elbert L., I:5392
Huber, George K., III:1253
Huckabee, Gloria Comstock, III:2307
Hudson, Henry, I:5051
Hudson, John A., II:198
Hudson, William Henry, I:4006; II:289; III:2176
Hudson River, I:5051
Hufeland, Otto, I:5038
Huff, Elizabeth, II:2369
Hufford, Harold E., I:1446–47; II:716, 898
Hughes, Charles Evans, II:2145
Hughes, Charles E., Jr., II:872
Hughes, Glenn, II:1611
Hughes, Lewis, I:4007
Hughes, Marija M., III:987
Hughes, Thomas, I:3385
Hughes Aircraft Company, III:1283
Huguenot Society of America Library, I:1085
Huguenots, II:961
Hulbert, Archer B., I:1101
Hull, Callie, I:2275
Hull, Francis, II:2746
Hull, P. D., III:1809
Hulsius, Levinus, I:233
Human engineering, II:1271
Human stress, III:1462
Hume, David, III:686
Hummel, Arthur W., I:1746, 3788–89, 4331; II:2355
Hummel, Ray O., Jr., II:2707; III:509
Humor, American, II:1635
Humphrey, Constance M., I:804
Humphrey, James, III, II:346, 1741, 1990
Humphrey, Kathleen Ann, III:3172
Humphreys, D. C., II:1503
Huneker, James Gibbon, II:289
Hungarian literature, II:1976; III:2743, 2781
Hungary, history, II:2339, 2343; III:2776–83
Hunnewell, James, II:2121, 3281, 3438
Hunt, Gaillard, I:4554
Hunt, Leigh, II:1840–41; III:2177–78
Hunt, Rachel McMasters, II:1121, 1123
Hunt, Mrs. Roy Arthur, II:1127
Hunter, Frederick J., III:1882, 1897
Hunter, R. M. T., III:2526
Hunter College Library: English fiction, I:3380; resources, II:107
Hunting, III:1907
Huntington, Edna, I:5039
Huntington, Thomas W., I:4298
Huntington Library: accounting, II:977; aeronautics, I:2548, 2556–57; American history, I:4447, III:3010; American imprints, I:698; American laws, charters and constitutions, I:1688; American literary manuscripts, II:1641; American maps, I:3870, 3872–73; American Revolution, I:4551, 4568; Americana, II:2472, 2475, 2478; art collections, II:2835; Barlow, Samuel L. M., III:2435; Battle Abbey, I:4275; Bibles, III:704; Blake, William, I:2949, II:1467, III:2138; Bradley, Will, II:1468; Bridgewater manuscripts, I:4260;

British history, III:2694, 2698; British paintings, I:2948; Bryant, William Cullen, II:1673; Brydges, James, I:4265; Byron, George Gordon, I:3440; California history, I:4736–38, 4746; California literature, II:1637; Caxton, William, I:655; Chaucer, Geoffrey, III:2149; Civil War, I:4612; collections, I:129–30, II:93, 99, III:154; colonial period, I:4505–07, 4511–12; Confederate imprints, I:699; Constitution, U.S., I:1835; Cruikshank illustrations, I:673; Daumier, Honoré, I:2959; Dickens, Charles, I:3461, III:2161; dime novels, II:1656; Donne, John, I:3465; Elizabeth II, II:2287; English architecture, I:2885; English ballads and broadsides, I:3353; English drama, I:3365–66, 3373–74, III:2126; English literary manuscripts, III:2119; English literature, I:3391, 3398, 3418–19, 4568; English novels, I:3379; English pamphlets, I:670; English poetry, I:3352, II:1775; Evelyn, John, I:3469; Garland, Hamlin, III:2013; Grabhorn Press, I:716; great books, II:284; Hastings family, I:4261, 4264, 4266; Illinois history, III:3187; incunabula, I:633, 654–55; Inquisition, III:3380; Kelmscott Press, I:673; Kitto Bible, I:703; Larpent plays, I:3365; legal manuscripts and books, I:1780–81, II:791; Lieber, Francis, I:1345; Lincoln, Abraham, I:4060; literary forgeries, I:3399; literary resources, III:1923; Loudoun papers, I:4512; manuscripts, I:490–91, III:430; maps, III:2361; medical history, I:2408; medical incunabula, I:2422; Merrymount Press, I:773; Mexican history, I:5299, II:2735, 2737; Mexican imprints, I:900; music, I:3011; New Mexico, II:2655; newspapers, I:390, 460; Overton, Richard, II:2191; Peoria, Illinois, imprints, I:737; Peru, history, I:5298; Pizarro, Gonzalo, II:2747; printing history, I:591–93; Prynne, William, II:576; Quakers, II:594; railroads, I:2557; rare books, III:453–54; research aids, I:128, 130; Royal primer, I:700; science history, I:2189; Scott, Walter, I:3512; Shakespeare, William, I:3521, II:1874, III:2214; Short title catalogue, supplement, I:669; sports, I:3130; Stowe collection, II:2288; theatre collection, II:1573; Thoreau, Henry David, II:1748, 1751, 1753; Turner, Frederick Jackson, II:2218; U.S. Navy, history, I:5449; Victorian manuscripts, II:1793; Washington, George, I:4110; Whitman, Walt, II:1758; women's education, I:2023
Hurlbert, Irene W., III:355
Hurley, Maryjane E., III:597
Hurst, Roger A., I:4832
Huss, Ralph E., III:1037, 2719, 2819, 2839, 2892–93, 3329, 3354

Hussey, Mary I., I:4205
Hussey, Minnie Middleton, II:1012
Hussey, Miriam, I:2731, 2736
Hussey, Roland D., I:5302–03
Hutchings, C. E., I:2324
Hutchins, Henry C., I:3454–56
Hutchins, Margaret, I:2549
Hutchinson, Edward P., I:1329–30
Hutchinson, Susan A., I:518–19
Hutson, Jean B., II:2440
Huxley, Aldous, III:2179–81
Hyatt, Thaddeus, III:2527
Hyde, Charles Gilman, II:1315
Hydraulic engineering, II:1310–12
Hydrography, I:3864
Hydroponics, I:2591
Hyer, Anna Harriet, II:1540
Hymnals, Catholic, III:755
Hymnody, III:1803
Hymnology, I:1047–50
Hynding, Alan A., III:2613

Iben, Icko, I:86–87; III:890
Ice cream, I:2599 (17)
Iceland, I:4252
Icelandic literature, I:3606–24; II:1928,
    1930–31
Ichthyology, II:1025
Idaho, history, I:4812–14; III:3179
Idaho State Library: government publications,
    III:37; Idaho history, III:3179;
    religion, III:689
Idaho, University, Library: Day, Jerome J.,
    III:2477; forestry serials, III:1680;
    humanities collection, III:1924; Jewett,
    George Frederick, III:2531; resources,
    II:103; science and technology,
    II:1015, III:1284; Scott, Walter,
    III:2206–07; serials, III:292; social
    sciences, III:785; special collections,
    III:144
———Southern Branch, Idaho history,
    I:4814
Ide, Simeon, I:692
Ifni, I:4380
Ike, Nobutaka, II:2416
Ikena, Richard J., III:2308
Illinois, history, I:4815–28; II:2604–12;
    III:3180–88
Illinois and Michigan Canal, I:2113
Illinois Central Railroad Company, I:2068,
    2096, 2102; II:987, 995
Illinois Civil War Centennial Commission,
    III:3085
Illinois Dept. of Agriculture Library: catalog,
    I:2605
Illinois Railroad and Warehouse Comm.
    Library: catalog, I:2099
Illinois State Archives: maps, III:2398; state
    records, II:2604
Illinois State Council of Defense, I:4821
Illinois State Historical Library: acquisitions,
    II:2606; Civil War, I:4608, II:2546;
    Davis, David, III:2475; Douglas,
    Stephen A., III:2481; genealogy,
    I:4150, 4156; Hennepin, Louis,
    I:4884; Illinois history, I:4817, 4822–
    24; King family, III:2540; Lincoln,

Abraham, I:4026, 4039, 4048,
    II:2492, 2546, 2605, 2610, III:2552–
    53; manuscripts, II:2612, III:3180–81;
    microfilms, III:3182; newspapers,
    II:187–88, III:317; Parsons, Lewis
    B., II:2191
Illinois State Library: archives, I:4826–27;
    catalog, I:213; county histories,
    III:3184; government publications,
    II:25, III:38; Illinois Constitution,
    III:1069; Illinois history, I:4825;
    Negroes, III:841
Illinois State Museum of Natural History:
    library catalog, I:2299
Illinois State University Library: juvenile
    literature, III:2321
Illinois Supreme Court, Law Library: subject
    index, I:1689
Illinois, University, Chicago Circle Library:
    Chicago history, III:3183
———Illinois Historical Survey: Illinois
    history, II:2607, 2609; New Harmony
    Community, II:2613; newspapers,
    II:199; western history manuscripts,
    I:4681, II:2567, 2609
———Institute of Labor and Industrial
    Relations: industrial relations
    bibliographies, III:964
———Library: aeronautics, I:2549; American
    humor, II:1635; architecture, II:1461;
    Bentley papers, II:256; Bibles, I:1024;
    Brazilian publications, III:3332;
    business records, III:890; Churchill,
    Winston, III:2462; Conservation
    Corps, I:2673; English fiction,
    III:2129; geography, II:2026; geology
    history, III:1396; grammars, II:1602;
    history research resources, I:4434;
    Hollander, Jacob, Library, II:719;
    incunabula, I:625; Italian history,
    I:4299, 4301; Italian plays, III:2255;
    jade, III:1765; Jewish books, I:1226;
    labor relations, I:1572; library
    publications, I:58; Lincoln, Abraham,
    II:2165, 2171–72; little magazines,
    II:161; Louisiana publications, I:755;
    manuscript collections, I:495, II:246;
    maps, II:2027; mathematics, I:2214;
    metallurgy, III:1697; Milton, John,
    I:3496, II:1865; municipal law, II:873;
    municipal publications, I:1878–79,
    1887; music, II:1532–34; newspapers,
    I:430; Pilgrims, I:4933; Proust,
    Marcel, III:2250; race relations,
    III:828; Richardson, Sir John, III:3397;
    Sandburg, Carl, II:1743, III:2065;
    school architecture, II:1460; science,
    II:1019; serials, I:316; II:225–26;
    Shakespeare, William, II:1877;
    III:2215; social sciences and
    humanities, III:789; special
    collections, II:280; subject distribution,
    II:79, 106; Turner, Tom, II:1799;
    United Nations, II:814; word lists and
    dictionaries, II:1601
———Music Library: resources, I:3015
———Ricker Library: architecture, I:2881
———Visual Aids Service: films and

transcriptions, I:3102; education films,
    III:1790
Illuminated manuscripts, I:498, 502–04,
    518–30, 566, 568–69, 572, 580,
    3135, 4274; II:265, 267–68, 270–71,
    274, 286, 542; III:433–35, 437, 464,
    1800
Illumination, I:2488, 2538
Illwitzer, R. P., III:363
Imaginary books, III:1920
Imbrie, B. V., I:5497
Imitatio Christi, I:1011
Immigration, U.S., I:1370–84; II:676–77;
    III:2412, 2423, 2425
Impeachment, I:1846
Imperial County, Cal., I:2628 (25)
Income statistics, I:2626 (73)
Income tax, I:1522, 1524, 1531
Incunabula, I:56, 146, 572, 578, 594, 596,
    607, 613, 615–63, 915, 956, 1041;
    II:94, 102, 282, 286, 294, 297, 302,
    305, 313, 318–44, 1001, 2274;
    III:452, 481–92, 1251, 1421;
    botanical, II:1121; Dominican, I:622;
    English, I:619, 624, 650, 655, II:343;
    Franciscan, II:603; French, III:485;
    German, III:486; Hebrew, I:632, 640,
    649, II:635, 641; Iberian, II:321;
    illustrated, II:325; legal, II:824;
    medical, I:2417–34; II:1251–52;
    miniature, I:638, II:327; Spanish,
    II:336
Indexes, I:1, 8, 10, 16; II:4, 17
Indexing systems, II:1263; III:1570
India, history, I:4193 (38); III:2828, 2839
Indian languages, I:3175–86
Indian primers, I:696
Indian publications, III:2838
Indiana: authors, I:3258; history, I:4829–42,
    II:2613–17, III:3189
Indiana Academy of Science: scientific and
    technical periodicals, I:2201–03
Indiana Civil War Centennial Commission,
    III:3086
Indiana Historical Society Library: McHenry,
    James, I:4066; manuscripts, I:4839
Indiana State Law Library: catalog, I:1690
Indiana State Library: catalog, I:214; early
    American furniture, I:2925; genealogy,
    I:4145, 4151–53, II:2256; government
    publications, II:26, III:39; Indiana
    history, I:4829, 4833–35, 4842;
    Indiana music, I:3059; manuscripts,
    I:4840–41, II:2615–16; newspapers,
    I:400
Indiana Supreme Court, Law Library: catalog,
    I:1691
Indiana, University, Audio-Visual Center:
    educational films, III:1791
———Folklore Institute: Afroamerican
    music, III:1840
———Libraries: African periodicals, III:364;
    business history, II:966; collections,
    I:131; Columbia Conserve Company,
    II:967; education, I:1959; Lane,
    Joseph, II:2160; Lindsay, Vachel,
    II:1722–23; little magazines, II:161;
    manuscripts, II:257; newspapers,

Indiana, University, Libraries *(cont.)*
I:400; Poe, Edgar Allan, II: 1737;
Slavic and East European literature,
III:2739; special collections, II:280
————Lilly Library: American patriotic
songs, III:1852; American poetry,
III:1965; collection, II:296; English
literature, III:2111; geography,
III:2362–63; great book lists, II:295;
history of science, III:1314; Housman,
A. E., III:2174–75; incunabula,
III:489; Indiana history, III:3189;
influential books, III:455; Latin
America, III:3303; manuscripts,
III:412; medical history, II:1232,
III:1486; medieval manuscripts,
III:431; Milton, John, III:2198;
Peruvian manuscripts, III:3388;
Philippine manuscripts, III:2913; Poe,
Edgar Allan, III:2054; quotations,
III:1925; sea novels, III:1936; Sinclair,
Upton, III:2069; Sterne, Laurence,
III:2223; Tennyson, Frederick,
III:2230; War of 1812, III:3070;
Wordsworth, William, III:2234
————Music Library: early keyboard sources,
III:1810
————School of Medicine Library: serials,
III:1535
Indianapolis Bar Assoc.: law library catalog,
I:1692
Indianapolis Public Library: Indiana authors,
I:3258; newspapers, I:400
Indic literature, I:3772–76
Indochina, I:4347; II:2406
Indonesia, II:2429–30; III:2840–42
Induction heating, I:2490
Industrial accidents, I:2344, 2355, 2359
Industrial diseases, I:1577
Industrial development, III:891
Industrial education, I:1992
Industrial mobilization, I:5410
Industrial plants, U.S., II:729
Industrial relations: I:1467, 1634–41; II:747–
81
Industrial surveys, I:2442
Inflation, economic, I:1488–90
Information services, government, I:2042;
II:690, 696–97
Infrared, II:1109, 1160
Ingersoll, Robert G., III:2528
Inglis, Margaret I., I:136
Ingold, Ernest, II:1877; III:2215
Ingpen and Stonebill, I:3381
Ingram, John Henry, I:1738
Inheritance, land, I:2602 (22)
Inheritance taxation, I:1523, 1531–32
Initiative, referendum and recall, I:1354
Injunctions, labor, I:1655–56, 1658
Inks, I:2797
Inland Empire Council of Teachers of English,
I:88
Inland waterways, III:921
Inoue, Hitoshi, III:2908
Inquisition, I:4231, 4241
Insignia, I:5413
Installment plan, I:2696
Institute of Aeronautical Science, I:2550–51

Institute of American Genealogy Library:
catalog, I:4154
Institute of Public Administration Library:
civil service and personnel, I:1857;
police science, I:1877; public
administration, I:1858, 1860
Institute of Transportation Library:
periodicals, II:1420
Insulating oil, I:2798
Insulation, electrical, I:2486
Insurance, I:1944–48; II:921; III:1235; farm,
I:2602 (47), 2626 (67), 2628 (24);
government control, I:1947–48;
group, I:1620; health, I:1621; life,
I:1622; unemployment, I:1617, 1623
Insurance Company of North America:
historical collection, I:2410; III:1235
Insurance Library Association of Boston:
catalog, I:1944
Insurance Society of New York: library
acquisitions, I:1945; life insurance
catalog, II:921
Interior decoration, I:2923–25, 2928, 2930,
2932; III:1604
International boundaries, III:1065
International Bureau of the American
Republics: Central America, I:5304;
Mexico, I:5305
International Colloquium on Luso-Brazilian
Studies, III:2794
International conferences, II:707, 815
International Geophysical Year, III:1372
International law and relations, I:1756, 1795,
1803–32; II:811–18; III:1058–68
International Science Foundation, III:1285
International Young Men's Christian
Association College: periodicals,
III:228
Internationalism, I:1355
Interstate commerce, I:2033–34
Inventors, I:2161
Investments, II:720; III:894; foreign, II:691
Iowa: authors, III:1956; history, I:4843–48;
III:3190
Iowa Archives: genealogy, II:2250
Iowa Historical, Memorial and Art Dept.:
early newspapers, I:420
Iowa State College Library: vocations, I:1990
Iowa State Historical Society: newspapers,
III:318
Iowa State Library: catalog, I:215
Iowa State University Library (Ames): Carver,
George Washington, II:2109; medical
periodicals, II:1211; Russian journals
in English, II:236
Iowa State University Library (Iowa City):
Hunt, Leigh, II:1840–41; Iowa state
publications, II:27; Iowa State
University history, III:1255; law
history, I:1693; Lincoln, Abraham,
II:2173; little magazines, II:161;
music, II:1534
Iowa, University, Libraries: American history,
III:3052; American Indian, III:3032;
Blunden, Edmund, III:2139;
Bonaparte, Napoleon, III:2579; Booth,
John Wilkes, III:2438; Ding Darling
cartoons, III:1754; Downing, J. Hyatt,

III:2000; English literature, III:2121;
folksongs, III:1842; Foster, O. D.,
III:2498; French Revolution, III:2711;
government publications, III:40; Greek
literature, III:2276; Griffin, Ray B.,
III:2511; Hunt, Leigh, III:2177–78;
Iowa authors, III:1956; Iowa land
records, III:3190; Italian plays,
III:2252; juvenile literature, III:2293,
2313; Latin American periodicals,
III:366; linguistics, III:1912; Long-
fellow, Henry W., III:2041; Meredith,
Edwin T., III:1612; oral history,
III:2681; Prairie Press imprints, III:546;
railroad history, III:923; rare books,
III:451; Riley, William F., III:1006;
serials, III:229; Suckow, Ruth,
III:2075; U.S. Presidents, III:2413;
Viereck, George Sylvester, III:2087;
World War I newspapers, III:3406;
Yewell, George Henry, III:1713
Ioway and Sac Mission Press, I:745
Iran, I:4351; II:2376, 2432; history, III:181,
2820
Ireland, William, I:3538
Ireland, history, I:4249, 4270
Irick, Robert L., III:2881
Irish and United States, II:677
Irish literature, I:3742, 4270; II:1785, 1795;
III:2120
Iron and steel, I:2497, 2787–89, 2805, 4193
(23); II:1427, 1430; III:1695
Iroquoian languages, I:3181
Iroquois Indians, II:1002, 2505–06
Irrigation, I:2601 (41); II:1372, 1410
Irving, Washington, I:3292–97; II:1632,
1710–11
Irwin, Margaret S., II:1421
Irwin, Theodore, I:2961
Isaac, Oliver B., III:3273
Isaacs, Lewis M., I:3327; II:1742
Ische, John P., III:1541
Isham, Ralph H., I:3427
Isidore of Seville, I:3721
Islamic manuscripts, II:276
Isle of Man, I:4272
Isle of Pines, I:5295, 5352
Italian bibliography, I:20
Italian drama, II:1941; III:2252, 2254–55
Italian fiction, II:1946
Italian literature, I:549, 3360–86, 3999;
II:1940–48; III:2107, 2252–56
Italian manuscripts, II:276
Italian Somaliland, I:4381
Italy, history, I:4297–4303; II:2316–18;
III:2724–29
Ives, Charles Edward, III:1864
Ives, Samuel A., I:496; II:1250
Ivins, W. M., I:941

Jaantila, Kirsti, II:2319
Jabbour, Alan A., III:1841
Jablonski, Stanley, II:1191
Jackson, A. V. W., I:537
Jackson, Andrew, I:4008–09, 4787–88;
II:2190; III:2529–30
Jackson, Anne, III:3165
Jackson, Donald, III:2642

Jackson, Donald F., III:2276
Jackson, Elisabeth C., I:2103
Jackson, Joseph, I:3302
Jackson, Margaret H., I:3672
Jackson, Sally, I:4865
Jackson, Sheldon, II:573–74
Jackson, Stuart W., II:2157
Jackson, W. Turrentine, I:4662, 4682, 5113, 5273
Jackson, William A., I:560–61, 3713, 4293, 4435; II:285–86, 1233
Jackson, William Vernon, II:79, 104–06, 1956–57; III:101–02, 3333–34
Jacksonville Public Library: genealogy, I:4155
Jacob, J. J., I:5246
Jacobius, Arnold J., II:1159
Jacobs, Wilbur R., II:2218
Jacobsen, Edna L., I:5028, 5040; II:661
Jacobsen, Phoebe R., III:745
Jacoby, Karl, I:3603
Jacoby, Robert L., II:2201
Jaffa, Aileen, II:1339
Jaggard, William, I:3527
Jahr, Torstein K. T., I:59
Jakhontov, Arkadi N., II:2321
Jakobson, Roman, II:1977
Jamaica, I:5283
James, A. E., I:3209
James, Alfred R., II:994
James, Edmund J., I:401
James, Eldon R., I:1782–83
James, Geraldine R., II:86
James, Henry, I:3299; II:1616, 1632, 1712–14; III:2033
James, James A., I:4555
James, Janet Wilson, III:1268
James, Josef C., I:5569
James, Margaret A., I:3457
James, William, I:3298–99; III:2033
James Jerome Hill Reference Library: periodicals, II:162, 169
James Prendergast Free Library, Jamestown, N.Y.: Swedish literature, III:2243
Jameson, Mary E., I:5456
Jamestown, Va., maps, I:3919
Janitz, John, III:2533
Janse, Renee S., II:1424
Jantz, Harold S., I:3223
Japan, II:2359, 2376; history, I:4337–43, 4356; II:2409–22; III:181, 2899–2908
Japan, Ministry of Foreign Affairs: archives, II:2409, 2419
Japanese-American evacuation, World War II, I:5541; II:2801
Japanese in America, I:1382, 2598 (3)
Japanese literature, I:3777–78, 3781, 3783–84, 3786, 3789–92; III:2860, 2908
Japanese prints, I:2963, 2967, 2974, 2987
Jarrell, Myrtis, I:4121
Jarrell, Randall, III:2036
Jeffers, Robinson, II:1715–18; III:2037
Jefferson, Thomas, I:266, 2602 (8), 4010–20, 4438; II:141, 1453, 1465, 2055, 2146–48, 2535, 2706; III:1260
Jefferson National Expansion Memorial, I:2891
Jelavich, Charles, II:480
Jenkins, Charles F., I:4556

Jenkins, Francis Briggs, II:1019; III:1286
Jenkins, Gwendolyn, III:2309
Jenkins, John Gilbert, III:2288
Jenkins, Marianna D., III:1716
Jenkins, Michael, I:4897
Jenkins, Myra Ellen, III:3226
Jenkins, William S., I:1433; II:47
Jenkinson, Richard C., I:602
Jenks, William L., I:3881, 3908
Jennings, Amy R., II:732
Jennings, Judson T., I:5027
Jennings, Pauline W., III:1610
Jensen, Howard E., II:680
Jensen, John H., II:2303; III:2710
Jerabek, Esther, I:32, 4695
Jesuits, I:4517; II:597, 610, 2524
Jet propulsion, I:2559
Jewett, George Frederick, III:2531
Jewett, James R., I:3767
Jewett, Sarah O., I:3300–01; II:1719–20; III:2038
Jewish music, I:3042
Jewish Theological Seminary of America Library: Biblical collection, I:1028, 1227; Hebrew manuscripts, I:1215, III:777; library history and resources, I:1217, 1228–29; polemical manuscripts, I:1233; Soncino books, I:649
Jews: in America, II:638–40, 644, 649; in drama, I:3769; in England, I:4253; in literature, I:3368–69; in Orient, I:4349
Jillson, Willard R., I:749–50, 4855, 4858–63; II:2058
Jiu-jitsu, I:3137
Joerg, W. L. G., I:3882
Johansen, Dorothy O., II:2732
John, Harry W., III:1173, 1193, 1197, 1224
John Crerar Library: abstract serials, I:8; acquisitions policy, II:1020; aeronautics, I:2552–53; amebic dysentery, I:2346; American history, I:4476; American trade union publications, I:1645–46; bakelite, I:2815; birds, I:2337; British Parliament papers, I:1434; Canadian Bureau of Statistics, I:1269; cancer, II:1144; catalogs, III:175–77; cellophane, I:2815; Century of Progress Exposition, I:2443; Chicago and Cook County publications, I:1875; civilian defense, I:5477; commerce directories, I:2039, 2816; cremation, I:2347; current serials, III:1335; decalcomania, I:2926; diorama, I:2887; dust explosions, I:2534; East Asiatic books, I:3790; education directories, I:1954; electrical insulation, I:2486; encyclopedias and dictionaries, I:7; engineering books, II:1265; feminist movement, I:2140; French economic documents, I:1459; French in Africa, I:4376; gages, I:2479; Greenland, I:5381; hibernation, I:2336; hydroponics, I:2591; incunabula, I:635–36; indexes, I:8; industrial arts, I:2444–45; industrial development, III:891; industrial

history, I:2445; industrial surveys, I:2442; Latin American history, I:5331; leukemia, II:1145; library history, I:132; maggot therapy, I:2349; magnetic recording, I:2487; medical libraries directory, III:1450; medicine, II:1143; metals, I:2282, II:1429, 1434–35, III:1698; military medicine, I:2351; mineral wool, I:2463; mining and mineral resources, I:2499; municipal government publications, I:1874–75; music therapy, I:2352; New Deal, I:1899; noise, I:2247; pediatrics, II:1203; periodicals, I:317–18; phobias, I:2350; Pluto, I:2234; radiant heating, I:2535; reading room collection, I:216; research service, II:1021; science books, I:2166–67; science glossaries, I:2165; science history, I:2192–93; scientific translations, II:1036; special bibliographies, I:6, 8; state government publications, I:1900, 1954; time and motion study, I:2684; translations, III:13; U.S. National Recovery Administration, I:1460; Venezuela, history, I:5335; weight reduction, I:2348; wine production, I:2795
John of Garland, I:3164
Johns, Alan B., III:476
Johns, C. H. W., I:4220
Johns, Gerald, III:1364, 1369
Johns Hopkins University, Applied Physics Laboratory: scientific-technical journals, III:1336
———Library: American trade publications, I:1645–47; architecture, III:1745; German drama, I:3580; Judaism, I:1230; rare books, III:444
———Tudor and Stuart Club: Spenser, Edmund, I:3548
Johnson, Alice S., I:4933
Johnson, Allen, I:4894
Johnson, Andrew, II:2149; III:2532
Johnson, Charles S., II:655
Johnson, Clifton H., III:829
Johnson, Donald Clay, III:2829
Johnson, Donald W., III:227
Johnson, Duncan S., I:2300
Johnson, E. D. H., I:2838
Johnson, Edgar A. J., I:2733
Johnson, Francis R., I:3548
Johnson, George F., III:2533
Johnson, H. Earle, I:3060
Johnson, Irma, II:1022
Johnson, J. W., II:1500
Johnson, James G., I:3242
Johnson, Josephine, III:2039
Johnson, Judith, III:2433
Johnson, Kathryn A., II:2647
Johnson, Lon, III:2534
Johnson, Lucia Porcher, II:2662
Johnson, Maizie H., III:1186, 1195–96, 1204, 1207, 1214, 1583–85
Johnson, Marion M., II:808–09; III:807, 944, 1030–33, 1036, 1068, 1100, 1182, 1305
Johnson, Marjorie J., III:621

Johnson, Martin and Osa, III:1954
Johnson, Neil M., III:2087
Johnson, Robert E., III:3397
Johnson, Robert K., III:1145
Johnson, Ruth, III:3112
Johnson, Samuel, I:3485–86; II:1597, 1842; III:2182–83
Johnson, Samuel (president, King's College), I:2011
Johnson, Thomas H., I:3970
Johnson, Thomas M., I:952
Johnson, Tillman D., II:2569
Johnson, Una E., II:1485
Johnson, Wanda M., I:1475
Johnson, Sir William, I:4498, 5025; II:2150
Johnston, David Claypool, III:1753
Johnston, Helen L., II:1352
Johnston, Joseph E., I:4021
Johnston, William D., I:89–90
Joint Comm. on Library Research Facilities for National Emergency, I:72
Joint University Libraries: historical documents, II:251; Latin Americana, III:3309; science serials, III:1337
Joline, J. F., I:4609
Jolly, David, II:2441–42
Jonah, David J., II:726
Jones, Catherine T., II:1715; III:2037
Jones, Cecil K., I:5306–07
Jones, Claud Lee, III:1536
Jones, Everitt L., III:3140
Jones, George, II:61
Jones, H. G., III:329–30
Jones, Harold W., I:2367, 2423
Jones, Helen D., I:1382, 1513, 1831, 2178, 2180, 2452, 2778, 3137, 4325; II:2427
Jones, James V., II:606
Jones, John P., I:4022
Jones, Joseph J., II:1744, 2464; III:2998
Jones, Mabel B., III:2265
Jones, Matt B., I:775, 993, 4435
Jones, Perrie, I:2586
Jones, Samuel A., I:3444
Jones, Silas P., I:3636
Jones, Theodore F., I:2010
Jones, Virgil L., I:4723; II:2585
Jones, Wesley L., I:5241
Jones family, III:2535
Jones Library, Amherst, Mass.: Dickinson, Emily, I:3282
Jonikas, Peter, II:59
Jopling, Carol, III:370
Jordan, Alice M., I:3809
Jordan, Casper Leroy, II:557, 685
Jordan, David Starr, II:951; III:2536
Jordan, Philip D., I:409, 3061, 3811
Jordan-Smith, Paul, II:1791
Jorgensen, Inge B., I:2535
Jorgenson, Chester Eugene, II:1746
Jorgenson, Margareth, I:5364; III:3368
Josephson, A. G. S., I:282, 636, 2191, 2445
Joslyn Art Museum, Omaha: West, history, III:3145
Journalism, I:480–82; II:237–39; III:404–06; religious, II:545–46
Joy, James F., II:2151
Joyce, James, II:1616, 1843–48; III:2002, 2120, 2184–88

Joyner, Fred B., III:2476
Judaism, I:1215–51; II:634–49, 1602, 2359; III:757–83
Judo, I:3137
Juhlin, A. P., II:1064
Julien C. Yonge Library, I:4786
Juniata College Library: American-German bibliography, I:1370
Junius, I:4258
Juvenal, I:3725
Juvenile delinquency, II:917
Juvenile literature, I:836, 3801–21; II:1993–2016; III:2287–2351; Confederate, III:2292
Juvenile periodicals, III:2339
Juvenile poetry, III:2302, 2335, 2340–41
Jwaideh, Zuhair E., III:1055

Kabelac, Karl Sanford, III:598
Kable, William S., III:2140
Kadrmas, Constance J., III:2628
Kahn, Herman, I:2636; II:2802
Kahrl, George M., I:3356
Kaige, Richard H., III:3184
Kaiser, Barbara J., III:1883
Kaiser, John B., I:1436
Kalamazoo College Library: Baptist collection, I:1060; Lincoln, Abraham, I:4058
Kalamazoo Public Library: Lincoln, Abraham, I:4058
Kaltenborn, H. V., III:2537
Kane, Grenville, I:620, 4456
Kane, Lucile M., II:2647; III:802
Kanick, Mary Joanne, III:568
Kann, Paul J., III:2271
Kansas: authors, III:1954; history, I:4849–53, II:2618–23
Kansas Association of Teachers of History, II:2619
Kansas City, University, Library: Missouri history, I:4982; transportation, II:1422
Kansas Court of Industrial Relations, I:1585
Kansas State College (Pittsburg): Kansas authors, III:1954
Kansas State Geological Survey: Kansas and Nebraska history, II:2623
Kansas State Historical Society Library: Anderson family, III:2430; Bristow, Joseph Little, III:2442; Brown, John Stillman, III:2444; Civil War, III:3080; collections, II:2621; Ewing, Thomas, Jr., III:2486; government documents, I:4852; Hyatt, Thaddeus, III:2527; index, II:2620; Kansas books, I:4853; Kansas imprints, II:390; Kansas newspapers and periodicals, I:389, 402–03; Long, Chester I., III:2555; McCoy, Isaac, III:2559; Meeker, Jotham, III:2569; New England Emigrant Aid Company, III:3191; Pratt, John G., III:2593; Robinson, Charles, III:2599; town and county histories, II:2618
Kansas State Library: catalog, I:217; government publications, II:28, III:41; Kansas public libraries, III:104; law catalog, I:1694

Kansas State Teachers College Library: William Allen White, III:2089
Kansas State University Library: religion, III:690
Kansas, University, Governmental Research Center: Kansas state publications, III:42
——Libraries: Amzalak, Moses Bensabat, II:725; Anglo-Irish literature, II:1785; Armenia, II:2323; Brown, John, II:2105; censored books, II:287; chemistry, II:1104; Chesterfield, Philip D. S., II:2110; Costa Rica maps, III:2364; English literature, III:2112; English pamphlets, II:348; French Revolution, II:2304, 2310; Gibson, Wilfred Wilson, II:1835; guide, III:145; herbals, III:1427; Jews in America, II:639; Joyce, James, II:1844; III:2187; Kansas history, II:2622; Latin America, III:3325; Latin American publications, III:3304; Law Library, II:783; Lawrence, D. H., II:1854; Linnaeus, Carolus, II:1050, III:1424–26; maps, II:2033–34, III:2365; medical botany, II:1140; medieval art, II:1442; microreproductions, II:98; Millay, Edna St. Vincent, II:1732; Mormon books, II:567; Near East, II:2362; O'Hegarty collection, II:1585; ornithology, II:1128–30, 1135; Pennell, J. J., photographs, II:1508; Poel, William, II:1583; Rafinesque, Constantine Samuel, II:1042; Ray, John, II:1051; Renaissance, II:670, 2278; Rilke, Rainer Maria, III:2241; Russian literature, II:1971; serials, III:230; Spanish plays, II:1954; Spanish Renaissance, II:2315; special collections, II:280; Synge, J. M., II:1896; vegetation maps, III:1665–66; women, II:1010–11; Yeats, W. B., II:1910–12
——Medical Center Library: Darlington, William, II:1227; hematology, II:1150; medical botany, II:1140; medical history, II:1226, 1236
Kantor, Harry, III:809
Kapitsa, Petr L., I:2249
Kaplan, Louis, II:754, 2081; III:161, 2411
Kaplan, Milton, I:4470; II:1496, 1510; III:2941
Kaplan, Mitchell M., I:1231
Kapsner, Oliver L., II:599, 607; III:749
Karcher, Carolyn L., II:2682
Karis, Thomas, III:2967
Karlson, Marjorie, II:1852
Karow, Otto, I:3778
Karpinski, Louis C., I:2215–16, 2235, 3837, 3844, 3888, 3909, 5393
Kase, Karel A., III:365
Kaser, Arthur L., II:1581
Kaser, David, II:262, 1581
Kaser, Jane, II:262
Kasinec, Edward, III:2754
Kastor, Robert, I:2168
Katterjohn, Catherine L., II:793

Katz, Joseph, III:1993
Katz, Willis, II:470
Kavanagh, Mary Whitney, III:581
Kavass, Igor I., III:1038
Kawai, Saburo, II:728
Kaye, F. B., I:458
Keast, William R., II:1878
Keating, George T., I:3450
Keats, John, I:3487; II:1849
Kebler, Geneva, III:797, 906–07, 931–32, 1230–31, 1240–42, 1399, 1488, 1590, 2391
Kebler, Leonard, I:3292
Keefer, Pearl M., I:351
Keeneland Association Library: horses, II:1377
Keener, Hazel, II:2394
Keep, Austin B., I:141
Keeweenaw Historical Society: Michigan history, I:4946
Kehl, Mary M., I:2685
Kehlenbeck, Dorothy, II:2109
Keidel, George C., I:404
Kelker, Luther R., I:5140
Kellar, Herbert A., I:4963
Kellar, Lucile, II:2184
Keller, Dean H., III:2631
Kelley, Maurice, III:2199
Kelling, Lucille, I:3544; II:1882
Kellis, Mary, II:434
Kellogg, Alfred L., II:1812
Kellogg, George, III:1924
Kellogg, Ira N., Jr., II:805, 2816
Kellogg, Louise P., I:5263–64
Kelly, Doris B., III:2130
Kelly, Harry F., III:1072
Kelly, Howard A., I:2319
Kelly, William M., III:599
Kelly, William W., III:2015
Kelmscott Press, I:572, 667–668, 673, 676; II:490, 492
Kelsey, Laura E., II:2068, 2072, 2767; III:868, 2379
Kelts, Lora Ives, III:1683
Kemble, Harold E., Jr., III:3216
Kemmerer, Donald L., I:5009
Kemp, Harold W., II:1460
Kenaf, II:1392
Kendall, John S., I:4885
Keniston, Hayward, I:3701, 5308
Kenk, Roman, II:1290
Kennedy, Edward G., I:937
Kennedy, Eugene, II:608
Kennedy, Frances B., I:3290
Kennedy, John Fitzgerald, III:2538
Kennedy, John Pendleton, II:2152
Kennedy, Lawton, III:3374
Kennedy, Marguerite K., II:900
Kennedy, Maxine E., II:1944
Kennerly, Sarah Law, II:2004
Kenney, Louis A., III:1368
Kenney, Mildred A., I:4156
Kenney, Sylvia W., II:1556
Kent, Donald H., I:5148; III:2580
Kent, George O., III:3011, 3416
Kent, Henry W., I:934
Kent County, Del., probate records, I:4144
Kent State University Libraries: children's

books, III:2287; newspapers, III:319; periodicals, III:231; Wright, Richard, III:2101
Kentucky: fiction, II:1661; history, I:4854–73, II:2624–28, III:3192; maps, I:3907, II:2058
Kentucky Court of Appeals, I:4860, 4863
Kentucky Dept. of Education Library: archives, III:1239
Kentucky gazette, I:749
Kentucky Library Association, I:405
Kentucky, Secretary of State, I:4864
Kentucky State Archives and Records Service: government publications, III:43
Kentucky State Historical Society: archives, I:4864; census records, II:2627; collections, I:4865; legislation, I:4860, II:792; manuscripts, II:2625–26
Kentucky State Land Office, I:4862–63
Kentucky State Library: catalog, I:218
Kentucky, University, Libraries: American history, III:3012; Civil War fiction, II:1661; English chapbooks, II:1792; folklore, II:1005; French plays, II:1936, III:2245; Hammer imprints, II:500; Harvey, William, II:1234; Kentucky law, II:792–93; manuscripts, III:413–14; maps, II:2058; postage stamps, III:80; Servetus, Michael, II:1234; Spanish plays, III:2264, 2268; Tibetan literature, II:1991; University archives, III:1254
——Medical Center Library: periodicals, III:1537
Kenya, Africa, III:2982
Kenyon, Carleton W., III:986, 994
Kenyon College Library: periodicals, II:170
Keogh, Andrew, I:637, 3545
Kephart, John E., II:563
Kepler, Johann, I:2229; III:1368
Ker, Annita M., I:48
Kerker, Ann Elizabeth, II:1029, 1116; III:1413, 1415, 1453–54
Kerlan, Irvin, II:2005
Kern, Alexander, I:1752
Kerner, Gaiselle, II:805–07, 857
Kerner, Robert J., I:4319
Kerr, Ruth A., I:164
Kerr, Willis, I:5450
Kevles, Daniel J., III:1365
Key, Mary P., III:500
Keyes, Jane Godfrey, III:2849
Keyes, Virginia, I:2342
Keynes, Geoffrey, I:2411, 3426, 3465, 3469; II:1810
Khazars, I:4350; II:2272
Kidd, Deborah Dove, III:514
Kidman, Ray, II:1051
Kielman, Chester V., III:1259, 3268
Kiemen, M. C., III:3378
Kilbourne, John D., III:2585
Kilgour, Frederick G., I:2194
Killebrew, Joseph Buckner, III:2539
Killeffer, D. H., I:2264
Killingworth, Charles T., I:1647
Kilmer, Kenton, I:3189
Kilroe, Edwin P., I:1925
Kilroy, William P., III:71

Kim, Stephen, III:1550
Kimball, Fiske, I:2888
Kimball, LeRoy E., I:3838
Kimball, Robert E., III:1866
Kimball, Stanley B., III:734
Kincaid, Elbert Alvis, II:2134–35
Kindilien, Carlin T., II:1644, 1871–72
King, Charles G., I:2945
King, Donald L., III:1088
King, Dorothy, III:2310
King, Frances, III:2311
King, Frank H. H., III:360
King, Joseph A., II:29
King, Judson, II:2153
King, Sarah B., II:406
King, Solomon, I:836
King family, III:2540
King's College (Columbia University): Columbiana, I:1998, II:947
King's College Library: Korson collection, III:1265
King's Mountain, I:5184
Kingsley, Charles, I:3385, 3405; III:2189
Kingston, N.Y., history, I:5068
Kinhead, Ludie, I:405
Kinken, Ann Daly, III:3249
Kinney, John Mark, III:738–39
Kino, Eusebio F., I:4746
Kipling, Rudyard, I:3415; II:1850; III:2190–92
Kirchman, Charles V., III:1192
Kirk, Rudolf, III:2031
Kirk, Sherri, III:819
Kirkham, E. Kay, II:519, 2247
Kirkpatrick, John, III:1872
Kirkpatrick, L. H., II:569
Kitchin, Claude, III:2541
Kites, I:2549
Klebs, A. C., I:2424
Kleist, Herbert, III:663
Klemme, Anna Carol, II:1953
Klesmont, Johannes, III:2723
Kletsch, Ernest, I:3739
Kline, Jane, III:2418
Klinge, Norma, I:1399
Klondike gold rush, II:1498
Klyberg, Albert T., III:3148
Knapp, Mary E., II:1834
Knapp, William I., I:3165
Knauss, James O., I:406–07
Knight, John E., I:4721
Knipp, Thomas, III:2101
Kniseley, Sherman P., II:1570
Knitting industry, I:2807
Knoepfmacher, I:4333
Knowles, Edwin B., Jr., I:3710
Knox, Bernard M. W., II:2270
Knox, Henry, I:4927
Knox College Library: Northwest history, I:4663–65
Koch, Michael S., II:1235
Koch, Theodore W., I:3676, 3679–80
Koeman, Cornelis, III:2366
Koerner, Alberta G. A., III:2401
Köhler, Herman, II:2297
Kolbet, Richard M., III:923, 3052
Kolchin, Morris, I:1520
Konstanzer, Marcia B., I:2542

Kopp, Jill, III: 2524
Koran, I: 1252; II: 1987
Korea, I: 4342; II: 2359; history, II: 2423–28,
      III: 2909–11; literature, III: 2860
Korn, Bertram W., II: 392
Kornhauser, Henrietta, I: 352
Korson, George, III: 1265
Koski, Leo G., II: 375
Kostrzewski, Lucien E., I: 4321
Kovacs, Suzanne, III: 494
Krader, Barbara, III: 456
Krader, Ruth, II: 2370
Krafft, Herman F., I: 5471
Kramer, Victor A., III: 1980
Krassovsky, Dimitry M., I: 4320
Krause, Sydney J., III: 1987
Krauskopf, Robert W., II: 2815
Krebs, Emil, I: 3146
Kreider, Harry J., II: 554
Krek, Miroslav, III: 2812
Kresge-Hooker Scientific Library: periodicals,
      II: 1110
Kress, Virginia E., III: 539
Kress Library of Business: business history,
      II: 962–63; East India Company,
      II: 975; Huguenot merchants, II: 961
Kreyenbuhl, Jeannine, II: 471
Krieger, L. C. C., I: 2319
Kristeller, Paul O., III: 2277
Kritzler, Charles, III: 3158
Krohn, Ernst Christopher, II: 1535
Krueger, John R., III: 2882
Krueger, Paul, I: 1754
Krug, Adele Jensen, III: 2312
Krull, Alan R., II: 1275
Krumbhaar, E. B., II: 311
Krummel, Donald W., III: 1812–13
Kruzas, Anthony T., III: 105–06
Kubal, G. J., III: 1627
Kucherov, Bertha, II: 1332
Küchler, A. W., III: 1665–66
Kudravetz, Barbara F., III: 569
Kuehl, John, III: 2049
Kuhlman, A. F., I: 31, 1928
Kuhn, John Clifford, Jr., II: 395
Kuhn, Thomas S., III: 1375
Kuhn, Warren B., III: 179, 1255
Kuiper, John P., III: 1782
Kulsrud, Carl J., I: 2620
Kuo, Leslie T. C., II: 1347, 1361
Küp, Karl, I: 2943; II: 609; III: 432
Kuri, Salme, II: 2341
Kurile Islands, III: 2902
Kuroda, Andrew Y., I: 3778
Kurtz, Charles L., III: 2542
Kvakovsky, Ivan, III: 1591
Kyle, Eleanor R., I: 848
Kyparissiotis, Niove, II: 1964

Labor, I: 4193 (10, 15), 1571–1668; II: 747–
      81; III: 786, 952–83; agricultural,
      II: 1368, 1374; disputes, I: 1651–58;
      law, II: 756; migratory, II: 764;
      newspapers, I: 1583–84; periodicals,
      I: 1583–84, 1638, II: 748, 776–77,
      779; III: 971; relations, public
      employees, III: 995; unions, I: 1645–
      50, II: 775–80, 1264, III: 956, 959

Lacefield, Arch Sanders, II: 1936
Lacey, Henry C., III: 2139
Lachman, Gisella R., II: 1438
Laciar, S. L., I: 3016
Lackschewitz, Gertrud, III: 1604
Lacy, Dan, I: 5103
Ladd, Mary B., I: 1651
Ladd, Richard S., II: 2047; III: 2373, 2404
Ladino literature, III: 780
Lafayette, Marquis de, I: 3936; II: 2154–57;
      III: 2543
Lafayette College Library: Lafayette, Marquis
      de, II: 2155, 2157; special collections,
      II: 2155
LaFontaine, Jean de, I: 3652
Lafreri, Antoine, I: 3856
Lagarde, Paul de, I: 237
LaGrange, Marie J., I: 2925
Lahontan, Louis Armand, I: 4524; II: 2463
LaHood, Charles George, Jr., II: 356, 1510
Lake Charles Public Library, Louisiana:
      newspapers, III: 321
Lake Superior, I: 4952
Lallou, William L., I: 1175
Lam, Katherine, II: 2006
Lamar, Mirabeau B., I: 5199
Lamb, Charles, I: 3488–90; II: 1851
Lamb, Ursula S., III: 3305
Lambert, Robert A., III: 559
Lamberton, John P., I: 319
Lammers, Sophia J., I: 3259
Lamont, Barbara G., I: 218
Lamont, Daniel Scott, II: 2158
Lampblack, I: 2345
Lancaster County Historical Society, I: 5143
Lancaster County, Penn., history, I: 5143
Lancour, A. H., I: 2842, 4166, 4168; III: 2412
Land, Emory Scott, II: 2159
Land, Robert H., II: 2208
Land, Roy, III: 2894
Land, William G., II: 2208
Land: drainage, I: 2601 (41); economics,
      III: 862–68; ownership, II: 1366;
      reform, II: 1375; settlement, I: 2602 (9),
      2621; titles, I: 2602 (21); utilization,
      I: 2622, III: 1637
Land Bank of 1740, I: 4921
Landa, Louis A., I: 3552
Landau, Baron Horace de, I: 3013
Landauer, Bella C., I: 2775
Landevennec Gospels, I: 521
Landor, Walter Savage, II: 1852
Landrey, Kathleen B., I: 3805
Landry, Hilton, III: 446
Landscape architecture, I: 2856–73; II: 1454–
      55; III: 1727–37
Landscape gardening, I: 2602 (35)
Lane, Joseph, II: 2160
Lane, M. Claude, III: 750
Lane, William C., I: 992, 2005, 3677, 3681,
      3960, 4105
Lang, Cecil Y., II: 1894
Lang, Elfrieda, II: 967; III: 3303
Lange, Otto, I: 1755
Langfeld, William R., I: 3296
Langmuir, Irving, III: 2544
Lanham, General Charles T., III: 2023
Lanning, John T., III: 2732

Lansing, Elizabeth, III: 2726
Lansing, John G., I: 994
Laos, III: 2828
Lapham, Ruth, I: 4574
Larason, Larry, III: 227
Larkey, Sanford V., I: 2408
Larkin, Thomas Oliver, II: 2590; III: 2545
Larouche, Leo O., III: 527
Larpent, John, I: 3365
Larrison, Earl J., III: 2207
Larsen, Henrietta M., I: 2734
Larson, Cedric, I: 3752
Larson, Esther E., III: 3013
Larson, Nellie G., II: 1345, 1350, 1355, 1370,
      1395; III: 1620, 1674
LaRue, Jan, II: 1486
Laskey, Julia H., I: 1164
Latham, Ernest H., Jr., II: 2317
Lathe, Mary H., I: 4178
Lathem, Edward C., II: 1705
Latimer, John R., II: 2399
Latin America, I: 4193 (9, 11); government
      publications, I: 43–48; history, I: 4290,
      5281–5370, II: 2716–55, III: 361,
      2730–31, 3294–3393; literature,
      II: 1949, 1951, 1959–61; maps,
      I: 3926–34
Latin literature, I: 237, 3724–29, 3731–33,
      3735–41; II: 517, 1601–03, 1963,
      1965–67, 1970; III: 2275, 2277–83
Latrobe, Benjamin H., I: 2888
Latta, Ann W., III: 66
Latvian literature, I: 3746
Laufer, Berthold, I: 3790–91
Lauritsen, Frederick M., III: 366
Laurvik, J. Nilsen, I: 2922
Lauterbach, Edward S., II: 1793
Lavoisier, Antoine Laurent, III: 1382
Law, Andrew, II: 2161
Law, Robert A., I: 133; II: 2260
Law, I: 183, 205, 220, 260, 273, 609, 1436,
      1669–1855; II: 782–833; III: 984–
      1057; administrative, III: 985; Africa,
      III: 1055; American Indians, I: 4487,
      4490; Argentina, I: 1734; Bolivia,
      I: 1735; Brazil, I: 1738; California,
      II: 785; Chile, I: 1734; China, I: 1752,
      III: 1054, 1056; Colombia, I: 1736;
      Connecticut, I: 1767; Cuba, I: 1737;
      District of Columbia, I: 1775;
      Dominican Republic, I: 1737; Ecuador,
      I: 1738; England, I: 1762, 1764, 1768,
      1772, 1780, 1789, 1796, 1800;
      European, I: 123, 1749, 1756; foreign,
      II: 819–27, III: 1046–57; France,
      I: 1758; Germany, I: 1759; Haiti,
      I: 1737; Indiana, I: 1794; international,
      II: 811–18, 823; Kentucky, I: 1785,
      II: 792–93; Korea, I: 1746; Latin
      America, I: 1732–45, III: 1057;
      libraries, I: 1761, III: 115, 984; library
      catalogs, I: 1669–1732; Mexico,
      I: 1739, 1742; Mohammedan, I: 1748,
      1750; municipal, II: 873; New York,
      I: 1770; Paraguay, I: 1740; periodicals,
      II: 822, III: 1038–45, 1052, 1056;
      Peru, I: 1741; philosophy, II: 794;
      Roman, I: 1754–55; Russia, I: 1751,

II:783, III:1052; Spain, I:1757, 1760; Tasmania, III:1049; Uruguay, I:1743; U.S. Civil War, I:1693; U.S. colonial, I:1675, 1688, 1716, 1770, 1783; Venezuela, I:1744; Virginia, I:1786

Law Librarians' Society of Washington, D.C.: legislative histories, II:710; periodicals, III:1041

Law Library Association of St. Louis: library catalog, I:1696

Lawrence, D. H., II:1853–58; III:2002, 2193

Lawrence, James, I:4023–24

Lawrence, T. E., III:2194

Lawrence Law Library: catalog, I:1697

Lawrence University Library: Scott, Sir Walter, III:2209

Laws, A. C., I:3682

Lawson McGhee Library: McClung historical collection, I:5179–80

Lazare, Edward, II:330–31

Lea, Henry C., I:4231, 4234, 4241

Leach, Howard S., I:3367

League of Nations, I:1819, 1829, 4361; II:813

League of Women Voters, II:675

Leake, Chauncey D., I:2375

Leake County, Miss.: I:2628 (27)

Lear, Edward, I:3491

Leary, Bernice M., III:2313

Leatherman, Marian, I:1879

Leavitt, Sturgis E., II:1960

Leder, Lawrence H., II:2509

Lederer, Alex, II:648

Lee, Arthur, I:4538, 4549

Lee, Guy A., I:1913, 2672

Lee, Hector, I:4194

Lee, Hwa-Wei, III:2942

Lee, Ivy, III:405

Lee, John T., I:4514

Lee, Richard H., I:4538

Lee, Robert E., I:4025

Lee, Samuel P., III:2546

Lee, Sidney, I:3536–37

Lee, Vernon, II:1859

Lee family, III:2547

Leech, James H., III:1323

Leech, John, I:3492

Leech, W. R., I:4089

Leeser, Isaac, I:1232

Lefferts, Marshall C., I:3503

Legal biography, I:1698

Legal fiction, I:1698

Legal medicine, I:2365

LeGear, Clara Egli, I:3839, 3871, 3883; II:2028–29, 2042–43, 2059, 2066; III:2375–76

Léger, Aléxis S., I:4188

Legienda di Sancta Caterina, II:319

Legislatures and legislation, I:1419–47, 1854–55; II:710–16

Lehigh University Library: Galileo, III:1315; Shakespeare, William, I:3538

Lehman, Herbert, III:2548

Lehman, Robert H., II:2443; III:2943

Lehmann-Haupt, Hellmut, I:909, 931; II:332

Leichtentritt, Hugo, II:1551

Leigh, Michael B., III:2917

Leikind, Morris C., I:2168, 2179, 2249, 2360; II:1333

Leisinger, Albert H., Jr., II:2493

Leisy, Ernest, I:3260

Leland, Charles G., I:3302

Leland, Waldo G., I:4477, 5506

Leningrad, battle, I:5553

Lennon, Donald R., III:3063

Lenox, James, II:291

Lenox Library: catalog, I:233; short title list, I:234

Lenski, Lois, III:2301, 2327

Lente, Helga, II:915

Lentz, Andrea D., III:2514

Leon, Stephanie, III:2629

Leonard, Carolyn M., III:124

Leonard, Katherine, II:681

Leonard, Lawrence E., III:124

Leptospirosis, II:1155, 1179

Lermontov, Mikhail Y., I:3754, 3762

Lescure, William J., III:972, 1084, 1111, 1125

Leslau, Wolf, I:3170–71

Leslie, Frank P., II:333

Leslie, Shane, II:1891

Lessing, Gotthold, I:3604

Letter-writing, I:3263

Letters, I:503

Lettish literature, II:1978

Leukemia, II:1145

Lev, Daniel S., II:2430

Levant, Muriel Roberta, III:639

Levin, Leah, II:745, 870

LeVine, Victor, III:2960

Levy, Babette M., II:540

Levy, Benjamin, II:392

Levy, Sharon, III:2314

Lewanski, Richard C., II:1604; III:1913

Lewinson, Paul, I:1393; II:755, 775; III:965

Lewis, Arthur O., Jr., II:1625

Lewis, Grace Hegger, II:1721

Lewis, Ida M., III:528

Lewis, John Allen, I:687

Lewis, John F., I:523, 541

Lewis, Sinclair, II:1613, 1721

Lewis, Virgil A., I:5249, 5253

Lewis, William D., I:2006, 3840, 5382; II:946

Lewis, Wilmarth S., I:134

Lewis, Wyndham, III:2040

Lewis and Clark expedition, I:4540

Lexington Public Library: Kentucky history, I:4866

Libbey, Elizabeth F., II:1859

Libby, Orin G., I:5265; II:2497

Liberia, I:1397, 4377

Liberty, I:1363

Liberty of conscience, I:1004

Libraries, Arizona, I:73, 96; Boston, I:103; California, I:92, II:73; Chicago, I:74; Colorado, I:73, III:124–25; Connecticut, III:90; directories, III:86, 100, 118, 135; District of Columbia, I:84, 98, 107, 109, II:87, III:103; federal, III:88, 132; Georgia, II:82; Idaho, I:73, 111; Illinois, I:66, III:97–98, 119; Indiana, I:106, III:131; Kansas, III:104; Los Angeles, I:97; Louisiana, III:120; Maine, III:111; Missouri, I:77, III:92, 113; Montana,

I:73, 111; Nevada, I:73; New England, III:123; New Jersey, I:93; New Mexico, I:73; New Orleans, I:94; New York, III:96, 108, 114, 117, 126, 133; New York City, I:62, 82, 89, 104, II:74, 84, III:91; North Carolina, III:93; Northwest, I:88; Oklahoma, I:87, 145; Oregon, I:111; Pacific Northwest, I:95, 111; Pennsylvania, III:110; Philadelphia, I:71, 105, II:86, III:129; Pittsburgh, II:85; public, II:59, 61; St. Louis, II:83; San Francisco, II:75; scientific, I:2176; South Carolina, III:112; Southeast, I:83, III:95, 107; Southern California, III:127; special, III:122; Texas, I:108, III:99; United States, I:78–81, 85, 99, 101–02, 110, 114–15; university, I:76, III:94, 115–16; Utah, I:73; Virginia, I:75, 112; Washington, D.C. I:84, 98, 107, 109; Washington (state), I:111; Wisconsin, III:109; Wyoming, I:73

Library architecture, I:2876

Library Association of Portland (Ore.): newspapers, III:332

Library Association of the City Colleges of New York: special resources, II:107

Library catalogs, I:177–280; II:8, 10, 126–42; III:163–200; law, II:810

Library Company of Philadelphia: American songs, III:1853; catalog, II:128; Shakespeare, William, III:2213

Library Company of the Baltimore Bar: Horwitz collection, I:1698

Library science, I:54–67; II:59–71; III:79–85

Library surveys, I:68–115; II:59, 72–125; III:86–162

Libya, I:4381

Lice, I:2598 (1)

Lichten, Frances, II:268

Lieber, Francis, I:1345

Liebert, H. W., II:288

Liebman, Olive K., III:1086, 1171, 1197, 1213

Liebman, Seymour B., III:3380

Liebmann, William B., III:2548

Liegey, Gabriel M., II:610

Lietz, Paul S., II:2758

Lievsay, John L., II:1945

Liles, Annette, II:1626; III:107

Lillard, John F. B., I:4641

Lilly, J. K., Library: collections, II:296; great book lists, II:295; Lindsay, Vachel, II:1723; medical history, II:1232; nautical fiction, III:1936; Poe, Edgar Allan, II:1737

Lilly Research Laboratories: serials, I:2446

Lima, Manoel de O., I:5310

Limited Editions Club, II:493

Limouze, A. S., I:461

Linares, Emma, II:63

Lincoln, Abraham, I:4026–60, 4438, 4827 (3); II:2162–79, 2540, 2546, 2605, 2610; III:412, 2549–53; music, II:1561

Lincoln, Benjamin, II:2225; III:2554

Lincoln, Charles H., I:497, 4022, 4497, 4499–4500, 4585, 5451
Lincoln, Jonathan T., I:2817
Lincoln, Robert T., I:4029, 4043–44
Lincoln, Waldo, I:451, 2584, 2950; II:1342
Lincoln Memorial University: famous collections, I:4041; photographs, I:4045; sheet music, II:1561
Lincoln National Life Foundation, I:3056
Lind, Genevieve R., III:2389
Lind, William E., II:556; III:730, 1083
Linda Hall Library, II:1031; III:1306; astronomy, III:1366; chemical technology, II:1105; chemistry, II:1106, III:1384; collections, I:2169, II:1023–24, III:1294; cybernetics, II:953; firearms, II:1283; floods, II:1310; geology, II:1111, III:1397; guide, III:1287; herbals, III:1427; Japanese, Chinese and Russian serials, III:367; mathematical programming, II:658; medical botany, II:1140; meteorology, II:1092–93; mining and metallurgy, II:1277; Oriental and East European serials, III:368; pharmacy, II:1146; physics, III:1316; psychology and psychiatry, II:510; serials, II:1065, III:1338–39; statistics, II:657
Lindbeck, John M. H., II:2395
Lindbergh, Charles A., I:4061
Linder, David H., I:2320
Lindfors, Bernth, III:2944
Lindgard, Elmer W., II:858
Lindley, Harlow, I:4836, 5120
Lindsay, Robert O., III:2712
Lindsey, Vachel, I:3303, II:289, 1722–23
Lingard, Elmer W., III:1296, 1579–81, 3040
Lingel, Robert, I:2124
Lingelbach, William E., II:2533
Lingenfelter, Richard E., III:320
Linguistics, I:237, 485, 3146–88; II:1595–1606; III:1909–17; Greek, III:1917; Philippine, II:1605, III:1914
Linnaeus, Charles, I:2326; II:1050; III:1424–26, 1433
Linton, Howard P., II:2396; III:108
Lion, Oscar, II:1765, 1767
Lippman, Walter, I:4062
Liquor, I:2718; laws, I:1869
Listeria, II:1156
Listeriosis, II:1156
Listrella, II:1156
Liszt, Franz, I:3050
Litchfield, Dorothy H., I:320
Litchfield, Hope P., III:609
Litchfield Historical Society: catalog, I:4764; Thomas Collier imprints, I:776
Literary Anniversary Club: Stevenson, Robert Louis, I:3550
Literary annuals, I:3207–09, 3212, 3266
Literary criticism, I:3191
Literary forgeries, I:3210, 3214, 3399, 3401, 3406, 3411, 3538; II:290, 1802–03; III:1930
Literary geography, I:3834
Literature, general, I:3189–3218; II:1607–1631; III:1918–43

Lithographs, I:2959, 2968, 2986; II:1489, 1493, 1496
Lithuania, II:2337; history, III:2770; literature, II:1978
Little, Brooks B., III:731
Little, Eleanor N., I:1784
Little, Homer P., I:2283
Little, Mary Lou, II:1532
Little, Thomas, I:3346; II:2202
Little magazines, I:331; II:161, 166; III:252
Little Red Riding Hood, I:3821
Littlefield, George E., I:777
Littleton, A. C., I:2772
Littleton, I. T., II:113; III:1345
Littmann, Enno, I:547
Litton, Gaston, II:2510
Liturgical literature, II:583; III:1821
Liu, Kwang-Ching, I:4329; II:2393
Liu, Po Ling, II:1984
Liu, Regina S. R., III:1376
Lively, Robert A., II:1657
Liveright, Frank I., I:2908
Livestock industry, I:2626 (62); II:1380; III:1660–61
Livingston, Dorothy F., I:3421
Livingston, Flora V., I:3446
Livingston, Luther S., I:3304, 3528
Livingston, Mary W., I:1599
Livingston, Robert, II:2509
Livingston, William, I:5014
Lizardo, José D., II:738; III:1124
Llewellyn, Karl Nickerson, III:1007–08
Llorens, Ana R., III:1915, 1928
Lloyd Library: botanical collection, I:2321; eclectic medical collection, I:2371–72; periodicals, I:2204; resources, I:2174–75
Lo, Anna, II:396
Loacker, E. M., I:3590
Lobel, Hildegarde, I:5552; II:2282
Local government, I:1872–94
Local transit, I:2132–37
Locke, Edwin, I:1256
Locke, Robinson, I:3110
Lockhart, Adelaide A., II:498
Lockwood, Sharon B., III:2977, 2980
Lodge, Ardis, III:137
Loeb, Jacques, III:1440
Loeffler, Charles M., I:3085
Loeffler, Mildred, II:727
Loehr, Rodney C., I:2735, 4964
Loening, Grover C., II:1331
Löfgren, Svante E., II:1934
Logan, Ida-Marie Clark, II:564
Logan, W. J. C., III:1639
Logsdon, Richard H., II:118
Lohf, Kenneth A., III:1994
Lokke, Carl L., I:5507; II:2305
London, Jack, II:1724
London, Samuel, II:425
London Naval Conference, I:5459
Long, Amelia R., I:5149
Long, Chester I., III:2555
Long, Huey P., III:2556
Long, John C., I:4515
Long, Marie Ann, III:109
Long, Wilbur, II:511
Long Island, N.Y., history, I:5084

Long Island Historical Society Library: almanacs, I:4696; bookplates, I:60; Brooklyn, N.Y. history, I:5041; genealogies, I:4157; manuscripts and early printed books, I:597; New York newspapers, I:384; resources, I:5039, 5042
Long Island University Library: periodicals, III:232
Longfellow, Henry Wadsworth, I:3251; II:1632, 1932; III:2017, 2041
Longhead, Flora H. A., I:92
Longyear, E. J., Co., I:2480
Longwood Library: DuPont family, II:2119–20
Loomis, Francis Butler, III:3350
Lope de Vega, I:3698
Lopez, Manuel D., III:298
Lord, Deane, III:1270
Lord, Robert A., I:5311
Lorenz, Denis, III:87
Loring, Rosamond B., III:662
Los Angeles, history, I:4738
Los Angeles Public Library: California history, I:4732; collections, I:135; early music, I:3017; films, II:1582; folk songs, I:3028; genealogy, II:2248–49; Japanese prints, I:2963; Latin America, III:3324; orchestral music, II:1536
——————Municipal Reference Library: city government, I:1380; city planning, I:2861; civilian defense, I:5478–87; police dogs, II:874; police helicopters, II:875; public employees, I:1573; race riots, I:1358
Los Angeles Railway Corporation Library: civilian defense, I:5488
Lotteries, I:971, 1503, 1526
Loughran, Clayton D., II:369
Louis, A. H., II:1742
Louis XVI of France, I:574
Louis XVII of France, I:3648
Louisiana: fiction, I:3243; history, I:4394, II:2629–31, III:3193–96
Louisiana Conservation Department, III:863
Louisiana Department of State: government publications, III:44
Louisiana Historical Assoc.: Davis, Jefferson, I:3969
Louisiana Historical Society: Cabildo archives, I:4875; colonial history, I:4886
Louisiana Library Association: Louisiana union catalog, III:3195
Louisiana Purchase, II:2534
Louisiana Secretary of State, II:30
Louisiana State Archives and Records Commission: colonial documents, III:3196; newspapers, I:321
Louisiana State Bar Assoc. Library: catalog, I:1700
Louisiana State Library: catalog, I:219; correctional institutions, III:1229; Louisiana books, II:2630
——————Law Department: catalog, I:1701
Louisiana State Museum: collections, I:4887; Louisiana history, II:2631

Louisiana State University, Department of Archives and Manuscripts: Hispanic Americana, III:3306
———Law Library: labor law, II:756; legal philosophy, II:794
———Library: Confederate letters, I:4607; Long, Huey, III:2556; manuscripts, I:4877, 4879; newspapers, I:408, II:200–01; III:322–23; oil and gas, II:1278; Rogers, Bruce, III:671; Romance languages, I:3163; scientific and technical serials, I:2205; seashells, III:1438; state publications, I:755
Louisiana Supreme Court, I:4882
Louisville Free Public Library: art collection, I:2839; Catholic books, I:1176; music collection, I:3018; Negroes, I:1394; Perry, Oliver Hazard, I:4592; U.S. history, I:4591
Louisville, University, Speed Museum: Lincoln, Abraham, I:4040
Lounsberg, Ralph G., I:5017, 5193
Lovejoy, Elijah P., I:4063
Lovelace Foundation Library: serials, III:1538
Loveless, Milo J., I:401
Lovett, Robert W., I:1636, 5540; II:964, 968–70, 998, 2757; III:881, 966, 2883
Low, Harriet, I:4331
Lowe, John A., I:2007
Lowe, Joseph D., III:2896
Lowell, James R., I:3251, 3304–05
Lowell City Library: French fiction, I:3637
Lowenhaupt, Warren H., II:62; III:81
Lowens, Irving, II:1562; III:1867
Lowenstein, Eleanor, II:1342
Lower California, I:5354; II:2587, 2742
Lowery, Woodbury, I:3892
Lowndes, William, III:2557
Loyal Legion Library: Civil War newspapers, I:4597
Lozano, Eduardo, III:3365
Lucas, E. Louise, I:2834, 2840; II:1446
Luce, Stephen B., III:2612
Lucey, William L., II:611–12
Luciani, Vincent, II:1946
Luckhardt, A. B., I:2412
Ludwig, Richard M., II:1681; III:2170
Luesing, Lois L., III:720
Lum, William Wong, III:3003
Lumbard, Emily C., II:1314
Lumber industry, I:2664; II:1406
Lundin, Dorothy, III:3033
Lundquist, M., III:1673
Lundy, Frank A., II:123
Luney, Alice W., II:407
Lunny, Robert M., III:2390
Luquiens, Frederick B., I:3708
Lurie, Edward, II:1052
Lusatians, II:1604
Luther, Martin, I:4064; II:2180
Lutheran church, I:184, 1086–90; II:553–54; III:724
Lutheran Historical Society Library: collections, I:1089–90
Luthern Theological Seminary, I:1089–90
Lutrell, Estelle, I:321, 3694, 4715; II:202
Lutz, Ralph H., I:5519

Lycanthropy, I:967
Lydenberg, Harry M., I:140; II:312
Lyell, Charles, II:1047
Lyles, Albert M., III:2154
Lyman, Susan E., I:5317
Lynch, Mary M., I:352
Lynch law, I:1851
Lynd, Robert S., III:2558
Lyon, Eunice M., III:2450
Lyons, John O., II:1818
Lyser, Alice I., I:4290

Ma, John T., II:534; III:716, 2879–80
Ma, Wei-yi, III:2885
Mabbott, Maureen C., I:2843, 3686, 4104
Mabbott, Thomas O., I:409
McAdam, Edward L., Jr., I:3486
McAdoo, William Gibbs, II:2181
Macalester College Library: periodicals, II:162, 169
McAnally, Arthur M., II:973, 1054
McAnear, Beverly, II:947
McAneny, Marguerite L., I:3315
Macao, I:4331
MacArthur, Douglas, I:4065
Macartney, George, II:2183
Macaulay, Neill, III:3307
McAvoy, Thomas T., II:613–14; III:751
McBride, Roberta, I:1635; II:750
McBurney, William Harlin, II:1778; III:2129
McCabe, Martha R., I:1966, 4365, 5368
McCain, William D., I:5508–10
McCalla, John M., III:313
McCann, Lewis P., II:1392
McCarter, Margaret Hill, III:1954
McCarthy, Betty Anne, III:993, 998
McCarthy, Charles, I:5266
McCarthy, Paul H., III:2416
McCartney, Hunter Pell, II:1841
McCarvel, Mary Kay, III:515
McClellan, William M., III:1845
McClelland, E. H., I:1552, 2529, 2782, 2786, 2790
McCloy, Elizabeth J., I:5541
McClung, Calvin M., I:5179–80
McColvin, Lionel R., I:3019
McComb, Ralph W., II:1794; III:110
McCombs, Charles F., I:601, 3434, 4114, 4571, 4938
McCombs, Lois F., I:2497
McConnell, Roland C., I:5104, 5431, 5435
McConnell, Winona, I:4491
McCorison, Marcus A., II:289; III:638, 640
McCormack, Helen G., I:5166
McCormick, Cyrus Hall, II:2184
McCormick, Jack, III:1666
McCormick Historical Association: agricultural history, I:2617
McCosker, M. J., I:2410; III:1235
McCoy, Donald R., II:717
McCoy, Garnett, III:1717
McCoy, Isaac, III:2559
McCoy, Mercer G., II:465
McCoy, Ralph E., III:146
McCracken, George E., II:2250
McCree, Mary Lynn, III:3185
McCrum, Blanche P., I:5421; II:2490–91

McCulloch, Champe C., I:2425
McCulloch, Samuel Clyde, II:532
McCusker, Honor, I:3063, 3286
McDaniel, Jane G., II:2738
McDarrah, Fred W., III:1718
MacDermot, Anne, II:948
MacDonald, Augustine S., I:4737
Macdonald, Duncan B., I:540
McDonald, Gerald D., II:2261
MacDonald, Grace E., I:38
McDonald, Jeanne, II:859
McDonald, Murray Frank, III:2315
McDonald, Norma B., I:5416
MacDonald, Pirie, I:2951
McDonald, Rita, III:1702
MacDonald, William, I:4008
McDonogh, John, I:4890
McDonough, John J., III:830, 892, 2713
MacDowd, Kennie, I:4752
MacDowell, Edward, I:3081–82
McDowell, Frederick P. W., III:2232
MacDowell, Lillian I., I:1958
McFarland, Marvin, I:2554, 5542; II:1324, 2094, 2121, 2241
McGarity, Mary Sue, II:1702
McGilvra, John J., III:2560
McGrath, Mary Kathryn, III:645
McGregor, Marylee G., III:3050
McGregor, Tracy W., I:4479; II:2473, 2496
McGrew, Ellen Z., III:798
McGuire, James C., I:1983
Machen, Arthur, III:2195–96
McHenry, James, I:4066
Machinery foundations, I:2478; II:1273
Machinery in industry, I:1594
Machlinia, William de, II:343
McIlwain, Charles H., II:2306
McIlwaine, Henry R., I:4158, 4557
McIntosh, Lacklan, III:2561
McIntyre, Helen, III:3331
Maciunas, Vincas, II:2337
McIver, John, III:2562
Mack, Wilmetta S., III:600
Mackall, Leonard L., II:4804
McKay, Alice A., III:601
McKay, George L., I:9; II:1890; III:2226
McKeen, Newton F., I:778
McKeen, Ona Lee, II:1505
McKelvey, Susan D., II:2322
McKenna, John R., II:1866
McKenna, Muriel, II:1201
McKenzie, Kenneth, I:3727
McKinley, William, III:2563
McKinly, Albert E., I:5141
McKinnell, Bettina, II:466
MacKinney, Loren C., I:4235
McKnight, William A., III:2265
McLaughlin, Andrew C., I:4436
McLay, Hannah H., III:2316
McLean, Hulda Hoover, III:2522
MacLean, John P., I:1189
McLean, M.D., I:5194
McLean, Philip T., I:4189
MacLeisch, Archibald, I:3306–08
McLendon, James H., II:2648
McLeod, Joyce, II:1011
McLeod, Malcolm, I:3103
McManaway, James G., I:671, 3374

McMillan, Audrey Yvonne, II:442
MacMillan, Dougald, I:3365
McMillan, Wendell, II:1365
McMillen, James A., I:322
McMullan, T. N., III:322
McMurtrie, Douglas C., I:323, 410–12, 638,
    712, 720–22, 728–29, 733–37, 740,
    745–47, 751–54, 756–58, 760, 786,
    788–90, 794–95, 799, 805, 810–11,
    819–33, 841–43, 846, 849, 852,
    856, 866, 869–70, 876, 878, 888,
    890, 892–93, 895, 901–02, 910–11,
    940, 1785, 2426, 4697, 4745, 4787–
    88, 4867, 5043; II:237, 426, 432, 435,
    792; III:499, 612
McMurtry, Robert G., I:4041
McNamara, Katherine, II:1454–55
McNay, Ralph R., I:2536
McNeal, Robert H., III:2763
MacNeice, Louis, III:2197
McNeil, Paul A., I:5312
McNiece, Jean, II:869
McNiff, Mary S., II:1795
McNiff, Philip J., II:127
McNutt, John C., I:1690
Macomber, Henry P., II:1053
Macon, Ga., Public Library: early newspapers
    and periodicals, I:305
MacPhail, Ian, III:1385
Macpherson, Harriet D., I:3650
Macpherson, James, I:3401
McRory, Mary O., II:1658
McVey, Ruth Thomas, II:2324
McVoy, Lizzie C., I:3243
Macy, George, II:493
Madagascar, I:4384–85; III:2979
Madan, Falconer, I:672, 3448
Maddox, J. Eric, I:1501; II:2810; III:1067,
    1080–81, 1132, 1178
Madigan, Angela M., II:376
Madison, Charles A., III:498
Madison, Dolly, II:2185
Madison, James, I:4067, 4438; III:2564
Magee, David B., III:2695
Maggot therapy, I:2349
Maggs Bros., London, booksellers, I:2555–
    56, 4558, 4746
Magicians, I:3114
Magnetic recording, I:2487
Magoun, Francis P., I:3498
Magriel, Paul D., I:3104, 3131
Magurn, Ruth S., I:2996; II:1487
Mahan, Alfred T., I:4068
Mahoney, Frances, I:2135
Maichel, Karol, II:214; III:14, 381
Maine, history, I:4892–96; III:3197–98
Maine Genealogical Society, I:4159
Maine State Library: Civil War, III:3087;
    government publications, II:31, III:45;
    law books, I:1702; library resources,
    III:111
Maine, University, Department of History and
    Government: Maine history, I:4895
———Library: Canada, III:2999; periodicals
    and newspapers, III:233
Maitland, Alexander, I:4451
Majakovskij, Vladimir, II:1977
Major, Charles, I:3309

Major, Ralph A., II:1236
Maki, Suiko, III:641
Malaya, I:4358, 5550, III:2828
Malikoff, G. E., I:362
Malleomyces pseudomallei, II:1157
Malloch, Archibald, I:2430
Malone, Miles S., I:5215
Malval, Joseph Fritz, II:2748
Mampoteng, Charles, I:1134
Management, II:657, 837, 844–45, 1413,
    1418; III:870; military, II:877, 883,
    1286
Manchester, Alan K., I:5313
Manchuria, II:2407
Manchus, I:4332
Mandates, I:1352, 1383
Manganese, I:2786
Mangler, Joyce Ellen, II:2161
Mango, I:2602 (29)
Mangosteen, I:2602 (32)
Manhattan College Library: incunabula,
    III:490
Mann, Charles, III:147, 2051
Mann, Thomas, I:3605; II:1616, 1916, 1926;
    III:2238–39
Manning, Mabel M., I:4789
Manny, Elsie S., II:1352
Manpower, I:5563
Manross, William W., II:585
Manucy, Albert C., I:4790
Manufactures, I:2807–28; Soviet Union,
    II:1438
Manuscripts, I:483–548; II:240–76; III:407–
    42; Arabic, I:531–32, 535–38, 540,
    546–47, II:276, 1986–87, III:442;
    Armenian, II:2323, III:439; British,
    I:512; Central European, II:269;
    Greek, I:546, 570, II:2266–68, 2270,
    III:699; illuminated, I:498, 502–04,
    518–30, 566, 568–69, 572, 580,
    3135, 4274, II:265, 267–68, 270–71,
    274, 286, 542, III:464, 1800; Indic,
    I:543, 545–46, 548; Islamic, II:276;
    Italian, II:270; medical, I:2417, 2431,
    2433; medieval, I:484, 496, 498, 502,
    506, II:254, 264–75, 282, 305, 1058,
    III:412, 452, 1499; medieval and
    Renaissance, III:428–38; Mongolian,
    II:2353; Oriental, I:531–48, III:439–
    42; Persian, I:534–35, 537, 544–46,
    II:276; Renaissance, I:496, 506,
    II:254, 264–75, 305, 1058, 1620;
    Spanish, I:492; Turkish, I:535, 537,
    540, 544–45, II:276
Manwaring, Elizabeth W., I:2862
Mao Tse-tung, II:2389
Maps, I:210, 2836, 3822–3934; II:305,
    2017–77; III:2352–2406; African,
    III:2396; Alaska, I:3893; American,
    I:3869–95, II:2052–77, III:2357,
    2382–2406; Boston, I:3896–98;
    California, I:3899–3903, II:2591;
    Canada, II:2053; Costa Rica, III:2364;
    Detroit, I:3904, III:2401; fire
    insurance, III:2397; Florida, I:3905,
    II:2064; Georgia, I:3906; Kentucky,
    I:3907, II:2058; Latin American,
    I:3926–34; maritime, III:2366;

marketing, II:734; Maryland, II:2055,
    2063; Michigan, I:3908–09; New
    Hampshire, III:2389; New Jersey,
    II:2056, III:2388, 2394; New York,
    I:3910–13, III:2392; North Carolina,
    I:3914; Ohio, I:3915; Pacific
    Northwest, I:3890–91, 3894, III:2405;
    Panama, III:2382; Pennsylvania,
    III:2393; Philadelphia, I:3916; Rhode
    Island, I:3917; Southeastern, II:2054,
    III:2385; Texas, III:2400;
    three-dimensional, II:2046, III:2378;
    treasure, II:2047, III:2373; U.S. cities,
    III:2403; Vermont, III:2389; Vineland,
    N.J., I:3918; Virginia, I:3919–22,
    II:2055, 2063, 2075, III:2384;
    Washington, D.C., I:3923–24; West
    Virginia, I:3925
Maquiso, Juanito G., II:56
Marblehead Historical Society: American
    Revolution, I:4559
Marchant, Anyda, I:1737
Marchman, Watt P., II:2142; III:2519
Marcinowski, Constance, III:602
Marco, Guy A., III:1814
Marcoux, Clara W., III:2317
Marcus, Jacob R., II:640
Marietta, Ohio, history, I:5120
Marietta College Library: American history,
    I:4410
Marin, Carmen M., III:1667
Marine atlases, II:2020
Marine Biological Laboratory Library: serials,
    III:1340
Marine biology, II:1025; III:1340
Marine borers, II:1290
Marine engineering, II:1289–93
Marine Historical Association: manuscripts,
    III:3127
———Library: Lawrence & Co., III:924;
    Mallory family, III:925; manuscripts,
    III:926; Talbot, Silas, III:2626
Marine paintings, I:2410
Mariners' Museum: library catalog, III:930;
    maps, III:927; marine photographs,
    III:928; marine prints and paintings,
    III:929
Marino, Samuel J., II:1558; III:369
Maritime history, II:998; III:924–30, 943,
    946, 948, 950–51, 3123
Maritime law, III:1000
Marke, Julius J., II:810
Marketing, II:734; III:896
Markham, Edwin, II:117
Marquette County Historical Society, I:4952
Marriage, I:980, 982
Marriner, Ernest C., I:3278; II:347, 1720
Marsh, George P., I:3216
Marshall, George C., III:2565
Marshall, John, I:4021
Marshall, Thomas M., I:4813
Marshall, William H., III:2148
Marson, Frank M., III:1372
Marston, Thomas E., I:639; II:313–14, 334–
    35, 344; III:1659
Martial law, II:833
Martin, Abbott Waite, III:552
Martin, Carolyn Patricia, III:3232

Martin, Edward F., II:1437
Martin, F. R., I:534
Martin H. Bradley, II:1736
Martin, John E., III:1024
Martin, John H., I:4496
Martin, Joseph W., Jr., III:2566
Martin, Lawrence, I:3825, 3841, 3884–85, 3927–28, 4859
Martin, Mamie R., I:787
Martin, Robert B., II:1869; III:2189
Martin, Roger M., II:1144
Martin, Thomas P., I:1395, 4294, 4437
Martin, William H., I:1786
Martineau, Harriet, I:3494
Martinez, Antonio, II:2186
Martinez, Patricia, III:516
Martinique, I:5362
Martinovitch, Nicholas N., I:535, 544
Marty, André, III:856
Marvin, H. M., III:664
Marx, Alexander, I:640, 1228–29, 1233
Marx, Karl, II:1616
Marx, Moses, II:641
Mary Washington College Library: art and architecture, III:1722; Asian history, III:2795
Maryland, history, I:4897–4914, II:2632–34; III:3199–3201; maps, II:2055, 2063
Maryland Court of Appeals, I:4901
Maryland Hall of Records: archives, I:4906; colonial records, I:4907; county records, II:2633; government publications, II:32; indexes, I:4902, II:2634, III:3199; Quaker records, III:745; state papers, I:4903–05, II:2632
Maryland Historical Society: American Revolution, II:2528; Baltimore and Ohio Railroad, II:994; Baltimore privateers, I:4909; Calvert papers, I:4908; early magazines, I:308; early newspapers, I:404; genealogy, III:2653; library catalog, III:3201; manuscripts, III:3200; Maryland history, I:4912; Maryland State Colonization Society, I:4900; Williams papers, I:4433
Maryland State Colonization Society, I:4900
Maryland State Library: catalog, I:220; Law Dept. catalog, I:1703
Maryland, University, Libraries: paleontology, III:1398; Stephen I, King of Hungary, III:2776
————Medical Library: library history, I:2402; medical history collection, I:2413
Masaryk, Thomas G., I:4069–70
Mascaro, Stephen A., I:1700
Masefield, John, II:1860–61
Maslyn, David C., III:2488
Mason, Alexandra, II:670; III:145
Mason, Elizabeth, III:3072
Mason, Janie E., I:2182, 5476
Mason, Julian D., III:2100
Mason, Philip P., II:768, 925, 952; III:967
Mason, Sara Elizabeth, II:2536
Masonic Library Association (Pa.), I:1942

Massachusetts, history, I:4915–41, II:2635; III:3202
Massachusetts Historical Commission: Timothy Pickering, III:2589
Massachusetts Historical Society, III:3202; American history, I:4438, III:3014; Civil War newspapers, I:4597; early American imprints, I:695, 772; Federalist party, I:1448; Forbes, Francis B., III:2496; Forbes, Robert Bennett, III:2496; handbook, I:4934–35; library catalog, I:4438; Lincoln, Benjamin, III:2554; Mather family, I:4076; New England history, I:4631; New England courant, I:387; Sargent, Winthrop, III:2607; Thomas Dowse library, I:221; Ward, Artemas, III:2638; Waterston papers, I:4438; Western Americana, II:2568
Massachusetts Horticultural Society Library: catalog, I:2606–07, III:1668
Massachusetts Institute of Technology Libraries: archives, II:948; art, II:1447; career literature, II:937; Chinese journals, II:1066, 1218, 2397, III:1549, 1341–42; civil and sanitary engineering theses, I:2536; collections, I:2796; glass industry, I:2796; Lincoln Laboratory Library, III:1377; science, II:1022; serials, II:163, III:1343; whaling prints, I:2964; Yeats, Jack Butler, III:1758
Massachusetts State Board of Agriculture Library: catalog, I:2608
Massachusetts State Library: catalog, I:222; foreign law, I:1747; government publications, III:46–47; legislation, I:1854; taxation, I:1515
Massachusetts, University, Library: African newspapers, III:370; serials, III:234–36
Massey, Linton R., III:2008
Masters, Edgar Lee, III:2042
Masterson, Isabel van Rensselaer, III:2220
Masterson, James R., I:2239, 4492, 5463–64, 5466–67
Maté, I:2628 (16)
Mathematics, I:495, 2158, 2209–28, 2235–36; II:1082–83; III:1292–93, 1566–67; periodicals, I:2206, 2227
Mather, Cotton, I:4072, 4625
Mather, Frank J., I:914, 2911–12
Mather, Increase, I:4073, 4625
Mather family, I:4071–76, 4523
Mathews, Thomas G., II:2749
Mathis, Treva, I:3055
Matica Srpska, III:2792
Matsui, Masato, III:2902, 2908
Matta, Seoud, III:2813
Mattern, Margaret, III:844, 1249
Mattfeld, Julius, I:3067–68
Matthews, Albert, I:324, 2008
Matthews, Brander, I:3205
Matthews, Charles D., I:536, 994
Matthews, Henry M., I:5245
Matthews, Jim P., I:4723
Matthews, Mary A., I:973, 975, 5389
Matthews, Sarah Wood, III:255

Matthews, William, II:2082–84
Maugham, W. Somerset, II:1862
Maumee Valley, I:5124
Maupassant, Guy de, III:2249
Maurer, Geraldine K., III:224
Maurer, Konrad von, I:3624
Maurer, Oscar E., II:219, 1796
Maury, Matthew F., I:4077–78
Mauseth, Viola, II:650, 2488
Maverick, Peter, II:1493
Mavro, Alexander P., II:702–03, 742; III:1063
Maxey, Samuel Bell, III:2567
Maxwell, Richard S., II:1452; III:1116, 2916
Maxwell, Samuel, III:2568
Maxwell, Sarah A., I:4640
Mayan manuscripts, III:408
Mayer, Claudius F., I:2414, 2427
Mayer, Hans, III:3061
Mayhew, George P., III:2228
Mayhew, Isabel, I:4672; II:2577
Maynard, George S., I:2543
Maynard, Julia M., I:4439
Maynard, Rosemary, II:397
Mayo Clinic Library: serials, I:2302
Mazarinades, I:3646
Mazzoni, Guido, III:2253
Meacham, Miriam D., III:633
Mead, Herman R., I:633, 995, 2422; II:336
Mead, Nelson P., I:4765
Meany, Edmund S., I:412, 5511
Mearns, David C., I:4042–44, 4054
Meat industry, I:2633; II:1380–82
Mechanic, Sylvia, III:56
Mecklenberg Declaration of Independence, I:4553
Mecklenberg Library Association: periodicals, III:237
Mecom, Benjamin, I:690
Mecom, Jane, II:2533
Medals, I:5413
Medical illustrations, III:1511
Medical libraries, III:115, 1450–51
Medical Library Association: German periodicals, I:2387; periodicals, III:1539; U.S. health science libraries, III:1451
————Southern Regional Group: periodicals, III:1540
Medical Library Center of New York: periodicals, III:1541; serials, III:1546
Medical portraits, III:1512
Medical prints, I:2434
Medical Society of County of Kings Library: incunabula, I:2428–29
Medicare, III:1465
Medici family, I:2721, 2724
Medicine, I:196, 306, 609, 2343–2434; II:1138–1252; III:1444–1562; aerospace, II:1162, 1172; Arabic, I:2414; aviation, II:1159, 1175; bibliography, III:14; biography, II:1138–39, 1147, 1238; catalogs, II:1203–10; caricatures, II:1244; eclectic, I:2371–72; history, II:1222–52, III:1307, 1389, 1472–1506; illustrations, II:1139, 1148, 1176; Latin American, I:2423; legal,

Medicine *(cont.)*
III:1551; military, I:2351, II:1168–71, 1181, 1220; periodicals, I:2385–2401, II:1211–21, III:293, 1526–62; portraits, II:1239, 1245, 1247; socialization, I:2356, 2358

Medieval history, I:2402–16, 4230–32, 4234–35, 4241, 4243–44, 4257; II:2273–74; III:2282–83, 2685–90

Medieval manuscripts, I:484, 496, 498, 502, 506; II:254, 264–75, 282, 305, 1058; III:412, 428–29, 431–32, 435–37, 452, 1499

Medina, José Toribio, II:475–76

Meehan, Thomas F., I:1177

Meeker, Jotham, I:746; III:2569

Meeks, Bernard, II:2005

Meeks, Carroll L. V., II:1462

Meeks, Leslie Franklin, II:377

Meier, Kathleen, III:2318

Meine, Franklin J., II:1635; III:2082

Meinecke, Bruno, I:2368

Meixell, Granville, I:2686

Mekeel, Arthur J., I:1148

Melioidosis, II:1157

Melish, John, III:2395

Mellen, George F., I:5180

Melville, Herman, I:3310–11; II:1725–30; III:2043

Melvin, Frank E., II:2304, 2310

Memminger, Christopher Gustavus, III:2570

Memphis Librarians' Committee: serials, III:238

Memphis State University Library: Anne Goodwin Winslow, III:2099

Mencken, Henry Louis, II:1731; III:2044–45

Mendeloff, Nathan N., II:451

Mendelsohn, Isaac, I:4200, 4202

Mendenhall, John C., I:3382; II:1781

Mendenhall, Thomas C., I:3843

Mengel, Robert M., II:1128–30

Menk, Patricia H., I:4405

Mennen, William G., II:1845, 1878

Mennonite Church, I:1091–93; II:547–48, 555; III:725

Mennonite Historical Library: catalog, I:1093

Mental illness, II:1158; history, III:1504

Mentally irresponsible persons, III:987

Mercantile Library Assoc. of the City of New York: fiction, I:3196, 3383, 3638; foreign language collection, I:3196, 3638

Mercantile Library of St. Louis: genealogy, I:4156

Mercantile marine subsidies, I:1545

Mercator, Gerhardus, II:2029

Mercer, George, II:2187

Meredith, Edwin T., III:1612

Meredith, George, I:3495; II:1863–64

Mereness, Newton D., I:4709, 5506

Meriwether, James B., II:1691, 1693; III:2006

Merril, Harold, I:1902

Merrill, William S., I:1178

Merriman, Daniel, II:1025

Merritt, Howard S., III:2635

Merritt, Percival, I:700

Merrymount Press, I:773

Mersky, Roy M., II:2103

Merz, Karl, I:3004

Meserve, Frederick H., I:4045

Meserve, Walter J., II:1583, 1732

Metallurgy, II:1277; III:1697–98

Metals, I:2793; II:1427, 1430–31, 1433–36

Metcalf, Frank J., I:1048–49

Metcalf, Jessie L., I:2301

Metcalf, Keyes D., I:1234; II:108–09

Meteorology, I:2294–95; II:1090–94; III:1372–74, 1567

Methodist Church, I:556, 1094–98; II:556–57; III:726–32

Metropolitan Museum of Art Library: book design, I:941; catalog, II:1448, III:1719; Italian woodcuts, I:2965; Japanese illustrations, I:2913; Junior Museum Library, III:1710; LaFontaine, Jean de, I:3652; Latin American art, I:2841; museums and museology, I:2170; Nizami manuscript, I:534; Persian manuscripts, I:537

Mettee, Andrew H., I:1699

Metzdorf, Robert F., I:509; II:252, 1804, 1885, 1900

Metzgar, Judson D., I:2963

Metzger, Ethel M., I:857

Mexican Americans, I:1372; III:823, 2929

Mexican literary journals, III:2267

Mexican War, I:4588, 5197

Mexico: constitution, II:2741; government publications, I:48; history, I:5299, 5314, 5318, 5369, II:2691, 2732–45, III:3138, 3268, 3296, 3371–87; literature, I:3694, 3696, 3703, 3716–19; literary journals, III:2267

Meyer, Herman H. B., I:1497, 2687, 2818, 2824, 3529, 4580

Meyer-Baer, Kathi, I:3020

Meyers, Charles L., I:2941

Mezzotints, I:2958, 2971

Miami Public Library: Floridiana, II:2600

Miami, University, Library: chemistry serials, II:1062; research resources, II:77

Miami University Library (Oxford, Ohio): Davis, Jefferson, III:2476; Ohio Valley history, I:5123

Mica, I:2279

Michel, Julian G., III:3308

Michelmore, G. W., I:2557

Michigan: history, I:4942–59, II:2636–45, III:3203–14; maps, I:3908–09

Michigan Board of Registration in Medicine, III:1487

Michigan Boys' Vocational School, III:1240

Michigan Bureau of Library Services: Michigan history, III:3205–06

Michigan Children's Institute, III:1243

Michigan Constitutional Convention, III:1070

Michigan Dept. of Aeronautics, III:1590

Michigan Dept. of Conservation, Geological Survey Division: cartographic records, III:1399

———Lands Division: cartographic records, III:2391

Michigan Dept. of Economic Development, III:906

Michigan Dept. of Education, Bureau of Library Services: newspapers, III:324

Michigan Dept. of Mental Health, III:1488

Michigan Dept. of Public Instruction, III:1242

Michigan Dept. of State: archives, I:4953

Michigan Executive Dept.: archives, I:4954

Michigan Girls' Training School, III:1241

Michigan Historical Commission: education manuscripts, II:925; Executive Office records, III:1072; government records, III:3208; Grand Army of the Republic, III:3088; manuscripts, III:3209; Michigan bibliography, I:4955; Michigan census, III:797; military history, III:1146; research collections, III:3207

Michigan Pioneer and Historical Society: Great Lakes region maps, I:3881; Michigan history, II:2641

Michigan Social Welfare Dept., III:1230

Michigan State Highway Dept., III:931

Michigan State Library: catalog, I:223; education of emotionally disturbed, III:1244; florists, III:1669; genealogy, I:4160; government publications, II:33, III:48; Law Dept. catalog, I:1704; Michigan books, II:2642; municipal government, I:1881; public archives, I:4959

Michigan State Planning Commission, III:907

Michigan State Prison, III:1231

Michigan State University Library: African collection, III:2934; Asian publications, III:2796; Douglas McMurtrie collection, III:499; early Western journalism, II:237; Latin American periodicals, III:371; Michigan history, III:3210; Negroes, III:831; serials, III:239; veterinary medicine history, II:1237

Michigan Turnpike Authority, III:932

Michigan, University, Asia Library: Asian publications, II:2356, 2797; Chinese collection, III:2885; Chinese gazetteers, III:2884; Chinese periodicals, III:372; Japanese bibliography, III:2903; Japanese local studies, III:2904–05

———Audio-Visual Education Center: catalog, I:3105

———Bureau of Industrial Relations: labor union periodicals, II:776

———Committee on Scientific Resources: serials, II:1069

———Law Library: periodicals, II:822, III:1042

———Libraries: Algeria, III:2946; Asian collections, II:2356–57; astronomy, I:2235; atomic power, II:1097; Bible, I:1029–31; Carlyle, Thomas, I:3444; collections, II:110; Dante, Alighieri, I:3683; Elzevir imprints, II:317; engineering, I:2464; folklore, II:1006; German archives, II:2297; German Foreign Ministry, II:2296; incunabula, I:641–42; insects, III:1439; Japan, II:2414; juvenile literature, III:2319; labor, I:1574; Maine history, I:4896;

Maltese printing, I:911; manuscripts, I:4947, III:440; mathematics, I:2235; medical history, II:1242; Mexican printing, I:903; Mexicana, II:2737; Michigan history, I:4956–57; military history, I:5393; Morocco, III:2947; mycology, I:2319; natural history serials, II:1067; Negroes, III:832; ostraca, I:4198, 4207; papyri, I:4206–10, III:440; polar collection, II:2764; Rau, Karl H., II:721; science serials, III:1344; Soviet science, II:1069; Spanish drama, I:3688; special collections, I:136, II:280; Stellfeld music library, II:1518–19, 1537–38, 1554; Swift, Jonathan, I:3551; theater collection, II:1586; Trollope, Anthony, II:1902–03; World War II, III:3413; zoology, I:2329

———Michigan Historical Collections: collections, II:2643, III:3212; early music books, II:1545; manuscripts, III:3211; natural resources conservation, III:864; Staebler papers, II:971; White, Andrew Dickson, II:2229

———School of Business Administration: resources, II:727

———William L. Clements Library, II:2482; Adams, Randolph G., III:2426; American drama, I:3234–35; American history, I:4395, 4406, 4440–46, 4504, 4518, III:3015; American Revolution, I:4533, 4560–67; Americana, II:2472; astronomy, II:1086; atlases, I:3844; British East Florida, I:4791; Canadian history, I:4390, 4392; Congregational Church, I:1077; Diaz, Porfirio, II:2732; early American printing, I:701–02; early printing, I:583; education, III:1245; English history, I:4267; facsimiles and forgeries, I:3210, II:290; Franklin, Benjamin, I:3983; Franklin passports, I:684; Grotius, Hugo, I:1807; Hamtramck, John Francis, II:2138; Harmar, Josiah, II:2138; historical hoaxes, I:3211; Hudson, William Henry, I:4006; ichthyology and herpetology, I:2338; Jefferson, Thomas, I:4013; Jesuits, I:4517; legal treasures, II:795; Lincoln, Abraham, I:4052–53; manuscript collections, II:253; maps, I:3879, 3886–89, II:2060; mathematics, I:2217; Maumee Valley (Ohio) history, I:5124; Mexico, conquest, I:5314; Michigan history, I:4958, II:2644; military history, I:5396; naval history, II:901; Negro history, III:833; Northwest Territory, I:4661; Ohio history, II:2667; Paine, Thomas, I:4087; Pennsylvania history, I:5148; Peru, conquest, I:5315; Pontiac, Indian chief, I:4493; Pontiac's War, III:3034; Presbyterian Church, I:1114; Roanoke colony, I:4516; Shelburne manuscripts, I:4248; South Carolina history, I:5171; Swedish in

Delaware, I:4770; Texas history, I:5195; Thomas, Isaiah, I:779; Virginia history, I:5213; War of 1812, III:3071; Western history, III:3148

Microbiology, II:1116
Microforms, I:12; II:1, 3, 6, 9, 98; III:9, 11, 15, 16
Microscopy, II:1150; III:1435
Mid-Appalachia College Council: periodicals, III:240
Middle East, II:2338, 2363, 2365; III:2809–23
Middlebury College Library: American literature, I:3256, 3261–62
Middleton, Arthur, II:2188
Middleton, J. E., I:4388
Middleton, Thomas C., I:1179
Midkiff, Jessie T., III:1174, 1213
Midland Terminal Railway Company, II:990
Midwest history, I:4646–53; II:2550–52
Midwest Inter-Library Center: Chemical abstracts project, II:1103; foreign newspapers, II:210
Midwest Regional Medical Library: medical history, III:1489
Milam, Carl H., I:1970
Milczewski, M. A., II:811
Miles, Ida R., II:1026
Milhollen, Hirst, I:1919, 4236, 4610; III:3103
Military administration, I:5420
Military biography, II:2088
Military conscription, I:5389
Military engineering, I:2470; II:1282–88
Military government, I:1828
Military history, I:5387–5495; II:900–912, 2805; III:1141–1226
Military law, I:5399
Military pensions, I:1867
Military science, I:2183, 2448; II:877–914; III:1141–1226
Military training, I:5391
Milkweeds, I:2598 (2)
Mill, John Stuart, II:1797
Millard, Alice, I:591
Millard, George, I:591
Millay, Edna St. Vincent, II:1732
Miller, Arthur, III:2046
Miller, C. William, I:680; II:283
Miller, Charles C., I:2639
Miller, Daniel, I:413–14
Miller, Dayton C., I:3021
Miller, Dorothy P., I:1406
Miller, E. Willard, II:2030
Miller, Edwin H., II:1764
Miller, Fred L., III:1066
Miller, George J., I:806
Miller, Joaquin, I:113
Miller, John Carl, II:1738
Miller, Nyle, II:2621
Miller, Perry, II:2553
Miller, Rosalind S., II:1764
Miller, Ruby M., II:2030
Miller, Samuel, II:1733; III:2571
Miller, William E., III:1874
Miller, Winlock W., Jr., II:2578
Milligan, Louise M., II:949
Millington, Yale O., I:415
Mills, George J., II:1449

Mills, Gordon H., II:1724, 1727
Mills, Hazel E., II:2673; III:3160
Mills, Helen M., I:5128–29
Mills College Library: Bender collection, I:598
Milnar, Virginia, II:443
Milojević, Borivoje Z., II:2049
Milstead, Mabel P., III:1172
Milton, George Fort, II:2189
Milton, John, I:233–34, 3496–99; II:1865; III:2198–99
Milwaukee County Historical Society: archives, III:3280
Milwaukee Municipal Reference Library: periodicals, I:325
Milwaukee Public Library: Great Lakes shipping, II:999
Miner, Dorothy E., I:498
Miner, Edward G., II:1224
Mineral resources, I:2499
Mineral wool, I:2463
Mineralogy, New Jersey, I:2284
Miniature books, I:590, 638
Minick, Amanda Rachel, II:408
Minimum wage, I:1603, 1609, 1615
Mining, I:2499; II:1277
Mink, Arthur D., I:427
Mink, James V., III:2408, 2604
Minneapolis, history, I:4969
Minneapolis Public Library: Minneapolis history, I:4969; Scandinavian literature, I:3631
Minnesota: government publications, I:32–33; history, I:4960–72, II:1504, 2646–47
Minnesota Historical Society: account books, I:4660; almanacs, I:4695; American Indians, III:3035; Brady photographs, II:1504; business history, II:2735; Dight papers, I:4674; Donnelly, Ignatius, III:2480; farmers' diaries, I:4964; government publications, I:32–33, III:49; home missions, I:1052; library catalog, I:4966; manuscripts, II:2646–47; Minnesota history, I:4972; Mississippi Valley, I:4967; music collection, I:3061; National Nonpartisan League, III:810; Neill papers, I:4962; newspapers, III:325; personal papers, I:4965; political science, III:802; Sioux missionaries, I:4971; Swedish immigration, I:4673; Taliaferro, Lawrence, III:2627; Taylor, James Wickes, III:2628
———Forest Products History Foundation: manuscripts, I:2653
Minnesota State Library: government publications, III:50; law books, I:1705
Minnesota, University, Biomedical Library: serials, III:1542
———Dept. of Audio-Visual Extension: 16mm films, III:1792
———Immigrant Archives: Ukrainian literature, III:2751
———Libraries: American newspapers, I:416–17; Bell, James Ford, II:2061–62, 2522–27; Bering Strait, II:2062; biology serials, I:2302; children's literature, II:2007; detective fiction,

Minnesota, University, Libraries *(cont.)*
    III: 1937; dime novels, II: 1659;
    economic history, III: 908–11; English
    history, I: 4268–69; Greek linguistics,
    III: 1917; immigration studies, III: 2423;
    James Ford Bell collection, III: 908–
    11; juvenile literature, III: 2320, 2323,
    2325; Loan Play Library, II: 1584;
    maps, II: 2031, 2061–62; newspapers,
    III: 326; rare books, III: 457; science
    serials, II: 1070; social science
    periodicals, I: 1257; South Asia,
    II: 2380–81, III: 2831–32; special
    collections, II: 280; World War II
    periodicals, I: 326
——Middle East Library: accessions,
    III: 2814
——Social Welfare Archives: collections,
    III: 1232; settlements and neighborhood
    centers, III: 1227; Survey Associates
    papers, III: 1228
Minniear, John Mohr, III: 1815
Minoan inscriptions, II: 2269
Minstrels, I: 3097; II: 1581
Mint Museum of Art Library: ceramics,
    III: 1696
Mires, Austin, III: 2572
Mish, Charles C., II: 1779
Mish, John L., II: 2382
Missar, Charles, II: 428
Missionary Research Library: Africa,
    III: 2943; catalog, III: 717;
    dissertations, III: 715; missions,
    I: 1054; periodicals, III: 716
Missions, I: 1051–55; II: 529–38; III: 712–18;
    African, III: 2933; American Indian,
    II: 560, 562, 570; Moravian, II: 560–
    62; Presbyterian, II: 570, 573–74;
    Protestant Episcopal, II: 587; Roman
    Catholic, II: 619
Mississippi, history, I: 4973–81; II: 2648;
    III: 3215
Mississippi delta, I: 2602 (40)
Mississippi Dept. of Archives and History:
    Civil War, II: 2539, III: 3073, 3089;
    collections, I: 4977; newspapers and
    pamphlets, I: 4976
Mississippi Historical Society, I: 4980–81
Mississippi River, I: 4652
Mississippi Secretary of State: government
    publications, III: 51
Mississippi State Library: catalog, I: 224
Mississippi, University, Library: lumber
    industry, II: 1406; Mississippi history,
    I: 4981
Mississippi Valley, I: 3888, 4652, 4663, 4967
Missouri, history, 4683, 4982–89; II: 2649–
    51
Missouri Baptist Historical Society:
    manuscripts, I: 1061
Missouri Botanical Garden Library: serials,
    I: 363; Sturtevant Prelinnean collection,
    I: 2323–24
Missouri Historical Society: acquisitions,
    II: 2649; Americana, II: 2650;
    genealogy, I: 4156; glass negatives,
    II: 1503
Missouri Library Association: serials, I: 327

Missouri State Historical Society: early
    imprints, I: 792; Missouri travel,
    I: 4987; newspapers, I: 418, III: 327;
    Western Americana, I: 4683
Missouri State Library: government
    publications, II: 34, III: 52; serials,
    III: 241
——Law Dept.: catalog, I: 1706
Missouri, University, Library (Columbia):
    Flack collection, I: 123; library science,
    III: 82; Punjab literature, III: 2830;
    Thomas Moore Johnson collection,
    I: 952; Western Americana, I: 4683
——(Kansas City): Missouri imprints,
    III: 580
Mitchell, Eleanor Drake, II: 457, 1384
Mitchell, Eleanor M., I: 1588
Mitchell, John, I: 3884–85
Mitchell, Philip Marshall, II: 481
Mitchell, Thornton W., I: 5462
Mitchell, William, I: 4079
Mittman, Sadie S., III: 949
Mix, David E. E., I: 3845
Mizener, Arthur, I: 3308; II: 1695, 1845
Mobility, military, II: 888
Mock, James R., I: 1396
Modern Language Association of America:
    manuscripts and rare books, I: 499–
    500
——American Literature Group:
    manuscripts, II: 1638
Moenkemeyer, Heinz, II: 1921
Moffit, Alexander, I: 743
Moghadam, Mohamad E., I: 545
Mohammedanism, I: 1252–53; II: 650
Mohr, Carolyn Curtis, II: 995
Moid, Abdul, III: 2833
Molière, Jean B., I: 3653, 3655
Moll, Wilhelm, II: 378
Moloney, Louis, III: 1361
Molyneaux, John L., III: 2547
Monaghan, Frank, I: 4123, 4452; III: 3017
Monaghan, James, I: 4046
Monaghan, Jay, II: 2164
Monell, Gary Elwyn, III: 1062
Money, I: 1476–1503
Mongan, Elizabeth, I: 2980
Mongolia, I: 4333
Mongolian literature, I: 3791
Mongolian manuscripts, II: 2353
Monitor and Merrimac, III: 3075
Monmouth County Historical Association:
    newspapers, I: 419
Monnette, Orra Eugene, II: 2249
Monongahela Valley, West Va., I: 5250
Monrad, Anna M., I: 1046, 1078
Monroe, James, I: 4080–81, 4438; II: 2190;
    III: 2573–74
Monroe doctrine, I: 1407, 1414
Monsanto Chemical Company Library: serials,
    II: 168
Montague, Gilbert H., II: 1309
Montaigne, Michel E. de, I: 3654–55
Montana, history, I: 4990–93
Montana Historical Society Library: catalog,
    I: 4992
Montana State Library, Law Dept.: catalog,
    I: 1707

Montana State University: government
    publications, II: 35
Montesquieu, Charles de S., I: 3656
Montessori, Maria, I: 2027
Montgomery, James, III: 3309
Montgomery, John W., II: 520, 541
Montignani, John B., I: 2841
Mood, Fulmer, I: 138; II: 111
Moody, Katharine T., I: 4161
Moody, Margaret, III: 1060
Moon, Charles F., II: 1230
Mooney, James E., III: 506
Mooney, Philip F., III: 1941
Moore, Geoffrey, II: 1835
Moore, Helen-Jean, II: 933
Moore, John, I: 3119
Moore, John H., III: 112
Moore, John Robert, II: 1826
Moore, John Trotwood, III: 2575
Moore, Julia A., I: 3312
Moore, Lillian, III: 1884, 1887
Moore, Mary T., II: 2628
Moore, Norman D., III: 1087, 1098, 1303,
    3271
Moore, Sue, II: 1816
Moore, Thomas, I: 4082
Morales, Phylliss, III: 2321
Moran, Leila P., II: 1076
Moran, Robert F., III: 622
Morand, Julia P. M., I: 1085
Moravian Church, I: 1099–1101, 5093;
    II: 558–62; III: 733; Archives,
    Bethlehem, Pa., II: 558–59, 561–62
More, Hannah, I: 997
More, Paul Elmer, III: 2047
More, Thomas, I: 3500; III: 2200
Moreland, Ellen D., III: 237
Moreland, Sara L., III: 1450, 1489
Morey, Charles R., I: 521
Morgan, Bayard O., I: 3591–92
Morgan, Dale L., II: 565–66, 2196; III: 3139,
    3149
Morgan, George, I: 4083
Morgan, J. Pierpont, I: 2922
Morgan, James D., I: 1165
Morgan, Katherine L., I: 466, 2206
Morgan, Morris H., I: 3728
Morgan, Paula, III: 1802
Morgan, S. Rowland, I: 962; II: 512
Mori, Hiroshi, III: 2904
Moriarty, John H., I: 4181
Morison, Samuel E., I: 2009, 4937, 5216
Morison, Stanley, I: 2917
Morize, André, I: 462, 3644
Morley, Charles, II: 2325
Morley, Christopher, I: 3313; III: 2048–50
Morley, James William, II: 2415
Mormon Church, I: 1102, 1212; II: 563–69,
    2699; III: 734; history, III: 3258
Morris, Raymond P., III: 691
Morris, Richard B., I: 4509, 5044; II: 2521;
    III: 3414
Morris, Richard T., II: 1101
Morris, William, I: 572, 605, 676;
    II: 490
Morrison, Hugh A., I: 445, 2114, 3190, 4611,
    4698, 4706
Morrison, Julia M., III: 1926

Morrison, Sibyl, II:2694

Morrissey, Eleanor F., III:1337

Morristown National Historical Park: manuscripts, III:426, 3061

Morrogh, Charles A., I:673

Morrow, John J., II:2444

Morsch, Lucile M., I:803, 807

Morse, Carleton D., II:726

Morse, Samuel French, II:1645

Morse, Willard S., I:113, 2914, 3336

Morse, William I., I:3348, 4389

Mortimer, Ruth, III:647

Morton, J. Sterling, III:2576

Mose, H. Einar, I:2166, 2347

Moseley, Elizabeth, II:1188

Moseley and Motley, I:2734

Mosely, Philip E., II:2326

Moser, Gerald M., II:2313

Moses, Richard G., III:2322

Mosher, Frederic J., I:15; II:238

Mosimann, Jeanne Denyse, II:456

Moskowitz, Harry, II:1286; III:1154

Moss, Roger W., Jr., III:1388

Mostecky, Vaclav, II:2327; III:888, 1052, 1061

Mote, Frederick W., II:2401

Mothers' clubs, I:1976

Mothers' pensions, I:1922

Motherwell, Sarah M., II:913

Motor fuels, I:2598 (10)

Motor transport, I:2035, 2136–37

Mott, David C., I:420

Mott, Frank L., I:480, 4846

Mott, Howard S., III:2136

Mott, Margaret M., I:3064

Mount, Huston Ellis, II:1434–35

Mount Athos, II:581

Mount Holyoke College Library: serials, III:234

Mountain Plains Educational Media Council: film catalog, III:1793

Mountaineers, I:1342, 2599 (28)

Mounteer, Honor, III:603

Moving pictures, I:1978, 2722, 3086, 3090, 3102, 3105, 3117–18; II:1574–77, 1582, 1587–89

Mowat, Charles L., I:4791

Moxon, Joseph, II:497

Mozart, Wolfgang Amadeus, III:1863

Mudd, Seeley W., Foundation, I:956

Mudge, Isadore G., I:90

Mugridge, Donald H., I:1836, 3984, 4615, 5420; II:2112, 2144, 2489, 2491, 2548; III:2419, 3062, 3101, 3103

Muir, John, III:2577

Mulcahey, Jasmine H., III:379

Mulhauser, Margaret, II:1791

Mulkearn, Lois, II:2187, 2683

Muller, Joseph, I:3065

Muller, Violette K., III:553

Mullins, Patrick Joseph, II:615

Multhauf, Robert P., II:1046; III:1274

Mumey, Nolie, I:5274

Munckmeyer, Charlotte, II:2070

Munden, Kenneth, I:5363, 5366–67, 5379; III:1737, 1908, 3106, 3343, 3386

Mundle, George F., III:964

Municipal law, II:873

Munk, Joseph A., I:4717–18

Munn, Robert F., II:2710; III:344, 1405, 3133

Munro, Isabel S., I:2942

Munsterberg, Margaret, I:3583, 3729, 5284

Muntz, Philip, III:3205

Murphy, Edgar Gardner, III:2578

Murphy, Francis, II:2008

Murphy, Henry T., III:1415

Murphy, Katherine, II:937

Murphy, Kathryn M., III:1094–96, 1122–23, 2508, 2783, 3344

Murra, Kathrine O., I:2016, 2025, 2178

Murray, C. Fairfax, I:2918

Murray, Deborah, III:1054

Murray, Keith, I:5241

Murrie, Eleanore B., I:3007

Muscle Shoals, I:2485, 2493

Museum Book Store, London, I:3872–73, 4447, 4568

Museum of Graphic Art: American prints, III:1766

Museum of the American Indian (New York), II:2737

Museums, I:2157, 2170; New York, III:1718

Mushabac, Ruth L., I:2996

Mushrooms, I:2601 (20)

Music, I:203, 234, 549, 552, 3000–85; II:114, 254, 1512–72; III:1795–1872; Afroamerican, III:1840; American, I:3051–85, III:1849–60; Burmese, II:1531; California, I:3052, 3066; education, I:3008, II:1517; libraries, I:3019, III:1811; manuscripts, III:464; Moravian, I:3069; Oriental, I:3035, 3040; periodicals, II:1564, III:1844–48; Portuguese, I:3025; prints, III:1796; religious, I:1047–50; therapeutics, I:2352

Music Library Association, Southern California Chapter: California music, I:3066

————Northern California Chapter: music periodicals, III:1846

Muskhogean languages, I:3182

Muss-Arnolt, William I:1118

Myers, Denys P., I:1808

Myers, Irene T., I:4868

Myrice, Mary Jane, III:3240

Mysticism, II:544

Naas, Bernard G., II:777

Nachbin, Jac, I:5316

Nadela, Ernestina C., III:1914

Naftalin, Mortimer L., III:1632–33

Nakayama, Yoshi, II:1343

Nall, Mabel Lexton, II:1147

Names, personal, I:4174; III:2254

Napoleon Bonaparte, I:4084–85, 4280, 4283; II:2300, 2309–10; III:2579

Narcotic habit, II:1149

Nasatir, Abraham P., III:1062

Nash, Gary B., III:2525

Nash, Ray, I:674, 800, 2024, 3285; II:1469–70, 1488; III:1944

Nashville, Chattanooga and St. Louis Railway, I:2060

National Academy of Design: library catalog, I:2927

National Academy of Sciences: scientific and technical societies, III:1288

National Association of State Libraries: government publications, I:34

National banks, I:1501

National bibliography, I:4

National Broadcasting Co.: dramatic scripts, I:3106

National Bureau of Casualty and Surety Underwriters Library: insurance, I:1946

National Carbon Co.: technical periodicals, I:2447

National Civil Service League, III:1074

National defense, I:72, 2087, 5391, 5394, 5411, 5417–18; II:846, 881, 887, 893–95, 1287

National Federation of Settlements and Neighborhood Centers, III:1227

National Gallery of Art: Georgia history, I:4808; Iowa centennial, I:4848; LaFontaine, Jean de, I:3652; Minnesota history, I:4970; Utah exhibition, I:5205; Wisconsin centennial, I:5267

National Genealogical Society: Long Island genealogy, III:2656

National Grange of the Patrons of Husbandry: records, III:1609

National Nonpartisan League, III:810

National parks, I:2870; III:1112

National planning, I:5446

National Research Council: astronomy, mathematics and physics, I:2236; biology, I:2303; chemistry, I:2265; geology and geography, I:2283; psychology serials, I:960; scientific groups, I:2171

National Science Foundation: science information services, III:1289

National Socialist Party, German, I:53

National Society of the Colonial Dames of America—Connecticut: Connecticut houses, I:2889

National union catalog, III:186–90

National Women's Trade Union League of America, II:778

Nationalism, I:1353

Natural resources, I:1504–08, 1537, 1570

Nauvoo, Illinois, I:4818

Naval architecture, I:2503, 5454

Naval history and science, I:2183, 2448, 5447–75, 5501; II:901, 909–14, 2805; III:1218–26

Naval History Society, I:5447, 5452

Nave, Andrew, II:2499

Navigation, I:2242–44; III:1370

Nazarene, Church, I:1194

Neafie, Nellie, III:2436

Near East, II:2362, 2364; III:2809–23

Neavill, Helen Aldena, III:560

Nebraska: authors, I:3259; history, I:4994–97, II:2623, 2652, III:3216–17

Nebraska Farmers' Alliance, III:811

Nebraska State Historical Society: archives and manuscripts, II:2652, III:3216–17; Chapman, Samuel M., III:2460; Furnas, Robert W., III:2501; Maxwell,

Nebraska State Historical Society (cont.)
    Samuel, III:2568; Morton, J. Sterling,
    III:2576; Nebraska Farmers' Alliance,
    III:811; newspapers, III:328
Nebraska State Library: catalog, I:225
Nebraska, University, College of Medicine
    Library: obstetrics and gynecology,
    II:1230
——Libraries: business periodicals, III:893;
    Nebraska authors, I:3259
Nece, Bernice M., III:1816
Needham, Wesley E., II:1985
Needlework, I:2929
Nef, Evelyn S., III:3399
Nef, John U., II:2306
Negley, Glenn, III:815
Negro authors, I:3265
Negroes, I:1385–1403; II:678–85, 2555;
    III:817–51, 2929–30; in armed
    services, I:5421; periodicals, III:840,
    851
Neiderheiser, Clodaugh M., II:1400
Neidinger, Maxine F., III:428
Neill, Wilfred T., II:2599
Neinken, Mortimer, II:2261
Neiswender, Rosemary, III:2755
Nekritz, Leah K., III:587
Nelen, Eleanor W., I:3730
Nelick, Franklyn C., II:348, 1912, 2110
Nelson, Cecil P., II:409
Nelson, Charles A., I:1950, 1998
Nelson, Dale, II:1879
Nelson, Horatio, I:4086
Nelson, Karen, III:2323
Nelson, William, I:421, 5010–12
Nemec, Dolores, III:1562
Nemec, Jaroslav, III:1551
Nemoy, Leon, I:538, 1235–37, 1249–50;
    II:344, 1986–87
Nepal, III:2828; publications, III:2920
Nerboso, Salvatore D., I:1597
Nesbitt, Alexander, III:1777
Netherland East Indies, I:4193 (12), 5386
Netherlands, history, I:4193 (3), 4443;
    III:2720–21
Netherlands Museum: Dutch in Holland,
    Mich., III:3213
Neu, John A., III:1314, 1389, 2712
Neubeck, Deborah K., III:810
Neuburger, Otto, I:53
Neurology, I:2394
Neustadt, Margaret Lee, III:2437, 2520,
    2541, 2578, 2583, 2624, 2640
Neutrality, I:1820
Nevada, history, I:4998–99; III:3150, 3218–
    21
Nevada Division of Archives, III:3218
Nevada State Library: catalog, I:226–27;
    government publications, II:36, III:53;
    Nevada history, III:3219
Nevada, University, Library: Burns, Robert,
    III:2147; Nevada history, III:3220;
    Western history, III:3150
Nevin, Ethelbert, II:1571
Nevins, Allan, III:3090
New Almaden Museum Library (California):
    catalog, III:173
New Bedford Free Public Library: catalog,

I:228; printing history, I:942; whales,
    I:2592
New Castle, Delaware, II:2594
New England, history, I:4624–33; II:2553;
    III:3123–27
New England Assoc. of Chemistry Teachers
    Library: catalog, I:2266
New England Board of Higher Education:
    microfilm collections, III:9
New England courant, I:387
New England Emigrant Aid Company,
    III:3191
New England Historic Genealogical Society
    Library: French heraldry, I:4163;
    Massachusetts history, I:4924
New England History Teachers' Assoc.,
    I:3846
New England Library Information Network:
    microfilm collections, III:9
New England primer, I:693, 697
New Hampshire: government publications,
    I:35; history, I:5000–04
New Hampshire State Library: catalog, I:229;
    government publications, I:35, II:37,
    III:54; New Hampshire history, I:5004
New Harmony, Ind., I:4832, 4837; II:2613
New Harmony Workingmen's Institute
    Library: New Harmony history, I:4837
New Haven Free Public Library: juvenile
    literature, I:3810
New Jersey: history, I:5005–14, II:2653–54,
    III:3222–25; maps, II:2056
New Jersey Archives and History Bureau:
    county archives, III:3222; municipal
    archives, III:3223
New Jersey Historical Society Library:
    genealogy, I:4164; manuscripts,
    II:2653; Newark imprints, I:802;
    railroads, II:984, 986; Stevens family,
    III:2623
New Jersey Library Association: Negroes,
    III:834; special collections, I:93
New Jersey, Secretary of State, I:5012
New Jersey State College Library (Trenton):
    New Jersey history, III:3224
New Jersey State Library: genealogy, III:2657;
    government publications, III:55; New
    Jersey history, I:5006, 5010
New Mexico, history, I:5015–21; II:2655–
    56; III:3226
New Mexico Historical Society: Southwest,
    history, I:5018
New Mexico State Records Center: Spanish
    archives, III:3226
New Mexico, University, Libraries:
    Luso-Brazilian collection, III:3331;
    manuscripts, II:2656; New Mexico
    history, II:2656; New Mexico
    newspapers, I:422; serials, I:328
——School of Medicine Library: catalog,
    III:1509
New Orleans Library Club: New Orleans
    libraries, I:94
New Orleans Public Library: fiction, I:3197
New Sweden, I:4770–72
New York: government publications, I:37;
    history, I:4634, 5022–89, II:2657–
    61, III:3227–30; maps, I:3910–13

New York Academy of Medicine Library:
    catalog, I:2373, III:1510; Davis
    collection, III:1444; dentistry, I:2353;
    illustrations, II:1148, III:1511;
    manuscripts and incunabula, I:2431;
    medical Americana, I:2430; medical
    biography, II:1238–39; medical
    history, II:1222; narcotics, II:1149;
    portraits, III:1512
New York Botanical Garden Library:
    botanists, biography, III:1428
New York City, history, I:1463, 5053–60,
    5080–81, 5085, 5089
New York College of the City of New York
    Library: Judaica, I:1238
New York City Council of Higher Educational
    Institutions: library directory, II:74
New York College of Pharmacy: library
    catalog, I:2369
New York Division of Archives and History:
    education, III:1246
New York Historical Society Library:
    American artists, II:1450; American
    Fur Company, I:4593; American
    history, III:3018; American
    Revolution, I:4579; Americana,
    I:4449, 4480, 4519; Bryant, William
    Cullen, II:1673; business history,
    I:2699; city directories, I:4183; early
    newspapers, I:442; Erskine, Robert,
    I:4552; Florida newspapers, I:406;
    Franco-American relations, II:708;
    Fulton, Robert, I:3991; Gallatin,
    Albert, I:3992; Green, Thomas, I:723;
    Hartford, Conn., imprints, I:723;
    Hawks-Niblo collection, I:4448; John
    McComb drawings, III:1743; Latin
    Americana, I:5317; Lawrence, James,
    I:4023–24; lottery collection, I:1503;
    Manhattan maps, I:3913; naval history,
    I:5447, 5452; New York history,
    I:5045–51; New York newspapers,
    I:384, 388; Pirie MacDonald portraits,
    I:2951; trade cards, I:2775; Trinity
    Church, I:1135
New York Law Institute: library catalog,
    I:1708; library history and resources,
    I:1787
New York Library Association: European
    history, I:4237; indexes, I:10
New York Mercantile Library Association:
    catalog, I:230
New York, New Haven and Hartford
    Railroad, I:2095
New York Public Library: aborigines, I:2310;
    aeronautics, I:2553; Aesop, II:1980;
    African history, I:4371, 4376; Age of
    Queen Anne, II:2286; Aldine imprints,
    II:323; Aleut language, III:3187;
    almanacs, I:4700; American
    Colonization Society, I:1397;
    American drama, I:3236; American
    history, I:4450–54, 4520–22, 4569–
    71, 4710, II:2262, III:3019; American
    imprints, II:357, 359; American
    literature, II:1636, 1787, III:1955,
    1959, 2113–15; American music,
    III:1850; American newspapers, I:423;

American poetry, I:3224–25; American political parties, I:1449; Americana, II:2479; Amhara history, I:4368; Arabian history, I:4369; Arabic literature, I:3770; Arents tobacco collection, II:1383, 1386; Armenia, I:4213; art auctions, I:2842; Arturo Toscanini archives, III:1838; asbestos, I:2465; Assyria, I:4214; Astor Library, I:231–32, 3796; athletics, I:3131–34; Atlantic neptune, I:2124; author as artist, III:1759; automobile tires, I:2542; Avery, S. P., I:2970; Babylonian history, I:4214; Bailey, Philip J., I:3423; Balkan States, I:4238; Baltic periodicals, I:464; baseball, I:3134; batteries, I:2543; Beaumarchais, Pierre, I:3650; beggars, I:1921; Bennett, Arnold, III:2137; Berg collection, I:3400, II:1622–23; Bible in literature, I:3368; Bibles, I:1034, 1037, II:526, III:708; Biddle, George, lithographs, II:1489; Blake, William, II:1809; blind impressions, II:312; book design, I:921–22, 943; book deterioration, I:61, 63; book illustrations, I:915–17; books in parts, II:1627, 1786, III:1927; botany, III:1429; boxing, I:3131; Brazilian folklore, I:2149; bridges and viaducts, I:2516; Brooklyn churches, I:996; Bryant, William Cullen, II:1673; Buddhism, I:1214; Bulletin, I:169; Bunyan, John, I:3434, III:2146; Canadian history, I:4391; canals, I:2112; caricatures, II:1474–75; catechisms, I:990; ceramics, I:2799; Cervantes, Miguel de, I:3714; chapbooks, I:2148, 2150; charities, I:1920; Chekhov, Anton P., I:3751, 3753; Christian art, I:2844; Circulation Dept., II:112, 164; Clough, Arthur Hugh, III:2150; coal mines, I:1504; collections, III:148; Columbus, Christopher, I:4508, 4521; Congreve, William, II:1824; constitutional conventions, I:1833; cooking, I:2587–88, II:1344; Cooper, Peter, I:3964; corn laws, I:1543; costume, I:2943; county government, I:1886; Crane, Stephen, II:1684; criminology, I:1926; Currier and Ives, I:2968; dance film collection, III:1873; dancing, I:3104, II:1578, III:1884, 1886–87; Declaration of Independence, I:4571; dehydrated food, I:2586; Dickens, Charles, I:3462, II:1829, III:2159, 2162; dictionaries, I:3147; dime novels, I:3244; drama, I:3192; drawing, I:2915; economic documents, I:1420–32; economics, I:1461–64; Egyptian history, I:4211–12, 4370; electricity, I:2489; Eliot, T. S., III:2001; Elliott, Mary B., I:3811; Emerson, Ralph Waldo, II:1690; Emmet manuscripts, II:2483; engineering, I:2466; English and American novels, III:2128; English

architecture, I:2928; English authors, I:3400; English literature, I:3225, 3368–69, II:1787–88, III:1959, 2113–15; English printing, I:675; engraving, I:2966–73, II:1484; Ethiopia, I:4367–68; etiquette, I:2154; fish, I:2339, 2637, 3145; folk music, I:3024, 3067; foreign official gazettes, III:19–20; Franklin, Benjamin, I:3985; French printing, I:912; French Revolution, I:4281–82; furniture, I:2928, 2930; Galaxy papers, I:239; gardening, I:2643, II:1384; Garrison, Lucy McKim, III:1865; genealogy, I:4165–68, II:2254; geography, I:3834, 3848–52, 3874, 3911–13, 3926; geography periodicals, I:3851; German American collection, I:1371; German literature, I:3592; gipsies, I:2155; Gissing, George, II:1836; glass, I:2799; Goudy imprints, II:504; grammars, I:3147; Greek linguistics, III:1917; Greenwood, John, I:2971; Gutenberg Bible, II:338; Harkness collections, II:299–300; Hawthorne, Nathaniel, I:3289, II:1701; Hebrew incunabula, II:635; Hebrew periodicals, I:289, 330; heraldry, I:4166; historical prints, I:4450, 4454; Hittites, I:4215; Holcroft, Thomas, I:3481; hornbooks, I:1983; Howells, William Dean, II:1708; hydraulic engineering, I:2522; Illinois history, I:4817; Illinois printing, I:737; illuminated manuscripts, I:520–22, III:1800; illumination, I:2488; incunabula, II:341; Indiana history, I:4938; industrial relations, III:957; inks, I:2797; insulating oil, I:2798; interior decoration, I:2928, 2930, 2932, III:1604; investment companies, II:720; Irish history, I:4270; Irving, Washington, I:3294; Isle of Man, I:4272; Italian fiction, II:1946; Italian libretti, III:1807; Italian literature, I:3667; Jackson, Andrew, I:4009; James, Henry, II:1713; Japanese-American relations, I:1406; Japanese history, I:4337; Japanese illustrated books, III:654; Japanese science journals, III:1327; Jewish Division, II:642, III:761; Jews in literature, I:3369, 3769; Jews in Orient, I:4349; journalism, I:481; Judaism, I:1239–40; juvenile literature, III:2324; Khazars, I:4350, II:2272; labor disputes, I:1652; labor history, III:958; Lafontaine, Jean de, I:3652; landscape architecture, I:2863–64; Latin American maps, I:3926; Latin American periodicals, I:463; Lenox Library, I:233–34, II:291; Lermontov, Mikhail Y., I:3754; letter-writing, I:3263; Library history and resources, I:139–40; linguistics, I:3147–49; literary annuals, I:3212; literary forgeries, I:3401; little magazines, I:331; Locke,

Robinson, I:3110; Lusatian dictionaries, II:1604; Lutheran Church, II:554; Maltese printing, I:911; Manchus, I:4332; manuscripts, I:501–02, 508, 520–22, 539, III:416; maps, I:3848–50, 3874, 3911–13, 3926; maritime collection, I:2119; Marlowe, Christopher, I:3493; marriage and divorce, I:980; Martineau, Harriet, I:3494; Masaryk, Thomas G., I:4070; Masefield, John, II:1861; mathematics, I:2218; mazarinades, I:3646; medical authors, III:1483; medieval and Renaissance manuscripts, III:432; Melville, Herman, II:1725, 1730; Meredith, George, II:1863; Mexican history, I:5318; Milton, John, III:2199; Mohammedanism, I:1252–53; money and banking, I:1478–83; Mongolia, I:4333; Montesquieu, Charles de S., I:3656; More, Hannah, I:998; Mormon Church, I:1102; Muhammadan law, I:1748; municipal documents, I:1882–83, 1885; music, I:3022–26, 3067–68, II:1555; music collection catalog, III:1817; music prints, III:1796; music rare books, III:1818; naturalization records, III:2425; naval history and science, I:5453–57; Near East, I:4238; needlework, I:2929; Negro collection, I:1391, II:679, 682; New England history, I:4633; New Jersey geology, I:2284; New Jersey history, I:5010; New Jersey maps, III:2388; New York City almanacs, I:4699, 4701; New York City churches, I:997; New York City libraries, I:62; New York directories, I:4179–81; New York Fire Dept., I:1884; New York health records, I:2370; New York history, I:5052–67; New York maps, I:3911–13; New York newspapers, I:384, 388; New York printing, I:816, 834–36; New York schools, I:1955–56; newspapers and gazettes, I:424; numismatics, I:2907; O'Casey, Sean, III:2201; occult sciences, I:963–67; occupational therapy, I:2354; O'Higgins family, I:5311; Olive Branch Petition, II:2293; Olympics, I:3133; O'Neill, Eugene, III:2052; opera, I:3023, 3068, III:1799; orchestral music, I:3022; Oriental collection, II:1988; Oriental literature, I:3799; Oriental manuscripts, I:539; Ottoman Empire, II:2348; pageants, I:3109; Pardoe, Julia, II:1868; Parsons, William B., I:2448; patents and trade marks, I:2776; peace and war, I:977; Pennsylvania Dutch art, I:2845; periodical indexes, I:329; periodicals, III:242; Persia, I:4351; Philippine Islands, I:5375; philosophy, I:953; photography, I:2997; plants in art, I:2931; Poe, Edgar Allan, I:3322; poetry, II:1608; Polish history, I:4321; Polish literature, I:3756; Portuguese history, I:4295; prices, I:1554; printing

New York Public Library (cont.)
history, I:599–601; prints, I:2966–73,
II:1490; prompt books, I:3107;
Provençal literature, I:3645, 3647;
psychology, I:961; Ptolemy, I:3852,
II:2036; public finance, I:1516–20;
Puccini collection, II:1558; Puerto
Rico, III:3341; railroads, I:2100–01;
Ramusio, Giambattista, II:2032; rare
books, I:562, III:458; Reference Dept.
acquisitions, II:7; Regerenes, I:4633;
religious periodicals, I:999; Riis, Jacob
A., III:2598; Robinson, Edwin
Arlington, I:3327, II:1742; Rogers,
Bruce, I:503; Royal primer, I:700;
Russian literature, III:2754; Russian
periodicals, I:464, II:225; Saint
Birgitta, II:609; sanitary engineering,
I:2537; Schomburg collection, II:2440,
III:835; scientific dictionaries, I:2172;
scientific management, I:2688;
Scotland, history, I:4271; seals,
II:2261; selenium, I:2267; Semitic
languages, I:3170–71; Shakers,
I:1190; Shakespeare, William, I:3530,
3541, III:2212; Shaw, George
Bernard, II:1881; shoe industry,
I:2823; shooting, I:3132; shorthand,
I:2689; Simple Simon, I:3813; slang,
I:3149; Slavic dictionaries, III:1913;
Slavonic bibliography, I:11; Slavonic
collection, II:1978; Social Security
Act, I:1604; sociology, I:1258–61;
South American newspapers, I:479;
Southeast Asia, II:2382; Southey,
Robert, I:3547; Spanish literature,
I:3690; Sproat, Nancy, II:2000;
starches, I:2800; Stimmer's woodcuts,
II:1486; Stravinsky, Igor, III:1889;
street railways, I:2134; submarines,
I:5456; technical books, I:2449,
II:1256, III:1563; Thackeray, William,
I:3556; theatre architecture, III:1746;
theatre collections, I:3107–10,
III:1880, 1885; Thoreau, Henry David,
II:1749; tobacco, I:2640–42,
III:1670–71; Tolstoy, Leo N., I:3757;
torpedoes, I:5457; Townsend Plan,
I:1605; Twain, Mark, III:2086;
type-specimen books, II:499;
typewriters, I:2822; typography,
III:665; ultra-violet rays, I:2248; union
lists, I:281; U.S. Exploring
Expedition, I:4594; U.S. Government
organization, I:1901; urban planning,
I:2864–68; Utamaro, Kitagawa,
I:2967; Van Vechten, Carl, II:1756;
Victoria and Albert etchings, III:1769;
Vinci, Leonardo da, I:2843; Virgil,
I:3731; Virgin Islands, I:5278; Virginia
history, I:5217–18; voyages, I:3847;
wages, I:1602–03; Washington,
George, I:4112–15, II:2223–24;
Webster, Noah, II:2228; Weitenkampf,
Frank, I:2972; welding, I:2820–21;
West Indies, I:5319; Western
Hemisphere, I:3874; Whitman, Walt,
II:1759, 1765, 1767, III:2093; women,

I:2141–42; William II, Emperor of
Germany, I:4129; Wood, Samuel and
Sons, I:3812; Woodberry, George E.,
I:3347; Wordsworth, William, I:3575;
World War I, I:5512, 5516, II:2768,
III:3405; World War II, I:5543,
II:2805; Yank, the Army weekly,
II:156; Yeats, W. B., II:1913;
Zacuto's Almanach perpetuum, II:320
———Library and Museum of the Performing
Arts, III:1888
New York Society Library: art collection,
I:2846; catalogs, I:235–36; early
newspapers, I:371, 384; Library
history, I:141–42
New York Southern Society Library: Southern
Americana, I:4641
New York State Court of Claims, II:796
New York State Historian: Clinton, George,
papers, I:3959; Kingston, N.Y.,
archives, I:5068; Suffolk County,
N.Y., archives, I:5069–70
New York State Historical Association
Library: Cooper, James Fenimore,
II:1679; manuscript diaries, II:2659
New York State Law Library: catalog,
I:1709; condominiums, III:1015;
Hand, Learned, III:1016; rare books,
I:1788
New York State Library: Allen, James E., Jr.,
III:2429; American history, I:4572–
73, II:2484; census records, II:661;
church records, I:1210; Clinton,
George, I:3959; colonial period,
I:5027, II:2520; fiction, I:3195;
Gotshall collection, II:292; government
publications, I:37, II:38–39, III:56–
57; Johnson, Sir William, I:5025;
Library history, III:149; Library
resources, III:114; Maine history,
I:4892; maps and surveys, I:3845; New
England genealogy, I:4136; New York
Constitution, II:830; New York
genealogy, I:4169; New York history,
I:5027–28, 5040, 5071–77, 5079;
New York maps, III:2392; New York
State Court of Claims, II:796; New
York statutes, II:711; science and
technology, II:1027; serials, II:165,
III:243; social sciences, II:651; South
Asian serials, III:373
New York State Medical Library: herbals,
III:1430; serials, I:2388, II:1212
New York State, Secretary of State: American
Revolution, I:4573; British history,
I:5075, III:2696; colonial history,
I:5076; Dutch history, I:5075,
III:2720; records, I:5077
New York State University, Downstate
Medical Center Library: medical
history, II:1235
———Libraries: serials, III:243–44
———(Binghamton): manuscripts, III:415
———(Buffalo): manuscripts, III:415
———(Geneseo): Huxley, Aldous, III:2180
New York Supreme Court Library: catalog,
I:1710
New York Times, I:425

New York University, Film Library: catalog,
III:1794
———Jewish Culture Foundation Library:
Judaica and Hebraica, II:643
———Libraries: Barnard, Henry, I:1961;
collection, I:2010: Dickens, Charles,
III:2163; dime novels, III:1938; early
American periodicals index, I:358,
3264; English and American fiction,
II:1615, III:2131–32; English legal
documents, I:1789; Frost, Robert,
III:2009; Gallatin, Albert, III:2502;
Hebraica, I:1241; Hegel, G. W. F.,
I:954; Lagarde collection, I:237;
Ottoman Empire, II:2348; Scott, Sir
Walter, III:2208; serials, III:245;
Tamiment library, III:786
———School of Law Library: catalog, II:810;
periodicals, III:1043
New Zealand, history, I:5372
Newark, Delaware, history, II:946
Newark, N.J., history, I:5013
Newark (N.J.) Free Public Library: business,
I:64, 2690–91; New Jersey maps,
II:2056; Newark history, I:5013;
Newark imprints, I:802; printing,
I:602; schoolroom decoration, I:2932
Newark (N.J.) Museum: numismatics, I:2908
Newbery, John S., II:1998
Newberry Library: American ethnology,
I:2311; American fiction, I:3245;
American history, I:4476, 4574,
III:3020; American Indians, I:3175,
4494, II:2511, III:3020; Americana,
II:2552, 2559; Anderson, Sherwood,
I:3275; Arabic and Turkish
manuscripts, I:540: Arthurian
romances, I:2151–52; Ayer collection,
I:3875, 4494, 5287, 5302; Balkan folk
music, II:1539; baseball, I:3134;
Bulletin, I:170; Bunyan, John, I:3435;
Burlington Railroad, I:2103;
calligraphy, I:2916–17, II:1471;
Cather, Willa, II:1675; Chicago
writers, II:1642; colonial period,
I:4503; constitutional conventions,
I:1837–38; copybooks and writing
manuals, I:2024; courtesy books,
I:970; Coverdale Bible, I:1035; Dante,
Alighieri, I:3684; early English
printing, I:677–78; East Asiatic
books, I:4352; encyclopedias, III:10;
English Bible, I:1035; English drama,
III:2124; English poetry, I:3357;
French pamphlets, II:2306–08; French
Renaissance, II:1937–38; genealogy,
II:2251; German literature, I:3592;
Goethe, Johann Wolfgang von,
II:1917; Greenland, I:5381; gypsies,
II:1007; Handbook, I:143;
Hispanic-Americana, I:5287, 5302;
Illinois Central Railroad, I:2096, 2102,
II:995; illuminated manuscripts,
III:433; incunabula, I:643–44; Italian
drama, II:1941; Italian literature,
II:1945; Kelmscott Press, I:676; Latin
American history, III:3295–96; little
magazines, II:166; manuscript

collections, II:254; manuscript maps, I:3875; Mexicana, II:2737; miniature books, I:638; Morris, William, I:676; municipal government, I:1874; music collections, II:1514, 1534, 1541, III:1812–13; Oriental books, I:3791; paper preservation, III:1386; Payne, W. M., II:238; Philippine history, II:2758–60; Philippine linguistics, II:1605; Portuguese history, II:2311, 2313–14; printing history, I:603, III:477–78; Probasco, Henry, I:563; rare books, III:462; religion in England, I:1004; Russian literature, III:2756; Silver collection, III:459, 461; South American periodicals, I:455; Spanish literature, II:1956–57; special collections, III:150; Taylor, Graham, II:918; Taylor, Thomas, I:955; theatre research, III:160; Venetian history, III:2724; Virgil, I:3732; Wagner, Henry Raup, III:460; Western history and travel, III:3137, 3151–52, 3154; Wing collection, I:929, II:315, 318

Newhall, Beaumont, II:1507
Newman, John, III:2413, 3406
Newman, John Henry, I:1186; II:604
Newnham, Anthony, III:2173
Newsome, Walter L., III:31
Newspapers, I:283, 297, 305, 310, 313, 321, 335, 341, 355–56, 359, 366–479, 942; II:187–215, 220–22, 226, 229, 231–33; III:168, 299–345; African, II:2459, III:370, 384; Alabama, II:194; Alaska, I:445; American, I:366–450, II:187–209, 2532, III:299–346; Arizona, I:321, 712, II:202, III:299; Arkansas, I:394, II:189, 198; Belorussian, II:231–32; Bermuda, I:451; Boston, I:369; British, II:211; California, I:442, II:197; Ceylonese, II:213; Chinese, III:360; Cincinnati, I:434; Cleveland, I:356; Colorado, I:432, 721, III:300; Confederate States, II:2537; Delaware, I:446; District of Columbia, I:415; East Central and Southeastern Europe, III:394; East European, II:221; English, I:454, 458, 460, II:215, 222, 233; European, I:469, 475–76; Federalist period, III:3064; foreign, I:297, 451–79, II:196, 201, 207, 210–15, 220–22, 226, 229, 231–33, III:304, 323, 335; French, I:459, 478, III:369; French-American, III:370; Georgia, I:305, 373; German, I:1371, II:229; German-American, I:407, 413–14, III:206; Haiti, I:456; Illinois, I:341, 401, 409, 4649, II:187–88, III:317, 346; indexes, I:372; Indian, II:213; Indiana, I:400, 435; Iowa, I:420; Irish, I:460; Jamaica, I:899; Kansas, I:389, 402–03; Kentucky, I:405, 435, III:313; labor, II:768–69; Latin American, II:220, III:350; Louisiana, I:323, 359, 397, II:201, III:321–23; Maine, I:386; Maryland,

I:404, 764; Masonic, I:1941; Michigan, I:399, II:203, III:324; Midwest, I:429; Milwaukee, I:892; Minnesota, III:325; Mississippi, I:392, 4976–77; Missouri, I:435, 4649, III:327; Monmouth County, N.J., I:419; Montana, I:442; Negro, I:376, II:684; Nevada, I:410, III:312, 320; New Brunswick, III:222; New Mexico, I:422; III:337; New York, I:384, 388; Newport, R.I., I:447; North Carolina, I:382, 426, III:329–30; Ohio, I:333, 427, 435, 444; Oklahoma, I:431; Oregon, I:442, III:332–33; Pakistani, II:213; Pennsylvania, I:413–14, 435, II:204, III:334–35; Philadelphia, I:395, 428; Philippine, III:362; Puerto Rico, III:350; Russian, I:453, II:214, 231–32; Scottish, I:460; Slavic, III:385; South Carolina, II:190, III:310; Soviet Union, III:381, 395; Spanish, III:389; Swedish-American, I:366; Tennessee, III:338; Texas, I:393, III:341; Turkish, I:469; Ukrainian, II:231–32; underground, III:331; Utah, I:313, 442; Virginia, I:378, 439; wallpaper, I:4597; Washington (state), I:411–12, 442, III:342; West Indies, I:451; Winchester, Va., I:374; Wisconsin, I:391, II:209; Wyoming, I:379
Newton, Isaac, II:2184; II:1043, 1053; III:1309, 1321
Nez Percé Indians, II:2515
Ng, Tung King, II:1989; III:2894
Niagara Falls, history, I:5043
Nicaragua, I:5304, 5321, 5341
Nicewonger, C. R., III:1846
Nicholas II of Russia, I:4314
Nicholes, Eleanor L., III:912
Nichols, Charles L., I:780, 4691, 4702–03, 5014
Nichols, Nelson, I:3547
Nicholson, John, III:2580
Nicholson, John B., I:4025
Nicholson, John P., I:4612
Nicholson, Natalie N., I:2467
Nickerson, Mildred E., I:3717
Nickles, John M., I:2289
Nicolosi, Anthony S., III:846
Nicolosi, Robert R., III:1119, 1133
Nicols, Lowell W., I:5155
Nietz, John A., II:935; III:1250
Nigeria, II:2454; III:2980
Nightingale, Florence, II:1141, 1225; III:1470
Nitecki, André, III:2784
Nitze, William A., I:2152
Nivert, Frank J., II:979
Nobel prizes, II:1246
Nobel, Frank H., I:1693
Noh, Toshio, II:2023
Noise, I:2247; II:1175
Nökel, Heidrun, III:1048
Nolan, James B., I:858
Nolan, Paul T., III:1879
Nolen, Eleanor W., I:3814
Nonpartisan League, II:2647
Nordbeck, Theodore M., I:2974

Norden, Eric, I:3914
Norfolk and Western Railway, I:2071
Norlie, Olaf M., I:1036
North Africa, I:4387
North Carolina: fiction, I:3248, II:1660; history, I:5090–5111, II:1643, 2662–64, III:3231–36; maps, I:3914
North Carolina College Library: race relations, I:1400, II:680
North Carolina Historical Commission: archives, I:5099; county records, I:5106; Cuban papers, I:5301; early newspapers, I:382; manuscript collections, I:5096, 5105
North Carolina Library Association: periodicals, II:167
North Carolina Museum of Art: painting and drawing, II:1479
North Carolina State Dept. of Archives: American Revolution, III:3063; census records, III:798; Civil War, III:3091–92; Florida history, I:4790; genealogy, II:2252, III:2658; manuscript collections, III:3233; newspapers, III:329–30; North Carolina history, II:2663; North Carolina maps, I:3914; records of state agencies, III:3234; Surry County records, III:3235; Tennessee history, III:3250
North Carolina State Library: archives, I:5099; catalog, I:238; 18th century imprints, I:844; genealogy, I:4170; government publications, III:58; newspapers, I:426; North Carolina history, I:5107, 5110
North Carolina State University Library: Negroes, III:836; North Carolina fiction, II:1660; science periodicals, II:1071; social science periodicals, II:652
North Carolina Supreme Court Library: catalog, I:1711–12
North Carolina union list of scientific serials, III:1345
North Carolina, University, Dramatic Museum: theatre collection, I:3089
———Hanes collection: incunabula, I:645
———Institute of Government: map resources, III:2367
———Library: art history, III:1712; Bartlett Yancy papers, I:5094; Berrien, John Macpherson, III:2437; Bragg, Thomas, III:2439; building arts, II:1459; Burke, Thomas, III:2448; Chinese literature, III:374; Chinese periodicals, III:374; Civil War novels, II:1657; collections, II:90, 113; detective fiction, III:1935, 1939; Dickens, Charles, II:1830; Dromgoole, Edward, III:2482; 18th century North Carolina imprints, I:844; Gaston, William, III:2504; Georgia history, III:3173; government publications, III:58; Green, Duff, III:2510; Herbert, Hilary Abner, III:2520; incunabula, II:325, 337; Kitchin, Claude, III:2541; Latin-American history, II:2716; Louisiana history, III:3193; Lowndes, William, III:2557; medieval and

North Carolina, University, Library *(cont.)*
Renaissance studies, III:2687–88;
Memminger, Christopher Gustavus,
III:2570; Murphy, Edgar Gardner,
III:2578; North Carolina history,
I:5092, 5094, 5108, 5110–11,
III:3232; North Carolina newspapers,
I:382; North Carolina state
publications, II:40; North Caroliniana,
II:2662, 2664; Outlaw, David,
III:2583; painting and drawing,
II:1479; Perry, Benjamin Franklin,
III:2588; political science, III:803; race
relations, I:1400, II:680; resources,
I:144; science serials, II:1071,
III:1345; sciences and social sciences,
III:1290; serials, III:246; Shaw,
George Bernard, I:3544, II:1882–83,
III:2220; social science periodicals,
II:652; South Carolina history,
III:3249; Southern history, I:4639,
4642, III:3130–32; Spanish plays,
III:2265; spoken-word recordings,
III:2678; state records, II:46; Stewart,
Ethelbert, III:2624; Weeks, Stephen
Beauregard, III:2644; Wolfe, Thomas,
II:1772–73; Yancey, Benjamin
Cudworth, III:2649
——Woman's College Library: North
Carolina composers, I:3055; science
periodicals, II:1071; social science
periodicals, II:652; women, I:2143,
II:1012
North Dakota, history, I:5112–13; III:3237–
38
North Dakota State Historical Society:
manuscript collections, III:3238
North Dakota State Law Library: catalog,
I:1713
North Dakota State Library Commission:
government publications, III:59
North Dakota, University, Library: Dakota
territorial records, III:3237; O. G.
Libby manuscripts, II:2497
North Texas State College Library: serials,
I:315; 20th-century music, II:1540
North-West Frontier Province, II:2358
Northeast Missouri State College Library:
Mark Twain, III:2083–84
Northeastern State College Library,
Tahlequah, Okla.: Cherokee Indians,
II:2499
Northeastern University Library: science and
engineering, III:1291
Northup, Clark S., I:3474; II:1837
Northwest, history, I:4657–74; III:3159–60
Northwest Passage, III:3049
Northwestern State College of Louisiana
Library: Cloutier family, III:2466;
Louisiana poets, III:1966
Northwestern University, Dental School
Library: serials, III:1543
——Library: African collection, II:2441–
42, 2445–46, III:2949–51; civil
defense, I:5489; collections, II:79,
104–06; Eliot, T. S., III:2002;
environmental pollution, III:1701;
Joyce, James, II:1846; little

magazines, II:161; manuscripts,
II:1797; South Africa, III:2948; South
American manuscripts, I:5316; Spanish
Americana, II:2754; special
collections, III:152; underground
newspapers, III:331; Venezuela,
history, I:5335; Vietnam War,
III:2851; women authors, II:2144
——School of Law Library: Chicago legal
collections, II:797; continental law,
I:1749; criminology, I:1933; foreign
and international law, I:1795, II:823;
rare books, II:798, III:1017
——Technological Institute Library: atomic
bomb, I:2502; heating, I:2490; radar,
I:2491; rockets, I:2559; transistors,
II:1275
——Transportation Center Library:
acquisitions, II:985, III:933
Norton, Charles E., I:3314
Norton, Jane E., I:3994
Norton, Margaret C., I:4827
Norway, history, I:4309
Norwegian American Historical Association,
I:1373
Nosek, Jindrich, II:821
Nosology, II:1198
Notre Dame, University, Library and
Archives: American Far East missions,
II:619; Brownson, Orestes Augustus,
III:2447; Catholic archives, III:752;
Catholic manuscripts, II:614;
collections, II:123; Dante, Alighieri,
II:1940; Ewing, Thomas, Sr., III:2485;
Sherman, William T., III:2616; South
Americana, I:5320
Novossiltzeff, George A., I:3169, 5544
Noyes, Crosley S., II:2987
Noyes, Nicholas H., II:2471
Noyes, R. Webb, I:760–61, 4896; II:398
Nuclear warfare, III:1156–57
Numismatics, I:2903–08; III:1775–76;
Oriental, I:2904–05
Nunn, G. Raymond, II:2357, 2371, 2414;
III:375, 2798, 2862–63
Nunns, Annie A., I:4103
Nuremberg chronicle, I:653
Nursing, I:2403; II:1141, III:1470; history,
III:1474–75; periodicals, III:1556
Nussbaum, F. L., I:4239
Nute, Grace L., I:4593, 4965, 4967–68
Nutrition, I:4193 (25); II:1343
Nuts, production and marketing, III:1673
Nutzhorn, Harold F., I:5317
Nyasaland, Africa, III:2931

Oakland Public Library: civil defense, I:5490;
music, I:3027; national defense,
I:5394; urban planning, I:2873
Oakleaf, Joseph B., I:4030
Oates, John F., III:441
Oberlin College Library: anti-slavery
propaganda, I:4613, III:837; Finney,
Charles Grandison, I:1211; labor,
I:1571; Spanish drama, I:3689
——Music Library: autographs and
holographs, III:1819
O'Brien, Genevieve S., III:1103

Obstetrics, II:1230
O'Callaghan, Edmund B., I:1037, 5075;
III:2720
O'Casey, Sean, III:2120, 2201
Occidental College Library:
Japanese-American relocation, I:5541;
Jeffers, Robinson, II:1717
Occult sciences, I:962–68; III:1385, 1390
Occupational therapy, I:2354
Ocean and lake transportation, I:2118–22,
2124–25, 2127–31; II:998–99, 1423
Oceania, II:2511
Oceanography, III:1401
Ochs, Robert D., I:2113
O'Connor, Thomas F., I:1180
O'Connor, William Van, III:2581
Oda, Wilbur Harry, II:444
Odd Fellows Library: catalog, I:1943
O'Dell, Sterg, II:1780
Odgers, Charlotte H., I:3890
Odland, Norine, III:2325
O'Donnell, Hugh F., III:2278
Oehlerts, Donald E., II:209; III:300, 784
Oey, Giok Po, II:2379
Official gazettes, I:51
Offset printing, I:947
O'Grady, Standish, II:1866
O'Hanlon, Mary Catherine, III:2326
O'Hara, John, III:2051
O'Hegarty, P. S., II:1585, 1785, 1910–11
O'Higgins family, I:5311
Ohio: history, I:4680, 5114–29, II:2665–69,
III:3239–40; maps, I:3915
Ohio Company of Virginia, II:2187
Ohio Historical Society: Brown, John, Jr.,
III:2443; Brown, Walter F., III:2445;
Garford, Arthur Lovett, III:2503; Gest,
Erasmus, III:2506; Harding, Warren
G., III:2514; Kurtz, Charles L.,
III:2542
Ohio Historical and Philosophical Society:
Ohio history, I:5127
Ohio Library Association: serials, I:332
Ohio Library Foundation: government
publications, III:60
Ohio River Valley, history, II:2552
Ohio State Archaeological and Historical
Society: county and local history,
I:5128–29; Joshua Reed Giddings
manuscripts, I:5116; manuscript
collections, II:2668; Ohio archives,
I:5122; Ohio newspapers, I:427;
Woodbridge-Gallaher collection,
I:5120
Ohio State Library: government publications,
II:41; Ohio history, III:3240
Ohio State University, Engineering
Experiment Station welding, II:1436
——Library: Algren, Nelson, III:1982;
American fiction, III:1973–75; Arabic
culture, III:2689; Beckett, Samuel,
III:1982; Cervantes collections,
III:2271; Charters, W. W., II:928;
chemistry, III:1387; Crane, Hart,
III:1993–94; French history, III:2714;
French-language dictionaries, III:1915;
government publications, III:60;
Hawthorne, Nathaniel, III:2019;

Hebraica and Judaica, III:778−79;
history of chemistry, III:1388; history
of science, III:1317; Homer, II:1969;
influential books, III:463; investment
literature, III:894; little magazines,
II:161; natural resources, III:865;
Negroes, III:838−39; periodicals and
newspapers, III:247; private presses,
III:500; Romance-language
periodicals, III:1928; special resources,
III:151; Thurber, James, III:2078−80;
welding, II:1436
Ohio Supreme Court Law Library: catalog,
I:1714
Ohio Valley, maps, II:2052
Ohio Wesleyan University Library:
periodicals, II:170
Ohl, John F., II:1541
Oil and gas law, III:1004
Oil shale industry, I:2794
Okfuskee County (Okla.), I:2628 (28)
Okinawa, II:2420
Okinshevich, Leo O., II:2729; III:3310
Oklahoma, history, I:5130−32; II:2670−72
Oklahoma A. and M. College Library:
criminology, I:1929
Oklahoma Historical Society: Oklahoma
newspapers, I:431; Whipple, Amiel
Weeks, II:1282
Oklahoma Library Commission: Oklahoma
libraries, I:145
Oklahoma State University Library: serials,
III:248
Oklahoma, University, Library: Bibles,
III:710; business history, II:972−73;
III:913; Lois Lenski collection,
III:2327; Oklahoma history, II:2670−
71; rare books, I:146; science and tech-
nology history, II:1054−57, III:1318;
serials, III:248−49; space law, II:799
Oko, Adolph S., III:682
Olcott, Thomas Worth, III:901
Old Northwest Territory, II:2550; III:3135
Oldfather, William A., I:3733−34; II:1966
Oldham, Ellen M., II:542, 644−45, 1827,
2126, 2750
Oldham, Kie, I:4720
Olearius, Adam, I:4311
O'Leary, Francis B., III:1545
O'Leary, John, II:1913
Olivart, Ramón de D., I:1809
Olive Branch Petition, II:2293
Oliveira Lima, Manoel de, I:5290
Oliver, L. M., II:1808
Oliver, Peter, I:3567
Olivera, Guido F., III:1039
Olmsted, Frederick L., I:2857; III:2582
Olson, Kenneth Donald, II:521
Olson, Mary E., III:206
Olson, Richard D., III:152
Olympics, I:3133
Omaha Public Library: Nebraska history,
I:4996
Omar Khayyám, II:1990
Ombudsmen, III:994
O'Meara, Eva J., III:1820
O'Neal, William B., II:1453
Oneida Community, III:3229

Oneida Historical Society of Utica (N.Y.):
library catalog, I:5078; manuscripts,
II:2661
O'Neil, Charles, III:2467
O'Neil, Perry, III:1927
O'Neill, Edward H., I:3937
O'Neill, Eugene, I:3315−16; III:2052
O'Neill, James E., III:2713, 3021−22
O'Neill, Maureen, III:561
Oneirocritica, I:961
Onondaga Historical Association: Syracuse
(N.Y.) history, I:5023
Open Court Publishing Co., III:684
Opera music, I:3023, 3036−37, 3068;
II:1530, 1532; III:1799
Ophthalmia neonatorum, I:2343
Ophthalmology, II:1152
Oppenheimer, Gerald J., III:1452
Optics, I:2250; II:1095; III:1293
Orchestral music, I:3016, 3022, 3039;
II:1515, 1528, 1536
Oregon, history, I:5133−39; II:2578, 2673−
74; III:3241−43
Oregon Historical Society: manuscripts,
I:5136; newspapers, III:332
Oregon State Library: catalog, I:240; foreign
languages collection, III:1929;
genealogy, II:2245; government
publications, II:42, III:62; newspapers,
III:332; Oregon history, II:2673−74;
Oregon Indians, III:3036; periodicals,
III:250; urban planning, I:2869
————Division of State Archives: agricultural
agencies, III:1611; legislative records,
III:3242; microfilms, III:3243
Oregon State University: archives, III:1256
————Library: biological serials, III:1414;
environmental pollution, III:1702;
forestry theses, II:1401, III:1681;
serials, I:334; University serial
publication, II:949
Oregon Supreme Court Library: catalog,
I:1715
Oregon Trail, I:4688
Oregon, University, Library: Aitchison, Clyde
Bruce, III:2428; American music,
III:1857; Andrews, T. Coleman,
III:2431; biological serials, III:1414;
Chaney, Ralph W., III:1400; Faulkner,
William, II:1692; Flynn, John T.,
III:2495; folklore, II:1004; forest
products, III:1682; French history,
III:2715; Indian records, I:4492;
newspapers, III:332−33;
transportation, III:934
Orel, Harold, II:1585
Oriental literature, I:237, 3767−3800;
II:1001, 1981−92
Orientalia, III:1261
Ornament, I:2931
Ornithology, I:2331−33, 2337, 2340−42;
II:1128−36; III:1441, 1443
Orthodox Eastern Church, II:579−81
Osborn, James M., I:3467
Osborn, Katherine W., II:1401
Osborne, Georgia L., I:4150
Osborne, Harriet, I:1016
Osborne, John W., III:2151

Osborne, Lucy E., I:613
Osgood, Herbert L., I:5079−80
O'Shaughnessy, Arthur, II:1867
O'Shea, Mrs. Henry, II:1711
Ossian, I:3401
Oster, Harry, III:1842
Ostrauskas, Kostas, II:2337
Ostrom, John W., I:3323
Ostvold, Harald, II:168
Ottenberg, Simon, III:2966
Ottersen, Signe, III:88
Ottoman Empire, II:2348−49
Outlaw, David, III:2583
Overman, William D., I:5122; II:974
Overton, Richard, II:2191
Owen, Doris H., III:2328
Owen, Robert, I:4837
Owen, Thomas M., I:4171, 4711, 4713−14,
4978
Owen, Wilfred, II:1607
Owens, James K., III:2515
Owsley, Harriet Chappell, III:2529, 3251−52
Oxford University, II:945
Ozarks, I:4643; II:2557

Pablo, Winifred O'Connor, III:529
Pace, Antonio, II:2098
Pacific Coast Gas Assoc. Library: catalog,
I:2801
Pacific islands, I:5383
Pacific Northwest: history, I:4666, II:2575−
78; maps, I:3890
Pacific Northwest Library Association: law
and medical libraries, III:115;
manuscripts, I:4667; special
collections, I:95
Pacific Ocean region, I:4193 (2); III:3394,
3396, 3400, 3404
Pacific, University, Pacific Center Library:
John Muir, III:2577
Pack, Roger A., III:2279
Packaging, I:2602 (42)
Packard, Frederick C., III:3213
Packer, Katherine H., II:934
Paganini, Nicolò, I:3048
Page, Alfred B., I:4704
Pageants, I:3109, 3116
Paget, Violet, II:1859
Paine, Barbara A., III:2329
Paine, Nathaniel, I:685−86, 765, 4523
Paine, Thomas, I:4087
Painter, William T., I:1959
Painting, I:2946−53; II:1476−82; III:1757−
59, 1761−62
Pajanovitch, Cecile, I:2823
Pakistan, II:2431; III:2828
Pakistani publications, III:2843
Paleography, I:191
Paleontology, I:2284, 2296; III:1398
Palestine, I:4386
Palha, M. Fernando, I:3702
Pallets, I:2459
Palmer, Foster M., II:1000
Palmer, George H., I:951, 3358, 3361
Palmer, Jane, II:814
Palmer, Philip Motley, II:1639
Palmer, R. R., I:4283
Palmer, Theodore Sherman, I:2340; II:1136

Palmer, Thomas W., Jr., I:1760
Palmerlee, Albert E., III:2364
Palmieri, Aurelio, I:3758
Palos Verdes, Calif., Library: California history, I:4741
Paltsits, Victor H., I:1033, 3284, 3289, 4115, 4524, 4705, 5058, 5063; II:291, 338
Paluka, Frank, III:1754, 1956, 2075
Pan, Ellen Chiang, II:1028
Pan American Railway, I:2079
Pan American Sanitary Bureau Library: Latin American medical and public health journals, I:2389
Pan American Union: Central American history, I:5321
———Columbus Memorial Library: accessions, II:129; bibliographies, III:4; Bolivar, Simon, I:3949–51; Bolivia, I:5323; economics, I:1465; education, II:926; fiction, I:3692; geography, I:3926, 3929–30; geology, I:2277; hemispheric defense, I:5395; inter-American relations, I:1408–09; international conferences, II:815; juvenile literature, I:3815; labor, I:1575; law, I:1733; Latin American history, I:5322, 5325–28; Latin American newspapers, I:465, II:220; Latin American periodicals, I:466, 2206, III:376; library science, I:65–66, II:63–64; maps, I:3926, 3930; Mexicans in U.S., I:1372; Monroe Doctrine, I:1407; newspapers, I:335; O'Higgins family, I:5311; periodicals, I:335–36, II:129; public administration, II:876; rare books, II:2719; resources, I:5324; tobacco, I:2644
Panama Canal, I:2114, 5353, 5355; II:2073; history, III:3349–50, 3352
Panofsky, Hans E., III:152, 2952
Pantle, Alberta, I:4696
Paolucci, Louis, II:1947
Papal documents, I:1157
Paper industry, I:2813, 2818; II:1405; III:479
Paper preservation, III:1386
Papyri, I:503, 546, 568, 4209, 4224, II:2264; Coptic, II:2271; Egyptian, I:4207–08, 4210, 4216; Greek, I:4201, II:2268, 2270; Latin, I:4206
Paraguay, history, I:5289; II:2755
Paraplegia, II:1199, 1201
Parcels post, I:2051
Pardoe, Julia, II:1868
Paré, Ambroise, I:2405
Parent-teacher associations, I:1976
Pargellis, Stanley, I:3150, 4512; II:254
Paris, France, history, II:2302
Paris Peace Conference, I:5518–19
Parish, John C., I:4735
Parish, William A., I:2885, 2959
Parker, Alice L., I:2975; II:1491, 1496
Parker, David W., I:4455
Parker, Ely S., II:2506
Parker, John, II:2522–23, 2526
Parker, Sheila M., II:1244
Parker, Susan Kay, III:949
Parker, Theodore, III:2584

Parker, Thomas F., III:3153
Parker, Wixie, II:1071
Parks, George B., II:2032
Parks, William, I:886
Parma, V. Valta, I:564
Parmelee, Gertrude, II:2688
Parrish, Michael, III:1147
Parrish, Morris L., I:923, 3384–87, 3447, 3463, 3557, 3562; II:1082–83, 1783, 1823, 1869, 1887, 1900
Parrish, Stephen M., II:2309
Parrott, Margaret Sangster, II:800
Parry, Albert, II:2426
Parsley, Gertrude Morton, II:80
Parsons, Arthur J., I:2976, 2988
Parsons, Elsie Clews, II:1003
Parsons, Lewis B., II:2192
Parsons, Wilfrid, I:56, 1038, 1181–82
Parsons, William B., I:2448, 2956
Partch, Clarence E., I:1984
Partington, D., III:2947
Parvin, T. S., I:1937
Parvin, Thomas, I:749
Pasadena Public Library: California history, III:3167
Pascal, Leo, I:1599, 5571; II:859; III:975, 1176
Past, Ray, II:1472
Patents, I:1567, 1671, 1724, 2453, 2776, 2780; II:1270; III:1003
Patrick, J. Max, III:2200
Patristics, I:191; II:595
Pattee, Fred L., I:3269; II:1734; III:2053
Patterson, Donald G., I:5529
Patterson, Eugenia, I:331
Patterson, Jerry E., II:2193, 2210, 2275, 2654, 2723–24, 2739–40, 2751–53
Patterson, John S., III:2028, 2440
Patterson, Lewis, II:1659
Patterson, Maureen L. P., III:2834
Patterson, Robert W., I:3737
Patton, Cornelius H., I:3576
Patton, John S., I:5234
Patton, Mollie M., I:3421
Paul, William G., III:3122
Pauli, A. F., I:3735
Paxson, Frederic L., I:4753
Paxton, Roger V., III:2772, 2779
Paylore, Patricia P., I:96; II:941
Payne, Loyal Frederick, II:1379
Payne, William Morton, II:238
Peabody, Francis G., I:1351
Peabody, George, I:2729
Peabody Institute Library, Baltimore: American imprints, II:352; architecture, decoration and furniture, I:2890; calligraphy, III:1778, 1780; catalog, I:242–43, III:178; collections, I:241; genealogy, III:2653; Kennedy, John Pendleton, II:2152; literary fraud, III:1930
Peabody Institute Library, Peabody, Mass.: catalog, I:244
Peabody Museum of Salem: Bowditch, Nathaniel, I:3952; Lawrence, James, I:4024
Peace, Glenda, III:819
Peace and war, I:972–79; II:507

Peach industry, II:1390
Peanut industry, I:2626 (80)
Pearce, Betty J., I:2269
Pearl, Orasmus M., I:4207
Pearlove, Shirley, I:161
Pears, Thomas C., Jr., I:1116
Pearson, Constance, I:3028
Pearson, James D., III:2799
Pearson, Justus R., Jr., II:239
Pearson-Lowenhaupt bookplate collection, II:62
Pease, Marguerite J., I:4681; II:199, 2567, 2607, 2609; III:3186
Pease, Theodore C., I:4828
Peat, I:2599 (12)
Peavy, Charles D., III:840
Peck, Charles R., III:1916
Peck, Deborah S., I:5476
Peck, Phoebe, II:1150
Peckham, Howard H., I:4442, 4563, 5396; II:388; III:1245
Peckham, Morse, I:3423–24
Pediatrics, II:1203; history, III:1482
Pedley, Avril J. M., III:3200
Peek, Philip M., III:1840
Peel, Bruce Braden, II:2465
Peery, William, II:1599
Pendell, Lucille, I:4475, 5433–34
Pendergrass, Margaret E., III:841
Penmanship, American, III:1944
Penn, Thomas, II:2585
Penn, William, I:4088; III:2586–87
Pennell, Elizabeth R., I:2589, 2977, 2979, 2989
Pennell, J. J., II:1508
Pennell, Joseph, I:2977, 2979, 2986, 2989
Penney, Clara L., I:594–95, 3293, 4090; II:310, 1711, 1955; III:3302
Penney, Freeland F., I:2672
Penniman, James H., I:1975
Penniman, Maria Hosmer, I:1952, 1957
Pennsylvania, history, I:5140–59; II:2301, 2675–84; III:3244–48
Pennsylvania Canal, II:1308
Pennsylvania Dept. of Internal Affairs: Pennsylvania history, II:2676
Pennsylvania Dept. of Public Instruction: library resources, III:116
Pennsylvania Division of Public Records: Pennsylvania history, II:2680
Pennsylvania Historical and Museum Commission: business history, III:914; county archives, I:5150; manuscripts, III:3246; military service records, III:2414; Nicholson, John, III:2580; Pennsylvania Canal, II:1308, III:3248; Pennsylvania history, II:2684, III:3247; Provincial Council, III:3245
Pennsylvania Historical Junto: Wister, Owen, II:1771
Pennsylvania Historical Society: business records, I:2709, 2731; colonial laws, I:1716; German printing, I:861; Lancaster County, I:5143; Leland, Charles G., I:3302; manuscripts, I:5146, 5151; New Sweden, I:4771; Penn, Thomas, III:2585; Penn, William, III:2587; Poinsett, Joel R.,

I:1410; prints and drawings, I:2978;
U.S. Constitution, I:4575
Pennsylvania Historical Survey: church
archives, I:1149; Pennsylvania
newspapers, I:428; Poinsett, Joel R.,
I:1410
Pennsylvania Horticultural Society Library:
catalog, I:2609
Pennsylvania Library Association:
newspapers, III:334
Pennsylvania Museum and School of
Industrial Art Library: catalog, I:2933;
Indian languages, I:3176
Pennsylvania State Archives: guide, III:3247;
Pennsylvania Canal, III:3248;
Provincial Council, III:3245
Pennsylvania State Library: business history,
I:2710; government publications,
III:63; law book collection, I:1717;
Pennsylvania autobiographies,
III:2415; Pennsylvania history,
I:5152−54; Pennsylvania law, I:1718;
water pollution, III:1703
Pennsylvania State University Library:
American literature, I:3269; Amy
Bonner papers, II:1670, III:1985;
annuals, I:3408; art and architectural
history, III:1720; Australian literature,
II:1794; Australiana, III:2756, III:3400;
Barnard, George Grey, III:1760;
Chinese plants, III:1431; 18th-century
library, III:147; emblem books,
II:1625, III:1931; English Civil War,
III:2697; English literature, III:2116;
Fielding, Henry, III:2169; German
literature, III:2236; heraldry, III:2659;
Hoffman, Arthur S., III:1957; Italian
literature, III:2256; Johnson, Samuel,
III:2183; maps, II:2030; Negroes,
III:842−43; O'Hara, John, III:2051;
Pattee, Fred Lewis, II:1734, III:2053;
Pennsylvania maps, III:2393; Roberts,
Dorothy, III:2102; serials, III:251;
Utopias, III:816
Pennsylvania Turnpike, I:2514
Pennsylvania, University, Law School
Library: space law, III:1019
————Libraries: Adams, John Quincy,
II:2190; American drama, II:1652−53;
American imprints, II:351; American
poetry, II:1646; Aristotle, I:3722,
II:1968, III:2280; Arrian's Anabasis,
II:1965; Bailey, Philip J., I:3423;
Bible, I:1039; Bird, R. M., II:1668−
69; British Renaissance books, III:493;
Brooks, Van Wyck, III:1986; Byron,
George Gordon, III:2148; Calhoun, J.
C., II:2190; catalog, I:245; chemistry
history, I:2252−55, 2268, II:1107;
Chinese collection, I:3779, II:2386;
Chronicle, I:171; Churchill, Winston,
II:2127; Dante, Alighieri, I:3682;
Dreiser, Theodore, II:1686−87;
education, I:1952, 1957; Elzevir
imprints, II:311; English drama,
I:3370, II:1777; English fiction,
I:3382, II:1781; Franklin, Benjamin,
I:3978, 3986, II:2127; French drama,

I:3633; French Revolution, II:2303,
III:2710, 2716; Furness, Horace
Howard, III:1874; Genizah fragments,
I:1219; German literature, II:1921;
German philology, III:3159; Great
Britain, history, I:4273; Harte, Bret,
II:1699; Hispanic literature, III:2259;
Hitler, Adolph, II:2295; Howells,
William Dean, III:2031; Indic
manuscripts and paintings, I:548;
Inquisition, I:4231, 4241; Italian
literature, I:3699; Legienda di Sancta
Caterina, II:319; Leland, Charles G.,
I:3302; Lithuania, II:2337; Louis XVI
of France, I:574; McCartney, George,
II:2183; manuscripts, II:275, III:411,
417; medical history, II:1223;
medieval history, I:4231, 4234, 4241;
Mexicana, II:2737; Monroe, James,
II:2190; Myrour to lewde men, II:272;
Orientalia, II:2376, 2410; Piccolomini
papers, II:2316; portraits, I:2946;
programmschriften, II:130−31,
III:1932; rare books, I:549, III:475;
resources, I:117, 155; Roberts,
Morley, III:2204; Russian literature,
I:3759; Sanskrit literature, I:3772;
Second Bank of the U.S., I:1476;
serials, I:320; Shakespeare, William,
I:3534−35; Sinclair, May, III:2221;
Smith, William, II:939; Spanish
drama, II:1958; Spanish literature,
I:3698, 3700; Swift, Jonathan,
II:1892−93; Torquemada, Tomás de,
II:601; university history, I:2002;
Werfel, Alma Mahler, III:2646;
Williams, William Carlos, III:2098
————Wharton School of Finance and
Commerce: Wetherill papers, I:2736
Penrose, Boies, I:2978, 4456
Pensions, I:1601, 1604−05, 1607, 1610,
1612−14, 1616, 1619, 1626, 1866−
67; II:773
Peoria Public Library: fiction, I:3195; German
literature, I:3593; Illinois printing,
I:737; music collection, I:3029
Peraza, Fermin, III:3363
Peraza Sarausa, Fermín, I:5329
Percussion music, III:1795
Perdue, Albert, III:2579
Periodicals, I:281−365; II:154−86; III:201−
98; African, I:473, 477, III:364, 380,
384, 387, 402; Alaskan, I:445; Arabic,
III:358; Arizona, I:321, II:202;
Australian, I:473, 477; Baltic, I:464;
Brazilian, III:359; British, III:256;
Buffalo, N.Y., I:342; California,
I:291; Ceylonese, III:373; Charleston,
S.C., I:314; Chinese, III:347−48, 351,
353, 355−56, 372, 374−75, 378,
398−99, 401; Cleveland, I:356;
Czechoslovak, III:365; East Asian,
III:377; East European, II:221, 230;
economic, I:2038; English, I:454, 458,
460−61, 666, 3409, II:215−16, 218−
19, 222, 233; European, I:471, 473,
475−77; foreign, I:451−79, III:347−
403; French, I:462, III:369; Georgia,

I:304−05, 307; German, I:468, 474−
76, 1371, III:382; German-American,
III:206; Illinois, I:341; indexes, I:329,
358, 2436; Indian, III:373; Indiana,
I:309; Indonesian, III:354; Irish, I:460;
Japanese, III:352, 398; Jewish, I:289,
330; Latin American, I:335−36, 452,
455, 463, 465−67, 470, 479, 2602
(5), 3701, 3703−04, II:223, III:361,
366, 371, 376, 400; little magazines,
II:161, 166; Louisiana, I:323, 359;
Maryland, I:308; Nepalese, III:373;
New Brunswick, III:222; New
England, I:324; New Orleans, I:312;
Ogden, Utah, I:313; Oklahoma, II:186;
Pakistani, III:373; Philippine, II:217;
Polish, II:234−35; Polish-American,
III:294; Portuguese, III:359; radical,
III:221; Russian, I:453, 464, II:224−
25, 227−28, 236, III:357, 363, 379,
386; St. Louis, II:159; scientific, I:471;
Scottish, I:457, 460; Slavic, III:349,
385; South Asian, III:373; Southeast
Asian, III:373, 403; Soviet, III:390−
91; Soviet and Eastern European,
III:396; technical, I:2435−36, 2440,
2446−47, 2450; women's, I:2145
Perkins, Frances, I:1582
Perkins, Henrietta T., I:2384
Perkins, Norton, I:3360
Perman, Dagmar Horna, II:2803
Permanent Court of International Justice,
I:1822, 1824
Perotti, Viola Andersen, III:580
Perros, George P., II:706, 854−55, 862, 868,
896, 906, 931, 1099, 1281, 1335,
1337−38, 2814; III:806
Perry, Benjamin Franklin, III:2588
Perry, Carmen, III:3262
Perry, Doris M., III:3224
Perry, Josepha M., I:2737
Perry, Matthew, II:2352
Perry, Oliver H., I:4592
Perry, Ralph B., I:3299
Perry, Ruth M., I:5513
Perry, Thomas Sergeant, III:2030
Persia, see Iran
Persian literature, III:2810
Persian manuscripts, II:276
Persius, I:3728
Person, Harlow S., I:4959
Person, Laura, III:715
Personnel administration, I:1857, 1861−62,
1864, 2602 (33), 2667 (2), 4193 (22,
37); II:840, 1349, 1414−15, 1417,
1419; III:871, 1073, 1076−77;
military, II:880
Peru, history, I:5289, 5294, 5298, 5311,
5315, 5333, 5359−60; II:2747, 2752;
III:3296, 3388−91
Peters, Charlotte H., I:2260
Peters, Harry T., I:2968
Petersen, Peter L., III:1612
Peterson, Agnes F., III:382, 2684, 2704,
2718, 3415
Peterson, Clarence S., I:1411
Peterson, Robert L., II:198
Peterson, Walter F., III:2209

Petrarch, Francesco, I:3685; II:2462
Petroleum, I:1559, 2281, 2500–01, 2803; II:1278–81; industry history, III:3265
Petroleum Research Company, Micro-Sort-Card Petroleum Geology Library: geology theses, II:1112
Pettengill, George E., I:1652
Pettit, Henry, I:3579
Pflug, Warner W., III:968
Pforzheimer, Carl, I:3402
Pfoutz, Donald R., II:8
Pharmacy, I:2321; II:1146; history, II:1250, III:1389; periodicals, II:1214, III:1562
Phelan, John Leddy; II:2760
Phelps, Ralph H., III:895
Philadelphia: history, I:4634; maps, I:3916; municipal archives, II:872
Philadelphia Academy of Natural Sciences: manuscripts, I:2188
Philadelphia Bibliographical Center: Union list of microfilms, I:9, 12; III:11
Philadelphia Board of Public Education Library: catalog, I:1958
Philadelphia College of Physicians Library: Harvey, William, I:2411; incunabula, I:2418–19
Philadelphia Free Library, Americana, II:2477; Bailey, Philip J., I:3423; Blackstone, William, II:801; careers, I:1987, 1991; common law, I:1719, III:1018; Dickens, Charles, I:3464; European manuscripts, I:523; fiction, I:3199; Fleischer music collection, I:3016, 3030, II:1542; fraktur, II:268; Fry, William H., I:3080; Gershwin, George, I:3079; Goldsmith, Oliver, I:3473; juvenile literature, I:3816, II:2011, III:2330, 2334; oriental manuscripts, I:541; Pennell, Elizabeth R. and Joseph, II:2979; periodicals, I:337; rare books, III:468; Shakespeare, William, I:3532; U.S. history, I:4525
Philadelphia Friends' Library: catalog, I:1150
Philadelphia International Electrical Exhibition, I:2492
Philadelphia Library Association of Friends: catalog, I:1151
Philadelphia Library Company, I:246–47; chess, I:3120; colonial history, I:4513, 4525; Fry, William H., I:3080; U.S. Constitution, I:4576
Philadelphia Mercantile Library Company: catalog, I:248
Philadelphia Museum of Art: Blake, William, I:2980
Philately: I:2044–48; II:978; III:80
Philippine Islands, I:485, 4193 (1), 4356, 5374–79; II:254, 694, 2511, 2757–60; III:2912–16, 3020
Philippine languages, I:3173
Philippoff, J. D., II:1276
Philips, William Pyle, II:283
Phillips, Albertine F., I:1701
Phillips, John C., I:2341
Phillips, Maurice T., III:1272
Phillips, P. L., II:2043

Phillips, Paul C., I:4993
Phillips, Philip L., I:3853, 3861, 3877–78, 3891–93, 3905, 3907, 3915–16, 3919–20, 3924, 3931, 4388, 4775, 5304–05, 5330, 5345–46, 5376
Phillips, Ulrich B., I:4805–06
Phillips, Venia T., III:1272
Phillips, Wendell, I:3317
Phillips, Academy Library: Vergil, I:3736
Philosophy, I:196, 306, 949–58, II:506–08, 511, 513–14, 651, III:681–84, 686; periodicals, I:958, II:514
Phobias, I:2350
Photo-facsimiles, I:18
Photo interpretation, II:1088
Photo-mapping, I:2292
Photographs: Civil War, II:1506; cowboys, II:1505; Detroit, II:1502; Kansas, II:1508; Klondike, II:1498; Minnesota, II:1504; Missouri, II:1503; Pacific Coast, II:1500; Washington, D.C., II:1506; Western history, II:1501
Photography, I:2990–91, 2994–99; II:1498–1511; III:1781–94
Physical sciences, III:1289
Physically handicapped, II:767; III:192, 194
Physics, I:2236, 2245–50; II:1095–99; III:1292–93, 1375–80, 1575–76; history, III:1375, 1380
Picasso, Pablo, II:1480
Piccolomini papers, II:2316
Picker, Martin, III:1868
Pickering, Timothy, I:1448; III:2589
Pictures, II:1443; collections, III:1725; medical, II:1139, 1244–45, 1247; U.S.A., II:2488
Pidhainy, Oleh S., III:2740
Pierce, Franklin, I:4089; III:2590
Pierpont, Francis H., I:5244
Pierpont Morgan Library: American history, I:4526; Andersen, Hans Christian, I:3632; Audubon drawings, III:1761; Babylonian, I:4217; Bible, I:1040; book design, I:941; Book of Common Prayer, II:582; bookbinding, I:924; British history, I:4274; Bunyan, John, I:3434; Central European manuscripts, II:269; children's literature, II:2009; Chinese calligraphy, III:1779; Cobden-Sanderson bindings, III:678; collections, II:92; Coptic manuscripts, I:4218–19, 4222; Cruikshank, George, I:2920; cuneiform inscriptions, I:4220; drawings, I:2918; English authors, English drama, I:3371; English poetry, II:1775; engravings and etchings, I:2961; fiftieth anniversary exhibition, II:293; Glazier, William S., collection, II:271; illuminated manuscripts, I:503–04, 524–30, III:434; incunabula, I:646–47; Italian manuscripts, II:270; Johnson, Samuel, II:1842; Lafayette, Marquis de, II:2156; Library history and resources, I:147–50; literary manuscripts, II:1619–20; liturgical manuscripts, III:1821; Maugham, W. S., II:1862; mezzotints, I:2958;

miniature incunabula, I:638; music collection, III:1822; Near Eastern seals, I:4203, 4221, 4223; papyri, I:4216; Piranesi, Giovanni B., I:2919; printing history, I:604–05; Protestant Episcopal Church, I:1136–37, II:586; rare books and manuscripts, I:565–69, III:464–65; Rembrandt, I:2982; Rousseau, Jean J., I:3658; Schreiber, L. W., I:2981; science, II:1058; Sprial Press, III:605; sports, I:3135; Swift, Jonathan, II:1891
Pierson, George Wilson, II:668
Pierson, Roscoe Mitchell, II:391, 543; III:723
Pierson & Company, II:969
Pietropaoli, Frank A., III:606
Pike, Albert, II:919–20
Pike, Charles B., I:2738
Pilgrim Holiness Church, I:1195
Pilgrim Society Library: catalog, I:4939
Pilgrims, I:4918, 4920, 4933, 4939
Pilling, James, I:3177–86
Pillsbury, Stanley R., I:4295, 4391
Pinger, W. R. R., I:3157
Pings, Vern M., III:1501
Pinkett, Harold T., I:1484, 2654, 2665, 2671; II:763, 1094, 1359, 1382, 1387, 1397–98; III:1686
Pinkett, Maude Moore, III:2953
Pinthus, Jurt, I:3111
Piranesi, Giovanni B., I:2919; III:1748
Pirates and piracy, II:2086
Pitts, Clyde E., III:2439, 2448, 2482, 2504, 2557, 2570, 2588, 2606, 2649
Pittsburgh Etching Club: Rembrandt etchings, I:2983
Pittsburgh, Pa., II:2678
Pittsburgh, University, East Asian Library: periodicals, III:377
————Libraries: Allen, Hervey, II:1663–65; American almanacs, II:2581; Archives of Industrial Society, III:915; Chinese history, III:2886; Cuban periodicals, III:3365; D'Happart papers, II:2301; economics, III:858. Foster, Stephen, II:1569; Gómez de la Serna collection, III:2272; Indian treaties, II:2512; manuscripts, III:418; Mercer, George, II:2187; Music Library, II:1570; Nevin, Ethelbert, II:1571; newspapers, III:335; Pennsylvania history, II:2683; Rumanian collection, III:2788; Sheldon, Thaddeus S., II:2209; textbooks, II:933, 935, III:1250; voting records, III:804
Pituitary-adrenocortical function, II:1184
Pizarro, Gonzalo, II:2747
Pizer, Donald, III:2013
Pizer, Irwin H., III:1544
Placzek, Adolf K., III:1747
Planning, government, I:1902
Plant culture, I:2640–50; II:1383–98; III:1664–78
Plant pathology, I:2599 (1–2, 8, 16)
Plasma substitutes, II:1185
Plastics, II:1425–26
Plato, III:2284–85
Platonism, I:955

Platt, Elizabeth T., I:3854, 3867
Play and playgrounds, I:1979
Playing cards, I:3127–28
Plenn, Abel, I:452
Plessis-Mornay, Philippe du, II:1937
Plimpton, Francis T. P., I:3672; III:1251
Plimpton, George A., I:570, 1951, 1985, 2219, 2221, 2223, 2226, 3151, 3404, 3531
Ploch, Richard A., III:1973–75
Plumb, Dorothy A., II:950
Plumb, Milton M., I:4578; II:778
Plummer, John, II:271
Plummer, Leonard B., II:2692
Plunkett, Mattie, I:224
Pluto (planet), I:2234
Poe, Edgar Allan, I:3264, 3318–23; II:1632, 1735–38; III:2054–56
Poel, William, II:1583
Poetry, I:3189–90; II:1607–09; III:2335, 2340–41; American, I:3219–31, II:1644–49, III:1964–70; English, I:3348–61, II:1774–76, III:2122; recordings, I:3213, 3229, II:1609, 1648, 1776, 1951, 1961, III:1942–43
Pogrund, Benjamin, III:2964
Pogue, Forrest C., III:2565
Poinsett, Joel R., I:1410
Point Four programs, II:692–93, 2374
Pol, Nicolaus, I:2420
Poland, history, I:4321; II:2344; III:2784–86
Polansky, Victor S., I:2246, 2514, 2786–89, 2791–92, 2808, 2810–11
Polar Regions, I:3833, 5380–81; II:2761–67; III:3395, 3397–99, 3401–03
Poleman, Horace I., I:542–43, 3775, 4353; III:2918
Police, I:1877, 5483; administration, II:874–75
Polish literature, I:3748, 3756, 3760; II:1974; III:2784
Polish Roman Catholic Union: Polonica in English, I:3760
Political associations, I:1925
Political parties, U.S., I:1448–51; II:717; III:808–12
Political science, I:1344–1451, 3943; II:651, 666–717; III:801–12
Polk, James K., III:2591
Pollak, Felix, II:1797, 2754; III:252
Pollard, Alfred W., I:616, 679, 3514
Pollard, W. Robert, III:836, 3173
Pollution, III:1700–05
Polo, Marco, II:2352
Polynesian languages, I:3172
Pombo, Jorge, I:5331
Pomfret, John Edwin, II:2478; III:154
Pomona College Library: Northwest coast maps, I:3894; Pacific area history, I:4344
Pomrenze, Seymour J., I:1913
Pondrom, Cyrena N., III:2117
Pontiac, Indian chief, I:4493
Pool, Eugene H., I:4023–24
Poole, Franklin O., I:4105
Poole, Herbert, III:746
Poor laws, England, I:4251
Poor Publishing Co., I:2701

Pope, Alexander, I:3501–04
Population, I:1272–1343, II:661–65; British Africa, I:1339; Europe, I:1335, 1340; France, I:1336; Germany, I:1337; Italy, I:1338; Sweden, I:1329; U.S., I:1272–1328, 1341–43
Population control, III:999
Population index, I:1331
Porada, Edith, I:4203
Porritt, Ruth K., II:114
Port Blakely Mill Company, II:955
Port of New York Authority, III:935
Porter, Cole, III:1866
Porter, Dorothy B., I:1398, 3226, 3265; II:2438, 2447; III:847
Porter, E. F., I:1713
Porter, John W., II:996
Porter, Patrick G., III:916
Porter, Peter B., III:2592
Porter, William A., I:1476
Porteus, Laura L., I:4888
Portland Cement Assoc. Library: catalog, I:2829
Portland Public Library: English fiction, I:3388
Portner, Stuart, I:5533
Portolan charts, I:3835–36
Portraits, I:2946–47, 2950–52
Ports, I:2118, 2125
Portugal, history, I:4295, 5310; II:2311–14; III:2731, 2733
Portuguese Africa, I:4382; III:2961
Portuguese literature, I:3695, 3702, 3705; II:2311, 2314; III:359, 2260–61, 2263, 2269
Posey, Merne H., III:1676
Posey, Sister Lauretta, II:445
Posner, Walter H., III:2682
Postal money order service, I:2049
Postal savings banks, I:1491
Postal service, I:2044–52; II:978–83
Potter, Alfred C., I:151, 250, 2645, 3305, 3372, 4075
Potter, David M., I:4047
Potter, Harriet S., I:3261
Potter, Margie, I:2380
Potter, Robert A., III:2168
Pottery, I:2851
Pottle, Frederick A., I:3427–28, 3501
Potts, E. Daniel, II:2494
Poultry husbandry, I:2601 (18), 2602 (12), 2626 (24); II:1378–79; III:1657
Pouncey, Lorene, III:3260
Pound, Ezra, II:1739; III:2057
Pound, Roscoe, II:802
Powell, Benjamin E., I:4683; II:1240
Powell, C. Percy, I:515
Powell, J. V., III:1673
Powell, John, III:1871
Powell, John H., I:3464
Powell, Lawrence C., I:119, 4190; II:115, 1854
Powell, Sarah, III:1186, 1191, 1198–99, 1215, 1601
Powell, William Stevens, II:426, 1660; III:2644, 3236
Power, Ralph L., I:97
Powers, Lyall H., II:1713

Powers, Zara J., I:4457
Prairie Press, III:546
Pratt, Harry E., I:4048; II:2192, 2546, 2610
Pratt, Ida A., I:1214, 1748, 4211–14, 4351, 4370
Pratt, John G., I:4850; III:2593
Pratt, Richard Henry, II:2508
Pratt, Willis W., I:3443; II:1820
Pratt Institute Library: schoolroom decoration, I:2932
Prayer books, I:985, 1118, 1137
Preibish, André, III:3313
Presbyterian Church, I:1103–17, 1212; II:570–78; III:735–37
Presbyterian Historical Society: American theological literature, I:1116; Bryan family, I:4869; Kentucky history, I:4858; library catalog, I:1115; manuscript collection, I:1117; missionary letters, II:570; special collections, II:571, III:736; U.S. western history, I:4684
Prescott, William H., I:4090; II:2193–95
Presidents, U.S., I:1907, 1909, 1912, 3938; II:836, 2078–79, 2087, 2089–90; III:805–07, 2409, 2413, 2419; campaigns, II:666; inaugurations, II:2089, 2494
Press, freedom, I:942
Presson, Mary Louise, III:2331
Preston, Katherine Emily, III:646
Price, Arnold H., III:12, 2701–02, 2705, 2722, 2954
Price, Francis W., I:3794
Price, Frank W., II:535; III:2943
Price, John M., III:2556
Price, Kathleen, III:1038
Price, Richard, I:4518
Price, Robert F., III:2792
Prices, I:1468, 1554, 1558, 1561, 2599 (5), 2626 (18, 48, 58, 79, 86), 2629
Prichard, Louise G., I:347
Priest, Joseph, I:4408
Priestley, H. I., I:4685
Priestley, J. B., III:2202–03
Priestley, Joseph, I:2260, 2270
Primary elections, I:1366
Primas, James E., III:1102, 1107, 1654, 2708–09, 2990, 3327, 3347, 3353
Primates, III:1409
Prime, George W., I:1041
Primers, I:696
Primm, James N., II:2651
Prince, Carl E., III:2502
Prince, Huberta, I:98
Prince, Thomas, I:4626, 4628
Prince, Toussaint L., II:855, 898
Princeton, Institute for Advanced Study: Gest Oriental Library catalog, I:4354
Princeton Theological Seminary Library: catalog, I:1000; religious periodicals, I:1001
Princeton University, Gest Oriental Library: Chinese history, III:2887; title index, I:4345
———Industrial Relations Section Library: resources, II:758; subject index, I:1637, II:757

Princeton University Library: American coins, I:2906; American history, I:4456, 4530, II:2485, III:3023, 3053; American illustrated books, I:914, II:486–87; American Indian, III:3037; American literature, I:3412; Americans in Paris, II:2085; Arabic manuscripts, I:532, 547, 3768; Asian history, III:2800; astronomy, II:1087; Audubon, John J., II:1131–32; Aztec and Mayan manuscripts, III:408; Bailey, Philip J., I:3423–24; baroque art, III:1721; Barrie, J. M., II:1807; Baruch, Bernard, III:2410; Beach, Sylvia, III:1933; Beardsley, Aubrey, I:2909, II:1473; Beauharnais, Eugene, I:4283; Berthier, Alexander, I:4558; Bibles, III:705; Blake, William, II:1811, III:1767; book illustration, III:655; bookbinding, I:923; Burr, Aaron, II:2107; Carroll, Lewis, I:3447, II:1082–83; catalog, I:251–52; Charles Scribner archives, III:501; chess, I:3122, 3124; China, II:2398; Christmas books, I:2156; Chronicle, I:172; Civil War, I:4609, 4614; Collins, Wilkie, I:3387, II:1823; Cowper, William, II:2155; Cozzens, James Gould, II:1681; Cruikshank collection, I:2911; cuneiform inscriptions, I:4225–26; Dickens, Charles, I:3463; Dickinson, Emily, III:1998–99; Dulles, John Foster, II:2118, III:2410; Edwards, Jonathan, II:2122; emblem books, II:1624; English drama, III:2123; English letters, II:1798; English literature, I:3412, III:2117; English novelists, II:1783; fables, I:3727; Faulkner, William, II:1691, III:2006; fiction, II:1616; fishing, I:3144; Fitzgerald, F. Scott, II:1695; Ford, Ford Madox, III:2170; Forrestal, James, III:2410; Franklin, Benjamin, II:2128; French portrait engraving, III:1768; German Reformation, I:4240; Ghana and Gold Coast, III:2955; Hemingway, Ernest, III:2022–23; Henry Holt archives, III:498; historical sources, III:2672; Hollis, Thomas, II:667; Homer, Winslow, I:2912; Horace, I:3737; Houston, William Churchill, III:2525; Hughes, Thomas, I:3385; illumination, I:2538; incunabula, I:620, 648; Julian Street Library, III:179; juvenile literature, III:2303; Kingsley, Charles, I:3385, III:2189; Kipling, Rudyard, III:2190–91; Lamb, Charles, I:3488–89; Latin America, III:3311; Lee, Ivy, III:405; Luther, Martin, II:2180; Machen, Arthur, III:2196; Mann, Thomas, III:2239; manuscript collections, I:487, 531–32, 544–47, II:243, 255; Maugham, W. S., II:1862; medieval manuscripts, III:435, 437; Melville, Herman, II:1728; military strategy, I:5397; Miller, Samuel, II:1733; Montaigne, Michel

E. de, I:3654; More, Paul Elmer, III:2047; Morley, Christopher, III:2049; New Jersey maps, III:2394; Nigeria, III:2956; One hundred American books, II:1640; O'Neill, Eugene, I:3315; oral history, III:2679; Oriental collection, II:1983; Oriental manuscripts, I:531; Ottoman Empire, II:2348–49; papyri, I:4224; Piranesi, III:1748; Princeton authors, III:1946; railroad finance, I:2054; rare books, III:449; Reade, Charles, I:3387, II:1869; Rochambeau, Count Jean, I:4541; Ruskin, John, I:3510; Russian bibliography, III:2757; Scheide Library, II:294; Schweitzer, Albert, II:2204; seals, II:2354; Shakespeare, William, I:3541, III:2211, 2216; Shang inscriptions, I:3780; space travel, III:1589; stamp collection, I:2047; Stevenson, Adlai, III:2410; Stevenson, R. L., II:1887; Street, Julian, III:2074; Tarkington, Booth, I:3334, II:1747; Thackeray, William, I:3557, II:1900; Trollope, Anthony, I:3561–63; Turkish and Persian manuscripts, I:544–46; Vergil, II:1967; Victorian literature, I:3405; Victorian novels, I:3384, 3386, III:2133; Virginia history, I:5238, II:2705; Western U.S. history, I:4688; Whit Burnett papers, III:1976; Wilde, Oscar, III:2231; William III (of Nassau), II:2289; Wilson, Woodrow, I:4132, II:2235, 2237, III:2648; Witherspoon, John, III:467; Wordsworth, William, I:3574; World War I, I:5514–17

———Marquand Art Library, I:2849

Printing: Abington, Va., I:885; Alabama, I:706–08; Albany, N.Y., I:826; Alexandria, Va., I:694; Allentown, Pa., II:444, III:620; Amherst, Mass., I:778; Antiqua, I:690, 901; Arizona, I:711–12; Arkansas, I:709–10; Atlanta, Ga., II:385; Auburn, N.Y., I:821, 832, III:598; Augusta, Ga., III:540; Augusta, Maine, III:551; Bangor, Maine, III:550, 553; Batavia, N.Y., I:818, 837; Belgian, I:908; Bethlehem, Pa., III:620; Boston, I:687; Brooklyn, N.Y., I:828; Buffalo, N.Y., I:819, 829, 839, III:596–97, 599–600, 602–04; Bulgarian, I:905; California, I:713–19, II:361–64, III:510–18; Canadian, II:483; Canandaigua, N.Y., I:824; Carlisle, Pa., I:864, II:444; Chambersburg, Pa., II:444, 447, III:619; Charleston, S.C., I:869, 872, II:455–56, III:631–32; Chicago, I:733, 736, II:386; Cleveland, Ohio, II:429, III:610–11; Colorado, I:720–22; Columbus, Ohio, III:608; Confederate States, I:699, II:298; Connecticut, I:723–25, II:365–66, III:519–34; Czechslovakia, II:479; Davenport, Iowa, II:389; Dayton, Ohio, I:849;

Delaware, I:726–27, II:367–69, III:535–36; Denmark, II:481; Des Moines, Iowa, III:545; Detroit, Mich., II:421; District of Columbia, I:728, II:370–84, III:537–38; Dover, N.H., III:581, 584; Dresden, N.H., I:800; Easton, Pa., II:438, 444; Economy, Pa., II:444; Ephrata, Pa., II:444; Erie, Pa., II:441; Fredericksburg, Va., I:885; French, I:912, III:647; French-American, I:688, II:355; Geneva, N.Y., I:820–22, 830; Georgetown, II:373; Georgia, I:729, II:385, III:539–42; German American, II:353, 412, 444, 469; Gettysburg, Pa., II:439, 444; Great Britain, I:664–83, II:345, 348–49; Greenland, I:913; Greensburg, Pa., II:444; Hanover, N.H., III:582–83; Hanover, Pa., II:444; Harrisburg, Pa., II:436, 442, 444–45, III:614–15; Hartford, Conn., I:723, III:520, 522–23, 526; Hebrew, I:599; Idaho, I:730–31; Illinois, I:732–38, III:543; Indiana, I:739–41, II:387–88, III:544; Iowa, I:742–46, III:545–47; Italian, I:648, III:650; Ithaca, N.Y., I:823, 833; Jamaica, I:899; Kansas, I:744–47, II:390; Kentucky, I:748–54; Latin American, I:896–904, II:475–77; Lexington, Ky., II:391; Lima, Peru, I:896–97; Los Angeles, I:719; Louisiana, I:755–58; Low Countries, II:484; Maine, I:759–61, II:393–99, III:548–56; Malta, I:910–11; Maryland, I:762–64, II:400–16, III:557–63; Massachusetts, I:765–84, II:417–20, III:564–72; Meadville, Pa., II:441; Mexican, I:900, 903–04, II:477; Michigan, I:785–86, II:421–22, 2636, III:573–74; Milwaukee, Wis., I:892; Minneapolis, Minn., II:423; Minnesota, I:787, III:575–78; Mississippi, I:788–91, II:424, III:579; Missouri, I:792–94, III:580; Montana, I:795; Morristown, N.J., I:805, 808, III:589; Nebraska, I:796; Nevada, I:797; New Bedford, Mass., II:418, 420, III:565; New Berlin, Pa., II:444; New England, I:687, II:355; New Hampshire, I:692, 798–801, III:581–84; New Haven, Conn., II:366, III:519, 521, 524–25, 527–34; New Jersey, I:694, 802–08, II:525, III:585–91; New Market, Va., I:882–83; New Mexico, I:809–12; New Orleans, I:756–57, II:392; New York, I:813–40, II:425, III:592–607; Newark, N.J., I:802; Norfolk, Va., II:465; North Carolina, I:841–44, II:426–27; North Dakota, I:845–46; Northampton, Mass., I:770; Northampton County, Pa., I:862; Ohio, I:847–50, II:428–29, III:608–11; Oklahoma, I:851, II:430; Oregon, I:852, II:431–35, III:612–13; Oxford, England, I:672; Pennsylvania, I:853–64, II:436–48, III:614–23; Peoria,

Ill., I:734, 737; Peruvian, III:649; Petersburg, Va., I:885; Philadelphia, I:694, II:437, 443; Philippines, I:907; Pittsburgh, Pa., I:853, II:440, 446–47, III:616–18, 621–23; Plymouth, Mass., II:419; Polish, III:648; Portland, Maine, III:548–49, 552, 554–56; Princeton, N.J., III:591; Providence, R.I., II:450, 453, III:625–26, 629; Reading, Pa., I:858; Rhode Island, I:865–68, II:449–54, III:624–29; Richmond, Va., II:462–63, III:643, 645–46; Rochester, N.Y., I:831, III:594–95, 601, 607; Russian, I:909; Sag Harbor, N.Y., I:827; St. Paul, Minn., II:423, III:576–78; Salem, Mass., I:784, III:566–68; Savannah, Ga., III:539, 541–42; Schenectady, N.Y., I:825; Singers Glen, Va., III:644; South Carolina, I:869–72, III:630–34; South Dakota, I:845; Southeastern, III:509; Spanish, III:2266; Spanish American, II:437; Syracuse, N.Y., III:592–93; Taunton, Mass., II:417; Tennessee, I:873–76, II:457; Texas, I:877, III:635–36; Trenton, N.J., III:585–87, 590; U.S., I:684–895, II:350–474, III:495–646; Utah, I:878, III:637; Utica, N.Y., I:817, 840; Vermont, I:692, II:458–61, III:638–42; Virginia, I:882–86, II:462–69, 643–46; Washington (state), I:887–88, II:470; Waterville, Maine, II:393; West Virginia, I:889–90, II:471–73; Winchester, Va., II:464; Wisconsin, I:891–93, II:474; Worcester, Mass., III:564, 569–72; Wyoming, I:894–95; York, Pa., I:856

Printing history, I:559, 580–948; II:308–505; III:477–680

Printing inks, I:2797

Prints, I:2836, 2838–39, 2954–93, II:1483–97, III:1763–74; historical, I:4450, 4454, 4466; railroad, I:2956

Priorities, I:5414

Prison labor, I:1580, 1593

Pritchard, James A., II:2196

Private presses, I:588, III:500, 659

Probasco, Henry, I:563

Prochovnick, Ammiel, II:1435

Proctor, Robert G. C., I:4527

Profit sharing, I:1606, 1611, 1624

Programming, II:658, 889

Programmschriften, II:130–31

Proportional representation, I:1365

Prosody, I:3153

Protestant Episcopal Church, I:1118–41, II:582–88, III:738–40

Protestant Episcopal Church Divinity School: theology, I:1003

Protestant Episcopal Church Historical Society: library resources, II:585

Protestant Reformation, I:986, 4233, 4240

Proust, Marcel, II:1616; III:2250

Provençal language, I:3162

Provençal literature, I:3645, 3647

Providence Athenaeum: library catalog, I:253

Providence Public Library: whaling, III:3126

Prynn, William, II:576

Pryor, Lewis A., III:517

Psalmody, II:542

Pseudonyms, I:15; II:1623

Psychiatry, I:2394, II:510, 1186; military, II:1170–71, 1189

Psychical research, II:509, 512

Psychological index, I:960

Psychological warfare, II:1284

Psychology, I:959–61, 2394, II:510, 651, III:685; periodicals, I:960; rural, I:2626 (78)

Psychopharmacology, II:1187

Ptolemy's Geography, I:3831, 3852, 3866; II:2036; III:2355

Public administration, I:1856–1916, II:834–76, 2804, III:1072–1140

Public Affairs Information Service, I:1261

Public finance, I:1515–42

Public health, I:2356, 2358, 2389, 5481

Public lands, U.S., II:2476

Public opinion polls, II:671

Public relations, I:2778

Public utilities, I:2030, 2036–37; III:889

Public welfare, I:1917–24; II:651, 915–18; III:1227–33

Public works, I:1591

Publishers and publishing, II:246, 256

Puccini, Giacomo, II:1558

Puerto Rico, I:5350, 5356–57, 5366, II:2749; history, III:3345–46

Puhvel, Jaan, III:2835

Pulaski, Count Kazimierz, I:4581

Pulitzer prizes, II:943

Pulliam, Marjorie, II:361; III:512

Pulling, Arthur C., I:1790–93

Pundeff, Marin V., III:2771

Punjab literature, III:2830

Purcell, George W., I:429

Purdue University Libraries: aeronautics, III:1591; agriculture, I:2610; biology, I:2610, II:1117, III:1413, 1415; biomedicine, III:1415; chemistry, I:2269, 2610; clinical medicine, surgery, and animal management, III:1453; company training programs, II:1417; engineering, I:2468, II:1072; Goss Library, II:1266; industrial engineering, II:1267; Major, Charles, I:3309; microbiology, II:1116; physical sciences, I:1072; railroads, III:936; Rogers, Bruce, I:739, III:666; science, II:1029; social sciences and humanities, III:787; sociology, II:656; vocational guidance, II:938

———Thermophysical Properties Research Center: science theses, II:1030

———Veterinary Science and Medicine Library: biomedical communication, III:1454; clinical medicine, surgery and animal management, III:1453

Purdy, Richard L., I:3480

Puritanism, II:540; III:741

Purviance, Samuel, I:4543

Pushkin, Aleksandr S., I:3755, 3763

Pushtu language, II:2358

Putignano, Andrew, II:818

Putnam, Herbert, II:2197

Putnam, Howard, II:927

Putnam, Samuel, III:3312

Pyle, Howard, I:2914

Pynson, Richard, III:343

Pyper, George Dollinger, III:2594

Quakers (Friends), I:1142–54, II:589–94, III:742–47

Qualey, Carlton C., I:1373

Qualls, LeRoy L., I:430

Quan, Lau-King, II:2360

Quatritch, firm, booksellers, I:3125

Quayle, William A., I:1016

Quebec, history, I:4388, 4392

Queen, Ellery, II:1740

Queens Borough Public Library: costume, I:2939

Queens College Library: Colombia, III:3360–61; periodicals, III:253; special resources, II:107

Quenzel, Carrol H., I:2739, III:1722, 2795

Quesada, Elwood R., II:1324

Quesnel, Louise, I:3330

Quigg, Dorothy, II:410

Quinby, Jane, II:1123

Quinn, Arthur H., I:3319, II:1653

Quinnam, Barbara, III:2332, 2344

Quintana, Ricardo, I:3440

Rabaut, Sister Palmyre, II:616

Rabinowitz, Louis M., II:288

Race relations, I:1358, 1362, 1364, 1400; II:680

Rackham, Arthur, III:1757

Racquet and Tennis Club Library: early American sport, II:1592; guide, I:3136

Radar, I:2491

Radcliffe College Library: American women, II:1009, 1013, III:1268–71; history and resources, II:114; university archives, II:948

Raddin, George G., I:3246

Rademacher, Elizabeth, III:1399, 2391

Rader, Hannelore B., III:1727

Radiant heating, I:2535

Radical organizations, III:808

Radin, Max, I:649

Radin, Paul, I:3718; III:1412

Radio, I:1868, 2484, 2494

Radioactive substances, I:2360

Radiology, history, III:1485

Radiotechnology, III:1377

Radoff, Morris L., I:4904; II:2633

Radyx, Sylvia G., III:578

Raff and Gammon, I:2722

Rafinesque, C. S., II:1041–42

Ragatz, Lowell J., I:5332

Ragsdale, Betty McFarland, III:634

Railroad literature, I:3206

Railroad prints, I:2956

Railroads, I:2054–2109, 2726, II:254, 984, 986–97, 2647; bibliography, I:2082; cars, I:2509, 2511–12; consolidations, I:2072, 2083; conventions, I:2084; economics, I:2054, 2057–58, 2067, 2069, 2072, 2074, 2076, 2080–81, 2085, 2109; electrification, I:2483; European, I:2097, 2108, II:993; gages,

Railroads (cont.)
  I:2510; government ownership,
    I:2055–56, 2077, 2101, 2106; Great
    Britain, I:2064; history, III:920, 923,
    936, 938, 939, 944–45, 947, 956;
    Iowa, I:2091; N.Y. City, I:2089–90;
    periodicals, I:2507; Scandinavian,
    I:2093; transport, I:2065; U.S., I:2098,
    2100, 2107
Railway motor cars, I:2511
Raines, C. W., I:5196
Raisig, L. Miles, II:1212
Raleigh, Walter, I:4091, 4516
Ramage, Allene, I:383
Ramalho, Américo da Costa, III:2723
Ramsaur, Edmund George, Jr., II:1830
Ramsey, Russell W., III:2850
Ramsey County, Minn., Medical Library:
    science periodicals, I:2302
Ramusio, Giambattista, Navigationi, II:2032
Rand Corporation: data processing, II:884
Randall, David A., II:295–96, 1737, 1887;
    III:1936, 2054, 2174
Randall, James G., I:4049
Randers-Pehrson, Justine (Davis), II:1241
Randers-Pehrson, N. H., I:2572
Randle, Martha Champion, II:1002
Randolph, John, I:4092; II:2198
Randolph County, Illinois, III:3186
Randolph-Macon Woman's College Library:
    Virginia women authors, I:2138
Raney, M. Llewellyn, I:120, 4050–51
Ranger, Edmund, I:920
Ranke, Leopold von, II:2318; III:2727–28
Rankin, Rebecca B., I:5060
Ranshaw, Carol Jean, II:2399
Rappaport, Gersten, III:1013
Rappaport, Philip, III:788
Rapport, Leonard, II:774
Rare books, I:549–79; II:277–307; III:443–
    76; law, II:790–91; medicine, II:1222,
    1237, 1242, 1251–52
Rastell Press, I:674
Ratchford, Fannie E., I:3406, 3411, 3504,
    3553, 3555
Ratcliff, John, I:920
Ratdolt, Erhart, printer, III:484
Rationing, I:2602 (3)
Ratliff, Alberteen, III:1815
Ratra, Paramjitk, III:530
Rau, Albert G., I:3069
Rau, Karl Heinrich, II:721
Rauch, John G., I:1794
Raw materials, I:1570, 5423
Ray, Gordon N., II:256, 1799; III:1960, 2134
Ray, Grace E., I:431
Ray, John, II:1051
Rayburn, Otto Ernest, II:2557
Raymond, Anne F., II:411
Read, Elizabeth Lumley, II:203
Read, Keith M., I:4602
Reade, Charles, I:3387; II:1869
Reading, Carolyn, II:500
Ready, James K., II:458
Real estate finance, I:2626 (60); II:738
Reapportionment, III:996
Rebec, Estelle, I:2043; II:772, 2811, 2817
Reciprocal trade, I:1546, 1550

Reclamation, I:2519
Recreation, I:5487
Recusant books, III:1947
Redfield, Robert, I:2311
Redgrave, G. R., I:679
Redlich, Fritz, II:2276
Redmond, John Oliver, III:608
Redwood trees, II:1399
Reed, Doris May, II:257, 1671, 1723
Reed, Grace W. W., II:2701
Reed, H. Clay, III:3171
Reed, Simeon G., I:2732
Reed College Library: Pacific Northwest
    economic development, I:2732
Rees, Philip Adrian, II:170
Reese, Rena, I:4837
Reeves, Dorothea D., II:975; III:855, 912,
    1613
Reeves, Harold, I:3019
Reeves, John K., II:1708; III:2032
Reference books, I:14; II:5, 15; III:1–2, 6–7,
    10, 12, 14
Reformation era, III:161, 452
Reformed Church, I:1103–04, 1107, 1110,
    1112–13; II:577–78
Refrigeration, I:2599 (10)
Rehabilitation, vocational, II:770
Reichard, Gladys A., II:1003
Reichenberger, Arnold G., II:1958
Reichert, William H., II:1113
Reichmann, Felix, I:859; II:412, 2746; III:117
Reid, Charles F., I:5278
Reid, George C., III:2595
Reid, Rosemary D., III:977
Reid, Whitelaw, II:2199
Reid, Winnifred, I:2270; II:824
Reilly, Joan, III:426
Reingold, Nathan, II:1059–60, 1089, 1357;
    III:1367, 1440
Religion, I:196, 237, 983–1253, II:513,
    515–650, III:687–783; periodicals,
    I:999, 1001, II:530, 534, 541, 545–46
Religious drama, I:3368
Religious education, I:1012
Relleve, Rosalie, III:570
Rembrandt van Rijn, I:2922, 2982–83;
    III:1770
Remer, Charles F., II:728
Remick, A. E., I:2271
Remmel, Harmon L., II:2104
Renaissance era, I:608, 4243–44; II:254,
    264–75, 278, 283, 305, 670, 1058,
    1599, 1620, 1624, 1937–38, 2278,
    2315; III:161, 1251, 1919, 2107,
    2283, 2685, 2687–88, 2690
Renstrom, Arthur G., I:2126, 2554, 2560–
    62, 2572, 2574, 2576, 2579; II:2241;
    III:1599
Renz, James H., II:2600
Reparations, I:5522, 5529
Reptiles, I:2338
Republican Party, II:717
Research, I:2178, 2180, 2451, 2626 (90)
Resins, II:1425–26
Reti-Forbes, Jean, III:1824
Revitt, Paul J., III:1803
Revolutionary War, fiction, III:1972
Rex, Frederick, I:1873, 2133

Rex, Wallace H., I:432
Rexroth, Kenneth, III:2058
Reynolds, James B., I:5081
Reynolds, John H., I:4724–27
Reynolds, Lawrence, II:1243
Reynolds, Lloyd G., I:1647
Reynolds, Michael M., III:1363, 1692
Rheinstein, Max, III:1009
Rhoads, James Berton, II:2051, 2069, 2073
Rhode Island: history, I:5160–63, II:2685–
    86; maps, I:3917
Rhode Island Historical Society: Americana,
    I:4458; Brown papers, I:2728;
    maritime history, II:2686; Rhode
    Island almanacs, I:4693; Rhode Island
    imprints, I:867–68, II:452; Rhode
    Island maps, I:3917
Rhode Island School of Design Library:
    history and resources, I:2934
Rhode Island State Archives: maritime
    history, II:2686
Rhode Island State Library: government
    publications, I:38, III:64
Rhode Island, University, Library:
    periodicals, III:254
Rhodesia, Africa, III:2931
Riant, Paul E. D., I:254
Ribero, Diego, I:3876
Riccardi, Saro J., I:2845, 2928; II:196
Ricci, Seymour de, I:13. 502, 506, 650;
    III:436
Rice, Carlton C., I:2038
Rice, Howard C., Jr., II:487, 1132, 1729,
    1733, 2122, 2398, 2705; III:437,
    1933, 2191, 3023
Rice, James E., Poultry Library: poultry
    husbandry, II:1378
Rice, I:2602 (31); II:1350; III:1672
Rice Institute Library: scientific and technical
    serials, II:1073
Rice University Library: Austro-Hungarian
    history, III:2706; scientific and
    technical serials, II:1073
——Regional Information and
    Communication Exchange:
    oceanography, III:1401
Rich, Edward P., III:1325
Richard, Father Gabriel, I:4945
Richards, Gertrude R., I:4300; II:2225
Richards, Kenneth W., III:3222–23
Richards, Laura E., III:2059
Richardson, Elmo R., II:2111
Richardson, Ernest C., I:99, 507–08, 1001,
    4228, 4459
Richardson, Helen R., I:2063, 2068, 2077;
    II:987–89
Richardson, Sir John, III:3397
Richardson, Louise, II:2473
Richardson, Mary H., I:2921
Richardson, Shirley J., II:1090
Richardson, William King, II:286
Richardson, Wilson G., I:179
Richart, Genevieve, I:1074
Richman, Irwin, III:3246
Richmond Area University Center:
    periodicals, III:255
Richmond, University, Library: Baptist
    Church, I:1072

Richter, Bodo L. O., II:1937–38
Richter, John Henry, III:80
Ricketts, C. Lindsay, III:431
Rickman, Marilee S., III:547
Rider, Fremont, I:165, 651–52
Ridge, Davy-Jo Stribling, III:469
Ridgely, Charles Goodwin, III:2596
Ridgely family, II:2200; III:2597
Rieck, Waldemar, I:3023
Rieder, Roland C., III:1105, 3369
Rieger, Morris, II:2448; III:965
Rier, Nadine S., III:531
Riffe, Nancy L., III:256
Riggs, J. M., I:1669
Riggs, John A., III:3024
Riggs, John B., II:2474
Riggs, John Beverley, II:2212
Riis, Jacob A., III:2598
Riker, Dorothy, II:2256
Riley, Franklin L., I:4981
Riley, Kathleen E., III:1125, 1170, 1185, 1212, 1750
Riley, Lyman Walter, II:544, 592, 1968; III:475, 2280
Riley, William F., III:1006
Rilke, Rainer Maria, II:1925; III:2240–41
Rimbaud, Jean Nicolas Arthur, III:2251
Rimington-Wilson, J. W., I:3126
Rinehart, Constance O., II:1242, 1586
Ringer, Barbara A., II:1269
Ringer, Gladys W., I:1692
Ringler, William, II:1775
Ringling Museum of Art Library: rare books, III:466
Rink, Ewald, III:535
Riordan, Margaret, II:2010
Riots and demonstrations, III:998
Ripley, S. Dillon, II:1133–34; III:1443
Ripley, William Z., I:2312
Rips, Rae Elizabeth, II:2639
Risorgimento, I:3663–64
Ristow, Walter W., I:3850, 3874; II:734, 2028, 2041–42, 2045–46, 2063; III:2368–69, 2374–75, 2378, 2395–97
Ritchie, George T., I:4055
Rivera, Rodolfo O., I:5333
Rivers, American, III:3006
Riverside Public Library: Colorado River, I:4686
Rivlin, Joseph B., I:3494
Ro, Regina S., III:374
Roach, George W., I:837, 5082
Road dust, I:2515
Roads, I:2517–18
Roalfe, William R., II:803
Roanoke Colony, I:4516
Roback, Abraham A., I:1242
Robbins, Caroline, II:669; III:2586
Robbins, Rossell H., I:3351; III:2122
Robbins, Roy M., I:338
Roberts, Dorothy, III:2102
Roberts, Edward Graham, II:171; III:1281
Roberts, Elizabeth Hiza, III:1362
Roberts, Elizabeth M., I:3324
Roberts, Ethel D., I:3509
Roberts, F. Warren, II:1721, 1855–56, 1858
Roberts, Jack, II:1286; III:1154

Roberts, Joseph K., I:2285, 3921
Roberts, Lily Melchoir, II:822
Roberts, Martin A., I:157, 703
Roberts, Morley, III:2204
Robertson, Giles B., III:119
Robertson, James A., I:4460, 4792–93, 5334, 5374
Robertson, Thomas W., I:3505
Robinett, Paul McDonald, II:902
Robinowitz, Grace, III:532
Robinson, Alexander C., I:5155
Robinson, Benjamin L., I:2325
Robinson, Charles, III:2599
Robinson, Edwin A., I:3325–27; II:1741–42; III:2060–63
Robinson, Evelyn B., II:679
Robinson, Francis W., I:3904
Robinson, Fred N., I:3744
Robinson, John, I:2905
Robinson, Kee, III:2042
Robinson, Stewart M., III:467
Robinson-Patman Act, II:732
Robison, Andrew, III:1748
Robson, Charles B., I:1345
Rochambeau, Count Jean, I:4541
Roche, Alphonse V., I:3645
Rochester Public Library: serial publications, I:339
Rochester Regional Research Library Council: serials, III:257
Rochester, University, East Asian Library: catalog, III:2864; history and resources, III:2861
———Libraries: bookplates, II:60; children's books, II:2015–16; Crapsey, Adelaide, III:1995; da Vinci, Leonardo, III:2635–36; Day, Mahlon, II:2015; Dewey, Thomas E., II:2116; education serials, II:1247; engineering, II:1578; fine arts serials, III:1723; Grabhorn Press, II:362; Hanson, Howard, scores, II:1572; herbals, II:1125; Howells, William Dean, II:1706; incunabula, II:1251; James, Henry, II:1714; manuscripts, I:509, III:415; medical history, II:1224; microscopy, III:1435; music, II:1534, 1552–53; Negroes, III:844; New York State history, II:2657; science collections, III:1292; science periodicals, III:1346; serials, III:259; Seward, William Henry, II:2206, III:2614; special collections, I:152; textbooks, III:1249
———Music Library, III:1837; Danish music, III:1836; Grainger, Percy, III:1870; Hart, Weldon, III:1869; liturgical music, III:1827
Rock, Kenneth W., III:2707, 2789
Rock Island Railroad, III:923
Rockefeller, George C., II:525; III:588
Rockets, I:2559; II:1296, 1299–1301, 1303–04; III:1588
Rockhill, William W., I:4355
Rockwell, William W., I:1002
Rockwell, Ford A., II:2086
Rocky Mountain region, history, II:2565, 2570, 2572; III:3142

Rocq, Margaret Miller, III:3166
Rodabaugh, James H., III:2519
Rodda, Dorothy J., III:692
Roden, Robert F., I:781
Rodger, Grace, I:3359
Rodgers, Cleveland, I:5060
Rodgers and Hammerstein Archives of Recorded Sound: recordings collection, III:1825
Rodionoff, Nicholas R., II:2048
Rodkey, F. S., I:4313
Rodriguez, Adelaide, II:413
Rodriguez, Antonio, III:649
Roe, Francis Asbury, III:2596
Roecker, Alan W., III:1414
Roehrig, Josephine Paula, II:2064
Roethlisberger, Marcel, III:703
Rogerenes, I:4633
Rogers, Bruce, I:739, 944; II:498, 503; III:659, 664, 666, 671
Rogers, D. M., II:596
Rogers, Francis M., I:3167
Rogers, Frank B., II:1151
Rogers, John, I:4633
Rogers, Paul P., I:3689
Rogers, Robert W., I:533
Rogin, Martin, II:2817
Rolfe, Franklin P., I:3461
Roller, Duane H. D., II:1054; III:1318
Rollins, Hyder E., II:1849
Romaine, Lawrence B., II:1257
Roman Catholic Church, I:1155–87, 1212, II:595–623, III:748–56; newspapers, I:1166; periodicals, I:1160, 1177, 1179, II:605, 611–12, 622–23
Roman de la Rose, I:3643
Romance languages, I:3162–67, 3216; periodicals, III:1928
Romans, Bernard, I:3905
Romansch language, I:3166
Rood, Arnold, III:1890
Roos, Charles, II:1168–72, 1189, 1220
Roosevelt, Franklin D., I:1418, 4407, 4471, II:2201, III:2600; Library, I:1418
Roosevelt, Robert B., I:1806
Roosevelt, Theodore, II:2202–03; III:1907, 2601–03, 2969
Roosevelt University Library: Africana, II:2441
Rose, Dean H., II:1391
Rose, Grace D., I:808
Rose, Kenneth, II:1563
Rose, Margaret, III:3238
Rose, William G., III:2040
Roseberry, Cecil R., III:149
Rosenbach, A. S. W., I:209, 1243, 2910, 3460, 3532, 3549, 3812, 3816; II:911, 2011
Rosenberg, Bruce A., III:1859
Rosenberg, Henry, I:153
Rosenberg Library: history and resources, I:133, 153
Rosenfeld, Alvin H., III:1967
Rosengarten, Joseph G., I:3987
Rosenthal, Elaine P., III:562
Rosenthal, Frederick John, II:895
Rosenthal, Robert, II:258; III:155

Rosenthal, Solomon, I:1241
Rosenwald, Lessing J., I:571, 3871; II:305, 484
Rosenzweig, Ben Zion, II:648
Rosicrucians, I:1934
Rosovsky, Henry, III:859
Ross, Allen M., II:1292
Ross, Earle D., III:1255
Ross, Ian, II:1819
Ross, John, II:2499
Ross, T. Edward, I:1039
Rossetti, Dante G., I:3506
Rossi, Matti M., II:1892
Roth, Catherine E., III:841
Roth, Elizabeth, III:1796
Roth, William M., I:3578
Rothacker, J. Michael, III:131
Rothfeder, Herbert P., III:3413
Rothrock, O. J., III:1768
Rothwell, C. Easton, II:116
Roulstone, John, bookbinder, III:677
Rousseau, G. S., III:2224
Rousseau, Jean J., I:3657–58
Rowell, J. C., I:3900
Rowell, Margaret K., III:211
Rowland, Buford, II:715, 2087; III:1126
Rowlandson, Thomas, I:2838
Rowse, Edward F., I:5083
Rowson, Susanna H., I:3328
Roy, Albert, II:978
Roy, G. Ross, III:2147
Roy, M. N., II:709
Royal primers, I:696, 700
Roylance, Dale R., III:656, 667, 1432, 2717
Rubáiyát, II:1990
Rubber, I:2827–28, 4193 (29), II:1425–26
Rubey, James T., I:1902, 5529
Rubincam, Milton, III:2650
Rubinstein, Joseph, II:287, 567, 670, 1061
Rubsamen, Walter Howard, II:1544
Ruddon, Elaine Marie, II:422
Rudge, William Edwin, III:659
Rudolph, Earle Leighton, I:3227; II:1647
Rudolph, G. A., III:1424, 1603
Rugby Colony, III:3251
Rugg, Harold G., I:880–81, 3407
Ruggles, Melville J., II:2277, 2327
Rumania, I:4323, II:730, 2347; history, III:2787–91
Rumball-Petre, Edwin A. R., I:1042; III:706
Rumford, Benjamin Thompson, II:1044
Rural electrification, II:1348, 1351; III:1641
Rural health, II:1352
Rural life, I:2603
Rush, Benjamin, II:2533
Rush, Charles E., I:144
Rusk, Ralph L., I:4648; III:1958
Ruskin, John, I:3507–10; II:1870
Ruskin, Mary Patricia, II:617
Russ, Nellie May, III:3167
Russell, Carl Porcher, III:2605
Russell, George William (AE), II:1871–72
Russell, J. Thomas, III:1166
Russell, John R., II:316, 362, 1224, 1714
Russell, Mattie, II:259; III:419
Russell Sage Foundation Library: pageants, I:3109; social work, I:1262

Russia, history, I:4310–17, II:2320–36, III:2748–67
Russian bibliography, I:21
Russian language, I:3169
Russian literature, I:3745, 3747, 3749–55, 3757–59, 3761–66, II:142, 1971–72, III:2744, 2750, 2753
Rutgers University Law Library: legal bibliographies, III:1020
————Library, I:173; American almanacs, II:2580; Bowles, William Lisle, II:1812; Bradford imprint, III:588; Civil War, III:3095; Cobbett, William, III:2151; Far East, II:2367; Handel, George Frederick, III:1868; literary annuals, I:3209; medieval history, II:2273; mission records, II:532; Negroes, II:834, 845–46; Neilson collection, I:2741; New Jersey fiction, III:1972; New Jersey history, III:3225; New Jersey maps, II:2056; Swinburne, Algernon, II:1894; textbooks, I:1984; U.S. Constitution, II:828
Rutherford, Livingston, I:838
Rutherford B. Hayes Memorial Library: resources, II:2142, III:2519
Rutledge, John, III:2606
Rutman, Anita, II:1704, 1718; III:2603
Ruysch, Johannes, II:2037
Ryan, Carmelita S., III:3117
Ryan, Garry D., III:1117, 1184, 1188, 1201, 1203, 3420
Ryan, Harold W., III:1134
Ryan, Milo, III:3421
Ryan, Pat M., Jr., II:1813
Rylance, Daniel, III:3237
Ryskamp, Charles, II:1811; III:1767, 2155
Ryukyu Islands, II:2417, 2420; III:2907

Sabin, Elizabeth, III:2349
Sabin, Joseph, Bibliotheca Americana, I:4404, 4461
Sacconaghi, Charles D., III:518
Sacket, Marie Hélène, II:1124
Sackton, Alexander, III:2003
Sadleir, Michael, II:1782; III:2135
Saegesser, Lee, III:1222, 1226
Safety, I:2344, 2355, 2359, 2602 (14), II:1033; at sea, I:5460
Safflower, III:1674
Sagas, Icelandic, I:3614–16, 3623
St. Armand, Barton L., III:2076
St. Aubin, Ernst, I:1625
St. Augustine, Fla., history, I:4795
St. Catherine's Monastery, II:579
St. Charles' Seminary, I:1183
St. Clement's Church, I:1003
Saint-Gaudens, Augustus, III:1756
St. John, Wallace, I:1004
St. John's Seminary Library: Estelle Doheny collection, I:572, II:297, III:3156
St. John's University Library: accounting history, I:2772
St. Lawrence seaway, I:2111, 2115, 2526, 2599 (30)
St. Leo Abbey, Florida, III:3172
St. Louis Mercantile Library: Missouri and

Illinois newspapers, I:401, 4699; Tennessee Baptist imprints, II:550
St. Louis Public Library: aeronautics, I:2563; American dialects, I:3152; architecture, I:2891–92; British and American poets, I:3359; criminology, I:1927; fur trade, I:1555; genealogy, I:4156, 4161, 4172, II:2253, III:2660; maps, I:3855; miniature scores, I:3031; national parks, I:2870; Negroes in America, I:1399; Shakespeare, William, I:3533
St. Louis University Libraries: Jesuits, II:597; Vatican Library, II:606; Vatican manuscripts, III:753
St. Mary's University, San Antonio: Spanish archives, III:3264
St. Olaf College Library: English Bibles, I:1036; periodicals, II:162, 169
St. Paul Public Library: periodicals union list, II:162, 169
St. Procopius College Library: Lincoln, Abraham, III:2550
Saito, Shiro, III:362, 3396
Sakanishi, Shio, I:3040
Sakhalin, Japan, III:2902
Sakr, Carmelita S., II:777
Salem Athenaeum, I:255
Sales tax, I:1529, 1539
Salisbury, Ruth, II:2581, III:334
Salishan languages, I:3183
Saliva, II:1161
Salk, Jonas E., II:1232
Salley, Alexander S., Jr., I:871, 5167–68
Salmagundi Club Library: costume, I:2944; Louis XVII, I:3648
Salmon, Lucy M., I:482
Salmonella, II:1190
Salmons, Ruth M., III:1547, 1607, 1614
Salmonsen, Ella M., I:2346, 2348–50, 2352, 2534, 2552
Salomão, Rosa, II:876
Salomon, Richard G., II:586
Salvador, I:5304, 5321
Salvation Army, I:1204–05
Salvemini, Gaetano, I:3668
Salverson, Carol, III:287
Sam Houston State College Library: Texas history, III:3263
Sammons, Vivian O., III:574
Samoa, I:5382, 5385
Sampley, Arthur M., I:340
Sampson, Francis A., I:4987
Samuels, Lee, III:2024
San Antonio, Texas, history, I:5194
San Antonio Public Library: circuses, I:3112, III:1902; U.S. Army, I:5398
San Bernardino Free Public Library: citrus fruits, I:2646
San Fernando Cathedral, Texas, III:754
San Francisco Art Assoc., I:2922
San Francisco Bay, maps, I:3902; II:2057
San Francisco Law Library, I:1720
San Francisco Public Library: English fiction, I:3389; music, I:3032; 19th century catalogues, I:256, 2173, 3817
San Jacinto Museum of History Assoc., I:5197

San Jose State College Library: biology,
III:1416
San Marcos Baptist Academy, III:721
Sanborn, Herbert J., III:668
Sanborn, Ruth A., I:2564
Sanchez, George I., II:927
Sanchez, Irene, III:799
Sánchez, José, I:2172
Sanchez, M., I:2208
Sanchez, Manuel S., I:5335
Sand, I:2280, 2288
Sandburg, Carl, I:3329; II:246, 1743;
III:2064–67
Sanders, Erhard, II:894
Sanders, Henry A., I:1029, 4206
Sandys, George, I:3511; II:1873
Sang, Philip D., II:2171
Sanitary and municipal engineering, II:1313–
23
Sanskrit literature, I:3772, 3776; III:2835
Santa Barbara Mission Archives, I:4733;
II:2655
Santa Fe Laboratory Museum, I:4654
Santamarina, Antonio, II:212
Santo-Tomás, Raúl, III:3294
Santos, Richard, III:754, 3264
Saponis, Leocadia Ann, III:589
Saranac Lake Free Library: Adirondackana,
III:3230
Sardinia, I:4302
Sargent, Ralph M., I:3313; II:283
Sargent, W. G., Company, II:970
Sargent, Winthrop, III:2607
Saricks, Ambrose, II:2304, 2310
Sarton, George, II:1049
Sassoon, Siegfried, III:2205
Satellites, artificial, II:1296–1303
Satorn, Choosri, III:3041
Sauer, Gordon C., II:1135
Saunders, Lyle, I:5019
Savage, Grace O., I:2240
Savage, J. B., Co., I:2730
Savage, J. E., I:2413
Savage, M. F., II:1561
Savannah Historical Research Assoc., I:4807
Savannah Public Library: Georgia history,
I:4811
Saville, Marshall H., I:2313
Saville, Russell, II:712
Savord, Ruth, I:351, 1810
Sawyer, Ellen M., I:1747
Sawyer, Rollin A., I:1478–79, 1482, 1504,
1519, 1886, 5454, 5512
Sayer, William L., I:942
Sayre, Francis Bowes, III:2608
Scandinavian countries, I:4193 (5); history,
I:4304–09
Scandinavian literature, I:254, 3216, 3606–
32; II:1928–34; III:2723
Scarich, Kathryn, III:828
Schaaf, Robert W., II:816
Schad, Robert O., I:593; II:284, 297; III:453
Schalau, Robert D., III:536
Schapiro, Israel, I:1244
Schatoff, Michael, II:214
Schecter, Abraham I., I:1246; II:647
Scheffler, Emma M., III:2398
Scheide, William H., II:294

Schekorra, Eva W., III:628
Schelling, F. E., I:3534–35
Schertz, Morris, II:339
Schick, Beth M., II:1030
Schick, Frank L., III:1451
Schiller, A. Arthur, II:2271
Schilling, Hugo K., I:3160
Schinz, Albert, I:3658
Schlinkert, Leroy W., I:5266
Schlundt, Esther M., I:2610; II:1116, 1267
Schmavonian, Arsiné, III:2492
Schmidt, Carl, I:1029
Schmidt, John F., II:555; III:725
Schmidt, John J., I:3747
Schmidt, Thomas V., III:623
Schmidt, Valentine L., III:466
Schmidt, William F., III:1256, 3216
Schmitt, Alfred R., II:131
Schmitt, Martin, II:1004; III:2428, 2431,
2495
Schmittou, Mary Jane, III:3345
Schneider, Heinrich, I:3596
Schneider, Herbert, I:2011
Schneider, Joyce B., III:851
Schnitzer, Martha, I:4173
Schnitzler, Mario C., II:2725
Schnorrenberg, John M., III:1724
Schoeffer, Peter, II:332
Schoessow, Mathilde Marthe, II:1545
Scholberg, Henry, III:2832
Scholes, Robert E., III:2186
Schomburg collection of Negro literature,
II:682, 2440
Schoneman, Ruth E., I:2830
Schons, Dorothy, II:1959
School lunches, I:2602 (26); II:1353;
III:1607–08
Schoolfield, George C., III:2241
Schools, Brooklyn, N.Y., I:1955; N.Y. City,
I:1956
Schorer, Mark, III:2193
Schoyer, George P., III:779
Schreiber, Carl F., I:3597
Schreiber, L. W., I:2981
Schrero, Morris, I:2258, 2497, 2666, 2781
Schroeder, Peter S., II:1347, 1361; III:1624,
1635, 1639
Schroeder, Rebecca, III:1854
Schroeder, Theodore A., I:1359; III:1071
Schubert, Franz, I:3045
Schullian, Dorothy M., I:2433; II:1151, 1252;
III:1319
Schultz, Charles R., III:924
Schulz, Herbert C., I:3870; II:1641; III:430,
2119, 2149
Schuman, Henry, II:1229, 1243; III:1482
Schurz, Carl, III:2609
Schwab, Marguerite J., I:302
Schwandt, Ernest, II:2800
Schwartz, Benjamin, I:4215
Schwartz, Harry, III:951, 1093, 1138, 1205–
06, 1220, 1222–23, 1226, 1371, 1457
Schwegmann, George A., Jr., I:368; II:207;
III:340
Schweinfurth, Edna, II:429
Schweitzer, Albert, II:2204; III:2610
Schwerin, Kurt, I:1795; II:797; III:1044
Sciarra-Colonna family, I:2717

Science, I:2157–2342, II:1015–1137,
III:1272–1443; bibliography,
III:1283; dictionaries, II:1024, 1032;
fiction, III:1940; history, I:2184–94,
II:1039–61, III:447, 1277, 1307–25;
translations, II:1036–37; USSR,
II:2335
Science, periodicals, I:2195–2208, 2385,
II:1062–81, III:1326–63; Chinese,
III:1341–42, 1354, 1357;
Czechoslovak, III:1347; Japanese,
III:1327, 1356–57; Russian,
III:1358–59
Scientific management, I:2687–88; II:1418
Scientists, biography, I:2161, 2168; II:1028
Scisco, Louis D., I:4910–11
Scotland, history, I:4271
Scott, Amreta Natalie, II:420
Scott, Dred, I:4615
Scott, Edith, III:540
Scott, Franklin W., I:341
Scott, John E., II:2178
Scott, Lorene L., I:3253
Scott, Mary A., I:3669
Scott, S. Morley, I:4392
Scott, Sir Walter, I:3512–13; III:2206–09
Scott, Temple, I:3473
Scott, Will, I:2201
Scott-Elliott, A. H., II:1474; III:1769
Scottish literature, II:2285
Scouten, Arthur H., I:1893
Scribner, Charles, publisher, III:501
Scribner, Lynette L., III:1443
Scrip, I:2629 (40)
Scripps College Library: Pacific area, I:4344
Scriven, Margaret, II:2611
Scroggs, William O., I:4889
Scudder, Samuel H., I:2296
Sculpture, III:1756, 1760
Sea novels, III:1936
Seabury, Samuel, II:586
Seager, Robert, II, II:976
Sealock, Margaret, II:1031
Sealock, Richard B., I:860, 5084
Seals, II:2261; Babylonian, II:2265;
Massachusetts Bay Colony, I:775;
Near East, I:4203, 4221, 4223;
western Asia, II:2354
Sealts, Merton M., Jr., I:3311; II:1730
Seattle Public Library: aeronautics, I:2565;
art, archaeology, and decorative arts,
III:1726; books for blind, III:200;
China, II:2391; European painting,
II:1477; harbors and docks, I:2523;
Northwest history, III:3159;
periodicals, I:364; soybeans, I:2647
Seattle University Library: Napoleon
Bonaparte, II:2300
Seattle World's Fair, III:1296
Seaver, William N., I:1464
Seawell, Mary Robert, III:2333
Secret societies, I:1934–43; II:919–20;
III:1234
Seeley, Pauline A., I:5084
Seelhammer, Ruth, III:2172
Seely, Caroline E., I:2227
Seidensticker, Oswald, I:861
Seidler, Richard D., III:1826

Selby, Carol E., II:1551
Selby, Mildred, III:689, 3179
Selby, Paul O., III:2083
Selekman, Benjamin M., III:882
Selenium, I:2267
Selfridge, Thomas Oliver, III:2611
Seligman, E. R. A., I:1452, 1458, 1466
Sellers, David Foote, III:2612
Selver, Paul, II:1979
Seminole Indians, I:4489
Semitic languages, I:3170–71
Semitic literature, I:3767–71
Semmes, Raphael, I:4912
Semple, Eugene, III:2613
Seneca, I:3738
Seniority, I:2693–94
Seris, Homero, I:3715
Sermons, I:4624, 4629; New England, I:1010, 4941
Servetus, Michael, II:1234, 2205
Sesame, I:2602 (20)
Seton, Grace T., I:2144
Seventh Day Adventist Church, II:624
Severance, Frank H., I:342
Severance, Henry O., I:137
Severance taxes, I:1537
Seversmith, Herbert F., III:2656
Sewage disposal, I:2530–31, 2537
Seward, William Henry, II:2206; III:2614
Sewell, Richard H., III:2512
Sewickley Public Library: Pennsylvania, I:5155
Sexton, Meta M., I:4299
Shaffer, Ellen, II:2011; III:468, 2334
Shaffer, Ellen K., I:653, 3336
Shafroth, John Franklin, II:2207
Shakers, I:1188–91; II:625
Shakespeare, William, I:233–34, 3390–91, 3514–43; II:1874–80; III:2210–18; promptbooks, III:2217
Shambaugh, Benjamin F., I:4847
Shanley, James Lyndon, II:1753
Shannon, Edgar F., Jr., II:1898–99
Shapiro, Karl J., I:3153, 3330; III:2036
Sharify, Meer Nasser, II:2431
Sharp, Freeman W., II:2806
Shattuck, Charles H., III:2217
Shattuck, Frederick C., I:4940
Shaver, Mary M., I:612
Shaw, Charles B., I:4462
Shaw, George Bernard, I:3544–45; II:1181–83; III:2219–20
Shaw, Gertrude M., I:3651
Shaw, Glenn, III:2901
Shaw, John Mackay, III:2302, 2335, 2340
Shaw, Nathaniel, I:2744
Shaw, Ralph R., I:2466; II:358; III:502–05
Shaw, Renata V., III:1762
Shaw, Robert G., I:3113
Shaw, Stanford J., II:2348
Shaw, Thomas, I:2744
Shaw, Thomas S., I:2900, 3329; II:68
Shaw, Virginia E., I:4768; II:2200; III:2597
Shay, Mary L., I:4301
Shea, James E., II:1274
Shearer, Augustus H., I:1837–38, 4228, 5156, 5208
Shearer, James F., I:872

Sheets, Marian L., I:2847
Sheffield, Joanne Wagner, III:541
Shelby, Charmion, I:467
Shelby, Isaac, II:2208
Shelby Iron Works, II:1430
Sheldon, Addison E., I:4997
Sheldon, Charles, I:2341
Sheldon, Charles M., III:1954
Sheldon, Thaddeus S., II:2209
Shell molding, II:1433
Shelley, Fred, I:4687; II:2095, 2653
Shelley, Percy B., I:3546
Shelley, Philip A., I:3408
Shelterbelts, I:2659
Shenandoah Valley, I:5215
Sheridan, Philip H., I:4093; III:2615
Sherman, Roger, I:4705
Sherman, Stuart C., III:3126
Sherman, William F., III:1092, 1648–49
Sherman, William T., I:4094; III:2616–17
Sherr, Paul C., III:1855
Sherrard, Elizabeth M., III:450
Sherrod, John, II:1258
Shetler, Charles, II:472, 2711–13; III:3094, 3121
Shewmaker, Kenneth E., III:2427
Shiel, Matthew Phipps, I:1884
Shields, Nancy C., I:3670
Shields, Sophie K., II:117
Shih, Bernadette P. N., III:378, 1342
Shih, Maria Huang, III:2336
Shih, Walter D., III:533
Shih-Chia, Chu, II:2400
Shillaber, Caroline, III:1730
Shilling, Charles W., III:1417
Shimanaka, Katsumi, III:2902
Shimmell, Lewis S., I:5142
Shinn, Josiah H., I:4727
Shipbuilding, I:2128, 2503–04, 5453–54
Shipman, Joseph C., III:1294
Shipping, I:2628 (6), 2749–63; II:1290–93, 1309, 1423
Shipton, Clifford K., I:2012–13; II:354; III:506, 1257
Shipton, Nathaniel N., III:3148
Shipwrecks, III:3051
Shirato, Ichiro, II:2390
Shirley, William W., I:1483
Shoe industry, I:2823
Shoemaker, Alfred L., I:862; II:204, 1360
Shoemaker, Michael, I:3881
Shoemaker, Richard H., II:358; III:502–05, 507
Shonkwiler, William F., II:905, 1334
Shooting, I:3132
Short, John C., I:5125
Shorthand, I:2689
Shriver, Harry C., I:5399
Shufeldt, Robert Wilson, III:2618
Shufelt, Edith Lord, II:160
Shufelt, Marcia, II:385
Shultz, Charles R., III:3127
Shumaker, Elizabeth M., I:1437
Shuster, E. A., Jr., I:2292
Sibley, John L., I:2014
Sicily, I:4302
Sickman, Lawrence, III:1779
Sidney, Phillip, II:1798

Siebert, Wilbur H., I:4242
Siedzik, John, II:2278
Siefer, Roxanna, III:331
Sifton, Paul G., III:2399
Signor, Nelle, I:1887; II:873
Sikkim, III:2828
Sikorsky, Igor I., II:1324
Silas Bronson Library, I:257
Sill, Edward R., I:4095
Silliman, Benjamin, I:1999
Sills, R. Malcolm, I:725
Silver standard, I:1480
Simkhovitch, V. G., I:554
Simkins, Thomas M., Jr., II:1621, 1762, 1821
Simmonds, Harney, III:1759
Simmons, J. S. G., II:501
Simmons, John, III:331
Simmons, John F., III:1303
Simmons College Library: historical maps and charts, I:3846
Simms, William Gilmore, III:2068
Simon, H., I:3046
Simonetti, Martha L., III:3247
Simons, Corinne M., I:2174–75, 2371–72
Simons, Lao G., I:2220
Simple Simon, I:3813
Simpson, Bernice, I:2165
Sims, Edith M., II:200
Sims, Grace, II:2013
Simsar, Muhammed A., I:541
Sinclair, Donald A., III:834, 845, 3095
Sinclair, May, III:2221
Sinclair, Upton, III:2069
Sinclair Refining Co., I:2802
Singapore, III:2828
Singer, Godfrey F., II:1781
Single tax, I:1519
Siouan languages, I:2184
Sioussat, St. George L., I:5125, 5181
Sit-down strikes, I:1652
Sizemore, W. Christian, III:260
Skaggs, Alma S., I:343
Skard, Sigmund, I:4305, 4308–09
Skarstedt, Marcus, I:184
Skau, Dorothy B., III:120
Skeel, Emily E. F., I:4125–27; II:2227
Skillin, Glenn B., III:2581
Skilton, Julius A., II:2738
Skin, II:1160
Skinner, Aubrey E., II:340, 1766
Skordas, Gust, I:4907
Slack, Charles G., I:4410
Slade, Bertha C., I:3468
Slade, William A., I:159, 1497
Slamecka, Vladimir, III:1347
Slang, I:3149
Slanker, Barbara O., III:96, 1396
Slate, Joseph E., III:2025
Slattery, William J., III:571
Slaughter, Peggy Ann, III:538
Slavery, I:3267, 4613, 4622; II:2555; III:846
Slavic history and literature, I:3745–66; II:1971–80; III:2734–92, 3313
Slavic languages, I:3168–69; III:1913
Slavonic bibliography, I:11
Sloane, Clarence E., II:604
Sloane, William, II:2014

Slocum, John J., II:1847
Slovak literature, II:1973
Slum clearance, I:2867, 2899
Slyfield, Donna Christensen, III:582
Small, Norman J., I:1895
Smart, James R., III:1835
Smet, Joachim, II:621
Smith, Adam, I:1455–56
Smith, Adelaide M., II:2286
Smith, Alice E., I:5268–69; III:3281
Smith, Ashbel, III:3270
Smith, Bernice F., III:1683, 1687
Smith, Charles L., I:207; II:1643
Smith, Charles W., I:95, 1374, 4667–72;
     II:2577
Smith, Clara A., I:3875, 4494
Smith, Courtney Craig, II:1800
Smith, Curtis R., III:192
Smith, David E., I:2212, 2221–27, 3798;
     III:2146
Smith, David R., III:1875, 3075
Smith, Dorothy, I:344
Smith, Dwight L., III:3154
Smith, E. Gene, III:2921
Smith, Edgar F., I:2252–55, 2268, 2274;
     II:1107
Smith, Edward E., III:2760
Smith, Edward R., I:2893–95
Smith, Elsdon C., I:4174; II:2254
Smith, Erwin Evans, II:1505
Smith, George D., booksellers, I:654
Smith, George Milton, II:1025
Smith, Gerrit, I:5031
Smith, Glenn C., I:441
Smith, Harold F., III:2370
Smith, Henry L., I:1959
Smith, Herbert F., III:3225
Smith, Hubert S., II:901
Smith, Idris, III:263
Smith, J. William, I:607
Smith, Joel S., I:3766
Smith, John, I:4096
Smith, John D., I:2315
Smith, Lester W., I:1474
Smith, Logan Pearsall, III:2070
Smith, Mary Alice Brown, II:379
Smith, Maurice H., III:1592
Smith, Murphy D., III:1278, 3028
Smith, Philip M., I:4182
Smith, Preserved, I:4064
Smith, Robert C., I:2848, 2854
Smith, Robert M., I:3538
Smith, Russell M., II:2149
Smith, Sharon C., II:2715
Smith, Solomon G., III:1705
Smith, Sophia, II:1014
Smith, Susan Sutton, III:1995
Smith, Thomas R., II:2033–34; III:2365
Smith, Wallace Bruce, II:1702
Smith, Walter George, III:748
Smith, William, II:939
Smith, William Jay, III:2341
Smith College Library: serials, III:234;
     women, II:1014
Smith College, Museum of Art: Winslow
     Homer, II:1492
Smither, Harriet, I:5198
Smithsonian Institution: aeronautics, I:2545;

botany, I:2315; Minnesota Centennial
     exhibition, I:4970; society & periodical
     publications, I:345
——Freer collection: Bible, I:1029–31
——Library: aeronautics, I:2566
Smits, Rudolf, II:224, 227; III:390–91
Smoke and smoke prevention, I:2529, 2532
Smoking and health, III:1464
Smyth, Herbert W., I:3724, 3740
Smyth, Sheila A., III:607
Snell, Joseph W., III:2430, 2442, 2444, 2486,
     2555, 2559, 2569, 2593, 2599, 3191
Snider, Helen G., I:3582
Snoddy, Alice Louise, II:459
Snow, Eliot, III:2619
Snow, Samuel, I:2737
Snuggs, Myrtle Ann, III:629
Snyder, Charles, II:1152
Snyder, Jacob R., I:4739
Snyder, Richard L., III:378, 1342
Snyderman, George S., II:2513–14
Social credit, I:1482
Social reform, I:1254, 1263
Social Science Research Council, I:1928
Social sciences, I:1254–2156, II:651–1014,
     III:784–1271; Chinese periodicals,
     II:653, III:791; Hungarian periodicals,
     III:790; serials, II:652–53, III:787–
     88, 790–91
Social Security Act, I:1604, 1626
Social welfare, III:1227–33
Social work, I:1262; III:1232
Socialism, I:1512–14, 1600; II:746, 754;
     III:786, 813–14
Socialist Labor Party of America, III:812
Societies, scientific, I:2171
Society for the History of the Germans in
     Maryland Library, I:4913
Society for the Propagation of the Gospel,
     II:532
Society of American Archivists: church
     records, III:693–94; college and
     university archives, III:1258
Society of American Foresters, III:1683
Society of California Pioneers, I:4739
Society of Friends, I:1142–54
Society of the New York Hospital, I:2373
Sociology, I:1254–68, 1344; II:654–56;
     III:795
Socolofsky Homer E., II:2619
Sodium nitrate, I:2257
Soil conservation, I:2665–73; II:1408–11
Soils, I:2599 (13, 14)
Sokol, Roberta A., III:1500
Solar heating, II:1272
Solberg, Thorvald, I:4296
Solomon, Barbara M., III:1271
Solyom-Fekete, William, III:2743, 2777
Somaliland, II:2457
Somers, Wayne, III:1324
Sommer, Francis E., I:2433; II:1252
Soncino, printers, I:649
Sondley Reference Library, I:154; American
     imprints, I:704
Songs, I:3007, 3051–54, 3057, 3064;
     English, I:3355; Negro, I:3220
Sonneck, O. G. T., I:3036–37, 3043, 3070,
     3072, 3081–83; III:1856

Sonnedecker, Glenn, II:1250
Sons and Daughters of Pioneer Rivermen,
     III:3006
Soriano, Frank S., III:2721, 2804–06, 2820,
     2846–47, 2992, 3356, 3358, 3390–
     91
Sotheby, Wilkinson and Hodge, I:655, 1796,
     3373
Sotheran, H. & Co., I:3154
Sotirin, Paul G., II:999
Součková, Milada, II:1979
Soule, Edmund P., III:1857
Sound recordings, II:1546, 2259; music,
     III:1825, 1828, 1835, 1841
Sousa, John Philip, III:1835
South, Aloha, III:1200
South, Charles E., III:3346
South, history, III:3128–34
South Africa, history, I:4371–72, 4374–75;
     III:2964
South America, history, II:2262, 2723
South Asia, III:2824–37
South Bend Public Library: Indiana, I:4838
South Carolina, history, I:5164–72; II:2687;
     III:3249
South Carolina Dept. of Archives and History:
     government publications, III:65
South Carolina Historical Society, I:5166
South Carolina, University, Library: Bridges,
     Robert, III:2140; Caroliniana, I:5170;
     rare books, II:298; II:469; Simms,
     William Gilmore, III:2068
South Dakota, history, I:5173–74; II:2688
South Dakota Library Association: serials,
     III:261
South Dakota State Library: South Dakota
     history, I:5174
South Dakota, University, Library: serials,
     III:215; South Dakota history, II:2688
South Manchurian Railway Company,
     III:2897
South Sea Bubble, I:1477
South Sea Company, III:905 ·
Southcott, Joanna, III:2620
Southeast Asia, III:2829, 2837
Southeastern Library Association: union
     catalogs, III:121
Southeastern United States: history, I:154;
     maps, II:2054
Southern California, University, Library:
     civilian defense, I:5480; folk songs,
     I:3028; Hamlin Garland, III:2014;
     Latin America, III:3324; philosophy,
     I:956, II:511, III:683; radio and
     television, III:1892; water resources,
     II:1317
Southern Connecticut State College Library:
     juvenile literature, III:2337
Southern fiction, I:3242
Southern Illinois University Library: catalog,
     III:180; Irish collection, III:2120; Latin
     America, III:3312; Lawrence, D. H.,
     II:1857; manuscripts, II:242; Mormon
     history, III:734; periodicals, III:262;
     philosophy, III:684; Schroeder,
     Theodore A., III:1071; special
     collections, III:146; travel literature,
     III:2370; Vietnam, III:2852

Southern Methodist University Library:
    Bibles, III:707; history of science,
    III:1320; incunabula, III:491–92;
    intellectual history, III:2673; rare
    books, III:470; serials, I:306, 315;
    Spanish collection, III:2266
Southern Mississippi, University, Library:
    Colmer, William M., III:2468
Southern states, history, I:4635–45; II:2554–
    57
Southey, Robert, I:3547; II:1885
Southwest, history, I:4654–56, 5018;
    III:3128–29
Southwest Missouri State College Library:
    Rimbaud, Jean Nicolas Arthur,
    III:2251
Southwest Museum: Arizoniana, I:4717–18
Southwestern Baptist Theological Seminary:
    serials, I:315
Southwestern Louisiana, University, Libraries:
    rice industry, III:1672
Sower, Christopher, I:859
Soybeans, I:2626 (74), 2647; II:1395;
    processing, III:1675
Spaatz, Carl, I:5542
Space law, II:799; III:1019
Space medicine, II:1172
Space travel and exploration, II:1297–1304;
    III:1588–89, 1595–97
Spain, history, I:4290–91, 4293–94, 4297;
    III:2275, 2730, 2732
Spalding, C. Sumner, I:3964
Spalding, Frances, II:266
Spanier, Lela M., III:1548
Spanish Africa, I:4380, 4383
Spanish American printing, I:594
Spanish Armada, I:4293
Spanish drama, I:3687–89; II:1953–54,
    1958; III:2258, 2264–65, 2268
Spanish fiction, I:3690–93
Spanish language, I:3165
Spanish literature, I:3687–3708; II:79, 100–
    102, 1950–58, 1961–62; III:2257–
    60, 2262, 2264–73
Spanish Morocco, I:4380
Spanish printing, I:594–95
Spanton, Albert I., I:3390
Spargo, John W., I:14, 782
Sparks, Jared, I:4415, 4439, 4463
Spaulding, Stephen, I:641
Spaulding, Thomas M., I:5393
Spear, Dorothea E., II:2486
Special collections, I:76–78, 86, 89–91, 93,
    95–96, 99, 101–02, 125–26; II:72–
    73, 77, 80–86, 95, 112–15, 121, 123
Special Libraries Association, I:101–04,
    2390; II:65, 81; Alabama Chapter,
    II:1213; Biological Sciences Group,
    I:2304; Boston Chapter, I:346, III:123;
    Boston Chapter Science and
    Technology Group, III:1348–49;
    Chemistry Section, I:2272–73;
    Cincinnati Chapter, I:347, II:1074;
    classification collection, III:83;
    Colorado Chapter, III:125; Connecticut
    Valley Chapter, II:172; directory,
    III:122; Geography and Map Division,
    II:2035, III:2371; Georgia Chapter,

II:82; Greater St. Louis Chapter, II:83,
    173; Heart of America Chapter,
    III:263; Illinois Chapter, I:348–49,
    2692, II:174; Kansas City Chapter,
    II:176; Michigan Chapter, I:350;
    Minnesota Chapter, I:2207, III:264;
    New Jersey Chapter, II:177, III:265;
    New York Chapter, I:351, II:84,
    III:126, 788, 896; Oak Ridge Chapter,
    II:1075; Pharmaceutical Section,
    II:1214; Philadelphia Libraries
    Council, III:129; Picture Division,
    III:1725; Pittsburgh Chapter, I:352,
    II:85; Rio Grande Chapter, III:266;
    San Francisco Bay Region Chapter,
    I:353, II:178, III:267, 1350;
    Science-Technology Group, I:2450;
    Social Sciences Group, I:1648;
    Southern California Chapter, I:354,
    II:1215, III:268; Special Libraries
    Council of Philadelphia, I:105, II:86;
    Technical book review index, II:1259,
    III:1564; Translation Center, III:13;
    Western New York Chapter, III:379
Speck, Frank G., II:1119
Speck, William A., I:3597–99
Spectacles, II:1241
Speech and hearing sciences, III:192
Speer, Klaus, III:1827
Speer, Lucile, II:35
Spehr, Paul C., III:3104
Spell, Jefferson R., I:3704, 3719
Spell, Lota M., I:5336; II:2726
Spence, Paul H., II:878
Spence, Thomas H., I:1104, 1212; II:577–78
Spencer, Helen, II:414
Spencer, Herbert, II:1797
Spencer, Marjory C., II:1178, 1184, 1193
Spenser, Edmund, I:3548
Sper, Felix, I:3409
Sperling, John G., III:905
Spielberg, Peter, II:1848
Spielman, Herbert, II:687
Spiller, Robert E., I:91
Spinning, I:2819
Spinoza, Baruch, II:506, 508
Spinoza, Benedictus de, III:682
Spiral Press, N.Y., III:605
Spivacke, Harold, I:3047–48
Spivey, Herman E., I:3277; II:1673
Spoerri, James F., II:1846
Sports, I:3129–38; II:1592–94
Spottswood, Richard K., III:1858
Spratt, Hereward P., I:2176
Sproat, Nancy, II:2000
Sprong, Olive T., I:3066
Sprudz, Adolf, III:1009, 1047
Spry, Betty, III:2840, 2912
Squair, Lyall, III:938
Squier, Ephraim George, II:2210
Stachlin, Robert H., II:423
Stahl, William Harris, II:2036
Stahler, Helen H., II:759
Stalin, Joseph, III:2763
Stallans, Thomas J., III:1134
Stallman, R. W., II:1683–84
Stanard, William G., I:5219
Standardization, I:2695

Standards of living, I:2625
Stanford University, Hoover Institution:
    African collection, II:2441, III:2936;
    African history, III:2957–68; African
    serials, III:380; Austria-Hungary,
    III:2704; Belgian publications, I:5513;
    British industrial relations, I:1639;
    Bukharin, Nikolai I., III:2759;
    catalogs, III:181; Chinese collection,
    II:2379, 2401–02; Chinese
    Communist movement, III:2888;
    Chinese history, III:2888–89;
    collections, I:4191, II:116; Communist
    International, III:813; East-Central and
    East Europe, II:221; French history,
    III:2718; German Africa, III:2962;
    German archives, II:2818; German
    industrial relations, I:1467; Germany,
    II:2298; Hoover, Herbert, III:2522;
    Hungarian history, III:2778; Japan,
    II:2413, 2416, III:2906; Library,
    I:4186, 4196; Menshevik Movement,
    III:2758; military records, III:1143;
    Nazi Party, III:3415; newspapers,
    III:336; ''Okhrana'', III:2760;
    Ottoman Empire. II:2348; Paris Peace
    Conference, I:5518–19; Polish
    underground, I:5545; Portuguese
    Africa, III:2961; resources, III:156;
    Russia, II:2328; Russian Imperial
    Army, III:1148; Russian publications,
    III:2761; Russian reference books,
    III:14; Russian newspapers and
    periodicals, I:453; Ryuku Islands,
    II:2417; Slavic collection, I:4320;
    Soviet armed forces, III:1147, 1149;
    Soviet disarmament policy, III:1150;
    Soviet newspapers, III:381; Stalin,
    Joseph, III:2763; statistics, III:796
———Libraries: anthropology, II:1118;
    Artigas, I:5281; Ashendene Press,
    III:669; Australian history, I:5371,
    III:2707; book design, III:658;
    Bulgarian history, III:2772;
    Czechoslovak history, III:2774;
    DeVoto, Bernard, II:1685; fine
    printing, I:606; German industrial
    relations, I:1467; German literature,
    I:3592; German periodicals, III:382;
    Grabhorn Press, II:502; Greenland,
    I:913; history of science, III:1321;
    Hungarian history, III:2779; industrial
    relations, I:1638; Jordan, David Starr,
    II:951, III:2536; Joyce, James,
    III:2184; Lawrence, D. H., III:2193;
    Maugham, W. S., II:1862; music,
    II:1546–47; Newton, Isaac, III:1309,
    1321; oral history, III:2680; Panama
    Canal, III:3350; Polish history,
    III:2785; railroads, I:2104; recordings,
    II:1546; Rumanian history, III:2789;
    serials, I:355, III:897, 1351;
    transportation, I:2764; undergraduate
    catalogs, III:182; U.S. government
    publications, III:66; Uruguay, I:5281;
    water resources, II:1317; Western
    Europe, III:2684
Stanhope, Philip, II:2110

Stanley, D. Keith, Jr., III:2281
Stanton, Madeline E., I:2416; II:2205; III:1490
Stanton, William R., II:2210
Staphylococcal infection, II:1192
Staples, Charles R., I:4869–70
Star, Morris, III:2043
Star spangled banner, I:3065, 3070
Starch, Taylor, I:3161
Starch, I:2800
Stark, Lewis M., I:2588, 3225; II:299–300, 341, 357, 359, 503–04, 526, 1344, 1765, 1767, 2224, 2228; III:708
Stark, Marie C., I:5574
Starke, Vivian A., II:467
Starkes, M. Thomas, III:2498
Starkie, Walter, II:2315
Starnes, DeWitt Talmage, II:1603
Starr, Edward C., I:1057, 1070–71; II:549; III:722
Starr, Herbert Willmarth, II:1837
Starr, Louis M., II:2259
Starr, Thomas I., I:4052–53
Starrett, Agnes L., II:1665
State government, I:1895, 1897–98, 1900, 1904
State rights, I:1903
State trade barriers, I:2628 (1)
Statistics, I:1269–1343; II:657–60; III:796; commercial, I:2041
Steam railways, I:2074
Steam turbines, I:2476
Steamboats, III:937
Stearns, Bertha M., I:1263
Stearns, Foster, II:599
Stearns, Mae I., I:677
Stearns, Margaret, III:787
Stearns, Samuel, I:4097
Steel, I:2497, 2782, 2786–89, 2805, 2810, 2826, 4193 (23); II:1427
Steele, Helen M., I:1576, 1578
Steele, Oliver L., III:2015
Steeves, H. Alan, I:943
Stefansson, Evelyn, II:2583, 2765
Stefansson, Vilhjalmur, II:2583, 2763, 2765
Steffan, T. G., I:3441
Stein, Barbara H., III:3311
Stein, Gertrude, I:3331–32
Stein, Gordon, III:2528
Steinbeck, John, III:2071
Steiner, Herbert, II:1922
Steinhoff, William R., II:1903
Steinitz, Kate Trauman, II:488, 1225, 1482
Stellfeld Music Library: catalog, II:1537–38; collection, II:1518–19, 1554
Stephen, Carol, II:1564
Stephen, Robert O., III:3265
Stephen F. Austin State College Library: Texas history, III:3261
Stephens, Alexander A., I:2046, 4098
Stephens, Fran, III:2152
Stephens, James, II:1886; III:2222
Stephens, Lola Wyckoff, II:913
Stephens, Stephen DeWitt, II:1493
Stephenson, Douglas R., I:2061, 2512, 2745
Stephenson, George M., I:4673
Stephenson, Richard W., II:2044; III:2384, 2402, 3102

Sterilization, III:999
Sterling, George, III:2621
Stern, Alfred Whital, II:2166, 2170, 2175
Stern, William B., I:1750; III:1045
Stern-Taeubler, Selma, I:1245
Sterne, Laurence, III:2223–24
Sterrett, Mary F., III:1140
Steuben, Baron von, I:4580
Steuernagel, Harriet, III:1544–45
Stevens, Harry R., I:433; II:2487
Stevens, Henry, I:3856, 3988; II:291, 2731
Stevens, Isaac Ingalls, II:2211; III:2622
Stevens, Rolland E., II:928, 1969; III:789, 2271
Stevens, Shirley, II:813
Stevens, Wallace, II:1645; III:2072
Stevens family, III:2623
Stevens Institute of Technology Library: Taylor, Frederick Winslow, II:1418; transportation, I:2748; Vinci, Leonardo da, I:4104
Stevenson, Adlai, III:2410
Stevenson, Edward L., I:3836, 3852, 3876
Stevenson, Noel C., III:130
Stevenson, Richard T., I:5126
Stevenson, Robert Louis, I:3549–50; II:1887–90
Stevenson, William E., I:5247
Stewart, Alice R., III:2999
Stewart, Bruce W., III:426, 3061
Stewart, Charles David, II:1744
Stewart, Donald H., III:3064
Stewart, Ethelbert, III:2624
Stewart, John H., I:4284
Stewart, Kate MacLean, II:2158, 2203, 2215; III:2969
Stewart, Powell, II:222
Stewart, Roland C., I:1574; II:1068
Stewart, William J., III:2600
Stieg, Lewis F., I:4237
Stieglitz, Alfred, II:1499
Stiles, Charles W., I:2374
Stiles, Jeanne N., III:2338
Stillwell, Charlotte B., III:1069
Stillwell, Margaret B., I:615, 656, 4113
Stimmer, Tobias, II:1486
Stimson, Henry L., II:2212
Stinnecke Maryland Episcopal Library, I:1139
Stipe, Robert E., III:2367
Stirling-Maxwell, William, II:2315
Stock raising, I:2599 (19)
Stockbridge, John C., I:3219
Stocking, Robert E., III:421
Stockton, Frank Richard, III:2073
Stockton, Patricia, III:583
Stoddard, F. G., III:2167, 2197
Stoddard, Roger E., III:609, 1968
Stohlman, W. Frederick, I:2849
Stokes, E. A., Jr., II:2556
Stokes, I. N. P., I:384, 4454, 5085
Stokes, William E., Jr., II:2198
Stoler, Mildred C., I:4839–41
Stoller, Leo, III:2077
Stone, Edna L., I:1580–81, 1609, 1613–14, 1650
Stone, Wilbur M., I:3812, 3818–19
Stonehill College Library: Joseph W. Martin, Jr., III:2566

Storage batteries, I:2543
Storkan, Charles J., I:356
Storm, Colton, II:2552; III:3152
Stoughton, Gertrude K., III:3167
Stover, Edna V., II:272
Stowe, Harriet Beecher, II:1745–46
Strandel, Constance A., I:2684, 5477
Stratman, Carl Joseph, I:1610; III:1893–96, 2125–26
Stratton, Porter A., III:337
Stratton, W. C., I:192
Stratton, William J., I:4826
Straus, Oscar S., I:4099; II:2213
Stravinsky, Igor, III:1889
Strawberry, I:2626 (28)
Strawbridge, Ruth, II:770
Street, Julian, III:2074
Street railways, I:2132, 2134, 2137; II:1000
Streeter, Floyd B., I:4651, 4955
Streeter, Mary E., I:258, 357; II:179
Streeter, Thomas W., I:4688; II:2474, 2693, 2696
Stricker, Thomas Perry, I:713
Strikes, I:1651–53, 1657; II:781
String music, II:1552
Strobridge, Truman R., III:942, 1652
Strohecker, Edwin C., III:2339
Strohm, Adam J., I:59
Strong, Katherine B., I:347
Stroupe, Henry Smith, II:545–46
Strout, Elizabeth, I:3795
Strunk, W. O., I:3071
Stryker-Roda, Kenn, III:2656
Stuart, Elizabeth C., II:2568
Stubbs, Carolyn, III:880
Student self-government, I:1980
Studer, William J., III:2063
Studley, Miriam V., III:2623
Stumberg, George W., I:1758
Stump, Vernon C., I:434
Stuntz, Stephen C., I:2611
Sturm, Rudolf, III:2775
Sturtevant, Charles G., I:5398
Sturtevant, E. Lewis, I:2323–24
Stutler, Boyd B., II:473
Subject collections in libraries, III:87
Subject headings, library, II:65
Submarines, I:5456; II:1309
Subsidies, maritime, I:2127, 2130
Subways, I:2133, 2137
Suckow, Ruth, III:2075
Suelflow, August R., III:693–94
Suez Canal, I:2114, 2123; II:2291
Suffolk County, N.Y., history, I:5069–70
Suffrage, I:1365–69
Sugar, I:1560
Sugar beet, I:2601 (16)
Sullivan, Frank, I:3500
Sullivan, Henry B., I:2277
Sullivan, Howard A., III:343, 1470
Sullivan, Joan Theresa, III:542
Sullivan, Louis Henry, III:1747
Sullivan, Majie P., I:3500
Summerall, Charles Pelot, II:2214
Summers, Natalia, II:701
Sumner, Charles, I:259
Sunday laws, I:1009
Sunflowers, I:2628 (20); III:1676

Surgery, plastic, III:1446
Surplus property, II:854—55
Surrealism, II:1476
Surry County, North Carolina, III:3235
Survey Associates, III:1228
Surveying, I:2726
Surveys, industrial, I:2442
Sussex County, Delaware, III:3169
Sutcliffe, Denham, II:1642
Sutherland, Bruce, III:3400
Sutherland, D. M., III:2246
Sutro Library: collection, II:94; Hebraica, III:764; Italian notarial documents, III:2725; Latin Americana, III:3297; Mexican imprints and manuscripts, II:2737
Suzuki, Seiko June, II:363; III:512
Suzuki, Yukihisa, III:2900
Swaengsugdi, Thanoo, II:2433
Swan, Bradford F., I:783; II:452, 482, 1731, 2037, 2685
Swan, Marshall W., I:3738; II:1932
Swanson, Donald C. E., III:1917
Swanson, Evadene B., I:4674
Swanton, Walter I., I:107
Swarthmore College, Friends Historical Library, I:1152—53, III:747; Quaker (Friends), II:589, 593, III:743
————Library: Addams, Jane, II:916; British Americana, I:4462; occult sciences, I:962; peace, I:972, 978—79, II:507; serials, I:320; Swarthmore collection, III:1253
Swartz, Jean M., II:468
Swearingen, M., I:4890
Sweden, history, I:4304, 4307
Swedish Americans, II:940
Swedish literature, I:3626, 3628—30; III:2243
Sweeney, David, II:618
Sweeney, John L., II:1609
Sweet, William Warren, I:1213; II:631
Swem, Earl G., I:478, 948, 1849, 2183, 2593, 2619, 2855, 2952, 3200, 3217—18, 3539, 3864, 3941, 3958, 4021, 5225—27, 5229
Swenson, Paul B., II:1901
Swider, Veronica, III:610
Swierenga, Robert P., III:3190
Swift, Jonathan, I:3551—54; II:1891—93; III:2227—28
Swift, Lindsay, I:3989, 4941
Swigart, Paul E., II:205
Swinburne, Algernon, II:1894—95
Swingle, Walter T., I:2326
Swisher, Bella French, II:157
Switzerland, history, I:4326; II:2350; III:2722
Sworakowski, Witold S., II:2328; III:813
Sydnor, Charles S., I:791
Sylvia, Esther, I:4297
Symbolism, religious, I:530
Synge, John Millington, II:1896—97
Syracuse Public Library: fine printing, I:607; genealogy and heraldry, I:4175; manuscripts and incunabula, I:607; Syracuse history, I:5023
Syracuse University Libraries: Africa, III:2970; African serials and newspapers, III:384; American history,

III:3025; Asian collection, III:2801; Balzac, Honore de, III:2247; Bourke-White, Margaret, III:1783; Braithwaite, William Stanley, III:2440; Camus, Jean Pierre, III:2248; Chaffee, Edmund B., III:2458; Corsi, Edward, III:2472; earth sciences, III:1402; economics, III:852; Falk, Sawyer, III:2488; Flanders, Ralph E., III:2492—93; Flick, Alexander C., III:2494; geology, III:1403; Harriman, Averell, III:2515; Hillyer, Robert S., III:2028; history of science, III:1322; Horton, S. Wentworth, III:2524; Johnson, George F., III:2533; Kipling, Rudyard, III:2192; Latin America, III:3313; Lorenzo collection, III:2416; manuscripts, III:415; maps, III:2372; mathematics history, III:1322; medieval and Renaissance history, III:2690; music recordings, III:1828; New York history, I:5031; O'Connor, William Van, III:2581; Oneida Community, III:3229; Philippine manuscripts, III:2913; political cartoons, III:1755; psychology serials, III:685; railroad history, III:938—39; rare books, III:471; religion serials, III:695; Rembrandt etchings, III:1770; Ryukyu Islands, III:2907; science fiction, II:1617, III:1940; serials, III:243; Slavic serials and newspapers, III:385; Southeast Asian periodicals, III:383; Taft, William Howard, III:2625; Thompson, Dorothy, III:2629; Venetian history, II:2318, III:2727—28
————State University College of Forestry Library: serials, III:1684
Syrett, Harold C., II:2137
Szabo, Andrew, III:2682
Szabo, György, III:438
Szajkowski, Zosa, II:646
Szczesnick, Boleslaw, II:619
Szilard, Paula, III:1577
Szladits, Lola L., II:1868; III:1759, 1959, 2164
Szporluk, Roman, III:2785

Taber, Thomas T., II:986
Taborn, Paul, II:818
Taft, Robert, II:1508
Taft, William Howard, II:2215; III:327, 2625
Taggard, Genevieve, I:3333
Taggart, W. T., I:2274
Taiwan, II:2404
Takeshita, K. Lillian, II:2418
Talbot, Silas, III:2626
Taliaferro, Lawrence, III:2627
Talkington, Gladys, II:973
Tallman, Johanna E., III:1295
Tammany, I:1925
Tang, Raymond N., III:2885
Tanganyika, Africa, III:2981
Tanis, James Robert, II:2578
Tanks, I:5407
Tannenbaum, Earl, II:1857
Tannenbaum, Samuel A., I:3493

Tanner, Earl C., II:2686
Tansill, William R., I:1445
Tanzy, C. E., III:2340
Tapley, Harriet S., I:784
Tapley, Priscilla M., III:584
Taracanzio, Timothy A., I:1751
Tarbell, Ida M., II:2163
Tariff, I:1536, 1543—51
Tarkington, Booth, I:3334; II:1747
Tartini, Guiseppe, II:1557
Tashjian, Nouvart, I:358
Tate, Allen, I:3228, 3230, 3324; II:1649
Tate, Vernon D., I:2796
Tauber, Maurice F., II:118
Tax exemption, I:1493, 1525; homestead, I:2628 (15)
Taxation, I:2626 (25); war, I:1520
Taylor, Archer, I:15, 608; II:10—11, 301, 1923
Taylor, Barbara, III:844
Taylor, Charles E., III:2121
Taylor, Charles M., III:2129
Taylor, Edith S., I:863
Taylor, Frederick Winslow, II:1418
Taylor, Graham, II:918
Taylor, Henry C., I:3843; III:1370
Taylor, Irwin, I:1710
Taylor, James Wickes, III:2628
Taylor, John, I:3819
Taylor, John E., III:1177
Taylor, Kanardy L., I:2591
Taylor, Kim, III:1899
Taylor, Louise M., I:1960, 4328
Taylor, Oliver A., I:984
Taylor, Robert H., II:1798
Taylor, Ruby L., I:1434
Taylor, Thomas, I:955
Taylor, Virginia H., II:2186
Taylor, Zachary, II:2216
Teachers and teaching methods, I:1976—81
Teachers pensions, I:1981
Teagarden, Lucetta, II:1948; III:2202
Technical reports, II:1258
Technology, I:2435—2829; II:1253—1440; III:1563—1602; periodicals, I:2195—2208
Tedrow, Joseph H., II:1422
Teggart, Frederick J., I:2104
Telephone, I:2053
Television, I:2484
Temple, Phillips, I:56
Temple University Library: De la Mare, Walter, III:2156
Tennent, Gilbert, II:572
Tennessee, history, I:5175—84; III:3250—56
Tennessee, Dept. of Archives, I:5181
Tennessee Historical Commission, III:3252
Tennessee Historical Society: Jackson, Andrew, III:2529
Tennessee, Secretary of State, I:5181
Tennessee State Library and Archives: Buell-Brien papers, III:2441; catalog, I:260, III:183; Cherokee collection, III:3038; Civil War, III:3096—97; county histories, III:3256; county records, III:3253; diaries and church records, III:3255; Dickinson, Jacob McGovock, II:2117, III:2479; Faw,

Walter Wagner, III:2490; genealogy, III:2661–62; government publications, II:43, III:67; Highlander Folk School, III:1266–67; Jackson, Andrew, III:2529; Jones family, III:2535; Killebrew, Joseph Buckner, III:2539; land records, III:3254; legislative reference, I:1435; McIver, John, III:2562; Moore, John Trotwood, III:2575; newspapers, III:338; popular music, II:1563; registers of personal papers, III:2417; Rugby papers, III:3251; Tennessee history, I:5181–82

Tennessee, University, Library: Congreve, William, III:2153–54; science collections, II:1026

Tennessee Valley Project, I:2871

Tenney, Mary A., I:4918

Tenney, S. M., I:4871

Tennyson, Alfred, Lord, I:3555; II:1898–99; III:2229

Tennyson, Frederick, III:2230

Terence, II:1970

Terner, Janet R., III:1372

Teton Mountains, I:5274

Texas, authors, I:3270

Texas, history, I:5185–5202; II:1472, 2689–96; III:3128, 3257–70

Texas A. & M. University Library: livestock industry, III:1660; serials, III:270

Texas Christian University: serials union list, I:315

Texas Engineers Library: catalog, I:2469

Texas Library Association, I:108

Texas list of scientific and technical serial publications, III:1353

Texas Southern University Library: Negro collection, II:683

Texas State College for Women: serials union list, I:315

Texas State Library and Archives: census records, III:799; genealogy, III:2663; government publications, II:44, III:68; Lamar, Mirabeau Buonaparte, I:5199; legislative reference collection, I:1436; maps, III:2386, 2400; Martinez, Antonio, II:2186; Maxey, Samuel Bell, III:2567; military history, III:1141; Texas authors, I:3270; Texas history, I:5188, 5196, III:3266; Texas imprints, I:877

Texas Tech University Library: Southwest collection, II:2694, III:3128–29

Texas, University, Humanities Research Center: Armitage, Merle, III:670; Bibles, II:427, III:709; Browning, Robert and Elizabeth Barrett, III:2141–42, 2144; Burns, Robert, II:1819; Dickens, Charles, III:2165–66; drama, II:1611; familiar books, II:302; Faulkner, William II:1693; Garnett family, II:1801; Hellman, Lillian, III:2020–21; history of science, III:1323; Hopkins, Kenneth, III:2173; Lawrence, D. H., II:1855, 1858; Lawrence, T. E., III:2194; Lewis, Sinclair, II:1721; Machen, Arthur,

III:2195; photography, III:1784; Pound, Ezra, III:2057; Priestley, J. B., III:2202–03; Queen, Ellery, II:1740; Sassoon, Siegfried, III:2205; Southcott, Joanna, III:2620; special collections, III:157; Steinbeck, John, III:2071; Texas history, III:3267; theatre and drama, III:1897; Traven, B., III:2242; Wise, Thomas J., II:1802
———Library: Agee, James III:1980; American sketch book, II:157; Anderson, Maxwell, III:1983–84; anesthesia, I:2375; archives collection, III:3268; Argentine acquisitions, III:3326; Ariosto, Ludovico, II:1948; Arkansas newspapers, II:198; Bolivian acquisitions, III:3328; Brazilian acquisitions, III:3335; British history, III:2699; British newspapers and periodicals, II:222; Byron, George Gordon, I:3441–43, II:1820; Canadian literature, III:2998; Canadiana, II:2464; Caribbean acquisitions, III:3342; Cather, Willa, II:1676; Central American acquisitions, III:3351; Chilean acquisitions, III:3359; Civil War, II:2555–56, III:3082; Coleridge collection, III:2152; Colombian acquisitions, III:3362; Confederate textbooks, III:3079; Cooper, James Fenimore, III:1992; Cuban acquisitions, III:3366; drama and theatre collections, III:1882; Dunsany, Lord, III:1267; Ecuadorian acquisitions, III:3370; education of Spanish-speaking people, II:927; Eliot, T. S., III:2004; Ercilla, Alonso de, II:1959; Fernandez de Lizardi, J. J., I:3718–19; forgeries, I:3411; Gandhi, Mahatma, II:2133; Geneva Bible, II:524; German literature, II:1923; Gondra, Manuel E., II:2755; Guatemala, III:3348; Hardy, Thomas, III:2171; Hebraica and Judaica, I:1246, II:647–48, III:757; Hemingway, Ernest, III:2024; herbal, I:2432; Hernandez, Francisco, II:1040; Hernandez, Jose, III:2273; Hergesheimer, Joseph, III:2025–26; Hertzog imprints, II:495; historical manuscripts, I:5202; Howells, William Dean, II:1707; Hudson, William Henry, III:2176; Hume, David, III:686; incunabula, II:340; indexes, I:16; Irving, Washington, II:1710; James, Henry, II:1712; Joyce, James, III:2188; Kipling, Rudyard, II:1850; Lamb, Charles, I:3490; Latin American collection, I:5289, 5336–37, II:2726, III:3314; MacNeice, Louis, III:2197; Masters, Edgar Lee, III:2042; Maupassant, Guy de, III:2249; Medina, Jose Toribio, II:475; Melville, Herman, II:1727; Meredith, George, II:1864; Mexican acquisitions, III:3384; Mexican history, II:2691, 2733, 2741, 2745, III:3381–84; Mexican literary journals, III:2267;

Mexican news-sheets, III:3379; Morley, Christopher, III:2048, 2050; Mormon history, III:3258; oil pioneers, III:3265; periodical, I:174; Peruvian acquisitions, III:3389; Poe, Edgar Allan, III:2055; Poe, Alexander, I:3502, 3504; rare books, I:573; serials, III:271; Shelley, Percy Bysshe, I:3546, 3553–54; Shiel, Matthew P., II:1884; 16th-century chronicles, II:2260; Spanish-American church history, I:988; Spanish-American literature, I:3704; Spanish documents, I:5194; STC English books, III:494; Stewart, Charles David, II:1744; Swift, Jonathan, I:3553–54; Swinburne, Algernon, II:1895; Tennyson, Alfred, I:3555; Texas history, II:2691–92, 2695, III:3258; Texas imprints, I:877; Thomason, J. W., Jr., collection, II:1472; U.S.-Mexican relations, I:1405; University of Texas archives, III:1259; Urena, Pedro Henriquez, II:2751; Uruguayan acquisitions, III:3392; Venezuelan acquisitions, III:3393; Victorian literature, II:219, 1796; war poetry, II:1607; Western history, III:3144; Whitman, Walt, II:1766; Wise, Thomas J., II:1803; World War I, I:5189; Wrenn Library, I:133, 3395, 3410; Yeats, W. B., II:1909

Textbooks, I:1982–86; II:932–35; III:1249–51; Confederate, III:3079

Textile industry, I:2817, 2824–25; II:1425–26, 1428

Textile Workers Union of America, III:983

Tezla, Albert, III:2780

Thackeray, William Makepeace, I:3415, 3556–58; II:1900–01

Thaden, J. F., III:831

Thai literature, III:2845

Thailand, II:2433; III:2828; history, III:2844–47

Thalberg, Irving, II:1575

Thalken, Thomas T., II:2145

Thatched roofs, II:1396

Thaxten, Roland, I:2327

Thayer, Evelyn, I:2342

Thayer, Gordon W., I:2153, 3188, 3355

Thayer, Henry, III:1709

Thayer, Lee, III:1709

Theater, I:3086–3119; II:1573, 1579–81, 1583–86, 1590–91, 1650–51; III:1873–1903; architecture, III:1746; periodicals, III:1893–94

Theatre Guild, II:1580

Theiss, Kay Thomas, III:554

Thelan, Esther, III:983

Thévenot, Melchisédech, I:233

Thibault, Roberta, III:2472

Thieme, Darius L., III:1832

Theis, Louis, I:2984

Thirty Years' War, II:2275–76

Thom, Emma M., I:2290

Thom, Ian W., III:2196

Thomas à Kempis, I:989

Thomas, Allen C., I:1154
Thomas, Bradford L., III:2365
Thomas, Daniel H., II:2279
Thomas, David L., III:2574
Thomas, David Y., I:4794–95
Thomas, Dylan, III:2002
Thomas, Elizabeth, I:1929
Thomas, Isaiah, I:180, 705, 766, 779–80, 3221
Thomas, Laura, III:3269
Thomas, Mabel W., I:4729; II:2589
Thomas, Martha Lou, III:1472
Thomas, Milton H., I:3956
Thomas, Roger, I:4905
Thomas, Sister Ursula, I:1184
Thomas, William S., I:4579
Thomas Gilcrease Institute of American History, III:3026
Thomases, Jerome, I:5429
Thomason, John William, Jr., II:1472
Thomason, Robert E., II:652
Thompson, Alma M., I:1400
Thompson, Arthur W., II:2470; III:3005
Thompson, C. Seymour, I:155, 574
Thompson, David W., I:864
Thompson, Donald E., I:4874; III:131
Thompson, Dorothy, III:2629
Thompson, Edgar T., I:1400
Thompson, Edith E. B., I:5220
Thompson, Francis, I:3559
Thompson, Glenn E., III:969
Thompson, Harold W., Jr., II:2155
Thompson, John Howard, II:415
Thompson, Laura A., I:1469, 1579, 1585, 1589, 1608, 1632, 1656, 1660, 1664–66, 2693
Thompson, Lawrence S., II:1005, 1661, 1960, 1991; III:2268
Thompson, Margaret S., I:4031
Thompson, R. T., I:2741
Thompson, Ralph, I:3266
Thompson, Ruth, I:4969
Thompson, Thomas P., I:4874, 4891
Thompson Products, Inc., I:1636
Thomson, H. W., II:977
Thomson, James, I:3560
Thomson, Peter G., I:5127
Thomson, Samuel H., I:4243–44
Thomson, Thomas R., I:2100
Thordarson, Chester H., library, I:2159, 2164; II:1048
Thoreau, Henry David, I:3251, 3256, 3335; II:1632, 1748–53; III:2076–77
Thornbrough, Gayle, II:2138
Thorndike, Israel, I:2711
Thornton, Mary L., I:5108; II:45, 2664
Thornton, Weldon, III:2188
Thorp, Willard, I:3510; III:1976
Thorpe, James, I:3412; III:1923, 2694, 3010
Thorpe, Thomas, I:4275
Thrash, James R., II:1108
Thrower, Norman J. W., III:2469
Thung, Yvonne, III:354
Thurber, Charles H., I:1951
Thurber, James, III:2078–80
Thurlow, Constance E., II:2148
Thursfield, Richard E., I:1961
Thurston, Ada, I:646

Thwaites, Reuben G., I:435, 4483, 4675
Tibbets, Robert A., III:666
Tibetan collections, III:2918, 2921
Tibetan literature, I:3791, 4355; II:1981, 1985, 1991
Tibetan Tripitaka, II:632
Tickhill Psalter, I:522
Ticknor, George, I:3695, 4100; III:2081
Ticknor, Margaret, II:1305–06
Tierney, M. Jeanne, III:572
Tilley, Nannie M., I:4638
Tillinghast, William H., I:2147; III:2109
Tilton, Eleanor M., II:1703
Tilton, Eva Maude, III:15
Tilton, McLane, III:2630
Time, III:1369
Time and motion study, I:2684
Timms, Walter, III:2458
Tin, I:2791, 4193 (23)
Tingley, Donald F., III:3187
Tinker, Chauncey Brewster, II:1804, 1831
Tinker, Edward L., I:359
Tinkler, Joan C., III:2487
Tippecanoe, Battle of, I:4591
Titley, Joan, II:1228; III:1513
Titus, Thomas R., III:563
Tobacco, I:2626 (75), 2640–42; II:1383, 1386, 2292; III:1667, 1670–71
Tobey, Leona E., I:4153
Tobin, James E., I:3552
Tocqueville, Alexis de, II:668
Tod, George-Anna, I:1399
Toda, Kenji, I:3781
Todd, Albert, I:5403
Todd, William B., I:3413; II:1802–03, 1895; III:2055
Toedteberg, Emma, I:60
Toelle, Gervase, II:621
Tohoku, Japan, III:2905
Toledo Public Library: union catalog, II:8
Tolles, Frederick Barnes, II:592, 594
Tolmachev, Mirjana, III:842
Tolstoy, Leo N., I:3757
Tomato industry, I:2628 (10)
Tomlinson, S. Arthur, I:1704
Tompkins, Hamilton B., I:3954, 4014
Toner, J. M., I:4116
Toovey, James, I:604
Torpedoes, I:5457; II:1309
Torquemada, Tomás de, II:601
Torts, II:787
Toscanini, Arturo, III:1838
Toth, Margaret K., II:1125, 2015
Totten, Ellsworth, I:261
Tourgée, Albion W., III:2631
Tower, Charlemagne, I:1716, 3759
Tower, Joseph T., Jr., I:3833, 3842
Tower, William H., I:2047
Towner, Isabel L., II:81
Towner, Lawrence W., III:150
Townsend, Dorothea, II:380
Townsend, George G., III:1815
Townsend, John W., I:748
Townsend, Rebecca D., I:683
Townsend Plan, I:1605, 1616
Toxicity, III:1463
Trachtman, Lester N., III:970
Tractors, agriculture, I:2628 (26)

Tracy, Lorna, III:2681
Trade cards, I:2775
Trade catalogs, I:2686; II:1257
Trade unions, I:1645–50; II:1264
Trademarks, I:2773, 2776; III:1003
Traffic Club of Chicago, I:2105
Transistors, II:1275
Translations, III:13
Transportation, I:2035, 2105, 2448, 2732, 2745–64, 4193 (36), 5488; II:984–86, 1420–24; III:920–51; of crops, I:2626 (81)
Transylvania College Library: rare books, I:575, 609, 3414
Trappists (monastic order), I:1156
Traven, B., III:2242
Treaties, I:1808, 1814, 1825; Indian, I:4488; international, III:1061; Latin American, I:1804
Tree nut production and marketing, III:1673
Trees, II:1393
Tregaskis, James, bookseller, I:3560
Tremaine, Marie, II:483; III:3401
Trent, Josiah C., II:1229, 1240, 1762
Trenton Public Library: Catholic catalogue, I:1185
Treworgy, Mildred L., III:843
Trienens, Roger J., III:508, 679
Triesch, Manfred, III:2020–21
Trimble, Robert Wilson, II:2217
Trinity College Library: natural history, I:2305; ornithology, III:1441; periodicals, union lists, I:360, II:180; rare books, II:303; religion, I:1005–06, 1098; sanitary science, I:2539
Trinterud, Leonard J., III:737
Trollope, Anthony, I:3405, 3561–63; II:1902–03
Tropical medicine, I:2395
Trotsky, Leon, II:2322
Trotter, Massey, I:2967
Troxell, Gilbert M., I:3415–16; II:1880
True, Rodney H., I:2618
Trumpeter, Margo, III:828
Trusts, I:1557, 1564
Tsao, Mary Ann, II:453
Tse-Chiukuo, Leslie, III:1624
Tsien, Tsuen-hsuin, II:2371, 2373; III:2865–66, 2872–73
Tsou, Rose Chiayin, II:2403
Tsuneishi, Warren M., III:2867
Tsunoda, Ryusaku, I:3784
Tubes, I:2811
Tucker, David A., Jr., II:1228
Tucker, Dorothy F., I:3457
Tucker, Ethelyn M., I:657, 2318
Tucker, Josiah, I:4518
Tucker, Louis L., III:158
Tucker, Mae S., II:1428
Tucker, Mildred M., III:3566
Tucker, Sara J., I:2314
Tufts University Library: Boston area archives, II:948; Confederate archives, I:4604; Eddy, Isaac, I:881; Holmes, John, III:2029
Tulane University Library: Davis collection, III:2407; Gallier, James, II:1466; Latin American collection, III:3315;

Louisiana history, I:4890, III:3194; manuscripts, II:249; Mexicana, II:2737; steamboats, III:937
———Middle American Research Institute, I:5338–41, II:2727
Tulley, John, I:4704
Tulsa Public Library: petroleum, I:2803
Tung, Shih-kang, III:2887
Turgenev, Ivan, II:1972
Turkish history, I:4238, 4327; II:2348–49; III:181, 2819
Turkish literature, III:2810
Turkish manuscripts, II:276
Turnbull, Robert J., II:2687
Turner, Ann, III:3086
Turner, Daniel S., II:1112
Turner, Frederick Jackson, II:2218
Turner, John, III:3228
Turner, Joseph B., I:1117
Turner, Lorenzo D., I:3267
Turner, Sylvie J., III:3168
Turner, Tom, II:1799
Turrill, Charles B., I:3899
Tuttle, Julius H., I:1007, 4076, 4438
Twain, Mark, I:113, 3336–37; II:1632, 1754–55; III:2082–86
Tweddell, Vera, II:2016
Twiggs, Levi, III:2632
Twining, William L., III:1007
Twitchell, Ralph E., I:5020
Tyler, John, III:2633
Tyler, Lyon G., I:5221
Typewriters, I:2822
Typography and book design, I:927–48; II:289, 297–98, 305, 489–505; III:658–74
Typothetae of the City of New York Library, I:945
Tysse, Agnes N., II:317, 1068; III:832

UFOs (unidentified flying objects), III:1598
Uganda, Africa, III:2983
Uhlendorf, Bernhard A., I:5171
Uhler, Katherine, II:1193
Ukraine, history, I:4315; III:2748, 2751
Ukrainian literature, I:3747
Ulasek, Henry T., II:809, 864, 1336, 2812, 2816; III:1124
Ulibarri, George S., III:1130, 3108, 3320, 3385, 3407
Ullom, Judith C., III:1981, 2345
Ulrich, Carolyn F., I:331
Ultra-violet rays, I:2248
Umbach, John P., I:5563
Umble, John, II:548
Unemployment, I:1659–63
Uniforms, I:5413
Union catalogs, I:70; III:121, 186–90
Union College Library: American Revolution, III:3065; history of science, III:1324
Union County, Miss., I:2628(27)
Union League Club: library catalog, I:261
Union Library Catalogue of the Philadelphia Metropolitan Area: Russian periodicals, III:386
Union lists of serials; I:281–364; II:154–86; III:201–98
Union Pacific Railroad, I:2075

Union Saint-Jean-Baptiste d'Amerique Bibliotheque: catalog, I:1375; resources, I:4632
Union Theological Seminary Library, N.Y.: British history and theology, I:4276–77; catalogs, II:522, 696–97; religious periodicals, I:999, 1001; serials, III:243
Union Theological Seminary Library, Richmond: catalog, I:1008; New Testament, I:1017
Unitarian Church, I:1192
United Brethren in Christ Church, I:1198
United Nations, I:1811; II:814, 817–18, 2279, 2331; publications, III:22
United Nations Educational, Scientific and Cultural Organization, I:1830–31; Latin American periodicals, II:223
United Nations Library: official gazettes, III:21
U.S. government publications, I:23–42; II:18–52; III:19–78
United States, history, I:4395–5280; II:2466–2715; III:3001–3293; Civil War, I:4595–4623, II:2065, 2536–49, 2555, III:821, 2549, 3072–3122; colonial period, I:4497–4532, II:2517–27, III:3045–53; regional, I:4624–90, II:2550–78, III:3123–60; Revolution and confederation, I:4533–86, II:708, 2156, 2293, 2528–31, III:3054–69; state and local, I:4708–5277, II:2582–2715, III:3161–3291; War of 1812, III:3070–71
U.S. Adjutant General: records, I:5434
U.S. Agricultural Adjustment Administration: records, I:2620, III:1652
U.S. Agricultural Marketing Service: acts, I:2628 (5); records, III:1647
U.S. Agricultural Research Service: records, III:1648
U.S. Agricultural Stabilization and Conservation Service: records, III:1649
U.S. Air Force, II:900, 2805; III:1208–15
U.S. Air Force Academy Library: falconry, II:1593; great generals, II:2088
U.S. Air Policy Commission: records, II:1336
U.S. Air University Library: air defense, II:1325; aviation history, II:1326; bombs, II:1294; film library, II:1327–29; Greece, II:2351; limited war, II:1285; medical periodicals, II:1217; military management, II:877; military periodicals, II:878–79, III:1209; services, III:1210; USAF historical archives, II:900, III:1208
U.S. Alien Property Custodian, II:2806
U.S. American Battle Monuments Commission: records, III:1188
U.S. American Commission for the Protection and Salvage of Artistic and Historic Monuments in War Areas: records, III:3418
U.S. American Expeditionary Forces (World War I): records, III:1189
U.S. Antarctic Service: records, II:2767
U.S. Argonne National Laboratory Library: serials, III:289

U.S. Armed Forces Staff College Library: Balkans and Middle East, II:2338
U.S. Armed Services Technical Information Agency: data processing, II:884; documents index, II:1260
U.S. Army, I:5398
———Library: national defense, I:5446
U.S. Army Air Forces: records, II:1212, 1214–15
U.S. Army, Chemical Corps, Technical Library: anthrax, II:1153; dengue and yellow fever, II:1154; leptospirosis, II:1155; listeria, II:1156; melioidosis, II:1157
U.S. Army Coast Artillery Districts and Defenses: records, III:1198
U.S. Army Commands: records, III:1186
U.S. Army Continental Commands: records, III:1199
U.S. Army Map Service Library, II:2038
U.S. Army Medical Library: American medical books, I:2379; Arabic medical literature, I:2414; catalog, I:2376; catalog cards, I:2381; congresses, I:2377; dental journals, I:2393; foreign periodicals, I:2391; Harvey, William, I:2411; history of medicine, I:2415; manuscripts, I:2433; medical bibliography, I:2392; medical films and periodicals, I:2397; medical incunabula, I:2421, 2425, 2433–34; neurology, psychology, and psychiatry journals, I:2394; new books and serials, I:2398; periodicals, I:2399; pre-1840 imprints, I:2423; serial abbreviations, I:2396; state and county society journals, I:2400; tropical medicine journals, I:2395
U.S. Army Military History Research Collection: catalog, III:1151
U.S. Army War College Library: catalog, I:5400; leadership, I:5402; maps, I:5400; Mexican War, I:4588; military bibliography, I:5401; South American maps, I:2277
U.S. Atomic Energy Commission: atomic energy, II:1098
U.S. Attorney General's Advisory Committee on Crime: records, I:1932
U.S. Bituminous Coal Division: records, III:1087
U.S. Board of Investigation and Research—Transportation: records, I:5571
U.S. Board of Surveys and Maps: collections, I:3857
U.S. Board of War Communications: records, III:1176
U.S. Bureau of Accounts (Treasury): records, III:1088
U.S. Bureau of Aeronautics: records, II:1334, III:1602
U.S. Bureau of Agricultural and Industrial Chemistry: records, III:1650
U.S. Bureau of Agricultural Economics: farm management, III:1656; records, II:1376
———Library: U.S. agriculture history, I:2615
U.S. Bureau of Agricultural Engineering: bibliography, I:2594; records, II:1357

U.S. Bureau of American Ethnology Library: linguistic manuscripts, I:3186

U.S. Bureau of Animal Industry: medical and veterinary zoology, I:2374, 2380; records, II:1382

U.S. Bureau of Customs: records, III:1089

U.S. Bureau of Dairy Industry: records, III:1662

U.S. Bureau of Entomology and Plant Quarantine: records, II:1397, III:1651

U.S. Bureau of Foreign and Domestic Commerce: Chinese law, I:1752; records, III:898

U.S. Bureau of Indian Affairs: biographical and historical index, III:3039; cartographic records, II:2068

U.S. Bureau of Insular Affairs: Dominican customs receivership, I:5363; Philippine Islands, I:5379; Puerto Rico, I:5366; records, II:856; U.S. in Cuba, I:5367

U.S. Bureau of Labor Standards: records, III:972

U.S. Bureau of Labor Statistics: labor in Ghana, III:970
————Library: industrial accident and disease prevention, I:2355

U.S. Bureau of Land Management: records, III:862, 867

U.S. Bureau of Medicine and Surgery: records, I:2382, III:1457

U.S. Bureau of Mines: petroleum, I:2500

U.S. Bureau of Naval Personnel: records, II:914, III:1226

U.S. Bureau of Navigation: American naval authors, I:5458

U.S. Bureau of Ordnance: records, II:905, III:1206

U.S. Bureau of Pensions: pension case files, III:2421; records, II:773

U.S. Bureau of Plant Industry, Soils, and Agricultural Engineering: publications, I:2599 (3); records, II:1398, III:1678

U.S. Bureau of Public Roads: Highway Transport File, III:949; records, III:942
————Library: automobile parking, II:1305; highways, II:1306-07, III:940

U.S. Bureau of Reclamation: irrigation projects, II:1410; records, II:1411

U.S. Bureau of Refugees, Freedman, and Abandoned Lands: records, I:4475, III:3118-20

U.S. Bureau of Ships: records, III:943, 951
————Technical Library: serials union list, II:913

U.S. Bureau of Supplies and Accounts (Navy): records, III:1224

U.S. Bureau of the Budget, Library: Bureau of the Budget, II:835; Executive Office, II:836; Federal reorganization, II:839; management audit, II:837; records management, II:838; wartime administration, II:2804

U.S. Bureau of the Census: cartographic records, II:2069; China, II:653; Hungary, III:790; records, III:800; statistical yearbooks, II:660

U.S. Bureau of the Mint: records, III:1090

U.S. Bureau of the Public Dept.: records, II:852, III:1091

U.S. Bureau of War Risk Insurance (Veterans' Bureau): records, III:1137

U.S. Bureau of Yards and Docks: records, I:5469, III:950

U.S. Capital Issues Committee: records, III:1092

U.S. Central Bureau of Planning and Statistics: records, II:857

U.S. Central Intelligence Agency: records, III:1093

U.S. Chemical Warfare Service: records, I:5568, III:1201

U.S. Circuit Court of Appeals Library: catalog, I:1721

U.S. Civil Aeronautics Administration: records, III:1600
————Library: airports, I:2567; wood in airplanes, I:2568

U.S. Civil Service Commission Library: executive training, II:840; holdings, III:1075; National Civil Service League, III:1074; personal improvement, II:929; personnel administration, I:1861-62, II:1419, III:1073

U.S. Civil War, I:4595-4623; II:2536-49; III:3072-3122

U.S. Civil War Centennial Commission, III:3098

U.S. Civil Works Administration, I:4427

U.S. Civilian Conservation Corps: bibliography, I:2670; camp papers, I:2673; records, I:1484, 2671, 4193 (30)

U.S. Coal Commission: records, III:1133

U.S. Coast and Geodetic Survey: records, II:1089; topographic and hydrographic sheets, I:2286

U.S. Coast Artillery School Library: catalog, I:5403

U.S. Coast Guard: vessel logs, I:5462

U.S. Collector of Customs: records, II:858

U.S. Combined Production and Resources Board: records, III:1191

U.S. Combined Raw Materials Board: records, III:1191

U.S. Command and General Staff College, Library Service: catalog, I:5404; leadership bibliography, II:880

U.S. Commerce Court: records, III:1034

U.S. Commissary General: records, I:5431

U.S. Commission of Fine Arts: records, II:1452

U.S. Commission on Intergovernmental Relations: records, III:1094

U.S. Commission on Organization of the Executive Branch of the Government: records, III:1095-96

U.S. Commissioner of Railroads: records, III:944

U.S. Committee for Congested Production Areas: records, II:859

U.S. Committee on Conservation and Administration of the Public Domain: records, III:1097

U.S. Committee on Fair Employment Practice: records, III:973

U.S. Commodity Credit Corporation: records, III:1098

U.S. Commodity Exchange Authority: records, II:736

U.S. Congress: apportionment, I:1440; bibliography, I:1441; congressional committee hearings, II:714; legislative process, II:713; organization, I:1445; records, II:715; women in Congress, I:1444
————House of Representatives Library: congressional committee hearings, I:1437, II:712
————Senate: bibliography, I:1419; Committee on Appropriations records, I:1446; records, I:1447, II:716; senators from Ohio, I:1443
————Senate Library: catalog, I:1438; congressional committee hearings, I:1439, III:1139-40

U.S. Constitution, I:4575-76, 4584; II:828, 2530

U.S. Constitution Sesquicentennial Comm.: broadsides, I:1839

U.S. Continental Congress, I:4565; issues, I:4546, 4554; official publications, I:4545

U.S. Corps of Engineers: North Pacific Division, III:1579; Portland District, III:1580; Seattle District, III:1581

U.S. Council of National Defense: records, I:5534

U.S. Counsel for the Prosecution of Axis Criminality: records, I:5572, III:3420

U.S. Court of Claims: records, II:805, 807

U.S. Defense Electric Power Administration: records, III:1099

U.S. Defense Materials Service: records, III:1178

U.S. Department of Agriculture: archives, I:4423; medical and veterinary zoology, II:1204, III:1514
————Library: agricultural books, II:1354; agricultural economics, I:2626-27; agricultural experiment station bulletins, I:2614; agricultural labor, I:1653, II:1368, 1374; Agricultural library notes, I:2596; agricultural marketing, I:2623-24; agricultural periodicals, I:2611; agricultural programs, I:2632; agriculture in defense, I:2597; aircraft in agriculture, II:1345; beef cattle, II:1381; Bibliographical bulletin, I:2598; Bibliographical contributions, I:2599; Bibliography of agriculture, I:2600, II:1346; botany, II:1126; Bulletin, I:2601; cacao, II:1394; Chinese periodicals, II:1218, 1361; citrus fruits, II:1391; contract farming, II:1370; cooperatives, II:1365, 1369; cotton, I:2648; drainage of land, II:1408; economic entomology, II:1385; Economic library lists, I:2628; farm forestry, I:2656; farm mechanization, II:1371; farmers'

prices, I:2629; fire and forests, I:2655; floras, II:1389; food control, I:2630; forest recreation, I:2657; forestry, I:2658, II:1402–04; freight rates, I:2631; history of agriculture, I:2615; irrigation, II:1372; kenaf, II:1392; land ownership, II:1366; land reform, II:1375; land settlement, I:2621; land utilization, I:2622; Latin American periodicals, I:467; Library lists, I:2602; livestock marketing, II:1380; low-income farmers, II:1373; meat industry, I:2633; peaches, II:1390; periodicals, I:2612, II:1361–63; personnel administration, II:1349; plant genetics, I:2328; plant pathology, II:1388; plant science, I:2649; rice, II:1350; rural electrification, II:1348, 1351; rural health, II:1352; rural living, I:2625; school lunches, II:1353; soil conservation, I:2667–69; Soviet periodicals, II:1076; soybeans, II:1395; space travel, II:1302; thatched roofs, II:1396; tree books, II:1393; urbanization, II:1367; Washington, George, I:4109; watersheds, II:1355; weather and crops, I:2595

U.S. Department of Commerce: archives, I:4424

——Library: European censuses, I:1340; price sources, I:1468

U.S. Department of Health, Education, and Welfare: records, III:1082

——Library: catalog, III:792–93; juvenile delinquency, II:917

U.S. Department of Housing and Urban Development Library: housing, III:1731; public transportation, III:941; urban planning, III:1732–36

U.S. Department of Justice: archives, I:4420; Court of Claims records, II:805

——Library: catalog, II:1722; Congress and legislation, II:713; foreign books, I:1753; strike settlements, II:781

U.S. Department of Labor: archives, I:4425, III:962

——Library: absenteeism in industry, I:1581; arbitration, I:1654; Australian and New Zealand pensions, I:1612; Canadian and New Zealand annuities, I:1607; Canadian pensions, I:1610; child labor, I:1664–66; collective bargaining, I:1589; convict labor, I:1580; employee stock owners, I:1606; employment of handicapped, I:1578; guaranteed annual wage, I:1608; hours of work, I:1630–32; industrial diseases, I:1577; injunctions, I:1655–56; Kansas Court of Industrial Relations, I:1585; labor and industry, I:1583; labor banks, I:1579; labor history, III:953; labor papers and journals, I:1584, II:779, III:971; labor profit sharing, I:1611; labor relations, I:1640; labor statistics, I:1586; leisure, I:1590; minimum wage, I:1609, 1615; "mothers' pensions," I:1922; national economic councils, I:1264; national

health care, I:2356; older workers, I:1587; pensions, I:1613–14; Perkins, Frances, I:1582; reconstruction, I:1469; resources, I:1576; right to strike, I:1651; seniority, I:2693–94; social welfare, I:1265; Townsend pension plan, I:1616; trade union journals, II:779, III:971; trade union publications, I:1645–46, 1649; unemployment, I:1660; unemployment insurance, I:1617; union security, I:1650

U.S. Department of State: archives, III:1064, 1085; Clark, George Rogers, I:4555; Jefferson, Thomas, I:4015; Madison, James, I:4067; maps, I:3882; Monroe, James, I:4080

——Library Division: Africa, II:2444; book acquisitions, I:1816; British foreign policy, II:2290; California broadside, I:4745; catalog, I:1812; Central America, I:5304, 5321; Chile, I:5330; Communist China, II:2395; Cuba, I:5346; current serials, II:182; Danubian Federation, II:2280; Evans, Luther, II:67; Far East, II:687; foreign investments, II:691; foreign relations, II:689; industrial plants, II:729; labor, USSR, II:760–61; Latin America, II:688; national law and diplomacy, I:1813, 1815; national strategy, II:881; Office of Intelligence Research, II:841; overseas information, II:690; Pakistan, II:2431; Point four, II:692–93, 1261, 2374; psychological warfare, II:1284; public opinion polls, II:671; Pushtu language, II:2358; Rumanian imprints, II:730; shipping, II:1423; Southeast Asia and Philippines, II:694; Soviet Union, II:2329–31; special agents, II:701; Suez, II:2291; treaties, I:1814; Vatican City, II:620; Washington, George, I:4112; Western Europe, II:2281; Western European agriculture, II:1356; world politics, II:695

U.S. Department of the Air Force: space law, III:1593

U.S. Department of the Army Library: Africa, III:2971–72; area bibliography, II:882; arms control and disarmament, II:885, III:1162–63; civil defense, III:1164; Civil War, II:2547, III:3099; Communist China, III:2890–91; Communist East Europe, III:2742; computers, II:883–84; constitutional and administrative law, II:831; current periodicals, III:1152; executives, II:1286; foreign law, II:825–26; foreign research and development, II:690; government procurement, II:842–43; informational activities, II:696; Latin America, III:3316–17; limited war, II:1285; manpower utilization, III:1154; martial law, II:833; Middle East, III:2815; military manpower utilization, III:1155; military power, II:887; missiles and space

travel, II:1295–1303, III:1211; mobility in warfare, II:888; National Guard, III:1153; national security, II:893, 1287, III:1160; nuclear warfare, III:1156–57; overseas bases, III:1161; personnel administration, III:1076–77; programming, II:889; psychological warfare, II:1284; science, II:1032; soil compaction, II:1409; South Asia, III:2836; Soviet Russia, II:891, III:2764–65; technological progress, II:886; theses, II:892, II:1159; U.S. Army Reserve, III:1158

——Office of Military History: study guide, II:902; World War II, II:2805

U.S. Department of the Interior: archives, I:4422; cartographic records, II:2072; centennial, I:4473; territorial papers, I:4662, 5113

——Library: acquisitions, I:263; American Indians, III:3039; catalog, I:262, III:184; management, II:844–45; natural resources, III:866; Nez Percé Indians, II:2515; petroleum, I:1279; safety, II:1033; Western history, I:4682

U.S. Department of the Navy: archives, I:4421, 5448, 5463; sesquicentennial, I:5470

——Library: naval history and biography, II:912

——Naval Operations Office: naval history, III:1218

U.S. description and travel, I:4414, 4452, 4540, 4594, 4690; II:2551, 2554, 2570, III:2404, 3008, 3013, 3052–53, 3136–37, 3146, 3149, 3154–55

U.S. Direct Tax Commission: South Carolina records, I:1541

U.S. District Court: Georgia, III:1021, 1024; Indiana, III:1025; Missouri, III:1023; Nebraska, III:1027; New Mexico, III:1028; New York, II:809; Oregon, III:1022; Pennsylvania, II:808; Western District of Virginia, III:1036; Wisconsin, III:1026

U.S. Economic Stabilization Agency: records, II:737

U.S. Emergency Relief Administration: archives, I:4428

U.S. Engineer Department Library: catalog, I:2470–71

U.S. Engineer School Library: aerial photography, I:2569; American wars, II:903; Arctic warfare, I:5405; construction, II:1440; dams, I:2524; disasters, II:1034; Engineer troops, I:5406; gas warfare, I:5390; guerrila warfare, II:1288; hydraulic engineering, II:1311; Korea, II:2424; Mexican war, I:4588; missiles and rockets, II:1304; Mississippi River and Valley, I:2287, 4652; national planning, II:846; periodical index, II:1268; petroleum pipelines, I:2501; Russia, II:2332; sand movement and beaches, I:2288; South African war, I:4372

U.S. Exploring Expedition, I:4594

U.S. Extension Service: records, II:860

U.S. Farm Credit Administration, I:1485; archives, I:4430; records, III:1653

U.S. Farm Security Administration: American survey, I:1256; prints and photographs, I:2990

U.S. Farmers Home Administration: records, II:1358

U.S. Federal Bureau of Investigation: records, III:1100

U.S. Federal Communications Commission: records, II:954, III:1101

U.S. Federal courts: archives, I:4417

U.S. Federal Extension Service: records, III:1102

U.S. Federal Fuel Distribution: records, III:1103

U.S. Federal Home Loan Bank System: records, III:1104

U.S. Federal Housing Administration: archives, III:1750; cartographic records, II:2070
——Library: urban housing, I:2896

U.S. Federal Inter-Agency River Basin Committee: records, III:1105

U.S. Federal Mediation and Conciliation Service: records, III:974

U.S. Federal Power Commission: records, III:1106

U.S. Federal Records Center, Kansas City: guide, III:1078

U.S. Federal Reserve System: records, III:1107

U.S. Federal Security Agency Library: disability benefits, II:771; Federal grants-in-aid, I:1840, II:770; group insurance, I:1618; mental illness, II:1158; social security, I:1619

U.S. Federal Supply Service: records, III:1108

U.S. Federal Trade Commission: records, I:2043
——Library: Clayton act, II:731; Robinson-Patman act, II:732

U.S. Federal Works Agency: records, III:1083
——Law Library: war public works, I:1591
——Library: automobile parking, I:2135

U.S. Federal Writers' Project: records, II:1629

U.S. Fish and Wildlife Service: records, III:1663

U.S. Food Administration: archives, I:5535; California, I:5502; Indiana, I:5536; Louisiana, I:5508; Missouri, I:5509; North Carolina, I:5510; Ohio, I:5539; Tennessee, I:5499; Virginia, I:5507; Washington, Oregon, Idaho, I:5511

U.S. Foreign Agricultural Service: records, III:1654

U.S. Foreign Broadcast Intelligence Service: records, II:704

U.S. Foreign Economic Administration: records, II:705

U.S. Foreign Funds Control: records, III:1066

U.S. Forest Service: archives, I:2665, III:1686; cartographic records, III:1685; prairie shelterbelts, I:2659; research units, archives, I:2654; Wisconsin, I:5267

——California Forest and Range Experiment Station: watershed management, II:1321
——Forest Products Laboratory: pulp and paper, II:1405
——Library: forest product marketing, I:2660; forestry index, I:2661; forestry serials, I:2663; precipitation and climate, I:2662

U.S. Fuel Administration: records, III:1134

U.S. General Land Office: cartographic records, III:868; land-entry papers, I:1540

U.S. General Services Administration: records, III:1084

U.S. Geological Survey: fossil insects, I:2296; Geologic literature, I:2289; North American geology, I:2290–91; photo-mapping, I:2292; Utah, I:5205
——Library: bibliographical lists, I:1902; catalog, I:1404; South American maps, I:2277

U.S. Government Printing Office Library, II:29

U.S. Grain Corporation: records, I:1553, III:1677

U.S. House of Representatives: Hungarians in Rumania and Transylvania, III:2743

U.S. Housing and Home Finance Agency: records, III:1749
——Library: cooperative housing, II:733; periodicals, III:1735

U.S. Housing Corporation: records, III:1751

U.S. Hydrographic Office: records, II:1312, III:1138
——Library: catalog, I:2237

U.S. Hygienic Laboratory Library: medical and veterinary zoology, I:2374

U.S. Immigration and Naturalization Service: records, III:2422

U.S. Industrial Incentive Division: records, I:5567

U.S. Information Agency Library: Moslems in U.S.S.R., II:650; U.S. pictorial books, II:2488

U.S. Inspector General: records, I:5432

U.S. Internal Revenue Service: records, III:1109

U.S. International Cooperation Administration: records, III:1067

U.S. Joint Army and Navy Boards and Committees: records, III:1173

U.S. Joint Chiefs of Staff: records, III:1184

U.S. Judge Advocate General (Navy): records, I:5467

U.S. Library of Congress, II:89; Abbe, Cleveland, III:1367; acquisitions, I:175; Adams, Abigail, I:3942; aeronautics, I:2570–71, II:1324, 1330; Aesop's fables, I:3730; African collections, II:2435, III:2938, 2941, 2954; African maps, III:2396; agricultural periodicals, I:2611; agriculture history, U.S., I:2615; Alabama, III:3161; Alaskan history, III:3162–63; Alaskan newspapers and periodicals, I:445; American Academy of Arts and Letters, II:247; American

and English genealogies, I:4176; American church history, II:627; American folk music, III:1858; American history, I:4413, 4436–37, 4459, 4464, 4466–67, III:3011, 3021–22; American maps, I:3878, 3883–84, 3891–92, II:2059, III:2395–97; American naval history, I:5451; American Negro, I:1401; American poetry, I:3228; American Revolution, I:4533–36, 4548, 4579, III:3062, 3066; American-Scandinavian relations, I:1411; American slaves, I:4596; American wood engravings, I:2954; Andersen, Hans Christian, II:1929, 1933; Apian map, II:2021; Army Medical Library catalog, I:2381; Arnold, H. H., II:2094; Arthur, Chester A., II:2095; ASTIA documents, II:1260; atlases, II:2028–29; Austria, III:2705; autographs, I:511; aviation medicine, II:1159; Bailey, Philip James, I:3423; Baker, Ray Stannard, I:3945; Balearic Islands, I:4296; Baltic states publications, III:2768–70; Batchelder collection, I:610–11; Beethoven acquisitions, III:.867; Bermuda, I:5343; Berryman, Clifford Kennedy, I:2921; Bible, I:944, 1027, 1043, II:264; Bolivar, Simon, I:3949–50; botany, II:1122; boxing, I:3131; Brady, Mathew B., photographs, II:1504, 1506; Brazil, I:5345; British belles-lettres, I:3417; British statutes, II:827; Bryant, William Cullen, II:1673; Bulgarian history, III:2771, 2773; Bulgarian imprints, II:480; Burmese literature, I:3787, II:1982; Burmese music, II:1531; California, I:4747; canal and railway routes, I:2114; catalogs, I:264–65, 267–68, II:132–40, III:185–90; Cattell, James M., II:922; Central America, I:5304, 5321; Cervantes, Miguel de, I:3709–10, II:1952; Chekhov, Anton P., I:3751; Chile, I:5330; China, II:2394–95; Chinese law. I:1752; Chinese manuscript, I:3788; Chinese medical periodicals, II:1218, III:1549; Chinese social science literature, III:791; Christian Science, I:1074; Civil War, III:3090, 3098, 3100; Civil War fiction, II:1661; Civil War newspapers, I:4597; Civil War photographs, I:4610; Clark, George Rogers, I:4555; Cleland, Thomas Maitland, III:668; collections, I:156, 158, 161–62, 4192; colonial costume, I:2941; Colorado, II:2593; Colorado imprints, I:722; Columbus, Christopher, I:3962; computers, II:883; Confederate publications, I:4611; Connecticut, I:4762; Continental Congress, I:4554; cookery, I:2589; Coolidge, Calvin, I:3963; Cooper, Peter, I:3964; Costa Rica, I:5296; county government, I:1890; cowboy photographs, II:1505;

Crimean War photographs, I:4236; Crittenden, John Jordan, I:3965; Croatian imprint, III:456; Cuba, I:5329, 5344, 5346; Cuban maps, I:3932; Custer, George Armstrong, I:3966; Cyrillic union catalog, III:2741, 2744; Czech and Spanish law, II:821; Czech imprints, II:479; Czechoslovak history, III:2775; Czechoslovakia and Poland, II:2344; dancing, I:3104; Daniels, Josephus, I:3967, II:2114; Declaration of Independence, I:4547; Delaware, II:2594; Detroit photographers, II:1502; directories, I:4182; District of Columbia newspapers, I:415; Eaker, Ira C., II:2121; early American imprints, III:508; early Americana, II:2518–19; 18th century American newspapers, II:193; Einstein, Albert, I:2245; Emancipation Proclamation, II:2543; European literature, III:2735; European scientific and technical journals, I:2208; Evans, Luther H., II:67; Far East, II:2366; Farm Security Administration survey, I:1256; films, II:1587–88, III:1782; finance and banking, III:892; fine arts acquisitions, I:2850; Finno-Ugrian languages, III:1, 1910, 2286; Fitch, John, I:3891; Florida, I:4778, 4789, 4796; Florida newspapers, I:406; foreign official gazettes, III:19; Franklin, Benjamin, I:3979, 3984, 3988, II:2129; Free Europe Committee, II:686; French and German engravings, I:2962; French consuls in U.S., III:1062; French fiction, I:3639–40; French history, III:2713; French incunabula, III:485; French literature, I:3649; French plays, I:3634; Gallaudet, II:2132; gas warfare, I:5390; Georgia, I:4802, 4808; German archives, II:2818; German bibliography, III:12; German government publications, II:53–54; German incunabula, III:486; German linguistics, I:3146; German literature, I:3592, 3594, II:1919; German serials, I:468; Gershwin, George, II:1568; Goethe, Johann Wolfgang von, II:1924; Goudy collection, I:939, 946; government archives, I:4465; Greek and Armenian manuscripts, II:580; Guiana and Venezuela maps, I:3931; Hale family, II:2136; Hans Breitmann bindings, III:679; Hartford, Conn., imprints, I:723; Harvard fiction, II:1654; Hawaii, I:5384; Hebrew collections, I:1244, 1247, Herrman, Augustine, II:2063; Hispanic literature, II:1950–51; Hispanica, II:2728; Hispano-Americana, I:5307; Historic American Buildings Survey, I:2897; Hotchkiss papers, I:3895; Houdini, Harry, I:3114; Housman, Alfred Edward, I:3482, II:1839; Howard, Francis, II:2144; Hughes, Charles Evans, II:2145; Hungarica, II:2339;

2343; Illinois, I:4817, III:3188; incunabula, I:623, 627, 658–61, 663, II:327; Indiana, II:2617; Indiana newspapers, I:400; Indic manuscripts and paintings, I:543, 548; Indic studies, I:3773; infrared, II:1160; international exchanges, II:2; Iowa, I:4848; Irving, Washington, I:3292; Island of Antigua imprints, I:901; Italian literature, I:3671; Italiana, I:4298; Jackson, Andrew, I:4008; Jakhontov, Arkadi N., II:2321; Japanese archives, II:2409, 2419, 2422; Japanese art, I:2987; Japanese collection, I:3778; Japanese Constitution, II:2418; Japanese picture scrolls, III:1762; Jefferson, Thomas, I:4011, 4015–17, 4020, II:141, 2146–48; Jefferson collection catalog, I:266; John of Garland, I:3164; Johnson, Andrew, II:2149; juvenile literature, I:3804, 3812, 3814, II:1999, 2001, 2003, 2006, 2008, 2010, 2012–13, III:2288–89, 2295–98, 2305–12, 2316–18, 2322, 2328–29, 2331, 2336, 2338, 2341–46, 2350–51; Kansas and Nebraska, II:2623; Kentucky map, I:3907; Kentucky rare books, I:750; Kepler, Johann, I:2229; Korea, II:2428; labor history, III:963; labor strikes, I:1651; LaFontaine, Jean de, I:3652; Lamont, Daniel Scott, II:2158; Landau, Baron Horace de, II:1532; Latin America, I:3815, 5334, 5342, III:3310; Latin American art, I:2848; Latin American bibliography, I:5306, III:4; Latin American government publications, I:47; Latin American imprints, II:476; Latin American maps, I:3926–28, 3930; Latin American periodicals, I:467, II:223; Latin American treaties, I:1804; Latrobe, Benjamin Henry, I:2888; law acquisitions, I:1797, II:804; law books, I:1723; Law Library centennial, I:1798; League of Women Voters, II:675; L'Enfant papers, I:1165; Lermontov, Mikhail Y., I:3754; Lewis, Sinclair, II:1613; Lincoln, Abraham, I:4029, 4035, 4042–44, 4054–55, II:2166, 2170, 2174–77, 2179, III:2551; literacy education, I:2025; literary geography, I:3834; Lithuanian history, III:2770; Loeb, Jacques, III:1440; Loeffler collection, II:1524; Los Angeles imprints, I:719; Louisiana Purchase, II:2534; Low, Harriet, I:4331; Low Countries imprints, II:484; Madison, Dolly, II:2185; Madison, James, I:4067; Maine, I:4896, III:3198; Mainz Bible, II:264; Malta imprint, I:910; Manhattan maps, I:3913; manuscript and rare book reproductions, I:499–500; manuscripts, I:508, II:260, III:422–25; maps, I:3825, 3853, 3858, 3871, 3878, 3883–84, 3892, II:2039–40, III:2368–69;

Massachusetts, I:4924; Matica Srpska, III:2792; Maugham, W. S., II:1862; Maury, Matthew Fontaine, I:4077; Mexican colonial imprints, I:903; Mexican government publications, I:48; Mexican war, I:4588; Mexico, I:5305, II:2743, III:3378; Michigan, I:4955, II:2645; microfilms, III:16; microreproductions, II:1; military training, I:5391; Minnesota, I:4970; missiles, rockets, and satellites, II:1299; Mississippi, III:3215; Mississippi drama, III:1879; Mississippi River and Valley, I:2287, 4652; mobility in warfare, II:888; Mongolian manuscripts, II:2353; Monroe, James, I:4080; Moore, Julia A., I:3312; motion pictures, I:3118, III:1891, 1900–01; Mount Athos manuscripts, II:581; music, I:3033, II:1548–49; music and phonorecords, III:1829–31; national bibliographies, II:12–13, III:17; National Women's Trade Union League, II:778; Nauvoo (Ill.) charter, I:4818; Nazi prints and photographs, I:2991; Near and Middle East, I:4346, II:2364; Negro history, I:1401, 4596, III:830, 847; Nekcsei-Lipocz Bible, I:1027; Nevada, III:3221; New Jersey maps, III:2388; New Mexico, Spanish archives, I:5020; new serial titles, II:183–85, III:290; New Sweden, I:4772; New York City newspapers, I:388; newspapers, II:191; North American ornithology, I:2332; Northwest Territory, I:4659; Northwestern Africa, III:2924; nuclear science, III:1378; offset printing, I:947; O'Higgins family, I:5311; Ohio, I:5125, II:2669; Ohio newspapers, I:333; oil shale industry, I:2794; Oneirocritica Americana, I:961; Oregon, I:5138; Oriental collection, I:3789, II:2355, 2359; Orientalia, I:3800; ornithologists, I:2340; Ottoman Empire, II:2348; Oxford lectern Bible, I:944; Pacific islands, I:5383; pageants, I:3109; Pakistan, II:2431; Panama maps, III:2382; papermaking, I:2818, III:479; Parker, Theodore, III:2584; Pennell, Joseph, I:2986; petroleum and natural gas, I:2281; Philadelphia maps, I:3916; Philippine government publications, II:57; Philippine imprint, I:907; Philippine Islands, I:5376; Philippine linguistics, III:1914; philosophy and religion, I:957, II:513; photography, II:1509; physiology of brain, II:1147; Poe, Edgar Allan, II:1735; poetry collections, I:3189; Polish bibliography, III:8; Polish history, III:2786; Polish imprints, III:648; political science, I:1346; population, I:1330–31; Portuguese collection, I:3705; postage stamps, I:2048; prints and photographs, I:2985, II:1191,

U.S. Library of Congress (cont.)
1494–95; Prints Division, I:2976; private circulation books, I:588; prosody, I:3153; psychological warfare, II:1284; public administration, II:876; Puerto Rico, II:2749; Putnam, Herbert, II:2197; railroad in literature, I:3206; rare books, I:564, 576, 589, II:304; Red Cross photographs, I:1919; Rembrandt van Rijn, I:2983; research collections, I:157, 159–60; Roberts, Elizabeth Maddox, I:3324; Robinson, Edwin Arlington, I:3325, III:2063; Roman law, I:1754–55; Roosevelt, Theodore, II:2203, III:1907; Russian acquisitions, II:2324, 2333–35; Russian Czar's Library, I:4314; Russian documents on U.S., III:3001; Russian early travel, I:4311; Russian publications, III:2766; St. Catherine's Monastery manuscripts, II:579; sand movement and beaches, I:2288; Sandburg, Carl, III:2066; Scandinavian collection, I:4305; Scandinavian literature, III:2723; science, I:2177, II:1016; science history, II:1059; scientific management, I:2687; sesquicentennial exhibit, II:66; Shaker literature, I:1189; Shakespeare, William, I:3529; Slavic acquisitions, II:2320, 2333–35, 2340–46; Slavic literature, I:3745, 3752, 3758, III:2738, 2745; Slavic medicine, II:1191; Slavica, I:4322; society and periodical publications, I:345; South American geology, I:2277; South Asia, II:2383; Southeast Asian publications, I:4348; Southeast Europe, III:2746; Soviet military power, II:891; Soviet newspapers, III:381; Soviet science, II:1038; Soviet sociology, III:795; Soviet war posters, I:5544; Spaatz, Carl, I:5542; space exploration, II:1297; space travel, II:1302, III:1593–95; Spanish archives, I:4294; Spanish drama, I:3687; Squier, Ephraim George, II:2210; state constitutional conventions, I:1833; state records, II:46–47; Straus, Oscar S., II:2213; Swiss history, III:2722; Taft, William Howard, II:2215; Tasmanian law, III:1049; technical reports, II:1258; Tennessee history, I:5183; Texas, I:5187, 5200; Texcoco map, III:2359; theater collection, I:3111; Thoreau, Henry David, I:3335; Tibetan books, I:4355; Tibetan scriptures, II:632; tobacco literature, III:1667; trade union publications, I:1645–46; 20th century world history, I:4188; Ukraine, I:4315; underground press, I:5546, 5578; U.S. and Europe, II:2263; USSR electric utilities, II:1276; urban development, I:2872; Utah, I:5205; Virginia archives, I:5319; Virginia Company of London, I:4502; Virginia maps, I:3919–20, 3922, III:2384; Virginia newspapers, I:439; Wales, I:4259; Walker-Washington map, III:2399; Walpole, Hugh, II:1613; Washington, Booker T., I:1388; Washington, George, I:4109, II:2222, III:2641; Washington, D.C., II:2595–96; Washington (State), II:2709; West Virginia, III:3278; Western history, I:4687; Whistler, James A., I:2975, 2977; White, William Allen, I:4128; Whitman, Walt, I:3342, III:2091, 2094, 2096; Wilson, Woodrow, I:4133–34, II:2232–34; Wisconsin, I:5267; Wister, Owen, III:2100; World War I, I:5516; World War I poetry, I:3190; World War II, III:3411; Wright, Wilbur and Orville, I:2554, II:2241

———Acquisitions Dept.: European World War II imprints, I:20

———Aerospace Technology Division: Chinese-English technical dictionaries, III:1594

———African Section: Africa, III:2973–89; African agriculture, III:1615; African collections, II:2996; African libraries, III:84; African music, III:1832; African periodicals, III:387; African studies, serials, II:2450; British East Africa publications, II:2449; Cameroons, III:2984; East Africa, III:2989; Ghana, III:2977; Kenya, III:2982; Madagascar, III:2979; Nigeria, III:2980; Portuguese Africa, III:2986; Rhodesias and Nyasaland, III:2987; Sierra Leone and Gambia, III:2985; Tanganyika, III:2981; Togo, III:2984; Uganda, III:2983; West Africa, III:2976; Zanzibar, III:2982

———American Libraries Book Procurement Center: Ceylon, III:2919; India, III:2838; Israel, III:2816; Karachi, III:388; Middle East, III:2817; Nepal, III:2920; Pakistan, III:2843

———Archive of Folk Song: African recordings, III:1841

———Arms Control and Disarmament Bibliography Section, III:1165

———Card Division: motion pictures and filmstrips, II:1589; non-GPO imprints, III:69

———Catalog Division: American doctoral dissertations, I:2015

———Census Library Project: Africa, I:1339, II:664; Americas, I:1334; demographic statistics, I:1332, II:662; Europe, I:1335, 1340; France, I:1336; Germany, I:1337; Italy, I:1338; state censuses, I:1341; statistics, II:659–60; U.S. census, I:1333, II:663

———Children's Book Section: juvenile literature, III:2341–45; Louisa May Alcott, III:1981

———Copyright Office: catalog of entries, I:19; design protection, II:1269; dramatic compositions, I:3237

———Division for the Blind and Physically Handicapped: adult talking books, III:197; braille books, II:146, 152–53; juvenile braille and talking books, II:145, 151, III:198; magnetic tape books, III:195; Moon books, II:149; reading for profit, II:150, III:196; talking books, II:147–48, III:199

———Division of Aeronautics: aeronautical collection, I:2546–47, 2581; Aeronautical index, I:2573; aeronautics, I:2545, aeropolitics, I:2126; air freight, I:2560, 2578; Alaska, I:2574; friction and flow, I:2575; investigations, I:2562; Langley collection, I:2566; 19th century Americana, I:2572; peacetime aviation, I:2561; periodicals and serials, I:2576; state publications, I:2577; U.S. policy, I:2579

———Division of Bibliography: accident prevention, I:2359, advertising, I:2779; Africa, I:4373–87; Alaska, I:5279; Aleutian Islands, I:5280; American almanacs, I:4706; American flag, I:1347; American Merchant Marine, I:2130; American Red Cross, I:5524; American women, I:3939; Anglo-Saxons, I:1266; arms limitation, I:1827; Australia, I:5373; automobile industry, I:2544; Bacon, Francis, I:3422; Balkans, I:4323; banking, I:1486–87, 1494–96; bankruptcy, I:1492, 1498; Barlow, Joel, I:3276; Belgian Congo, I:4373; Benjamin, Judah Philip, I:3947; Benton, Thomas Hart, I:3948; Bill of Rights, I:1841, 1848; Boer War, I:4374; British Honduras, I:5348, British in Africa, I:4375; British in Caribbean, I:5349; Burney, Fanny, I:3436; Burton, Theodore Elijah, I:3955; business cycles, I:2031; camouflage, I:5412; Canada, I:4393; capital punishment, I:1850, 1852; cartularies, I:4285; child labor, I:1667–68; children and war, I:5547; China, Japan, and Philippines, I:4356; Chinese immigration, I:1381; circus, I:3115; civil service, I:1864–65; Civilian Conservation Corps, I:2670; civilian defense, I:5491–92; coal, I:2293; colonization, I:1378; Colorado, I:4754; Colorado River, I:4689; commerce, federal control, I:2033–34; community centers, I:2898; Congress, I:1441; Constitution, I:1845, 1847; containers, I:2777; cooperation, I:1510–11; copper, I:2806; cost of living, I:1561; cotton, I:2825; county government, I:1888–90; criminal justice, I:1930–31; Custer, George Armstrong, I:3966; Danish West Indies, I:5351; defense financing, I:1521; Denmark, I:4306; disarmament, I:1817; District of Columbia, I:1891; drug abuse, I:2357; dye-stuffs, I:2804; economic planning, I:1562; economic reconstruction, I:1473; 18th amendment, I:1844; election corruption, I:1369; electoral

college, I:1367; embargoes, I:1853; employers' liability, I:1643–44; English and U.S. cabinets, I:1915; Ethiopia, I:4379; Europe and international politics, I:4245; executive branch reorganization, I:1905; fairs and expositions, I:2452; Far East, I:4357; federal aid, I:1842; federal budget, I:1534; flags and insignia, I:5413; flood control, I:2525; Florida, I:4797; Ford, Henry, I:3973; foreign aid, I:5548; foreign budgets, I:1530; foreign commerce, I:2040–41; foreign debt collection, I:1528; foreign language-English dictionaries, I:3155–56; 14th and 15th amendments, I:1402; freedom of expression, I:1360; freedom of seas, I:1818, 1820; French in Africa, I:4376; French in American Revolution, I:4582; Furuseth, Andrew, I:1592; Garfield, James A., I:3993; German militarism, I:5549; Germans in U.S., I:1380; gliding, I:2580; Gorky, Maxim, I:3761; government centralization, I:1903; government finance, I:1863; grants-in-aid, I:1923; Greece, I:4325; Grey, Lady Jane, I:3995; group insurance, I:1620; Guianas, I:5358; handicrafts, I:2935; handwriting, I:3214; health insurance, I:1621; Hopkins, Gerard Manley, I:4003; hours of work, I:1633; House of Representatives, I:1440; housing, I:2899; Houston, Samuel, I:4005; humor, I:3215; Ifni, I:4380; immigration, I:1376–77, 1379; impeachment, I:1846; income tax, I:1522, 1524, 1531; industrial arbitration, I:1641; industrial education, I:1992; industrial machinery, I:1594; industrial mobilization, I:5410; industrial research, I:2451; inflation, I:1488–90; inheritance tax, I:1523, 1531–32; initiative, referendum and recall, I:1354; installment plan, I:2696; insurance, government control, I:1947–48; international arbitration, I:1821; international courts, I:1822, 1824; international law, I:1823; internationalism, I:1355; iron and steel, I:2805, 2826; Isle of Pines, I:5352; Italians in Africa, I:4381; Japan, I:4338–39; Johnny Appleseed, I:3268; judo and jiu-jitsu, I:3137; Kentucky, I:4872; knit goods, I:2807; labor disputes, I:1657–58; League of Nations, I:1819; legislatures, I:1442; Lermontov, Mikhail Y., I:3762; Liberia, I:4377; life insurance, I:1622; Lindbergh, Charles A., I:4061; liquor control, I:1869; London Naval Conference, I:5459; lotteries, I:971, 1526; Lower California, I:5354; lumber industry, I:2664; lynching, I:1851; MacArthur, Douglas, I:4065; MacLeish, Archibald, I:3306; Madagascar, I:4384–85; Malayan

campaign, I:5550; mandates, I:1352; marine engineering, I:2503; marriage and divorce, I:981–82; Maryland, I:4914; medical care, I:2358; mercantile marine subsidies, I:1545; military government, I:1828; military pensions, I:1867; military priorities, I:5414; military training, I:5408–09; Mississippi, I:4979; Mitchell, William, I:4079; monetary question, I:1497; Monongahela Valley, I:5250; Monroe doctrine, I:1414; Moore, Thomas, I:4082; motion pictures, I:3117; motor transport, I:2136; municipal government, I:1892–94; Muscle Shoals, I:2493; national defense, I:5411, 5417–18; nationalism, I:1353; natural resource taxes, I:1537; natural resources conservation, I:1505, 1507; Negroes, I:1402–03; neutrality, I:1820; Nevada, I:4999; New Deal, I:1910; New York, Philadelphia, and Washington, I:4634; New Zealand, I:5372; Newman, John Henry, I:1186; North Africa, I:4387; North American Indians, I:4495; Ohio senators, I:1443; O'Neill, Eugene, I:3316; Ozarks, I:4643; pageants, I:3116; Palestine, I:4386; Panama Canal, I:5353, 5355; pensions, I:1866; petroleum industry, I:1559; Philippine Islands, I:5377–78; Phillips, Wendell, I:3317; photography, I:2998; political parties, I:1450–51; political systems, I:1348; Portuguese in Africa, I:4382; postal money orders, I:2049; postal savings banks, I:1491; postal service, I:2050–52; powdered metals, I:5416; presidential powers, I:1909; presidential terms, I:1907; presidents, U.S., I:3938; primary elections, I:1366; prison labor, I:1593; profit sharing and bonuses, I:1624; proportional representation, I:1365; public relations, I:2778; public utilities, I:2032, 2036; Puerto Rico, I:5350, 5356–57; Pulaski, Count Kazimierz, I:4581; Pushkin, Aleksandr S., I:3763; radio broadcasting, I:1868, 2494; Randolph, John, I:4092; railroads, I:1546; reciprocity, I:1355; resale prices, I:1558; research administration, I:2178; road building, I:2517; Robertson, Thomas William, I:3505; St. Lawrence project, I:2115, 2526; sales tax, I:1529; Samoa and Guam, I:5385; Sandburg, Carl, I:3329; Saratoga campaign, I:4583; Scott, Walter, I:3513; sea safety, I:5460; senatorial election, I:1368; Sheridan, Philip Henry, I:4093; Sherman, William T., I:4094; ship subsidies, I:2127; shipping and shipbuilding, I:2128, 2131, 2503–04; Sicily and Sardinia, I:4302; Sill, Edward Rowland, I:4095; Southern U.S., I:1527, 4644; Soviet economic policy, I:1472; Soviet Russia, I:4316; Spanish

in Africa, I:4383; standardization, I:2695; state government, I:1904; state taxation, I:1535; statistical methods, I:1270; Steuben, Baron von, I:4580; sugar, I:1560; Sunday legislation, I:1009; Supreme Court, I:1906, 1911; Sweden, I:4307; Switzerland, I:4326; tanks, I:5407; tariffs, I:1536, 1544, 1547–48; tax exempt securities, I:1493; tax exemption, I:1525; telephone, I:2053; Tennessee Valley project, I:2871; Texas, I:5201; textile machinery, I:2824; transportation, I:2035; treaties, I:1825; trusts, I:1557; Twain, Mark, I:3337; unemployment insurance, I:1623; unemployment relief, I:1662–63; U.S. banks, I:1495; U.S. consuls, I:1826; U.S. economic conditions, I:1470–71; U.S. foreign relations, I:1412–13; U.S. government costs, I:1533; U.S. government departments, I:1908; U.S., Mexico and Central America, I:1416; U.S. Navy, I:5461; U.S.-U.S.S.R. relations, I:1415; urban planning, I:2871; urban transportation, I:2137; Vermont, I:5209; Virginia and Maryland, I:5222; wartime cost of living, I:1556; Washington, D.C., I:4776–77; Washington (State) and Oregon, I:5242; water power, I:1563; water rights, I:1506; waterways, I:2116–17, 2129; West Africa, I:4378; West Virginia, I:5251; western hemisphere defense, I:5415; White House, I:4778; women in Congress, I:1444; wool tariffs, I:1549; workmen's insurance, I:1595; world governments, I:1843; World War I, I:5520–27; World War II, I:5547–51; Wyoming, I:5275; youth movements, I:1267

————Division of Documents: German official publications, I:53; World War I state publications, I:5528

————Division of Fine Arts: colonial architecture, I:2874

————European Affairs Division: Africa, II:2452; displaced persons, I:5552, II:2282; Egypt, II:2451; Europe, II:2283; European press, I:469; Finland, II:2319; freedom of information, I:1361, II:697; German political science, II:672; textbooks, I:1986; U.S. and postwar Europe, I:4246–47

————Far Eastern Law Division: Chinese law, III:1056

————General Reference and Bibliography Division: Africa, II:2453–57, III:2991; American history, II:2489–91; American poetry, I:3230, II:1648–49; American Revolution loyalist exiles, I:4586; Antarctica, II:2766; art and war, II:1451; atomic energy, I:2179; Balkan and Slavic countries, I:4324; Bedford County (Pa.), I:5157; British Malaya and North Borneo, I:4358; cartels, combines and trusts,

U.S. Library of Congress, General Reference and Bibliography Division (cont.)
I:1564; China, I:4334; civil defense, II:894–95; Civil War, II:2548, III:3101; college graduates' earnings, I:2016; Columbus, Christopher, II:2112; communal settlements, I:1513; date production, I:2650; demobilization, I:5554; dictionaries, II:1600; Dred Scott decision, I:4615; Duplin County (N.C.), I:5109; Evans, Luther H., I:1830, 3972; Falkland Islands, I:5361; Federal-state relations, II:848; firearms and explosives, I:5419; foreign affairs, II:698; foreign governments, I:1916; foreign information services, I:2042; Formosa, II:2404; France, I:4286; German Communists, I:1514; Henderson, James Pinckney, I:4001; humanities, II:1628; international fairs, II:1262; international meetings, II:816; Iran, II:2432; Italy, I:4303; item veto, II:847; Japan and Far East, I:4340; Japanese in U.S., I:1382; juvenile literature, I:3820; Kapitsa, Petr L., I:2249; Kennedy, John F., III:2538; Leningrad defense, I:5553; liberty, I:1363; library architecture, I:2900, II:68; Library of Congress, II:69; library periodicals, II:70; literary recordings, III:1943; MacLeish, Archibald, I:3307; military administration, I:5420; national bibliographies, II:13; Nazis, I:5555–56; Negroes in U.S. armed services, I:5421; Netherlands East Indies, I:5386; Nigeria, II:2454; non-self governing areas, I:1383; patents, I:2453; philosophical periodicals, I:958, II:514; post-war problems, I:39; presidential inaugurations, I:1912, II:2089, III:805; race relations, U.S., I:1362, 1364; recorded poetry, III:1942; reference books, II:15; research finance, I:2180; Russian belles-lettres, I:3764; Ryukyu Islands, II:2420; Scandinavia, I:4308; science, social impact, I:2181; Slavic languages, I:3168; Southern U.S., I:4645; Soviet bibliographies, I:21, II:14; state theaters, II:1590; Stuart and Jacobite exiles, I:4278; Turkey, I:4327; UNCIO library, I:1811; UNESCO, I:1830–31; union list of serials, III:291; U.S.S.R. fuel utilization, I:1565; U.S. biography, III:2418; U.S. Presidents, III:2419; U.S. reference books, I:1271; universal military training, I:5422; war contracts, I:1870; Washington, D.C., I:4779; weather and war, I:2294; White House, II:2492
——Geography and Map Division: American city maps, III:2403; Detroit maps, III:2401; maps, III:2373–78; U.S. county maps, III:2402; U.S. explorers' routes maps, III:2404

——Hispanic Foundation: Cuba, III:3367; Handbook of Latin American studies, II:2720; Ladino books, III:780; Latin American belles-lettres, I:3706; Latin American books, III:3318; Latin American fine and folk arts, I:2852–53; Latin American periodicals, I:470; Prescott, William H., II:2194; Spanish and Portuguese translations, III:2269; Spanish literature, II:1961–62; Spanish newspapers, III:389
——International Organizations Section: guide, III:1297
——John Boyd Thacher Collection: catalog, I:578
——Korean section: Korean history, III:2909
——Law Library: African law, III:1055; Anglo-American legal bibliographies, I:1800; Chinese law, III:1054, 1056; collections, I:1773, 1797–99, 1801; current acquisitions, III:1029; District of Columbia law, I:1775; French law, I:1758; German law, I:1759; international and continental law, I:1756; Latin American law and legal literature, I:1734–45; Latin American legislation, III:1057; Mexican history, III:3377; Mexican law, I:1739, 1742; military law, I:5399; Spanish law, I:1757, 1760
——Legislative Reference Service: Alien Property Custodian, II:2806; atomic energy, I:2182; building and loan associations, I:1500; cartels and international patents, I:1567; civil defense, I:5476, 5493; Communism, III:814; Congress, I:1445; District of Columbia research facilities, I:109; educational systems, II:930; employment, I:1566; executive branch reorganization, I:1896; federal taxation, I:1538; foreign aid, II:699; intergovernmental relations, II:849; international federations, I:1832; labor management, II:762; legislation, I:1855, 1937–39; patents, II:1270; small businesses, I:2697; state governments, I:1895; synthetic rubber, I:2827; war political economy, I:1453; war production, I:1568; wartime labor, I:1596; wartime raw materials, I:5423; Washington, George, I:4121; Washington, D.C., II:850; World War II, I:5557–66
——Library of Congress Office: East Africa, III:2983; Indonesian publications, III:2842
——Loan Division: District of Columbia libraries, II:87
——Manuscript Division, III:407; Allen, Frederick Lewis, II:2092; Allen, Henry T., II:2093; American historic documents, I:4584; American history, I:4469; American Revolution naval records, I:4585; Arthur, Chester A., III:2432; Baring, Alexander, II:2096; Berge, Wendell, II:2099; Bonaparte,

Charles Joseph, II:2101; Brent, Charles Henry, II:587; Callan, John Lansing, III:2451; Carnegie, Andrew, III:2452; Casey, Silas, III:2456; Cattell, James McKeen, III:2457; Chambers, Washington Irving, III:2459; Cherokee archives, I:4486; Cleveland, Grover, III:2464; Colhoun, Edmund Ross, III:2467; Confederate muster rolls, II:2542; Connally, Tom, II:2113; Coolidge, Calvin, III:2471; Corey, Herbert, II:1680; Crittenden, John Jordan, I:3965; Culbertson, William S., III:2473; Cushing, Leonard F., III:2619; Davenport, Marcia, III:1996; Davis, James J., II:2115; Dulany, Bladen, III:2483; Farragut, David G., III:2489; Fisher, Walter L., II:2124; Fiske, Minnie Maddern, III:2491; Frankfurter, Felix, III:2499; Franklin, Benjamin, I:3990; Freeman, Douglas Southall, II:2131; Gleaves, Albert, III:2507; Grant, Ulysses S., III:2509; Harriman, Florence, II:2139; Harrison, Benjamin, III:2516–17; Harrison, William H., II:2140; Hooper, Stanford Caldwell, III:2456; Horner, Gustavius R. B., III:2483; Jackson, Andrew, III:2530; Johnson, Andrew, III:2532; Jones, John Paul, I:4022; King, Judson, II:2153; Land, Emory Scott, II:2159; Langmuir, Irving, III:2544; Lee, Samuel P., III:2546; Lincoln, Abraham, II:2176; Loening, Grover C., II:1331; Lynd, Robert S., III:2558; McAdoo, William G., II:2181–82; McKinley, William, III:2563; Madison, James, III:2564; manuscript collections, I:512–17; Marshall, George C., III:2565; Milton, George Fort, II:2189; Monroe, James, I:4081, III:2573; Negro history, I:1395; Olmsted, Frederick Law, III:2582; O'Neil, Charles, III:2467; Palmer, Theodore S., II:1136; Patterson, Daniel Todd, III:2483; personal papers, I:4468; Peru, Pizarros and Almagros, I:5360; Pierce, Franklin, I:4089; III:2590; Polk, James K., III:2591; presidential papers, II:2090; Reid, Whitelaw, II:2199; Ridgely, Charles Goodwin, III:2596; Roe, Francis Asbury, III:2596; Roosevelt, Theodore, III:2602; Sayres, Francis Bowes, III:2608; Schurz, Carl, III:2609; Selfridge, Thomas Oliver, III:2611; Sellers, David Foote, III:2612; Sheridan, Philip H., III:2615; Sherman, William T., III:2617; Shufeldt, Robert Wilson, III:2618; Snow, Elliot, III:2619; Summerall, Charles P., II:2214; Taylor, Zachary, II:2216; Van Buren, Martin, I:4101; Vernon, Edward, I:4102; Waite, Morrison R., II:2219; Walker, John Grimes, III:2596; Washington, Booker T., II:2220; Washington, George,

I:4117–20, III:2643; Watson, John Crittenden, III:2451; White, Wallace H., II:2230; Woolley, Robert W., II:2240

——Map Division: American maps, I:3877; Alaska and northwest North America, I:3893; Antarctic maps, II:2044; atlases, I:3861, II:2043; aviation cartography, II:2041; Boston maps, I:3898; California and San Francisco maps, I:3902; cartography, I:3862; Civil War maps, II:2065, III:3102; collections, I:3839, 3858, 3863, II:2045; Disturnell's map, I:3934; foreign large scale maps, I:3859; Hispanic America, I:3933; historical cartography, II:2042; Laferi's atlas, I:3856; marketing maps, II:734; Ohio, I:3915; three-dimensional maps, II:2046; treasure maps, II:2047, III:2373; U.S. atlases, II:2066; Washington, D.C., I:3923–24; World War I maps, I:3860

——Music Division: acquisitions, III:1834; American folk music recordings, I:3074–75, II:1565–66, III:1843; American popular songs, I:3064; autograph scores and letters, II:1550; Brahms and Chausson manuscripts, I:3047, 3049; Clementi manuscripts, I:3046; dramatic music, I:3037; early American music, I:3072; early music books, I:3034–35; English language folk songs, I:3077; flute, I:3021; Foster, Stephen C., I:3083; Gershwin, George, I:3084; Harold Bauer collection, III:1826; Horace de Landau collection, I:3013; Latin American folk music, I:3073, 3075, II:1565, III:1843; Latin American music, I:3076, III:1833; Liszt manuscript, I:3050; Loeffler, Charles Martin, I:3085; MacDowell, Edward, I:3082; music collections, I:3033, 3038; opera librettos, I:3036; orchestral music, I:3039; Paganini, Nicolo, I:3048; Schubert song autographs, I:3045; Sousa Band, III:1835; Star spangled banner, I:3065, 3070; 20th century English poetry, I:3229

——National Referral Center for Science and Technology: Federal Government, III:1298; physical sciences, III:1299; social sciences, III:794; toxicology, III:1455; water, III:1582

——Navy Research Section: OSRD reports, II:1289

——Near East Section: Arab history, III:2818; Arabic manuscripts, II:442; Middle East, II:2363

——Netherlands Studies Unit: Dutch bibliographies, II:16

——Orientalia Division: Arabian Peninsula, II:2458; Burma, I:4359; Chinese and Japanese books, I:3792; Chinese Communists, II:2390; Chinese gazetteers, I:4336; Chinese local histories, I:4335; Chinese Section,

II:2405; Chinese works index, I:3793; East Asiatic books, I:3792; East Asiatic music, I:3040; Orientalia, III:2803; Southeast Asia, I:4360, II:2384–85, III:2837

——Photoduplication Service: Americana photographs, I:4470; Negro newspapers, II:684; Norwegian culture, I:4309

——Photograph Section: microfilms index, I:2999

——Prints and Photographs Division, I:2976; American prints, III:1771; Americana photographs, II:1510; Civil War photographs, III:3103; Fenderich, Charles, II:1496; Hubbard engravings collection, I:2988; Latin American art, I:2854; prints and photographs, I:2990, III:1772–74; research resources, II:1483; Whistleriana, I:2989

——Processing Department: British manuscripts, II:261; East European accessions, II:2284; Russian accessions, I:3765, II:142; Russian periodicals, II:225; state publications, I:40, II:58, III:70

——Rare Book Division: acquisitions, III:473; Castlemon, Harry, I:3803; early music books, I:3010; Evans titles, II:360; gastronomy, I:2582; guide, III:472; incunabula, II:342

——Reading Rooms: American fiction, I:3247; democracy, I:1357; economic planning, I:1569; Edwards, Jonathan, I:3971; Russian dictionaries, I:3169; Sino-Japanese dispute, I:4361; Welsh in America, I:1384; World War I reparations, I:5529

——Reference Department: Africa, II:2461; African newspapers, II:2459; African periodicals, II:2460; Asia, II:2360; chemical warfare, I:5424; civilian defense, I:5494; Congressional hearings, II:714; economic assistance, II:700; foreign newspapers, II:226; Indochina, II:2406; Korea, II:2425–27; Manchuria, II:2407; Martinique, I:5362; poetry recordings, II:1776; prints and photographs, II:1497; Russia, I:4317; Soviet aeronautics, II:1332; Soviet geography, II:2048; Soviet manufactures, II:1438; Soviet serials, II:227, III:390–91; Soviet Transportation, II:1424; Whitman, Walt, II:1768

——Rosenwald Collection, I:571; acquisitions, I:558, 577; Belgian books, I:908; fine books and manuscripts, I:558; incunabula, I:627; Philippine imprint, I:907; reference works, I:550

——Science and Technology Division: abstracting and indexing services, III:1355; aeronautics and space, III:1595; Air Force research, III:1596; air pollution, I:1704; Antarctic region, III:3403; Chinese publications, III:1354, 1357; Chinese serials,

II:1080; directories, III:1300; fish protein, III:1605; IGY bibliography, III:1372; Japanese-Chinese journals, II:1077; Japanese publications, III:1356–57; mainland China organizations, III:1301; radioactive materials, I:2360; Russian serial translations, II:228; saliva, II:1161; science serials, II:1078, 1081; scientific literature, II:1035; Scientific Translations Center, II:1036; Soviet science, III:1302; Soviet serials, II:1079, III:1358–59; space science, III:1597; UFOs, III:1598; ultrashort waves, III:1379; weather modification, III:1373; Wright, Wilbur and Orville, III:1599

——Serial Division: African newspapers, III:392; American newspapers, I:436–37; European serials, I:473, 475–77; foreign newspapers, I:472; German newspapers, II:231; German periodicals, I:474; Latin American newspapers, III:393; newspapers, I:438, II:205–06, III:339; U.S. government reports, III:71

——Slavic and Central European Division: East European newspapers, II:232; East European periodicals, II:230; East Germany, II:2299; Estonia, II:2341; Latin America, II:2729; newspapers, III:394; periodicals, III:396; Rumanian history, III:2790; West German libraries, II:85; Yugoslav geography, II:2049

——Stack and Reader Division: Civil War motion pictures, III:3104; library motion pictures, II:71

——Technical Information Division: aerospace medicine, II:1162; air pollution, II:1323; Diesel engines, II:1274; human engineering, II:1271; infrared, II:1109; marine borers, II:1290; photointerpretation, II:1088; polar regions, II:2050; visibility, II:1333

——Union Catalog Division: Horace, I:3739; newspapers on microfilm, II:207, III:340; scientific and technical periodicals, I:471

——Vollbehr Collection: Gutenberg Bible, I:661; incunabula, I:658–61, 663

U.S. Light-house Board Library: catalog, I:2527

U.S. Marine Corps: cartographic records, II:2074; Latin America, III:3307; records, I:5468, III:1204; World War II unit histories, II:2805

U.S. Marine Corps Museum: Butler, Smedley Darlington, III:2450; Cochrane, Henry Clay, III:2465; Miller, Samuel, III:2571; Tilton, McLane, III:2630; Twiggs, Levi, III:2632

U.S. Maritime Commission: records, III:946

U.S. Maritime Labor Board: records, I:1597

U.S. Military Academy Library, II:904; catalog, I:5426, III:1167; history of science, III:1325; manuscript

U.S. Military Academy Library (cont.)
collection, III:1166; manuscripts, rare
books and memorabilia, I:5428;
Military Academy history, I:5425;
resources, I:5427
U.S. Military Tribunals, Nuernberg: records,
III:3419
U.S. Mint: records, II:869
U.S. National Advisory Committee for
Aeronautics: records, III:1601
U.S. National Agriculture Library: activated
charcoal, III:1699; aircraft in
agriculture, III:1616; barometric
pressure, III:1619; beautification of
land, III:1617; bibliography, III:1618;
catalog, III:1630; Chinese agriculture,
III:1639; Chinese medical journals,
III:1549; Chinese publications,
III:1624–25; contract farming,
III:1626; cooperatives, III:1620–21,
1623, 1627, 1629, 1634; drainage,
III:1631; freeze-drying of foods,
III:1606; historical works, III:1632–
33; Japanese serials, III:1635; Korean
publications, III:1636; land utilization,
III:1637; Linnaeana, III:1433; parity
prices, III:1614; pesticides, III:1628,
1638; rural electrification, III:1641;
safflower, III:1674; school lunches,
III:1607–08; soybean processing,
III:1675; special collections, III:1610;
sunflowers, III:1676; tree nut
production, III:1673; veterinary
medical periodicals, III:1547;
zoological science serials, III:1442
U.S. National Archives: Adjutant General,
I:5434; Africa, II:2448; Agricultural
Adjustment Program, I:2620; air
accidents, II:1338; Air Policy
Commission, II:1336; Air Services,
II:1337; airmail, II:983; American
Commission to Negotiate Peace,
II:2051; American Expeditionary
Forces, I:5531; American Indian,
II:2510; American Revolution,
III:3067–68; American-Scandinavian
relations, I:1411; Antarctic Service,
II:2767; anthropology, I:2314;
Argentina, III:3327; Arizona
Superintendency of Indian Affairs,
III:3044; Army records, I:5429,
III:1175; Asian history, III:2804–06;
atomic energy, II:1099; Attorney
General's Crime Committee, I:1932;
audio-visual records, III:1080;
Austria-Hungary, III:2708–09;
Aviation Policy Board, II:1335;
Belgian history, III:2719; Bibles,
III:711; Board of Investigation and
Research-Transportation, I:5571;
Bolivia, III:3329; Boston Navy Yard,
I:5465; Brady, Mathew B.,
photographs, II:1504; Brazil, III:3336;
British Africa, III:2990; Bureau of
Aeronautics, II:1334; Bureau of
Agricultural Engineering, II:1357;
Bureau of Animal Industry, II:1382;
Bureau of Entomology, II:1397;

Bureau of Indian Affairs, II:2068,
III:3041; Bureau of Insular Affairs,
II:856; Bureau of Medicine and
Surgery, I:2382; Bureau of Naval
Personnel, II:914; Bureau of
Ordnance, II:905; Bureau of Pensions,
II:773; Bureau of Planning and
Statistics, II:857; Bureau of Plant
Industry, II:1398; Bureau of
Reclamation, II:1410–11; Bureau of
Refugees, Freedmen, and Abandoned
Land, I:4475; Bureau of the Census,
II:2069; Bureau of Yards and Docks,
I:5469; Burma and India, III:2839;
business history, III:900; census
records, III:800; Central America,
III:3356; Chemical Warfare Service,
I:5568; Chief of Naval Operations,
II:2071; China, II:2400, III:2892–93;
citizenship records, III:2420; Civil
Service, II:862; Civil War, III:3105–
06; Civilian Conservation Corps,
I:1484, 2671; climatological records,
I:2238; Coast and Geodetic Survey,
II:1089; Coast Guard vessels, I:5462;
Collector of Customs, II:858;
Colorado, II:2593; Commission of
Fine Arts, II:1452; Commodity
Exchange Authority, II:736; company
history, III:902; Confederate States
records, II:2549; congested production
areas, II:859; Costa Rica, III:3353;
Council of National Defense, I:5534;
Counsel for Prosecution of Axis
Criminality, I:5572; Court of Claims,
II:805, 807; Cuba, I:5364, 5367,
III:3368–69; Direct Tax Commission,
I:1541; District of Columbia, I:4773;
District Courts, II:808–09; Division of
Insolvent National Banks, I:1501;
Dominican customs receivership,
I:5363; Dominican Republic, III:3343;
Economic Stabilization Agency,
II:737; El Salvador, III:3354, 3357;
executive agencies' authority, II:868;
Executive Mansion, II:1463; Extension
Service, II:860; Far East, II:687;
Farmers Home Administration,
II:1358; Federal agencies, I:1913;
Federal Communications Commission,
II:954; Federal Housing
Administration, II:2070; Federal
medical records, I:2383; Federal Trade
Commission, I:2043; Federal Writers'
Project, II:1629; Florida, I:4780, 4788;
Food Administration, I:5535; foreign
aid, II:706; Foreign Broadcast
Intelligence Service, II:704; Foreign
Economic Administration, II:705;
foreign service post records, II:702–
03; III:1063; Forest Service, I:2654,
2665; France, II:2305; Franklin D.
Roosevelt Library, I:1418, 4471,
III:2600; genealogy, I:4171, III:2664–
66; General Land Office, I:1540;
geographical exploration, II:2067;
Georgia, I:4808; German archives,
II:2771–2800, 2803, 2818; German

Foreign Ministry, III:3416; Goethals,
George Washington, III:2508; Grain
Corporation, I:1553; Guatemala,
III:3355, 3358; guide to records,
I:4472; Haiti, III:3344, 3347; Henry S.
Wellcome papers, III:3043; history of
science, II:1060; House of
Representatives, II:715; Hungarian
refugee relief, III:2783; Hydrographic
Office, II:1312; immigrant records,
III:2412; Inaugural Committee (1961),
III:807; Indian land cessions, III:3033;
Indian treaties, I:4496; Indiana Food
Administration, I:5536; Industrial
Incentive Division, I:5567; Industrial
Records Branch, II:1147; Inspector
General, I:5432; Interior Department,
I:4473, 4662; international boundaries,
III:1065; international conferences,
II:707, III:1068; international military
agencies, III:1172; International
Military Tribunal for the Far East,
III:1192; interservice agencies,
III:1085–86; interstate railroads,
II:996; Iowa, I:4848; Irish, II:677;
Italian armed forces, III:1168; Italian
history, III:2729; Japanese records,
II:2415; Jefferson, Thomas, I:4018;
Kansas and Nebraska, II:2623; Labor
Dept. Wage and Hour Division,
I:1625; labor history, III:960; Latin
America, II:2721, III:3319–20;
Liberia, III:2992; Louisiana Food
Administration, I:5508; map archives,
I:3882; Marine Corps, I:5468, II:2074;
Maritime Labor Board, I:1597; Maury,
Matthew Fontaine, I:4078; Mexico,
II:2742, III:3385–86; Michigan,
II:2645; microcopies, I:4474, II:2493,
2495; Middle East, II:2365; migratory
labor, II:764; military archives,
III:1169; Minnesota, I:4970; Mint,
II:869; Missouri Food Administration,
I:5509; national defense, II:898;
National Guard Bureau, I:5430;
National Recovery Administration,
II:739, 744; National Resources
Planning Board, I:1474, II:851, 867;
National War Labor Board, I:1598;
Naval Observatory, I:2239; Navy,
I:5448, 5463–64, 5466–67, 5470,
5570; Navy Board for Production
Awards, I:5567; Negro studies, I:1393,
1396; Netherlands history, III:2721;
New Mexico, I:5017; North Carolina,
I:5104; North Carolina Food
Administration, I:5510; Office for
Agricultural War Relations, II:1359;
Office for Emergency Management,
II:864; Office of Civilian Defense,
I:5495; Office of Commissary General
of Subsistence, I:5431; Office of
Government Reports, II:865; Office of
Inter-American Affairs, II:2730; Office
of Pardon Attorney, II:806; Office of
Price Administration, I:5577, II:735,
741, 743, 863; Office of War
Information, II:907; Office of War

Mobilization, II:908; Ohio Food Administration, I:5539; Oklahoma, II:2672; Oregon, I:5138; Pacific Basin, III:3404; Pacific Northwest maps, I:3890; Panama Canal, II:2073, III:3352; Paymaster General, I:5435; Pennsylvania, I:5144, 5159; Persian history, III:2820; Peru, III:3390–91; petroleum, II:1280–81; Philippine Islands, I:5379, III:2915–16; pictures, III:1081; plant industries, II:1387; population, II:665; Postmaster General, II:979–82; postwar military policy, II:896; presidential inaugurations, II:2494; presidential nominations, III:806; Price Decontrol Board, II:740; Public Building Service, II:1464; public debt, II:852; Public Works Administration, II:866; Puerto Rico, I:5366, III:3345–46; range cattle industry, I:2636; real estate bondholders, II:738; Reference circulars, I:4193; Retraining and Reemployment Administration, II:765; Rhode Island, II:2686; Rubber Survey Committee, I:2828; Rumanian history, III:2791; Russia, II:2336; Santo Domingo, I:5365; Secret Service, I:1871; Secretary of the Interior, II:2072; Secretary of War, I:5433; seized enemy records, III:1187; Selective Service System, I:5532, II:897; Senate records, I:1446–47, II:716; Ship Building Stabilization Committee, II:1293; Shipping Board, II:1291; Siam, III:2846–47; Soil Conservation Service, I:2672; Solid Fuels Administration, II:1437; special agents, II:701; Strategic Bombing Survey, I:5437; Supreme Court, II:784; surplus property, II:854–55; Tennessee, I:5183; Tennessee Food Administration, I:5499; Texas, I:5187, 5193; Turkish history, III:2819; United Nations, II:817–18; Utah, I:5205, III:3271; Virgin Islands, II:861; Virginia Food Administration, I:5507; Wage Adjustment Board, II:774; War Department, I:5387, 5392, II:906; War Department Claims Board, I:5533; War Food Administration, II:763; War Industries Board, I:5573–74; War Labor Board, I:1599, II:772; War Production Board, I:5569, 5575; War Shipping Administration, II:1292; War Trade Board, II:742; wartime health and education, II:931; Washington, Oregon and Idaho Food Administration, I:5511; Washington (State), II:2709; Washington Superintendency of Indian Affairs, I:4492; Weather Bureau, II:1094; Western history, III:3155; Wisconsin, I:5267, II:2714; Works Progress Administration, II:853; World War I, I:5530, II:2769, III:3407–09; World War II, II:2807–17, III:1170, 3410, 3417–20; Wyoming, I:5273

U.S. National Bituminous Coal Commission: records, III:1110
U.S. National Board of Health: records, III:1456
U.S. National Bureau of Standards: records, III:1111
U.S. National Clearinghouse for Smoking and Health Library: smoking and health bibliography, III:1464
U.S. National Commission on Law Operations and Enforcement: records, III:1031
U.S. National Conference on Outdoor Recreation: records, III:1908
U.S. National Guard Bureau: records, I:5430, III:1202
U.S. National Institutes of Health Library: periodicals, III:1553; reference aids, II:1163; resources, II:1164
U.S. National Labor Relations Board, Library: Labor management relations act, II:766
U.S. National Library of Medicine, II:1151; aerospace medicine, II:1162; Art Section, II:1139; aspirin, II:1165; biomedical computer applications, III:1458; biomedical serials, II:1219–20, III:1548; bone, II:1193; burns, II:1183; cancer, II:1173; catalogs, II:1205–10, III:1513, 1515–19; Chinese journals, II:1218, III:1549–51; dentistry, III:1461; encephalitis, II:1166; film guide, II:1176, III:1459; fungus infections, II:1177; gas gangrene, II:1178; Gesner, Conrad, III:2505; guide, II:1182; Harvey, William, II:1248; history of medicine, III:1491–99; incunabula, II:1252; leptospirosis, II:1179; medical caricatures, II:1244; medical portraits, II:1245, 1247; medical reviews, II:1167, III:1552; medicolegal serials, III:1551; MEDLARS services, III:1460; military medicine, II:1168–69, 1181; military psychiatry, II:1170–71, 1189; Nobel prize winners, II:1246; noise and hearing, II:1175; physiology of brain, II:1147; pituitary-adrenocortical function, II:1184; plasma substitutes, II:1185; psychiatry, II:1186; psychopharmaca, II:1187; reference books, II:1174, 1188; Salmonella, II:1190; scientific translations, II:1037; Slavic medicine, II:1191; Southern Asia, II:1180; Southern Asia publications, II:1202; Soviet medicine, III:1462; space medicine, II:1172; Staphylococcal infection, II:1192; toxicity, III:1463; viral genetics, II:1194
U.S. National Park Service: records, III:1112; Utah centennial, I:5205; Virginia history, I:5223
U.S. National Recovery Administration: bibliography, I:1460; records, II:739, 744
U.S. National Resources Committee: urban planning, I:2872
U.S. National Resources Planning Board: records, II:851, 867; reports, I:1474

U.S. National Security Agency Library: writing aids, II:1630
U.S. National Security Resources Board: records, III:1113; World War II production control, I:5575
U.S. National War College Library: catalog, I:5438–39, 5445; Civil War, I:4616–19; limited war, II:1285; Mexico, I:5369; military biographies, I:5442; psychological warfare, II:1284
U.S. National War Labor Board: records, I:1598, II:2811; wage stabilization, II:772
U.S. National Youth Administration, I:1267
U.S. Naval Academy: historic objects, I:5471
————Library: catalog, I:5473–74; log-books, I:5475; naval literature, I:5472
————Museum: manuscripts, II:909–11
U.S. Naval Districts and Shore Establishments: records, III:1222
U.S. Naval Observatory: records, I:2239, III:1371
————Library: catalog, I:2241; Maury, Matthew Fontaine, I:4077; resources, I:2240
U.S. Naval Research Laboratory Library: periodicals, III:1216; resources and services, III:1217
U.S. Navy, I:4585, 5447–49, 5451–52, 5461, 5463–75; II:909–12, 914; III:1216–26
U.S. Navy Board for Production Awards: records, I:5567
U.S. Office for Agricultural War Relations: records, II:1359
U.S. Office for Emergency Management: records, II:864; synthetic rubber, I:2827
U.S. Office of Censorship: records, II:2812
U.S. Office of Civilian Defense: records, I:5495
U.S. Office of Contract Settlement: records, III:1114
U.S. Office of Education: federal libraries, III:132
————Library: biographical directories and college catalogs, I:1997; city school systems, I:1971; college and student publications, I:2017; education economic value, I:2029; education in depression, I:1966; education publications, I:1968, 1974; education research, I:1963–65; education theses, I:1967; elementary education, I:2026; Far East, I:4362–65; higher education, I:2018; home economics, I:2590; Latin America, I:5368; library facilities, I:1969; Library leaflet series, I:1970; Montessori method, I:2027; motion pictures, I:1978; parents' groups, I:1976; play and playgrounds, I:1979; post-war planning, I:1973; public library catalogs, I:177; rural life, I:2603; rural schools, I:2028; secondary education, I:1996, 2026; state departments and associations, I:1972; student government, I:1980;

U.S. Office of Education Library (cont.)
subject bibliographies, I:1962;
teachers' pensions, I:1981; teaching
profession, I:1977; vocational
education, I:1993; vocational
guidance, I:1994; women in wartime,
I:5576
U.S. Office of Experiment Stations:
agricultural experiment station
bulletins, I:2614; records, I:2613,
III:1655
U.S. Office of Geography: records, III:2379
U.S. Office of Government Reports: records,
II:865
U.S. Office of Indian Affairs: archival maps,
I:3882; Washington Superintendency
of Indian Affairs, I:4492
U.S. Office of Intelligence Research: reports,
II:841
U.S. Office of Inter-American Affairs:
records, II:2730
U.S. Office of Price Administration:
Accounting Dept., II:735; Enforcement
Dept., II:743; Information Dept.,
II:863; Office of Personnel, III:1115;
Price Dept., II:741; Rationing Dept.,
II:2813
U.S. Office of Public Buildings and Grounds:
White House, III:1737
U.S. Office of Science and Technology:
records, III:1303
U.S. Office of Scientific Research and
Development: records, III:1304;
reports, II:1289
U.S. Office of Strategic Services: records,
III:1193
U.S. Office of Territories: records, III:1116
U.S. Office of the Chief of Chaplains:
records, III:1117
U.S. Office of the Chief of Engineers:
records, III:1583
U.S. Office of the Chief of Finance (Army):
records, III:1179, 1207
U.S. Office of the Chief of Naval
Operations: cartographic records,
II:2071; U.S. naval history,
III:1218–19
U.S. Office of the Chief of Ordnance: records,
III:1194
U.S. Office of the Chief Signal Officer:
records, III:1221, 1225
U.S. Office of the Commissary General of
Prisoners: records, III:1118
U.S. Office of the Inspector General: records,
III:1203
U.S. Office of the Judge Advocate General
(Navy): records, III:1223
U.S. Office of the Pardon Attorney: records,
II:806
U.S. Office of the Quartermaster General:
records, III:1195–96
U.S. Office of the Special Adviser to the
President on Foreign Trade: records,
III:1119
U.S. Office of War Information: records,
II:907, III:1181
U.S. Office of War Mobilization and
Reconversion: records, II:908

U.S. Ordnance Department Library: catalog,
I:5436
U.S. Patent Office: law library catalog,
I:1724; library catalog, I:2780
———Scientific Library: periodicals, III:1360
U.S. Paymaster General: records, I:5435
U.S. Petroleum Administration, I:1902 (3);
records, II:1280, III:1120
U.S. Post Office Department: records,
III:1121
U.S. Postmaster-General: records, II:979–82
U.S. Presidential Railroad Commission:
records, III:945
U.S. President's Advisory Commission on
Presidential Office Space: records,
III:1123
U.S. President's Advisory Committee on
Government Organization: records,
III:1122
U.S. Presidents, campaign songs, III:1849
U.S. President's Committee on Employment
of the Physically Handicapped:
bibliography, II:767
U.S. President's Committee to Study the
United States Military Assistance
Program: records, III:1182
U.S. President's Materials Policy
Commission: records, III:1124
U.S. President's Organization on
Unemployment Relief: records, III:975
U.S. President's Scientific Research Board:
records, III:1305
U.S. Price Administration Office: OPA
bibliography, I:5577
U.S. Price Decontrol Board: records, II:740
U.S. Prison Industries Reorganization
Administration: records, III:1125
U.S. Provost Marshal General's Bureau (Civil
War): records, III:3109–16
U.S. Public Roads Administration: automobile
parking, I:2135
U.S. Public Works Administration: records,
II:866
U.S. Public Works Housing Division, I:1902
(2)
U.S. Railroad Administration: records, III:947
U.S. Rent Commission of the District of
Columbia: records, III:1126
U.S. Retraining and Reemployment
Administration: records, II:765
U.S. Rubber Survey Committee: records,
I:2828
U.S. Secret Service: records, I:1871, III:1135
U.S. Secretary of the Air Force: records,
III:1213
U.S. Secretary of the Army: records, III:1180
U.S. Secretary of the Interior, Division of
Finance: records, III:1079
U.S. Secretary of War: records, I:5433
U.S. Securities and Exchange Commission:
records, III:1127
———Library: collection list, I:1502; public
utilities, I:2037
U.S. Selective Service System: records,
I:5532, II:897
U.S. Senate: records, II:716
———Library: Congressional committee
hearings, III:1139–40

U.S. Shipping Board: records, II:1291, III:948
U.S. Smaller War Plants Corporation: records,
III:1183
U.S. Smithsonian Institution: records, III:1128
U.S. Social Security Administration: records,
III:1129
———Library: Medicare, III:1465; social
security, I:1626
U.S. Soil Conservation Service: records,
I:2672
U.S. Soil Erosion Service, I:1902 (4)
U.S. Solders' Home: records, III:1136
U.S. Solicitor of the Treasury: records,
III:1130
———Library: catalog, I:1725
U.S. Solid Fuels Administration for War:
records, II:1437, III:3417
U.S. Strategic Bombing Survey: records,
I:5437
U.S. Supreme Court, I:1906, 1911;
biographies of justices, II:2080;
opinions index, III:1030; records,
II:784, III:1032–33
U.S. Surplus Marketing Administration:
records, III:1131
U.S. Tariff Commission: foreign commercial
and economic periodicals, I:2038
———Library: raw materials, I:1570;
reciprocal trade, I:1550; tariff, I:1551
U.S. Temporary National Economic
Committee: records, III:860
U.S. Tennessee Valley Authority: records,
III:1132
U.S. territorial possessions, I:4411, 4455,
5278–80
U.S. Treasury Department: archives, I:4418
———Library: catalog, I:1914; Federal-
state-local relations, II:870; national
wealth and income, I:1475, II:745
U.S. Veterans Administration: archives,
I:4426; pension case files, III:2421
———Libraries: aged, II:1196; bibliotherapy,
II:1195; brain surgery, III:1467; care
of veterans, II:1197, III:1466; civil
defense, II:899; fair employment
practices, III:977; medical journals,
II:1221, III:1554; nosology, II:1198;
paraplegia, II:1199; popular medicine,
II:1200; traumatic paraplegia, II:1201
U.S. Wage Adjustment Board: records, II:774
U.S. Wage and Hour and Public Contracts
Division: records, III:976
U.S. War Ballot Commission: records,
II:2815
U.S. War Department: archives, I:4419, 5392;
Claims Board records, I:5533;
McHenry, James, I:4066; Military
Affairs Committee investigation,
II:906
———General and Special Staffs: archives,
I:5387, III:1197
———Library: acquisitions, I:5439–40,
5445; catalog, I:5438; Civil War,
I:4616–19; Mexican war, I:4588;
Mexico, I:4588, 5305, 5369; military
biographies, I:5442; national defense,
I:5446; reference works, I:5443;
serials, I:5441, 5444

U.S. War Food Administration: records, II:763

U.S. War Industries Board: records, I:5573–74

U.S. War Labor Policies Board: records, I:1599

U.S. War Minerals Relief Commission: records, III:1185

U.S. War Production Board: production control, I:5575; records, I:5569, III:1205

U.S. War Refugee Board: records, II:2816

U.S. War Relocation Authority: records, II:2817

U.S. War Shipping Administration: records, II:1292

U.S. War Trade Board: records, II:742

U.S. Weather Bureau: climatological and hydrological records, II:1094; meteorological records, III:1374
————Library: meteorology, I:2295

U.S. Works Progress Administration: archives, I:4429; records, II:853

United Transportation Union: railroad labor history, III:956

Universal languages, I:3148

Universalist Church, I:1193

University of the South Library: special collections, I:143

Untermeyer, Louis, III:2010, 2063

Upanishads, II:633

Updike, Daniel B., I:773

Upton, William T., I:3072, 3078, 3080

Urban planning, I:2856–73, 2875; II:1454–55, 1458; III:1727–37

Urbanization, II:1367

Urdu literature, II:2833

Urena, Pedro Henriquez, II:2751

Urology, history, III:1476

Uruguay, history, I:5281, 5289; III:3392

Ustick, Stephen C., I:694

Utah, history, I:5203–05; II:2697–99; III:3271

Utah Genealogical Society: microfilm program, II:2697

Utah State Federation of Labor: records, III:978

Utah State Industrial Union Council: records, III:978

Utah State Library: catalog, I:269; government publications, II:48

Utah State Library Commission: government publications, III:72

Utah State University Library: Mormons, II:568

Utah, University Libraries: genealogy, III:2667; government publications, III:73; labor unions, III:978; Mormons, II:568–69; music, II:1551; Pyper, George Dollinger, III:2594; Western Americana, II:2569; Whitaker, John Mills, III:2647; Yiddish collection, III:781
————Middle East Center Library: Arabic collection, III:2821
————Utah Humanities Research Foundation: archives, I:4194

Utamaro, Kitagawa, I:2967

Utica Public Library: Sullivan's expedition, I:5086; Utica history, I:5087

Utley, George B., I:4476

Utopias, I:1351; III:815–16, 2200

Uyehara, Cecil H., II:2419

Uzdrowski, Mel R., III:2346

Vail, Robert W. G., I:1010, 2742, 3295, 3328, 4396, 4528, 4624, 4748; II:425

Vale Press, II:346

Valentine Museum: newspapers, I:440

Valinger, Leon de, Jr., I:4768; II:2200

Value, theory, I:1461

Vambery, Joseph, II:454

Van Buren, Martin, I:4008, 4101

Vance, John T., I:1739

Vance, Joseph C., II:2182

Vanderbilt, Paul, I:2991; II:1497, 1511, 2177

Vanderbilt University Library: catalog, I:270

Vandergrift, Barbara P., III:555

Van Derpool, James Grote, I:2901; II:1456

Van Doren, Mark, III:2066

Vander Velde, Esther, II:2231

Van Duzer, Henry S., I:3558

Van Gaasbeek, Peter, III:3228

Van Gulick, R. H., III:2634

Vanilla, I:2602 (13)

Van Lennep, William, II:1591

Van Male, John, II:110–11

Vann, William H., I:3484

Van Name, Addison, I:614

Van Neste, W. Lane, II:1464

Van Patten, Nathan, I:913; II:1547

Van Schreeven, William J., I:5536

Van Sinderen, Adrian, I:3343

Van Tyne, Claude H., I:4477

Van Vechten, Carl, II:1631, 1756

Van Volkenburg, Ellen, II:1586

Varney, Edith, I:1555

Vassar College Library: periodical press, I:482; rare books and manuscripts, I:612; Vassariana, II:950

Vatican City, II:620; Library, II:606

Vatshaug, Tordis O., II:1175

Vaughn, Evelyn L., III:3184

Vaughan, John, I:4566, 5021

Vecoli, Rudolph J., III:2423

Vedelen, Harold C., I:4814

Venezuela: history, I:5335, II:2754, III:3296, 3323, 3393; maps, I:3931

Venice, history, II:2318; III:2724, 2727–28

Vergil, II:1967

Vermont, history, I:5206–10; II:2700–01; III:3272

Vermont Historical Society: Civil War, III:3093

Vermont Secretary of State: archives, II:2700; III:3272

Vermont State Library: Hartford imprints, I:723

Vermont, University, Fleming Museum: early American maps, I:3869
————Library: catalog, I:271; Ira Allen papers, I:5210; Romance languages and Scandinavian literature, I:3216

Verner, Coolie, II:2055, 2075, 2147, 2706; III:3069

Verner, Mathilda, II:460

Verner, Sarah A., II:240, 1715, 2143, 2537; III:2037

Vernon, Edward, I:4102

Verrett, Mary Camilla, III:755

Vesalius, Andreas, I:2404; III:1319

Veterinary medicine, I:2374, 2380; II:1204, 1237; III:1514; periodicals, II:1211, III:1547

Veto, II:847

Viaducts, I:2516

Victoria, Queen, III:2691, 2695, 2700

Victorian literature, II:219, 1783, 1790, 1793, 1796, 1799; III:2106, 2133, 2691, 2695, 2700

Vienna, history, III:2703

Viereck, George Sylvester, III:2087

Vietnam, II:2828, 2848–52

Vilas, William F., I:4103

Viles, Jonas, I:4988–89

Vincent, Claire, III:104

Vinci, Leonardo da, I:2843, 3686, 4104; II:1474, 1482; III:2635–36

Vineland, N. J., maps, I:3918

Vineland Historical and Antiquarian Society Library: history, I:5005; maps, I:3918

Viola, Herman J., III:3044

Virgil, I:3731–32, 3736

Virgin Islands, II:861

Virginia: history, I:5211–38, II:2702–07, III:3273–76; maps, I:3919–22; II:2063, 2075

Virginia Baptist Historical Society: Baptist Church records, I:1072; manuscripts, I:1067

Virginia Company of London: records, I:4502, 4529

Virginia Historical Society Library: archives, I:5219; George Rogers Clark papers, I:4555; manuscripts, I:5212, 5224; Virginia newspapers, I:439

Virginia Polytechnic Institute Library: Maury, Matthew Fontaine, I:4077

Virginia State Library: agriculture, I:2593, 2619; American history, I:4478; American Revolution, I:4557; Bill of Rights, I:5231; biography, I:3941; Confederate publications, I:4611, 4620; debating, I:3218; fiction, I:3200; French newspapers, I:478; genealogy, I:4158, 4177; geography, anthropology and hydrography, I:3864; George Rogers Clark papers, I:4555; government publications, I:41, II:49, III:74–75; history, I:4195; language and literature, I:3217; Maury, Matthew Fontaine, I:4077; music, fine arts and photography, I:2855; newspapers, I:440; 19th century directories, II:2707; parish records, I:1141; printing and books, I:948; science and technology, I:2183; Shakespeare, William, I:3539; Shenandoah Valley, I:5215; social sciences, I:1268; Southeastern broadsides, III:509; taxation, I:1542; Virginia archives, I:5219; Virginia conventions and constitutions, I:1849; Virginia history, I:5212, 5220–21, 5226–30, 5232;

Virginia State Library *(cont.)*
    Virginia imprints, I:885; Virginia
    maps, I:3922; Virginia newspapers,
    I:439
Virginia, University, Library: American
    history, I:4405, 4479, II:2496;
    American literature, I:1632, 1634;
    American poetry, III:1970; American
    writer in England, III:1960; botany,
    II:1127; Brooks, Charles Timothy,
    II:1672; business records, I:2743;
    Bynner, Edwin Lassetter, III:1989;
    Cabell, James Branch, II:1674; Carter,
    Landon, III:2453; Carter family,
    III:2454; catalog, I:272; Charles I,
    II:2292; Chinese classics, II:1989;
    Chinese collection, III:2894;
    collections, I:91, 97, 120; Davis,
    Richard Harding, III:1997; directories,
    II:2707; early newspaper, I:441;
    English books, I:680; Faulkner,
    William, II:1694, III:2007–08; foreign
    newspapers, III:397; Franklin,
    Benjamin, II:2130; Frost, Robert,
    III:2011; Fry and Jefferson map,
    II:2055; Garnett Library, II:119;
    Glasgow, Ellen, III:2015; Glass,
    Carter, II:2134–35; Gothic novels,
    I:3375; Hamond, Sir Andrew Snape,
    III:2513; Harte, Bret, II:1700; Holmes,
    Oliver Wendell, II:1704; Howells,
    William Dean, II:1709; Hunter, R. M.
    T., III:2526; James, Henry, III:2035;
    Jeffers, Robinson, II:1718; Jefferson,
    Thomas, I:4010, 4012, 4019–20,
    II:1453, 1465, 2055, 2148; John
    Powell music collection, III:1871;
    Lafayette, Marquis de, II:2157; Lee
    family, III:2547; missionary records,
    III:718; Monroe, James, III:2574;
    optics, I:2250, II:1095; parish records,
    I:1140–41; Poe, Edgar Allan,
    II:1738, III:2056; printers' ornaments,
    II:491; Randolph, John, II:2198;
    Roosevelt, Theodore, III:2603;
    Sandburg, Carl, III:2067; special
    collections, III:159; Sterling, George,
    III:2621; Stockton, Frank Richard,
    III:2073; Switzerland, II:2350;
    Tennyson, Alfred, Lord, II:1899,
    III:2229; Thoreau, Henry David,
    III:1961; University records, I:2019;
    Virginia authors, III:1962; Virginia
    folksongs, III:1859; Virginia gazette
    day books, III:3274; Virginia history,
    I:5233–35; Ward, Elizabeth Stuart
    Phelps, III:2639; Whitman, Walt,
    II:1760, III:2095
———Medical School Library: serials,
    III:1555–56
Virginia War History Commission, I:5236
Virtue, Ethel B., I:4971
Virus diseases, II:1194
Visibility, II:1333
Vivian, James F., III:2791
Vocational education and guidance, I:1987–
    94; II:150, 936–38
Vogel, Emil, I:3041

Vogler, Richard A., III:2158
Vogt, George M., I:3360
Volcanoes, I:2278
Völgyes, Ivan, III:2778
Volta Bureau Library: Bell, Alexander
    Graham, I:3946; deaf periodicals,
    I:1924
Von Chorba, Albert, Jr., II:1646, 1652
Vormelker, Rose, I:102
Vosper, Edna, I:4566
Vosper, Robert, I:163
Voss, Thomas H., III:1988
Voyages, I:3843, 3847

Wabeke, B. H., I:5578
Wachovia Historical Society: Moravians,
    I:5093
Wadden, Anthony T., III:2000
Wade, Alfred Byers, II:1488
Wade, Allan, II:1913
Wade, Evelyn, III:1137, 1169
Wade, James C., II:381
Wade, Joseph S., I:3335
Wade, Louise C., II:918
Wager, Charles, I:4102
Wages, I:1602–03, 1608–09, 1615, 1625;
    II:772, 774
Wagner, B. M., I:56
Wagner, Frank S., III:1361
Wagner, Henry R., I:113, 718, 812, 900,
    904, 3865, 3894, 4655–56, 4690,
    4749; II:477, 2568, 2570, 2725, 2731
Wagner Lutheran College Library, II:117
Wainwright, Alexander D., I:4530; II:1733,
    1783
Wainwright, J. C. J., I:3123
Wainwright, Nicholas B., III:2587
Wait, Martha H., I:4621
Waite, Morrison R., II:2219
Wajcicka, Janina, II:230
Wakashan languages, I:3185
Wake Forest University Library: Charles Lee
    Smith library, I:207, II:1643; Mark
    Twain, III:2085; North Carolina
    history, I:5110
Wakefield, Roberta P., II:2255
Waldbott, Sigmund, I:2204
Waldron, Rod, III:1702
Waldron, Vincent G., II:1088
Waldseemüller, Martin, II:2031
Wales, history, I:4259
Walker, Audrey A., III:2981–83, 2985,
    2987
Walker, Ella K., I:2873
Walker, Evans, III:1099, 1116
Walker, John W., I:3418
Walker, L. Evans, II:866
Walker, Mary A., I:741; II:536–38
Walker, Richard L., II:1992
Walker, Rosemary L., III:1915
Walker, William, I:5341
Walker, John Grimes, III:2596
Wall, Alexander J., I:442, 1503, 2902, 4701,
    5088
Wallace, Anthony F. C., II:1119
Wallace, Carolyn Andrews, III:3131
Wallace, David H., II:1450
Wallace, John M., III:341

Wallace, Marlene, III:3272
Wallace, Paul A. W., II:560–62
Wallace, Sarah Agnes, II:2185
Wallace, William H., III:2637
Wallace, William S., II:208
Wallach, Kate, II:1278
Waller, Salvador B., II:446
Wallis, Talbot H., I:1674
Walls, Howard L., I:3118
Walpole, Horace, I:3564–66
Walpole, Hugh, II:1613, 1797
Walsh, John, III:1306
Walsh-Healey Act, I:1588
Walsworth, Bertha L., I:4686
Walter, Frank K., II:2524
Walter, Yvonne, I:3359
Walter Reed Army Medical Center:
    biomedical periodicals, III:1557
Walters, Henry, I:662
Walters, Mary D., III:838–39
Walters Art Gallery: bookbinding, II:505;
    calligraphy, III:1780; incunabula,
    I:662; manuscripts and rare books,
    I:498
Walton, Clarence E., I:67, 2020, 3300
Walton, Clyde C., II:2173, 2612;
    III:2553
Walton, Ivan Henry, II:1006
Walton, Izaak, I:233, 3567
Walton, Robert P., I:61, 2800
Wan, Weiying, III:2873
Wang, Chi, III:1301, 1378
Wannarka, Marjorie Bernice, III:1468–69
Wanning, Andrews, I:4004
War: contracts, I:1870; economic aspects,
    I:1453, 1464, 1556, 1568, 1596, 1639;
    industry, I:5561; limited, II:1285;
    poetry, II:1607; posters, I:5496, 5503,
    5517, 5544; production, I:1568;
    profiteering, I:5389; referendum,
    I:1350
War of 1812, I:4447
War Services Program, Louisiana, I:1343
Ward, Artemas, III:2638
Ward, Christopher, I:3840
Ward, Elizabeth Stuart Phelps, III:2639
Ward, Marietta, III:1726
Ward, Philip R., III:1677
Ward, Robert E., II:673
Ward, William H., I:4221
Ward, William S., II:233
Warden, David B., I:4590
Wark, Robert R., II:1467
Warmbrodt, Carole Sue, III:981
Warmoth, Henry Clay, III:2640
Warner, Donald F., II:2527
Warner, John E., III:2103
Warner, Robert M., III:3211
Warnow, Joan Nelson, III:1380
Warrell, William H., I:4227
Warren, D. Michael, III:364
Warren, Katherine, I:3119, 3238
Warren, Louis A., I:4056
Warrington, James, I:1050
Washington, Booker T., I:1388; II:2220
Washington, George, I:2599 (22), 3936,
    4105–22, 4438; II:2221–25, 2535;
    III:1851, 2399, 2641–43, 3065

Washington, D.C., II:850; history, I:4634, 4773–79, II:2595–96; maps, I:3923–24

Washington (state) history, I:5239–42; II:2578, 2708–09; III:3277

Washington State Department of Conservation, Division of Mines and Geology: Washington geology and resources, II:1113

Washington State Library: books for blind, III:200; catalog, I:273; government publications, I:42, II:50, III:76; legal collection, I:1726; Negroes, III:848; newspapers, III:342; Northwest history, III:3160; public welfare, III:1233; resource conservation, I:1508; roads, I:2518

Washington State University Library: Brown, William Compton, III:2446; Carty, William Edward, III:2455; early English books, I:664; Hill, Knute, III:2521; Horan, Walt, III:2523; Johnson, Lon, III:2534; Mexican history, III:3387; Mires, Austin, III:2572; Pacific Northwest maps, I:3890; Russell, Carl Porcher, III:2605; serials, III:292

Washington University Libraries (St. Louis): Chinese and Japanese periodicals, III:398–99; Chinese-Japanese collections, III:2895; Gardner, Isabella, III:2012; Johnson, Josephine, III:2039; Latin America, III:3321–22; Latin American serials, III:400; manuscript collections, II:262; Middle East and North Africa, III:2822; music, II:1535; scientific periodicals, III:1362; serials, I:363, II:168

——School of Medicine Library (St. Louis): catalogs, III:1520–24; periodicals, III:1558; William Beaumont, III:1500

Washington, University, Far Eastern Library (Seattle): Chinese books, II:2403; Chinese literature, II:1984; collections, II:2370; Japanese literature, III:2908; Tibetan collection, III:2921

——Forest Resources Library (Seattle): bibliography, III:1683; forestry economics, III:1687; manuscripts, III:1679; reference works, III:1688; theses, III:1691; tropical forestry, III:1689; woodworking, III:1690

——Law Library (Seattle): resources, I:1769

——Libraries (Seattle): art and archaeology, III:1726; Asian collection, III:2807; Bagley family, III:2433; Ballinger, Richard A., III:2434; bookbindings, III:680; Brainard, Erastus, II:2102; Burke, Thomas, II:2106; business history, III:917–19; China, II:2391; Chinese gazetteers, III:2896; Indian records, I:4492; Italian literature, II:1944; Japan, II:2421; Klondike photographs, II:1498; Löfgren, Svante E., II:1934; McGilvra, John J., III:2560; Manning

Ferguson Force, III:2497; manuscripts, III:427; Oregon Improvement Company, III:918; Pacific Northwest history, I:4668; Pacific Northwest maps, I:3890, III:2405; periodicals, I:364; Port Blakely Mill Company, II:955; science, II:1028; Semple, Eugene, III:2613; Shakespeare, William, II:1879; Stevens, Isaac Ingalls, II:2211, III:2622; Upanishads, II:633; Wallace, William H., III:2637; Washington history, III:3277; Washington Mill Company, III:919; Wesley L. Jones papers, I:5241

——Phonoarchive (Seattle): World War II, III:3421

Watanabe, Ruth, II:1552–53, 1572; III:1836–37, 1869

Watch papers, II:2486

Water, I:2667 (3); III:1568; fluoridation, II:1322; pollution, II:1318, III:1700, 1703, 1705; power, I:1563; resources, II:1313–21; rights, I:1506; softening, I:2477; supply, I:2533; transportation, II:998–99

Water-glass, I:2258

Waters, Edward N., I:3049–50, 3084–85; II:1550

Waters, Margaret R., I:4151

Waters, Willard O., I:698–99, 719, 1688, 3901

Watersheds, II:1321, 1355

Waterston, Robert, I:4438

Watertown Library Association: Americana, I:4531

Waterways, I:2110–17

Watkins, Carleton E., II:1500

Watkins, Jessie B., III:1402–03, 1418–19, 2372

Watkins, V. G., I:2200

Watkinson Library: Connecticut authors, I:3252; Connecticut imprints, I:724; Connecticut local histories, I:4758; Hartford imprints, I:723; rare books, II:303, III:474; serials, I:365; Spanish literature, I:3707; special collections, I:164

Watling, John W., II:1902–03

Watrous, Roberta C., II:1394

Watson, Alice G. H., III:3323

Watson, John Crittenden, III:2451

Watson, Ritchio O., III:2510

Watt, Lois B., III:2342

Wauchope, Robert, II:2727

Wayne State University Libraries: anthropology, II:1120; archives, II:952; biology serials, I:2301; guide, II:121; juvenile literature, III:2347; labor history, III:968; labor newspapers, II:768; labor unions, II:780; Negroes, III:849; newspapers, III:343; Nightingale, Florence, III:1470; serials, III:293; Spanish plays, III:2258; Thailand, II:2433; Thoreau, Henry David, III:2077

——Kresge-Hooker Scientific Library: periodicals, II:1110

——Medical Library: history of medicine, III:1501; serials, III:1559–61; union catalog, III:1525

Wead, Eunice, I:925–26

Wead, Mary E., I:3444

Weaks, Mabel C., I:5052

Weather, I:2294, 2595; III:1373–74

Weaver, Clarence L., I:5128–29

Weaver, Warren, II:1082–83

Weaver, William D., I:2482

Weaving, I:2819

Webb, Alexander S., I:4123

Webb, Allie Bayne, III:671

Webb, David S., III:2083

Webb, Erna Mae, II:416

Webb, James W., I:4123

Webb, Robert E., III:1176

Webb, Samuel B., I:4123

Webb, Willard, I:3639, 3895

Webber, Mabel L., I:4707

Webbert, Charles A., III:785, 2477

Weber, Albrecht F., I:3776

Weber, Carl J., II:2953, 3273, 3301, 3477–78, 3483; II:1990

Weber, Clara C., I:3301

Weber, David C., II:122, 871

Weber, Francis J., III:3156

Weber, Hilmar H., I:1349, 3604

Weber, Jessie P., I:4822

Weber, Shirley H., II:1967

Webster, Daniel, I:4124

Webster, Noah, I:4125; II:2226–28

Webster, William, I:3330

Weedon, George, I:4537–38

Weeks, Stephen Beauregard, I:844, 5110–11; III:2644

Weeks family, III:2645

Weems, Mason L., I:4126–27

Wegelin, Oscar, I:839, 3231, 4183, 4480, 4809

Weichlein, William J., III:1847

Weidensall, Robert, I:4606

Weidman, Lucy E., I:5430, 5532

Weigand, Hermann J., I:3601–02; II:1925

Weights and measures, I:2740

Weinberg, Allen, II:872

Weinberg, Gerhard L., II:2297, 2818

Weinberger, Bernhard W., I:2353

Weiner, Jack, II:1333

Weinert, Janet, III:1034–35, 3409

Weingart, Harry L., III:1078

Weinstein, Walter W., II:1312; III:1115

Weis, Frederick L., I:2947

Weiss, Harry B., I:63, 836, 961, 998, 2148, 2150, 3263, 3812–13, 3821

Weiss, Herbert J., III:2959

Weitbrec, Robert F., II:992

Weitenkampf, Frank, I:916, 2844, 2868, 2971–72, 2992, 5059; II:1475

Welch, d'Alte A., III:2348

Welch, Doris, I:3173

Welch, Walter L., III:1828

Welding, I:2820–21; II:1436

Welfare work, I:1917–24; II:915–18; III:1227–33

Welland, Dennis, III:2086

Weller, Sam and Lila, III:2700

Wellesley College Library: Browning, Elizabeth Barrett, I:3431, II:1817; Browning, Robert, I:3431; English poetry, I:3361; Grabhorn Press, II:364; Italian literature, I:3665, 3672; Ruskin, John, I:3509, II:1870; Yeats, W. B., II:1914

Wells, Carolyn, I:3342; III:2092

Wells, H. G., II:246, 1833

Wells, James M., II:318; III:10, 160

Wells, Lester G., III:1940

Wells, Margo A., III:2934

Wells, Rulon, III:2284

Welsh, Charles, I:2147; III:2109

Welsh, Doris Varner, II:1605, 2307–08, 2314, 2759

Welsh, John R., III:2068

Welsh Americans, I:1384

Wemyss, Stanley, I:4481

Wendel, Carolynne, II:2256

Wentz, A. R., I:1090

Wentz, Charles H., I:5157, 5424, 5494

Wentz, Loretta Ann, III:590

Wepsiec, Jan, II:234–35; III:294, 2932, 2993

Werewolves, I:967

Werfel, Alma Mahler, III:2646

Werner, Eric, I:3042

Werner, William L., I:3269; II:1734

Wesley, Charles, III:728

Wesley, John, III:728

Wesley Theological Seminary Library: serials, III:286

Wesleyan University Library, I:165; classical languages and literature, I:3735; French Revolution, I:4287; periodicals, II:180; reference materials, II:5

Wesson, Ernest J., I:4057

West, Clarence F., I:2275

West, Elizabeth H., I:4101, 5199

West, Herbert F., I:3280, 3303, 3453

West, history, I:4675–90; II:2558–78; III:2225, 2549, 3137–60

West Africa, III:2976; languages, I:3188

West Indies, I:4102, 4394, 5284, 5319; II:2750; III:3338–39; Danish, I:5351

West Point, I:5425–28

West Virginia: history, I:5243–56, II:2710–13, III:3278–79; maps, I:3925

West Virginia Archives and History Department, I:5256; Arthur I. Boreman letters, I:5243; government publications, II:51, III:77; Henry Mason Matthews letters, I:5245; West Virginia history, I:5252–53; William E. Stevenson letters, I:5247

West Virginia State College Library: Lincoln, Abraham, II:2178

West Virginia State Library: law books, I:1727

West Virginia University Library: Appalachians, III:3133; bibliographic center, III:18; business history, I:2739; Civil War, III:3094, 3121; coal industry, III:1405; Cook, Roy Bird, III:2470; forestry, III:1692; geology, III:1406; Kentucky newspapers, III:313; legal publications, I:1728; manuscript collections, I:5254–55,

II:2712; newspapers, III:345; serials, III:295, 1363; Southern mountaineer in literature, III:1963; West Virginia history, II:2710–13, III:3279; Wharton, Edith, III:2088

Westbrook, Max, III:2024

Westchester County, N.Y., history, I:5038

Westcott, Mary, I:383

Western Kentucky State College Library: Kentucky history, II:2628, III:3192

Western Michigan College of Education Library: Lincoln, Abraham, I:4058

Western Michigan University Library: Michigan history, III:3214

Western New York Library Resources Council: serials, III:296

Western Pennsylvania Historical Society: manuscripts, I:5158, III:3244

Western Pennsylvania Historical Survey: American newspapers, I:443; manuscripts, I:5158

Western Reserve Historical Society Library: collections, I:4646, III:3239; costume, I:2945; French history, I:4284; genealogy, I:4135; Herrick, Myron T., I:4002; Lincoln, Abraham, I:4034; manuscripts and maps, I:4653; Ohio newspapers, I:444; serials, I:357, II:179

Western Reserve University Library: architecture and art, III:1752; biographical material, I:3935; China, II:2394; classification collection, II:65; English ballads and songs, I:3355; French history, I:4284, 4288; Henry Adams collection, I:258; periodicals, I:357, II:179

————Morley Chemical Library: journals, II:1108

Westlake, Neda M., III:475

Weston, Karl Ephraim, III:1970

Westwood, Thomas, I:3145

Wetherill, Samuel, I:2736

Wetmore, Hester A., I:2272

Wetzel, Charles McKinley, II:1594

Whaling, I:2592, 2964; II:726, 1729; III:3126

Wharton, Edith, III:2088

Whatley, W. A., I:5202

Wheat, Carl Irving, I:3903, 4750; II:2076–77

Wheat, James Clements, III:2406

Wheat, I:2626 (33)

Wheatley, Phillis, I:3338

Wheaton College Library: Mormonism, II:563

Wheeler, Helen E., I:5576

Wheeler, Joseph T., I:763

Wheeler, W. Gordon, III:489

Whelan, Joseph G., III:814

Whicher, George F., I:3282, 3540

Whimpey, Albert, II:1280

Whipple, Amiel Weeks, II:1282

Whistler, James A., I:2975, 2977, 2989

Whitaker, John Mills, III:2647

Whitaker, William A., II:1830

Whitby, Thomas J., II:1038

White, Andrew Dickson, I:4233; II:2229

White, Don, III:1023

White, Elaine G., III:2455

White, George W., III:1396

White, Helen, III:2099

White, Helen McCann, II:1407; III:2480, 2627

White, James Fellows, II:1926

White, James M., I:4981

White, John G., II:1001

White, Viola C., I:3262

White, Wallace H., II:2230

White, William Allen, I:4128; II:2231; III:2089

White, William Augustus, I:3419, 3541

White, William Chapman, III:133, 3230

White House, II:1463, 2492; III:1737

Whitefriars Hall Library: Carmelitana collection, II:621

Whitehill, Walter Muir, II:277, 598

Whitelock, Margaret M., II:591

Whitfield, Francis J., I:4315

Whiting, Brooke, III:2168

Whitman, Walt, I:3251, 3264, 3339–43; II:1632, 1757–69; III:2090–97

Whitmore, Eugene, III:1902

Whitmore, William H., I:4626

Whitney, Dorman H., III:3270

Whitney, Edward A., I:5537

Whitney, James L., I:2876, 3695; III:2260

Whitney, Philip, III:3004

Whittemore, Caroline, I:801

Whittier, John G., I:3344–45

Whittingham, W. R., I:1138–39

Whittlesey, Walter R., I:3083

Wichita City Library: pirates and piracy, II:2086

Wick, Peter A., III:657

Wickersham, Cornelius W., II:2293

Wickersham, James, I:445

Wickes, Forsyth, II:708

Wickes, George, III:2179

Widener, Harry E., I:209, 274, 2910, 3460, 3549

Wiener, Minnie, I:1591

Wigglesworth, Michael, I:993

Wight, Ruth N., III:2463

Wigmore, John H., I:1933

Wilberforce University Library: African Methodist Episcopal Church, II:557; U.S. Negro history, II:685

Wilborn, Elizabeth W., III:3091

Wilbour, Charles E., I:4199

Wilbur, Clarence Martin, II:2388, 2390

Wilbur, Ray Lyman, I:4196

Wilcox, Benton H., II:2714

Wilcox, Fannie M., I:3270

Wilcox, Jerome K., I:1460, 1899–1900, 1954, 2039, 2167, 2234, 2442–43, 2463, 2499, 2553, 2795, 2814–16, 2887, 2926

Wilcox, Robert C., I:4002

Wilde, Oscar, I:3568–69; II:1904–05; III:447, 2231

Wilder, Bessie E., III:42

Wilder, Elizabeth, I:2848

Wilder, Thornton, II:1770

Wilgus, A. Curtis, I:3692, 3930, 5237, 5370

Wilhelm, Jane, III:2045

Wilkie, Florence, I:850

Wilkin, R. H., I:1689

Wilkins, Ernest H., II:2462

Wilkins, Madeleine J., II:1159
Wilkins, Otto, II:399
Wilkins, Robert P., II:2497
Wilkinson, Billy Rayford, II:1773
Wilkinson, Richard T., III:2046
Wilkinson, W. W. J., I:56
Willard, Charles B., II:1769
Willard, Helen D., III:1903, 2218
Willard, James F., I:4755, 5276
Willey, Robert H., I:1485
Willging, Eugene P., II:622–23; III:756
William II, Emperor of Germany, I:4129
William III (of Nassau), King of England, II:2289
William Allen White Library, II:2231
William and Mary College: Jefferson, Thomas, III:1260
————Library: American Revolution, II:2529; dogs, I:2638; Johnston, Joseph E., I:4021; Marshall, John, I:4021; portraits, I:2952; Virginia history, III:3276
Williams, Dolores T., II:382
Williams, Edwin E., I:114; II:88, 109; III:134
Williams, Ernest W., Jr., II:997
Williams, Evan, III:1424
Williams, Frederick W., I:3794
Williams, J. F., I:4972
Williams, Jeane M., III:710
Williams, John, III:3272
Williams, John C., I:840
Williams, Nicholas M., I:5283
Williams, Otho H., I:4433
Williams, Philip L., III:1871
Williams, Ralph C., I:3640
Williams, Roger, I:4130–31
Williams, Samuel W., I:4721
Williams, Schafer, II:2743
Williams, Sidney H., I:3448
Williams, Stanley T., I:3297, 3343
Williams, T. Harry, III:2556
Williams, Terrence, III:1426
Williams, William, I:840
Williams, William Carlos, III:2098
Williams, William P., III:690
Williams College, I:2007
————Chapin Library: alphabets, III:480; Butler, Samuel, I:3439; English book design, III:672; French book design, III:673; history of biology, III:1420; history of writing, III:480; short-title list, I:613; Terence, II:1970
————Library: catalog, I:275; early American imprints, II:350
Williamson, Charles C., I:932, 1603
Williamson, Roland, I:1801
Willis, William H., III:2282–83
Willocks, R. Max, III:297
Willson, Robert W., I:2232
Wilmington Institute Free Library: Delaware history, III:3171; Delaware newspapers, I:446; finding list, I:276; Pyle, Howard, I:2914
Wilson, Angus, III:2232
Wilson, Bernard E., II:1554
Wilson, Carmen, I:2487
Wilson, Carroll A., I:3283, 3536
Wilson, Clyde N., Jr., I:3130

Wilson, Dorothy Gwendolyn, II:427
Wilson, James, I:3838
Wilson, Louis N., I:5498
Wilson, Louis R., I:3248, 4197; II:123
Wilson, Nancy, I:5256
Wilson, Patrick, II:674, 709
Wilson, Samuel, Jr., II:1466
Wilson, William J., I:506, 2276, 5577; II:1249
Wilson, Woodrow, I:3251, 4132–34, 4484; II:2181–82, 2232–37; III:2648
Wimersberger, Evelyn, II:236
Winchell, Constance M., I:115
Wine, I:2795
Wineman, Walter Ray, III:2453
Winfrey, Dorman H., II:588; III:1838
Wing, Donald G., I:681; II:349, 1905
Wing, John M., Foundation, II:315, 318; III:477
Winiecki, Mary Alice, II:383
Winkler, Ernest W., I:877; II:2695; III:635–36
Winkler, Robin L., II:2427
Winks, Robin W., III:3000
Winship, George P., I:447, 479, 579, 663, 1011, 2021, 3274, 3314, 3452, 3577, 3957
Winslow, Anne Goodwin, III:2099
Winsor, Justin, I:968, 3542–43, 3866, 3878, 4415, 4482
Winter, E. C., I:1191
Winterich, John T., II:1615; III:2132
Winters, William H., I:5089
Winther, Oscar Osburn, II:2160
Winthrop, Albert W., II:954
Winthrop, James, I:180
Winthrop, John, I:235
Wire, I:2812
Wirick, Harriet P., I:738
Wisconsin: authors, I:3271; history, I:5257–71; II:2714–15; III:3280–91
Wisconsin Center for Theatre Research: resources, III:1883
Wisconsin, Land Office: archives, I:5265
Wisconsin Legislative Reference Library: historical manuscripts, I:5268
Wisconsin, State Department: archives, I:5265
Wisconsin State Historical Society: archives and manuscripts, I:4483, 5269, 5271, II:2715, III:3283–89; catalogs, I:5270, III:3282; Civil War, I:4622–23, 5257, III:3122; Confederate publications, I:4611; education, III:1248; genealogy, III:2655; George Rogers Clark papers, I:4555; German literature, I:3588; government publications, II:52, III:78; Hillquit, Morris, III:981; Illinois history, I:4817; Kentucky history, I:4858, 4869, 4873; labor history, I:1600, II:769, III:961, 969, 979, 982; labor newspapers and periodicals, III:980; McCormick, Cyrus H., II:2184; maps, III:2360; Michigan history, I:4955; Milwaukee imprints, I:892; newspapers, I:333, 448–49; periodicals, I:333; religion, II:521; Socialist Labor Party of America, III:812; Tennessee history, I:5184;

Textile Workers Union, III:983; theses, III:3290–91; Vilas, William F., I:4103; Virginia history, I:5237; Washington, George, I:4122; Wisconsin authors, I:3271; Wisconsin history, I:5257, 5263–64, 5266, III:3281; Wisconsin imprints, I:893; Wisconsin newspapers, II:209
————Mass Communications Center: collections, III:406; H. V. Kaltenborn, III:2537
Wisconsin State Library: law books, I:1729
Wisconsin, University, Agriculture Library: apiculture, I:2639
————Department of Hebrew Studies (Milwaukee): pamphlets, III:782
————Engineering Library: serials union list, III:1586
————Libraries: Baudelaire, Charles, II:1939; European labor, II:754; French socialist congresses, II:746; German literature, I:3592; little magazines, III:252; pharmacy, history, II:1250; religion, II:521; science and technology, I:2159, 2164; science history, II:1048, III:1389; special collections, II:380, III:161; Swahili collection, III:2994; Tanzanian collection, III:2995; Wordsworth, William, II:1908
————Pharmaceutical Library: periodicals, III:1562
Wisdom, Donald F., III:71, 389
Wisdom, William B., I:3346
Wise, John S., II:2238
Wise, Karen, III:1726
Wise, Murray M., I:470
Wise, Thomas J., I:3399, 3406, 3410–11; II:1802–03
Wiser, Vivian D., I:5567; II:1376; III:1656
Wish, Harvey, I:4842
Wistar Institute: biological serials, I:2306; serials, I:320
Wister, Owen, II:1771; III:2100
Wit and humor, I:3215
Witchcraft, I:963–65, 968
Witcher, Esther, II:186; III:2327
Witherell, Julian W., III:2976–77, 2979, 2984, 2996
Witherspoon, A. M., I:3499
Withington, Mary C., I:1975, 2744; II:2573
Witmark, Isadore, I:203
Witten, Laurence C., III:1385
Wittenberg College Library: Berkenmeyer parish library, II:520
Wofford College Library: biography, III:2424; geography and travel, III:2380; hymns and hymnody, III:1839; juvenile literature, III:2349; 17th-century imprints, III:476
Wolanin, Alphonse S., I:3760
Wolf, Edwin, II, I:523, 3652, 4532; II:649, 1810, 2108, 2127; III:1853
Wolfe, Don M., II:2191
Wolfe, Richard J., II:1555; III:1860, 2412, 2425
Wolfe, Thomas, I:3346; II:1772–73
Wolfson, Harry A., I:1248; III:783

Women, I:2138–46, 3939; II:114, 1008–14; III:1268–71; as physicians, I:2146; education, I:2023; in Congress, I:1444
Woo, Irene, III:356
Wood, Charles A., III:2630
Wood, Marjorie P., I:3673, 3740, 5538
Wood, Richard G., I:5159, 5465, 5469, 5570; II:897
Wood, Samuel and Sons, I:3812
Wood, Samuel S., II:976
Wood engraving, I:2954, 2957, 2960, 2962, 2965, 2993; II:486–87, 1485–86, 1492
Woodall, Nancy, II:366
Woodard, Clement M., I:3162
Woodberry, George E., I:3347
Woodman, Edwin R., Jr., III:2181
Woodress, James, II:1747
Woodress, James L., Jr., I:4289
Woodring, Carl R., II:1851
Woodrow Wilson Foundation Library, I:4484
Woodruff, William E., II:2239
Woods, William R., III:3324
Woods Hole Oceanographic Institution: serials, III:1340
Woodard, Clair D., II:1517
Woodward, Gertrude L., I:678, 3374
Woodward, Wilma J., II:1319
Woody, R. H., I:5172
Woody, Robert H., III:3134
Woody, Thomas, I:1957
Woolcock, Judy, III:2488
Woolley, Robert W., II:2240
Woolridge, Geraldine, III:611
Worcester County Law Library: catalog, I:1730
Worcester Historical Society: manuscript collections, I:4929
Wordsworth, William, I:3360, 3570–77; II:1906–08; III:2233–34
Work, Robert L., II:1137
Workers' leisure, I:1590
Workingmen's Institute Library: New Harmony, Ind., history, I:4832, 4837
Workingmen's insurance, I:1595
Workmen's compensation, I:1642–44
World government, I:1355–56
World War I, I:4004, 5189, 5496–5539; II:2768–69; III:1189–90, 3405–09; poetry, I:3190
World War II, I:4193 (39), 5540–70; II:2295, 2270–2818; III:1170, 3410–21
Worley, Ted R., II:189, 2097, 2123, 2239, 2584
Worthington, Edna M., I:4059
Wrenn, John H., I:3406, 3410
Wright, Albert Hazen, III:2392
Wright, Almon R., I:5539
Wright, Charles H. C., I:3655
Wright, Dora L. E., III:711
Wright, Doris Marion, II:2560
Wright, Edith A., I:2026; II:273, 2195
Wright, Frank Lloyd, III:1747
Wright, Frank V., I:1684
Wright, John, I:1044–45
Wright, John Buckland, III:1764
Wright, John C., I:3823
Wright, John K., I:3867

Wright, Lottie M., III:642
Wright, Louis B., I:5238; II:124, 307; III:162
Wright, Lucille N., II:1378; III:1657
Wright, Lyle H., I:128, 2548, 3130, 3249, 4060; II:1662; III:1977–79
Wright, Marcia, II:2179; III:2517
Wright, Marjory H., II:1180, 1194, 1202
Wright, Muriel Hazel, II:2516
Wright, Norman E., III:2668
Wright, Orville and Wilbur, I:2554; II:2241; III:1599
Wright, Richard, III:2101
Wright, W. E., II:350
Wrigley, Elizabeth S., II:1806
Writing: aids, II:1630; history, I:539, III:480; manuals, I:2024; technical, II:1254
Wrone, David R., III:346
Wroth, Lawrence C., I:647, 764, 886, 2242–43, 2993, 3272, 3868, 4394, 4403, 4485, 4798; II:2744
Wu, K. T., I:3040
Wu, Eugene, II:2402; III:2889
Wu, Joan, II:448
Wu, Kuang-Tsing, III:2872
Wunderlich, Charles E., III:1848
Wust, Klaus German, II:469
Wust, Louis G., II:1630
Wyckoff, Lola A., I:1578
Wycliffe, John, II:528
Wyer, Malcolm G., II:2564, 2571–72; III:3143
Wyles, William, II:2164
Wyman, Roger E., III:3290
Wymberley Jones DeRenne Georgia Library: catalog, I:4810
Wynar, Lubomyr R., III:2670
Wynkyn de Worde, II:343
Wynne, Allen, III:125
Wynne, Marjorie Gray, I:3138; II:17, 1888–89
Wyoming, history, I:5272–80
Wyoming Historical Society: early newspapers, I:379
Wyoming State Library: law books, I:1731
Wyoming Stock Growers' Association: records, I:2635
Wyoming, University, Archives Department, I:5277
——Library: European history, I:4239; Stock Growers' Association records, I:2635

X-ray, I:2246
Xylographica, I:605, 625, 646

Yagello, Virginia E., III:1317, 1387
Yakima Indian War, II:2501
Yakobson, Sergius, I:4315
Yale College: College history and graduates' biography, I:2001
Yale Theological Seminary: religious periodicals, I:1001
Yale University, Beinecke Library: papyri, III:441
——Brothers in Unity Library: catalog, I:1055
——Divinity Library, III:691

——Divinity School, Day Missions Library: catalog, I:1055
——Elizabethan Club, II:1880; rare books, I:3420; Shakespeare, William, II:1880
——Law Library: manual, I:1802; William Blackstone collection, I:1732
——Library: African collections, III:2935; African periodicals, III:402; agricultural history, I:2618; air and water pollution, III:1705; alchemy and occult sciences, III:1385, 1390; Aldine Press, II:314; American game mammals and birds, I:2341; American history, I:4399, 4457, 4466; American literature, I:3416, III:1950; American Revolution, I:4550; American theater, II:1650–51; Arabic manuscripts, I:538, II:1986–87; architecture, II:1462; Audubon, John J., II:1134; Babylonian seals, II:2265, III:2809; Bacon, Francis, I:3421; Bailey, Philip James, I:3423; Balbus' Catholicon, II:334; Barlow, Joel, II:1666; Barrie, J. M., III:2136; Baskerville imprints, I:683; Beckford, William, II:1667; Bibles, I:1045; bookplates, II:62, III:81; Boswell, James, I:3427; botanical illustrations, III:1432; Brady, John G., II:2582; Brandeis, Louis D., II:2103; Bryant, William Cullen, II:1673; Buchan, John, III:2145; Canadiana, III:3000; catalog, I:279; Caxton, William, II:322; Chaucer, Geoffrey, II:335; China, I:3794; Chinese Communist literature, II:1992; Chinese periodicals, III:401; Civil War wall-paper newspapers, I:4597; Clare, John, II:1822; collections, I:134; Congregationalism, I:1075, 1078; Conrad, Joseph, I:3450–51; Cuba, II:2753; Defoe, Daniel, I:3454, 3456; De Forest, John Hancock and John William, I:4589; Dickens, Charles, III:2160; early books, I:614; East Asia, III:2865; education rare books and manuscripts, I:1975; Eliot, George, II:1831; engineering serials, I:2472; English Bibles, II:528; English landscape gardening, I:2862; English literature, I:3416; English periodicals, II:216; English plays, I:3374; English poetry, I:3352; English voyages, I:3843; Fernandez de Lizardi, J. J., I:3718; Fielding, Henry, I:3470–71; Fisher, Irving, III:853, 861; Franklin, Benjamin, I:3975–76, 3980; French book design, III:667, 674; French history, III:2717; French in Africa, I:4376; Galsworthy, John, II:1833; Gazette, I:176; German literature, I:3587, II:1920, 1927, III:2235; Goethe, Johann Wolfgang von, I:3597–99; Greek and Latin literature, I:3741; Greek manuscript, II:2270; guide, II:125; Hardy, Thomas, I:3480; Hartford, Conn. imprints, I:723; Harvey, Perry Williams, I:682; Hawthorne, Julian, III:2016; Hebrew

collection, I:1235–37, 1249–50; Heine, Heinrich, I:3601–02; Hispanic America, maps, I:3926; horses, III:1659; House, Edward Mandell, I:4004; illuminated manuscripts, II:274; illustrated books, III:656–57; incunabula, I:639, II:313, 343–44; indexes, II:17; Irving, Washington, I:3297; Italian legal incunabula, II:824; Ives, Charles Edward, III:1864, 1872; James, Henry, III:2034; Japan, I:3777, 4341; Jeffers, Robinson, II:1716; Johnson, Samuel, I:3486; Joyce, James, II:1847; Juvenal, I:3725; Kipling, Rudyard, I:3415; Lafayette, Marquis de, II:2154; Landor, Walter Savage, II:1852; Latin Americana, III:3305; Lawrence, D. H., II:1853; Lincoln, Abraham, I:4047; Linton, W. J., I:725; Lippman, Walter, I:4062; MacLeish, Archibald, I:3308; Mann, Thomas, I:3605, II:1916, 1926; manuscript collections, II:252, 263; Masefield, John, II:1860; Mason music library, III:1820; Maugham, W. S., II:1862; medical serials, I:2401; Mencken, H. L., II:1731; Meredith, George, I:3495; Mexican history, II:2737, 2739–40; Mexican imprints, II:477; Milton, John, I:3499; navigation and piloting, I:2244, III:1370; Negroes, III:850; New Jersey, II:2654; newspapers, I:450; Northwest Territory, II:2550; Oregon imprints, II:433; Orient, I:3795, II:2361; ornithology, II:1133, III:1443; Oxford books, I:672; Pacific Northwest, II:2578; Pequot Library, II:2498; Peru, II:2752; Picasso, Pablo, II:1480; Plato manuscripts, III:2284–85; political science, II:2535; Pound, Ezra, II:1739; Rabinowitz collection, II:288; religious education, I:1012; Rilke, Rainer Maria, II:1925; Rogers, Bruce, II:498; Roman de la Rose, I:3643; Ruskin, John, I:3507; Scandinavian collection, I:3625–26; science, II:1025; Shakers, II:625; Shakespeare, William, III:2213; Shaw, George Bernard, I:3545; Shaw, Nathaniel and Thomas, I:2744; Silliman, Benjamin, I:1999; Slavica, I:3766; South America, II:2723–24; Southeast Asia, III:2829; Southeast Asian serials, III:403; Southey, Robert, II:1885; Spanish American literature, I:3708; sporting collection, I:3138; Stein, Gertrude, I:3331–32; Stevens, Wallace, II:1645; Stevenson,

Robert Louis, II:1888–90, III:2225–26; Stieglitz, Alfred, II:1499; Stimson, Henry L., II:2212; Swift, Jonathan, I:3551; Texas imprints, II:2696; Thackeray, William Makepeace, I:3415; theatre collection, III:1877; Theatre Guild, II:1580; Thirty Years' War, II:2275; Thoreau, Henry David, I:3336; Tibetan collection, II:1985; Tinker, Chauncey B., II:1804; Tocqueville, Alexis de, II:668; Van Vechten, Carl, II:1631; Webb, Samuel Blatchley, I:4123; Wells, H. G., II:1833; Western Americana, I:4678, II:2558, 2573–74, III:2225, 3147; Western history, III:3157–58; Western travel, III:3146; Whitman, Walt, I:3343; Wilde, Oscar, II:1905; Wilder, Thornton, II:1770; Wood, Samuel S., II:976; World War I naval history, I:5501; World War I posters, I:5496; World War II, III:3412; Yale College history, I:2001; Yeats, William Butler, I:3578

——Linonian and Brothers Library: catalog, I:280
——Medical Historical Library, III:1490
——Medical Library: guide, III:1471; Harvey Cushing collection, I:2364, 2384; history of medicine, III:1502–06; Nicolaus Pol library, I:2420; surgical anesthesia, I:2416
——School of Forestry Library: catalog, III:1693; handbook, III:1694
——Sheffield Scientific School Library: mathematics, I:2228
Yamak, Labib Z., III:2823
Yamey, B. S., II:977
Yanagihashi, Minoru, II:2421
Yancey, Bartlett, I:5094
Yancey, Benjamin Cudworth, III:2649
Yang, Key Paik, II:2428
Yang, Teresa S., III:2808
Yang, Winston L. Y., III:2808
Yarmolinsky, Avrahm, I:3187, 3755, 4070; II:1980, 2272
Yassukovitch, Antonina, I:3757
Yates, Dora E., II:1007
Yates, Garard F., I:1187
Yeats, A. W., II:1850
Yeats, Jack Butler, III:1758
Yeats, William Butler, I:3578; II:1909–14; III:447, 2002, 2120
Yellow fever, II:1154, 1224
Yenawine, Wayne S., I:2673, 4811
Yewell, George Henry, II:1713
Yiddish drama, III:1967
Yiddish literature, I:1242

Yiddish poets, III:1967
Ynsfran, Pablo Max, II:2745; III:3381
Yohannan, Abraham, I:537
Yonge, Ena L., III:2381
Yorktown, Va., history, I:5223
Yoshipe, Harry B., I:1540
Young, Edward, I:3579
Young, F. G., I:5139
Young, James H., I:4098
Young, John, II:2422; III:2897
Young, Louise M., II:675
Young, Lucien, I:5458
Young, Malcolm O., I:2022
Young, Patricia Miller, III:556
Young, Perry, I:2118
Youth, I:2626 (17, 65)
Youth movement, I:1267
Youtie, Herbert C., I:4207
Yuan, T. L., II:2405
Yüan, T'ung-li, III:2898
Yugoslavia, history, I:4323; II:2347

Zabriskie, Christian A., II:910
Zabrosky, Frank, III:804, 915
Zacour, Norman P., III:417
Zafren, Herbert C., II:637
Zahm, Albert F., I:2581
Zaid, Charles, III:947, 973, 1456
Zakrzewski, Esteban A., III:534
Zalewski, Caroline, III:298
Zangwill, Israel, II:1915
Zanzibar, Africa, III:2982
Zeitlin, Francis, III:2261
Zeke, Zoltan, II:461
Zellars, W. C., I:3693
Zenger, John Peter, I:838, 5065
Zens, Mildred L., III:2350
Zeydel, Walter H., II:827
Ziemke, Earl, II:384
Zikeev, Nikolay T., III:1359, 1373
Zimmer, John T., I:2333
Zinc, I:2792
Zinner, Ernst, III:1364, 1369
Zinsser, William K., III:148
Zion Research Library: catalog, I:1013
Zionist Archives and Library: Palestine and Zionism, I:1251
Zito, Anthony, III:3210
Zola, Emile, II:1935
Zoology, I:2329–42, 2374, 2380; II:1128–37; III:1434–43; medical and veterinary, II:1204, III:1514; periodicals, I:2329
Zorn, Roman J., II:2104
Zubatsky, David S., III:400, 3321–22
Zugby, Lillian C., III:2351
Zumwinkle, Richard, III:2058
Zuwiyya Yamak, Labib, III:2811

Composed by Automated Office Systems Inc. in Times Roman with
Bodoni display type on a Text Ed/VIP phototypesetting system

Printed on 60-pound Warren's 66, a pH neutral stock, and bound in
C-grade Holliston Roxite cloth by Braun-Brumfield, Inc.